United Germany and the New Europe

United Germany and the New Europe

Edited by
Heinz D. Kurz

Professor of Economics
University of Graz, Austria

Edward Elgar

Published by
Edward Elgar Publishing Limited
Gower House
Croft Road
Aldershot
Hants GU11 3HR
England

Edward Elgar Publishing Company
Old Post Road
Brookfield
Vermont 05036
USA

A CIP catalogue record for this book is available from
the British Library

Library of Congress Cataloging-in-Publication Data
United Germany and the new Europe/edited by Heinz D. Kurz.
    352 p. 23 cm.
    Includes index.
    1. Germany—Economic conditions—1990– 2. Germany—Economic
policy—1990– 3. Germany—History—Unification, 1990. 4. Europe—
Economic integration. I. Kurz, Heinz Dieter.
HC286.8.U55 1993
337.4304—dc20   92–41279
                                                          CIP

ISBN 1 85278 584 5

Printed and Bound in Great Britain by
Hartnolls Limited, Bodmin, Cornwall.

Contents

Figures

Tables

Contributors

Dieter Frey	Professor of Psychology, University of Kiel, Germany; in the academic year 1988–89 Theodor Heuss Professor, The Graduate Faculty, The New School for Social Research, New York.
Bernd Görzig	Senior Member of the Research Staff, Deutsches Institut für Wirtschaftsforschung, DIW (German Institute of Economic Research), Berlin.
Harald Hagemann	Professor of Economics, University of Hohenheim, Stuttgart, Germany.
Peter Kalmbach	Professor of Economics, University of Bremen, Germany.
Hugo M. Kaufmann	Professor of Economics, Queens College, New York and Center for European Studies at City University of New York.
Eva Kigyóssy-Schmidt	Senior Research Fellow, German Academy of Sciences (1968–1991), Berlin (East), and Hungarian Academy of Sciences, Budapest.
Heinz D. Kurz	Professor of Economics, University of Graz, Austria; in the academic year 1990–91 Theodor Heuss Professor, The Graduate Faculty, The New School for Social Research, New York.
Michael A. Landesmann	Senior Research Officer, Department of Applied Economics, University of Cambridge and Fellow, Jesus College.
Edward J. Nell	Professor of Economics, The Graduate Faculty, The New School for Social Research, New York, USA.
Karl-Dieter Opp	Professor of Sociology, University of Hamburg, Germany; in the academic year 1991–92 Theodor Heuss Professor, The Graduate Faculty, The New School for Social Research, New York.
Ulrich K. Preuss	Professor of Law, University of Bremen, Germany.
Emanuel Richter	Lecturer in Political Science, University of Kassel, Germany.

Christine Rider	Associate Professor of Economics, St John's University, New York.
Wolf Schäfer	Professor of Economics, University of FAF, Hamburg, Germany.
Hélène Seppain	Cambridge, England.
Gunther Tichy	Professor of Economics, University of Graz, Austria.

Foreword

Marion Countess Dönhoff

In history it is not so much the facts that matter but the perception people have of those facts. Hence, when the two superpowers were fed up with the Cold War and with the escalation of defence spending which both could no longer afford, they took to the contrary perception: cooperation instead of enmity – consequently the whole artificial postwar set-up broke down everywhere, as the following examples demonstrate:

1. The bipolarity restricting the self-determination of a Germany divided into East and West to an extent unknown elsewhere, is now a thing of the past. The map has been radically altered. The postwar order in Central and Eastern Europe has broken down. Peoples from the East and the West can again come together unhindered.
2. Europe, for whose benefit Germany has renounced essential degrees of her sovereignty (commercially in favour of the EC, and militarily for NATO), will now be even more closely integrated.
3. The collapse of the Wall and of the Iron Curtain have made possible the unification of the two parts of Germany. Understandably enough, this is the greatest of all changes for us, but surprisingly also the most difficult. For the next three to five years it is going to demand the full attention of the government and all its resources.

Purely emotionally and without serious reflection, Germans in both parts of the country had thought that once Wall and barbed wire had been removed, everything would once more be as before. There is, of course, no question of this. Some glib propagandists had labelled the GDR as the avant-garde of the Eastern Bloc and maintained that it was one of the ten leading industrial nations of the world. This was just as absurd as the fiction that Iraq was the fourth largest military power in the world.

But it now turns out that the industry of the GDR, which had for decades been shielded against the world market and thus had never been exposed to competition, was completely obsolete; that the towns are dilapidated, the infrastructure will have to be basically renovated and that agriculture is in a pitiful condition. All this will require in the next few years financial support on a previously unheard-of scale. In 1991 grants of over DM 120 billion had to be made and in each of the next two years it looks like being about 150 billion.*

Coping with the economic disaster places enormous demands on the government and the citizens of the former Federal Republic; but the psychological defects of the GDR populace are even more difficult to compensate. They require a high degree of patience and sensitivity from all concerned.

It is almost impossible simply to reunite two generations who have grown up in different systems, whose respective societies proceed from alternative sets of values and whose objectives are differently conditioned. It would be far easier for the FRG to merge with Belgium than with the GDR. For the communists recognized only one alternative: friends or enemies. They did not think in terms of right – right is only a means of power in the hands of the ruling class – but in terms of struggle. In their view, the historical process is nothing but a class struggle. The friends are 'fraternal parties', the enemies the capitalists and imperialists who must be destroyed. The population of the former GDR, brought up with these opinions, finds it difficult to digest this anticlimax: no longer progressive citizens of the technological age, as they had been assured for forty years, but like backwoodsmen, to be limping along 50 years behind developments. Backwoodsmen who have suddenly become dependent on those who were previously reviled as capitalists and exploiters.

They themselves – the 'Wessis' – frequently conduct themselves with all the arrogance of a typical 'Mr Know-all', and this naturally helps to aggravate the inferiority complex of the 'Ossis'. This awareness crisis between the Germans is a psychological wall which is almost as difficult to surmount as the one previously erected by the communists.

The material problems are also gigantic. According to statistics, the former GDR regions are among the 'poorest regions of the European Community'. The per capita gross domestic product in the GDR at the collapse of the Wall was two-thirds lower than in the Federal Republic. Furthermore, a completely new administration had to be established; at present more than 10 000 Federal civil servants work in the five new Länder, and the old Länder and municipalities have sent about the same number there. But these numbers are still not enough. This process entails all sorts of difficulties, for instance the questions of salaries and wages. The level of wages in the former GDR is in general about 60 per cent that of the Federal Republic. For Western civil servants, prepared to serve in the East, this in many respects entails downgrading (separation from family, apartment, comfort). For this reason an

---

*Note: Throughout this book reference is always to US billion (i.e. 1,000 million).

allowance is added to their Western salary, which, of course, widens even more the psychological gulf between West and East.

However, the most serious of all problems is that a large percentage of all firms operate uneconomically or produce goods of such inferior quality that they are not saleable anywhere. Trade with the Eastern Bloc, which previously bought a large proportion of these goods, has more or less collapsed. Consequently one-third of all firms had to be closed.

The remaining two-thirds of the firms are so overstaffed that everywhere 20–30 per cent of the workforce will have to be laid off. The Damocles Sword of unemployment, a phenomenon unknown for 40 years in the East, is leading to a general feeling of insecurity, lack of hope and psychological depression.

And it is not only workers who will be unemployed but also intellectuals, judges, diplomats and policemen. To give you some sort of idea, the well-known East Berlin publishing house 'Volk und Welt' had to dismiss 90 of their staff of 130. Full employment in the communist states has always been achieved purely by subsidies. Nobody needed to count the cost, and this also applied to the bureaucracy. To take one example: in the FRG (population 62 million) the establishment of the Foreign Office, from ambassadors to drivers, amounted to 7 000 persons. In the GDR (population 17 million) the figure was 14 000, exactly double.

Anyone who has experienced the last two years with their surprising changes will be very reluctant to answer the question of Germany's role in the future. I have described in some detail the economic situation and the psychological state of the GDR because, in my opinion, they indicate that the two notions currently held are absurd:

that Germany through its unification has become an economic world power;
that Germany will succumb to the temptation of using this economic potency for realizing political ambitions and striking out on her own.

Apart from the difficulties I have described, which will occupy Germany's whole powers of concentration and financial resources for the next few years, there is also one fact which protects her from national ambitions and irrationality, namely the changed character of the Germans. This can be summarized as follows:

1. They have nothing more in common with the idea of the nineteenth century nation state. They are like the Swedes, who – exhausted by Charles XII's expansionist campaigns – have since then had only one wish, to be left in peace, to trade and occasionally to indulge in good works.

2.   The Germans do not seek power – on the contrary, they avoid it; they
     would prefer to dissociate themselves from any position of power and
     play no role in power politics. Trading and earning money, yes. But to
     aim at a position of power with their commercial potency, no! They are
     tired of heroism.

Another word on foreign policy. Germany will continue her commitment to
European integration. Those who doubt her motives, and insist on seeing the
negative aspects, may think that Germany only wants to conceal her past in
this peaceful guise.

   Furthermore, if developments in the East proceed more or less normally,
Germany's function as a bridge between East and West will increasingly
emerge. Germany will regain her old sphere of influence in eastern and
south-eastern Europe. For hundreds of years, up to the time of Adolf Hitler,
German was the lingua franca in these countries. Today they are showing an
eager interest in close relations with Germany. There are universities in
Poland where a growing number of students study German; joint ventures
are much in demand, as are German instructors in management courses.

   One can only wish that America would rate Germany's function as media-
tor not as disloyality to the Alliance but as a sensible division of labour in
the difficult East–West relationship. For now everything depends on helping
the East Europeans who have succeeded in casting off the communist yoke
to build up a democracy: an objective for which the West has struggled for
forty years. This struggle will have been in vain if we do not succeed in
saving these countries from collapse. They cannot manage this alone.

Acknowledgements

The idea for this volume was born when I held the Theodor Heuss Chair in the Graduate Faculty of Political and Social Science of the New School for Social Research, New York, in the academic year 1990–91. This chair was donated by the West German government partly as a tribute to the Graduate Faculty which had its origin as the 'University in Exile' in 1933. It provided a refuge to many German, Austrian and other European émigré scholars after the Nazis had taken over power in Germany. The chair bears the name of the first president of the Federal Republic of Germany.

One of the duties of the holder of the Theodor Heuss Chair is to contribute to the promotion of German studies in the United States. There are of course many different ways to approach this task, and being an economist I generally share my fellow economists' concern with alternative choices. However, in the present case I happily accepted the fact that there was no real alternative: one month after my arrival in New York, on 3 October 1990, in line with article 23 of the West German constitution, East Germany declared itself part of the Federal Republic of Germany. 'Il y'a des problèmes qu'on se pose et des problèmes qui se posent,' as the French mathematician Poincaré had put it. The idea was close at hand: to try to foster German studies by holding a conference dedicated to the problem of German unification and European integration.

'The Germans,' Goethe once said, 'make everything difficult, both for themselves and for everyone else.' While this may be true in general, there are exceptions to the rule. I am grateful to the Goethe Haus, New York, and especially to Dr Jens-Uwe Ohlau, then its Director, for making everything easy for me. The Goethe Haus kindly provided financial support for the conference and also helped with the organization. The conference, 'German Unification and European Integration', took place on 2–3 May 1991, in the New School for Social Research, New York. The present volume contains the proceedings of the conference.

I am also indebted to the Graduate Faculty at the New School for Social Research and to the American Council on Germany (ACG) for co-sponsoring the conference. I should like to thank Robert A. Gates, then Associate Dean, and Mr Carroll Brown, President of ACG, for their valuable help and advice. I appreciate the support from the German Consulate General in New York;

special thanks go to Dr Gudrun Sräga-König and Dr Manfred Kölsch. I am grateful to Dr Hans Decker of Siemens Corporation, New York, for his early support and the useful discussions we had. Dr Marion Countess Dönhoff, editor of the German weekly *Die Zeit*, kindly wrote the Foreword to the present volume.

Christian Gehrke and Mark Knell were of great help in organizing the conference. Günseli Berik, Ira Katznelson, Will Milburg, Amantia Pollis, Willi Semmler, Anwar Shaikh, Charles Tilly and Aristide Zolberg, all of the Graduate Faculty, and Carroll Brown kindly volunteered as chairs or discussants. Ernest Auerbach, A. Bernett, Hans Decker, J. Kenneth Hickman and William H. Janeway kindly participated in round-table discussions. I thank them all.

It goes without saying that the conference could not have been organized in the way it was, had there not been the support and assistance of the Department of Economics in the Graduate Faculty. I am particularly grateful to Anwar Shaikh, Chairman of the Department, and to Karin Ray and Julie Barnes, not only for the help and services they provided, but also for the friendly atmosphere they created, which proved invaluable for my well-being and my work. I tremendously enjoyed the privilege of being a member of a department with such a rich history, and for being able to teach and do research amidst such long-standing friends as Robert Heilbroner and Edward J. Nell.

Last but not least I should like to thank Christian Gehrke for his editorial assistance and Heidelinde Hofer for preparing the final typescript.

Heinz D. Kurz

Introduction

Heinz D. Kurz

In his *Über die ästhetische Erziehung des Menschen in einer Reihe von Briefen* (On the Aesthetic Education of Mankind in a Series of Letters), written in 1793–95, the German poet and historian Friedrich Schiller expressed concern about the revitalized spirit of nationalism in the aftermath of the French Revolution, which in his view was a potential threat to individual freedom. His view earned him hostile criticism and public attacks from nationalists. In order to answer his critics, during the winter of 1795–96 Schiller joined forces with his fellow poet and friend Johann Wolfgang von Goethe in writing several hundred epigrams, 414 of which were published in the *Musenalmanach* in 1797. Following a suggestion of Goethe's, the epigrams were called *Xenien* (gifts to guests). One of the best known is 'Deutscher Nationalcharakter' (German national character) and reads:

> Zur *Nation* euch zu bilden, ihr hofft es, Deutsche, vergebens;
> Bildet, ihr könnt es, dafür freier zu Menschen euch aus.[1]

Recent events appear to have falsified the message contained in this distich. German unification not only re-established a unique German nation. Ironically, it was the East German yearning 'to be freer human beings' that eventually resulted in the achievement of a goal which Schiller and Goethe had considered unattainable.

With the lessons of history in mind, one should beware of premature judgements. Too often events, which at the time were frenetically applauded by many people, eventually turn out to be but a step towards another sociopolitical catastrophe. Whether the 'experiment' of German unification will lead to an entirely new understanding of the role of the Germans in contemporary history and redefine the concept of tension between the formation of a single German nation state and political freedom, cannot be answered yet. We simply do not know.

What we *do* know, however, is that the emancipatory potential of an age can only be realized if simultaneous destructive tendencies are effectively warded off. For the East Germans 1989 and the beginning of 1990 were the

1

years of the light at the end of a long tunnel, but in the second half of 1990 East Germany entered a new tunnel with no end in sight. The destructive tendencies at work were felt with vigour. Monetary union between the two German states, which in important respects anticipated complete German unification, became effective on 1 July 1990. It sent the East German economy into a tailspin. Unification did not bring quick economic success and growth in the former GDR but dizzying decline – a plunge into depression unparalleled in modern history. Mass unemployment appeared and it does not look as if it will go away soon. At the political fringes there is a radicalization, with neo-Nazis trying to apply measures of mass intimidation. Those who remember the history of the Weimar republic are aware of the destructive tendencies of large-scale unemployment which culminated in the seizure of power by Hitler and the Nazis.

Yet despite these bewildering events, those responsible for the politics of unification seem to be paralysed and unable to act in a way which effectively addresses the core problem: unemployment and social distress in the five new Länder. It cannot even be excluded that Schiller and Goethe's above epigram will eventually prove correct because another epigram of the two, 'Das Deutsche Reich' (The German Reich) applies:

> Deutschland? aber wo liegt es? Ich weiss das Land nicht zu finden.
> Wo das gelehrte beginnt, hört das politische auf.[2]

The present volume attempts to contribute to a better understanding of the opportunities and risks of German unification and its possible impact on the process of European integration. Due to the multifaceted nature of the problem an interdisciplinary approach is indispensable, at least in the sense of bringing together the points of view of representatives of several social sciences. The people contributing to this volume include scholars doing research in political science, sociology, social psychology, history, law and economics.

The book is divided into five parts. Part I is dedicated to a discussion of the economic and political developments in the former GDR that eventually led to the 'peaceful revolution' in autumn 1989 that brought down the Berlin wall and paved the way to German unification. In Chapter 1 the sociologist Karl-Dieter Opp argues that the revolution was the outcome of a spontaneous cooperation of individuals. The chapter focuses on explaining the protests in the GDR in 1989. It first specifies the set of incentives which were significant in explaining these protests and then shows how these incentives were changed by events inside and outside the GDR so that an increasing willingness to protest could be expected. Finally, he examines how the individual readiness to participate was coordinated so that extensive demonstrations could emerge. In Chapter 2 Eva Kigyóssy-Schmidt analyses the aftermath of the demise of the socialist regime and the economic and political problems the East Germans are confronted with. Emphasis is on the institutional and legal reforms which are a prerequisite for a successful transformation of a command economy into a market economy. In this context the human factor turns out to be of crucial importance.

Part II deals with political, constitutional and social psychological aspects of German unification. In Chapter 3 the political scientist Ulrich K. Preuss addresses the problem of the constitutional alternatives available to the East Germans prior to unification. He argues that a unique historical opportunity was missed by not symbolizing the birth of the new German polity in terms of a new constitution which reflects the polity's goals and aspirations. It is through constitutions that the distinctiveness of a historical situation is transmitted to later generations. Seen from this perspective, the constitutional aspects of German unification reveal a failure to perceive the uniqueness and confront the deeper meaning of this event. In Chapter 4 Dieter Frey examines German unification from the point of view of a social psychologist. His main concern is with the mental and motivational deficiencies generated by totalitarian regimes in general and the former 'socialist' regime in East Germany in particular. He provides an explanation of why and how totalitarian regimes can survive for a long time. In his view social psychology may contribute to overcoming the deficiencies mentioned: the chapter provides a set of 'remedies' to this effect. In Chapter 5 the political scientist Hélène Seppain investigates the special relationship between Bonn and Moscow. In her view, 'buying peace' is the key to understanding the economic content of *Ostpolitik*. She argues that the Bonn–Moscow relationship will be a crucial factor in the construction of the New Europe and that German unification will in all probability lead to very little change in Germany's economic approach to the Community of Independent States (CIS). Germany is once again to become a 'bridge' between East and West. This will inevitably revitalize traditional Western suspicions, which can only be neutralized with Germany being an integral part of the European Community.

Part III addresses the economic problems and perspectives of Germany; emphasis is on the five new Länder. All contributions in this part are by economists. Harald Hagemann deals with the macroeconomic consequences of German unification in Chapter 6. He first provides an account of the deep economic crisis in East Germany triggered by monetary union and then compares the East German situation with that of West Germany after the currency reform in 1948. It is argued that because of marked differences between the two it is improper to draw analogies between them. Then follows a discussion of the long-term perspectives of the East German economy and an investigation of some international macroeconomic impli-

cations of German unification. In Chapter 7 Bernd Görzig provides a detailed quantitative account of the different aspects of the economic crisis in
East Germany. The chapter summarizes the findings of a research project
carried out by the German Institute of Economic Research in collaboration
with the Institute of World Economics (Kiel) and of a recent economic
outlook on East Germany elaborated by the five leading institutes of applied
economics in Germany. The institutes forecast a further collapse of production
in manufacturing and persistently high levels of unemployment in Eastern
Germany. In Chapter 8 Peter Kalmbach discusses three types of wage policies
for Eastern Germany: the rapid adjustment to Western German wages; a
wage policy oriented toward economic development as reflected in productivity growth; and a policy of wage subsidies which aims at lowering costs
borne by firms. Type one is the wage policy actually carried out. It involves
massive transfer payments to the new Länder and contributes to the rapid
growth of public debt. With rising rates of interest a general economic
depression in Germany cannot be excluded. Whether this pessimistic scenario will materialize depends of course on a variety of additional factors, in
particular the development of the world economy. Heinz D. Kurz in Chapter
9 is concerned with the distributive aspects of German unification. It is
argued that the terms of unification triggered a huge conflict over the distribution of wealth and income which is detrimental to social peace and cohesion in Germany as a whole and to a quick recovery and restructuring of the
East German economy. In is contended that a major error was the adopted
route to privatization which deprived the population of the new Länder of
that part of the 'property of the people' which is left after compensating the
post-1949 expropriations. Understandably, the East Germans try to minimize
this loss by demanding large wage increases and substantial transfer payments.
However, rapidly rising East German wages are not only detrimental to the
competitiveness of the existing capital stock and employment in the new
Länder; they also retard and decelerate the formation of new capital, which
is badly needed in order to restructure the East German economy.

Part IV deals with European Economic and Monetary Union. In Chapter
10 the economist Gunther Tichy discusses various criteria defining an optimal integration area. Whichever criterion is adopted, the European countries
are still surprisingly heterogeneous. Hence, for almost any combination of
them integration can be expected to entail not only benefits, but also substantial costs. Several theoretical arguments plus some empirical findings
are provided to explain wealth-decreasing effects of economic integration;
emphasis is on the diversion of trade and investment. It is conjectured that a
currency union among all EC members plus perhaps all EFTA members may
be wealth-decreasing due to a lack of harmonization of national policy
goals, institutions, inflation rates and the absence of fiscal federalism. It is

concluded that the project of a European monetary union should be given time and should be seconded, for example by the introduction of an EC-income surtax to finance unemployment subsidies. Chapter 11, by the political scientist Emanuel Richter centres around the concept of 'community building'. Attention focuses on whether German unification tends to increase or diminish the tensions accompanying the process of European integration. The author first discusses the ambivalence between the goal of German national unity and that of supranational integration in the postwar period. He argues that the changing forms of community building have gradually softened that ambivalence. Given the persistent demands for national unity and democratic political identity, which expressed themselves anew in the recent upheavals in all of Eastern Europe, there can be no supranational integration without national unity. From this point of view German unification is considered a necessary precondition of European integration. The chapter concludes with a critical outlook emphasizing the role of political cohesion for the emerging new European order. The next two chapters are by economists. In Chapter 12 Hugo M. Kaufmann is concerned with the opportunities and risks of European economic and monetary union, with German economic and monetary union as a major sideshow. The author begins by reviewing some of the central thinking that preceded the creation of the European Monetary System (EMS) and then addresses the consequences of German economic and monetary union and the challenge posed to economic policy. He points out that when it came to German monetary union, Germany somewhat ironically ignored its own position and insight which made it oppose the 'monetarist' point of view in the discussions prior to the establishment of the EMS. After a brief summary of the theory of optimum currency areas the author discusses the future of the EMS, taking into account expected monetary developments in conjunction with the completion of the European internal market set to start on 1 January 1993. In Chapter 13 Wolf Schäfer addresses the question of how the economic integration of the two Germanies will affect the nominal and real exchange rate of the Deutschmark. It is argued that in order to answer this question one has to take into account the necessary structural adjustments in the real sector of the economy. In this context the distinction between internationally tradable and non-tradable goods turns out to be of great importance. Taking into account the probable development of wages relative to labour productivity it is concluded that in the medium run a general real appreciation of the DM is to be expected.

Part V concludes with a general analysis of the political and economic reforms in Central and Eastern Europe. In Chapter 14 Edward J. Nell asks: where is the Keynes of Eastern Europe? He starts with an investigation of the causes of the breakdown of the Soviet-style economies of Eastern Europe, contending that the difficulties of these economies were not essentially due to socialism, nor to the lack of, or interference with, markets. In his view it was the persistent pressure of excess demand that brought these systems down. The natural tendency to create excess demand is taken to change the incentives facing firms. Because firms operate in a sellers' market, costs don't have to be kept down and quality standards will erode. The Keynes of Eastern Europe would have to develop incentive-compatible policies to manage excess demand in a way similar to that in which Keynes developed policies to manage a lack of effective demand in capitalist economies. In Chapter 15 Christine Rider starts from the premise that the economic and political restructuring of the former 'socialist' economies in Eastern Europe, German unification and the process of European integration are closely related phenomena. She argues that merely introducing the price mechanism will not suffice to generate economic success. Nor will it suffice to open the EC's door to new entrants. Eastern European countries applying for full EC membership will have to fulfil a set of requirements in order to be accepted. Yet, due to the partial nature of the reforms in some countries and the time needed for the reforms to work themselves out, it is to be expected that several countries will not, at least within the foreseeable future, meet these requirements. Finally, in Chapter 16 Michael Landesmann examines the industrial restructuring in Eastern Europe and East–West trade integration. He starts with a number of comparisons of industrial structures and of past experiences of structural change across East and West European countries. Taking the composition of industry in West European countries as a bench-mark, he shows that considerable diversity exists across East European countries, reflected in different distances of their composition of industry from the benchmark composition. The author then elaborates a long-run and a short-run scenario of East–West European trade integration. While the long-run scenario presupposes a convergence of export performance of East European economies with those of West European economies, in the short-run export growth patterns may deviate significantly from longer-term specialization.

NOTES

1.   See Schiller (1966, vol. II, p. 737). An English translation provided by Craig (1983, p. 289) reads: 'You hope in vain, Germans, to make yourselves a nation. – Train yourself rather, you can do it, to be freer human beings.'
2.   'Germany? but where is it located? I cannot find the country. Where the learned one begins, the political one ends' (Schiller 1966, vol. II, p. 737).

REFERENCES

Craig, G.A. (1983), *The Germans*, New York: Meridian.
Schiller, F. (1966), *Werke in drei Bänden*, edited by H.G. Göpfert in collaboration with G. Fricke, Munich: Carl Hanser.

PART I

Peaceful Revolution in the Former GDR
and its Aftermath

1. Spontaneous Revolutions: The Case of East Germany in 1989

Karl-Dieter Opp*

---

1 INTRODUCTION

The collapse of the communist regime in the GDR in 1989 has brought about numerous books and articles. Nevertheless the question of why this revolution could emerge has not been answered in a satisfactory way. Standard explanations emphasize, for example, the high extent of deprivation the population was exposed to. Apart from the well-known free rider problem, this explanation does not answer the question of why the revolution did not occur until October 1989 although discontent was high and increasing long before. Further, the protests increased after discontent decreased when after 9 October some political liberalization began. Other explanations emphasize that the great number of citizens who left the country, and Gorbachev's new politics, were major causes of the revolution.[1] It is left open why a single citizen should be motivated to participate in the large-scale protests because Gorbachev came into power in 1985 and because other citizens emigrated to the FRG. An answer could be that these events raised discontent. This leaves us with the problem of the grievance hypothesis mentioned above.

This chapter focuses on explaining the emergence of the extensive protests in East Germany in 1989. I begin with an account of the development of the protests in 1989, propose a general explanatory model specifying the factors that promote protest, then show how these factors changed in 1989 and by which processes the widespread willingness to protest led to a spontaneous revolution that was neither intended nor predicted.

2 THE DEVELOPMENT OF THE PROTESTS IN THE GDR

Since the establishment of the GDR, protests of various kinds have occurred again and again, albeit on a smaller scale. These protests mainly consisted of demonstrations. The number of demonstrations and participants began to increase from May 1989. On 7 May a local election took place in the GDR, the results of which were obviously tampered with. Several demonstrations followed, directed against these falsifications. From the end of September 1989 there was a dramatic upsurge in the number of demonstrations and participants. An example of this was the number of participants taking part in the Monday demonstrations on the Karl-Marx-Platz in Leipzig. These demonstrations took place subsequent to the prayers for peace that had been held in the Nikolai Church since 1982. The demonstrations in Leipzig were the point of departure for the revolution in the GDR, and as such are of particular interest. Approximately 800 to 1 200 people took part in the Monday demonstration on 4 September. The development from 25 September is shown in Table 1.1.[2]

Table 1.1:   The Number of Participants in the Monday Demonstrations in Leipzig, 1989

Date	Lowest estimation	Highest estimation	Medium estimation
25. 9	5 000	8 000	6 500
2.10	15 000	25 000	20 000
9.10	70 000	70 000	70 000
16.10	>100 000	120 000	>110 000
23.10	150 000	300 000	225 000
30.10	200 000	500 000	350 000
6.11	400 000	500 000	450 000
13.11	150 000	200 000	175 000
20.11	>100 000	200 000	>150 000
27.11	200 000	200 000	200 000
4.12	150 000	150 000	150 000
11.12	100 000	150 000	125 000
18.12	150 000	150 000	150 000

Sources: Fischer-Weltalmanach, 1990; Schneider, 1990; Tetzner, 1990; Wimmer et al., 1990; Zimmerling and Zimmerling, 1990, parts 1 to 3; *Spiegel Spezial*, 1990; *Zeit Magazin*, 29.12.89.

All the demonstrations before 9 October were immediately stopped or impeded by security agents, for example the demonstrators were arrested. The demonstration on 9 October 1989 was the largest demonstration in the GDR since 17 June 1953 and the first demonstration that was not dispersed by the regime. On this day demonstrations were also held in other towns in the GDR, but with far fewer participants. Both the demonstrations in Leipzig and in almost all the other cities were non-violent. All demonstrations were illegal, as they had been neither registered nor permitted.

Apart from demonstrations, there was a *second* type of political measure directed against the SED (Socialist party) regime: the establishment of or an appeal to establish oppositional groups. For example, on 13 August about 400 members of various oppositional groups met together in the community hall of the Confessional Church in Berlin-Treptow. On 26 August it was called upon to found a social democratic party and on 9–10 September to establish the New Forum.

A *third* method of opposing the SED regime was that individual groups, e.g. artists, church groups or workers' groups, wrote and distributed declarations, open letters or petitions demanding reform.

A *fourth* form of opposition was 'exit' (Hirschman, 1970). Since July 1989 emigration was resorted to by an increasing number of GDR citizens as a reaction to the political and economic situation in the GDR.

All types of protest – demonstrations, establishment of opposition groups, drafting declarations and emigration – increased in the course of the year 1989.

3   AN EXPLANATORY MODEL FOR POLITICAL PROTEST

Theoretical Foundations

In order to avoid *ad hoc* explanations of the kind mentioned above, it is useful to apply a theoretical approach that provides information about the factors that could have led to the emergence of the revolution. This approach must be able to take account of the fact that the extensive protests on the part of the citizens had an *evolutionary* origin: they were the unplanned and unforeseeable result of *spontaneous cooperation* of an increasing number of individuals who found themselves in a similar situation.

A widely accepted theoretical approach in sociology is the resource mobilization perspective.[3] The basic idea is that actors in the political process try to mobilize resources to achieve their political aims. Those resources mainly consist of the support of political important societal groups. Collective action of a large number of persons 'is rarely a viable option because of lack of resources and the threat of repression. ... When deprived groups do mobilize, it is due to the interjection of external resources' (Jenkins and Perrow, 1977, p. 250). This theoretical idea does not hold for the protests in the GDR in

1989. An increasing number of citizens engaged in the protests without having been members of protest-encouraging social groups and in spite of severe state sanctions. There was no 'interjection of external resources'.

In order to explain the spontaneous cooperation of a large number of citizens another theoretical approach seems preferable: *the individualistic approach in the social sciences was particularly successful in explaining evolutionary processes.*[4] The basis of such an explanation is a theory that explains the individual decisions of the actors taking their respective social situation into consideration. One such theory is value-expectancy theory, a variant of the model of rational action which will be applied in the following considerations. According to this theory, individuals perform an action if they value the respective expected consequences to a high extent and if they attribute a relatively high degree of certainty to the occurrence of these consequences.[5]

If one applies this theory to explain the protests in the GDR, two questions arise: (1) What behavioural consequences were important for the protests? (2) How and for what reasons did the respective behavioural consequences (i.e. their evaluations and subjective probabilities) change in the course of 1989? It is necessary to answer these questions in such a manner that not only the increase of protest is explained but also two further facts: (1) Why did the demonstrations initially arise in Leipzig and not in other cities? (2) Why were the protests non-violent?

Preconditions for Citizens' Protests

Empirical research on political protest and social movements has shown that protest can be adequately explained by a certain set of action consequences to be outlined in this section.

The extent of citizens' political involvement first of all depends on their *dissatisfaction* with the prevalent political and economic situation. However, the effects of discontent depend on (1) the extent to which an individual actor assumes that his or her protest will contribute towards the provision of collective goods; and (2) the extent to which he or she expects the collective protest to be successful. Political dissatisfaction and these factors that can be summarizingly labelled as *perceived political influence* to realize certain political goals via protest have a multiplicative effect on participation in protest actions: the higher the perceived political influence, the stronger the effect of dissatisfaction.[6]

Empirical investigations of the effects of *official sanctions* on protest have shown that these have to be regarded as costs, thus having a deterrent effect. However, governmental sanctions also trigger off solidarization effects. For example, protesters exposed to repressive acts receive to a high extent informal positive social sanctions, i.e. positive incentives for protest increase. This is especially the case if sanctions are regarded as illegitimate. The stronger the governmental sanctions, the more dominant the deterrent effects (see in particular Opp and Roehl, 1990b, with further references).

Internalized norms are of central importance not only for social action in general but also for political protest.[7] The kind of such *protest norms* influences the kind of political action resorted to. If the citizens of a country generally only regard non-violent forms of political action as morally justified, non-violent acts of protest are more likely to occur than in a situation where violence is generally regarded as a justified form of political action. Norms are linked to specific situations. An individual will, for example, not feel obliged to resort to non-violent protest actions if these entail high risks or appear futile.

Empirical investigations have shown that participation in protest actions is highly dependent on *incentives emanating from the social environment*, for example from expected positive sanctions on the part of friends and acquaintances.[8] Political groups in particular are the source of such incentives. The social environment is a source not only of positive incentives for protest but also of negative ones. Whether the social environment resorts to positive or negative sanctions with regard to certain political actions depends on the situation. Violent forms of protest are likely to entail negative sanctions. It can be further assumed that political involvement will be negatively sanctioned if protest is linked to extremely high costs in the form of governmental repression: the 'price' is regarded as being too high. Only if governmental repression is not too extreme will negative sanctions for protest decrease and positive sanctions rise. Positive sanctions will not emerge if the protest is regarded as futile.

In order to explain the development of protest within a group, it is of particular importance to examine the *distribution* of the above-mentioned incentives within the group. In the literature, focus is frequently placed on the role of the so-called *political entrepreneurs*.[9]

Research into political protest normally does not presuppose that the citizens consider leaving their country as a possible reaction to dissatisfaction with the economic and political situation. For GDR citizens the behavioural alternative 'emigration' was existent in 1989 via the channels of exit permits or became possible from July 1989 via other Eastern Bloc countries to which one could legally travel. This, however, entailed high costs: one had to reckon with long waiting periods if one applied for an exit permit, and it was very uncertain whether or not such a permit would be granted. Applicants also had to expect various repressive measures on the part of governmental bodies during the processing of their applications. Due to the extreme frontier protection measures, it was virtually impossible and highly dangerous to

leave the country without permission. In any case, leaving the country automatically severed existing social ties and meant leaving behind all posses-
sions. As the costs of emigration were relatively high, few citizens resorted

Table 1.2:   Changes in the Causes of Protest in the GDR

Factors	until May 1989	May– 9 Oct. 1989	10 Oct.– end 1989
Dissatisfaction	high	high	increasing (low dynamics of change)
Perceived influence	low	increasing	continually increasing
Governmental sanctions	high	decrease or remain (Chinese solution)	no longer existent
Protest norms	low	increasing	continually increasing
Positive social incentives	low	increasing	increasing
Negative social incentives	high	decreasing	decreasing
Political entrepreneurs	few	increasing (formation of new groups)	increasing
Action alternatives	restricted mobility	fewer restrictions	from 9 Nov. open borders
Macro-events	start of liberalization in Eastern Europe (Poland, Hungary, USSR)	increasing liberalization (Czechoslovakia, Bulgaria, Romania, extended possibilities of travel), termination of the democracy movement in China	

to leaving the country, so it is regarded as justified to refrain from explaining why certain citizens preferred emigration to opposition or doing nothing.

This concludes the outline of those factors that research on political protest and social movements considers significant for the emergence of protest. I assume that these factors have also been significant in explaining the protests in the GDR in 1989. The question thus becomes how these factors changed in 1989.

4   CHANGES IN PROTEST DETERMINANTS IN 1989

In this section I will first describe the situation prevalent at the beginning of 1989 and then show to what extent the incentives for protest effective in the situation changed after 7 May 1989. The considerations are summarized in Table 1.2.

The Situation at the Beginning of 1989

The degree of satisfaction prevalent among the citizens of a given country depends on the extent to which their demand for everyday commodities, for an adequate physical environment and for freedom of choice is met. In the GDR these conditions were extremely rare. A representative survey carried out in January 1990 assessing the level of satisfaction among GDR citizens generally indicated a high degree of dissatisfaction with all areas referred to (Winkler, 1990). Extensive dissatisfaction was also evident in the slogans on the banners carried during demonstrations (Schneider, 1990). Here particular criticism was directed towards the extent of East German state security (or Stasi) supervision, the lack of alternatives in political decision-making and travelling restrictions.

The extent of dissatisfaction depends among other things on the groups one compares oneself to. GDR citizens primarily compared their situation with that prevalent in the FRG, a factor which can be attributed to the following reasons: (1) both countries share a common language; (2) goods in demand in the GDR were widely available in the FRG; and (3) GDR citizens are relatively well informed on the situation in the FRG, not least because the majority of them can receive West German television programmes. When comparing their economic and political situation to that prevalent in the FRG, the level of deprivation was probably relatively high.

With regard to the *economic situation* citizens will compare the present situation with past and future situations in their own country. Even low supply levels are not necessarily regarded as depriving, if improvements are expected for the future. In the GDR as in all other Eastern Bloc countries, however, the economic supply had deteriorated in the course of time and an amelioration of the situation was not in sight.

Other socialist countries served as a comparison too. Again a relative dissatisfaction was the result, as in several of these countries processes of democratization had taken place.

In sum, the discontent of a GDR citizen with the political as well as economic situation was high at the beginning of 1989.

At that time there was a low degree of perceived *influence* with regard to the possibility of changing the situation via involvement in politics. The power was solely concentrated in one party that strictly opposed political reforms and suppressed political opposition. Given these circumstances, it appeared relatively improbable that the situation could be changed as a result of the individual getting involved in politics. From the citizens' point of view, the same probably applied to the influence that groups such as the church could have on reform (Heinze and Pollack, 1990).

At the beginning of 1989 the expectation of governmental sanctions was rated relatively high. Political involvement opposing the dominating political line was answered with severe sanctions. Opposition to the regime was linked to arrest, imprisonment, occupational downgrading or not being promoted and being denied educational opportunities. Sanctions also extended to direct members of families (children, spouse) and even to friends.

The expected sanctions were not only severe, they were highly likely to be effected. There was an extensive system of private informers.[10] Before liberalization in the USSR, large-scale political actions would automatically have brought about the intervention of Warsaw Pact troops (an example being on 17 June 1953). Although in 1989 the GDR population probably did not expect the intervention of foreign troops as a reaction to protests, there was widespread fear of a 'Chinese solution' (severe sanctions following the pattern of the suppression of the democratic movement in China), as the SED had positively commented on the suppression of the protests in China. Accordingly, it was to be expected that the SED regime would suppress general upheavals as it had always done in the past.

Protest norms were probably not effective in a situation where governmental repression was highly likely to occur as a result of political protest and where personal involvement appeared futile.

Given the high costs of political involvement to be reckoned with, only negligible *positive social incentives* for protest were likely. Due to the high risk and uncertain outcome of political action, there will hardly have been positive incentives, such as rises in status and esteem, in the case of involvement. *Negative social sanctions* of protest are more likely to have dominated: an individual will certainly attempt to dissuade his or her friend or partner from participating in protests if these are likely to jeopardize their career or access to university.

Although *political entrepreneurs* did exist in the form of members of opposition groups, the high costs of participating in protests prevented them from mobilizing any substantial share of the population in this direction (Heinze and Pollack, 1990).

The Change in the Situation Subsequent to 7 May 1989

Two kinds of event brought about a change in the situation after 7 May 1989: (1) external events, i.e. certain decisions of third countries; and (2) internal events, i.e. certain decisions of political bodies in the GDR. According to the above outlined explanatory model, *such macro events are only relevant if they affect the individual determinants of political action*, since protests are actions of individual actors. It is therefore necessary to ascertain what events occurred since May 1989 and how these events have affected the incentives to political action on the individual level.

The following *external events* played a significant role in the increase of protest-enhancing incentives after May 1989: (1) There was a continuation of liberalization processes in other Eastern Bloc countries. On 2 May Hungarian frontier police started to pull down border fortifications on the Austrian border. (2) On 4 May the first demonstrations were held in Beijing; on 3 and 4 of June the democratic movement in China was terminated by government repression. (3) Starting from 15 July, GDR citizens sought refuge in various FRG embassies (Budapest, Prague, East Berlin) with the aim of leaving their country. Emigration from the GDR increased tremendously when Hungary and Czechoslovakia allowed emigrants from the GDR to pass through their borders to reach the FRG. What were the effects of these events on the incentives to protest outlined above? With regard to emigration, the existing possibilities of leaving the GDR were perceived by the citizens and made use of by an increasing number. This, in turn, gave those who remained the impression that the GDR regime was in trouble: the large number of emigrants created even more problems in many social sectors, for example in the economy, medical care, and in the educational sphere. The population probably expected the regime to adopt certain liberalization measures in order to put a stop to the exodus. This led to a further increase in dissatisfaction in 1989 as well as to a rise in the perceived influence of being able to bring about changes by means of personal involvement. Due to the GDR regime facing difficulties as a result of extensive emigration, the population probably also expected fewer governmental sanctions: a regime that is in trouble is likely to decrease the extent of repression.

Increasing liberalization in Poland and in Hungary probably had the same effect, leading to an increase in relative dissatisfaction with the regime among the GDR population. It also strengthened citizens' expectations that the regime in the long run would have to effect certain reforms. This, in turn, raised the probability of changing the situation by personal involvement.

Many citizens, on the other hand, were afraid of a 'Chinese solution', as mentioned above. Such a solution was not improbable, as it had been explicitly approved by the SED regime. The increasing number of those involved in the protest movement in the course of 1989 decreased the likelihood that this solution would be adopted. This assumption is further substantiated by the fact that more and more citizens demanded reforms in resolutions without being subjected to sanctions.

Internal events leading to a rise in protest-enhancing incentives in the course of 1989 comprise, among others, the fact that the outcome of the communal elections held on 7 May had obviously been tampered with. This increased the population's dissatisfaction with the regime, as did the celebrations of the 40th anniversary of the GDR held on 7 October. Within the framework of the latter event, the 'achievements' of socialism in the GDR were highly acclaimed, although the discrepancy between the regime's claims and reality were becoming more and more obvious.

This situation – increasing dissatisfaction, increasing political influence and decreasing or at least not increasing expected repression – led to the following consequences: (1) Protest norms became applicable to a higher degree. The individual will feel more and more obliged to become involved in politics if there is an increase in the dissatisfaction and in the expected success, as well as a decrease in the risk of political involvement. (2) The same conditions will result in an increase in positive social incentives for participation in protest actions and to a decrease in negative social incentives.

Accordingly, the increase in demonstrations and other protest actions could be expected. These protests may in turn have changed the incentives in question: the population increasingly assumed that a rise in involvement would lead to reforms being granted by the regime. If there is an upsurge in the extent of protest, a regime that, according to its ideology, is supposed to represent the interests of the population cannot, in the long run, oppose the demands of the citizens. A citizen will assume this to hold true, even if the SED completely rules out any reforms in a multitude of announcements and via the party newspapers. Simultaneously, faced with the increasing establishment of political groups in 1989, GDR citizens had reason to assume that the influence of these groups and their personal influence had risen.

The growing number of protests will have enticed a growing number of citizens to feel obliged to get involved. The greater the number of citizens fighting for political reform, the realization of which would be beneficial to each individual, the more the individual citizen will also feel obliged to get involved.

After 9 October there was another upsurge in protests, as this was the first time that no governmental repressions had occurred. The cost of participation thus decreased considerably. In addition there will have been a relatively high expectation of political change after this date. As these changes, however, were not effected as quickly as the population had expected, there was a further increase in political dissatisfaction due to the low dynamics of change.

A successive alteration in incentives thus took place: at a certain point in time certain external and internal changes led to an increase in protest-enhancing incentives, which in turn resulted in a rise in protest. This again brought about a further rise in protest-enhancing incentives. The consequential increase provoked internal events, such as changes in the sanctioning behaviour of the government. In addition further external events ensued, leading to a change in protest-enhancing incentives, and so on. It is impossible to explain the exact course of this process, as this would require exact information on changes in the perceived action consequences for a multitude of points in time in 1989.

This information can no longer be procured. One can therefore only ascertain that a process of the kind described above and displayed in Figure 1.1 took place.

5 THE PROCESS OF THE REVOLUTION

The changes in protest-enhancing incentives that took place in 1989 do not explain how the behaviour of a great number of individuals was coordinated in such a manner that demonstrations could be staged at certain places and times, for example on Monday evenings on the Karl-Marx-Platz in Leipzig. Four possible processes might have channelled the willingness to protest into these demonstrations.

First of all it is possible that the demonstrations were organized by one person or group. Such an *organization model* does not apply to the demonstrations in the GDR, as governmental bodies would have prevented even the announcement of the time and place of any large-scale demonstrations.

Secondly, the demonstrations could have had their origin in the decision of a certain group to have a demonstration at a certain place and time. This group passes this information to other persons or groups, asking them to pass this information together with the request to join the demonstration. However, such a *micromobilization model* does not apply to the situation in the GDR, as there was no such group that initiated the demonstrations.

Figure 1.1: The Process of the Revolution in the GDR in 1989

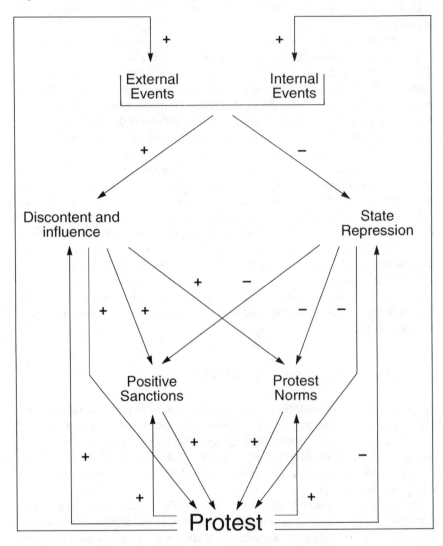

Note: + and – denote proposed positive and negative causal effects.

Both models presuppose that the demonstrations were planned by individual persons or groups, a fact not assumed in the following two models. One of these, which I have labelled the *threshold model*, proceeds from the assumption that certain actions such as participation in demonstrations become less costly if other persons have already adopted them.[11] The process of participation in demonstrations could, according to this model, be described as follows. In the initial phase those persons participate who gain a very high (net) utility from participation in demonstrations. This lowers the cost of participation for others until their threshold for participation is reached. They will participate in the next demonstration to be staged. A greater number of participants leads in turn to the participation threshold of another group of persons being reached, and so on. Such a process can explain the progressive increase in protest up until 6 November, albeit not the decrease in protests ascertainable thereafter (see Table 1.1). The major weakness of the model is that it does not explain how the protests were coordinated. It presupposes that the protests have been coordinated in some way, at least the first time. Then it may be assumed that all participants in subsequent protest actions behave as the participants in the first one.

This critique of the threshold model does not imply that the number of protesters is irrelevant to the costs and benefits of participating. As I argued earlier, the costs that depend on the number of protesters are only one part of the total costs (or benefits) of protest.

The most plausible model is the *spontaneous cooperation model*. Uniform behaviour of a large number of persons often occurs when various individuals independently arrive at the same decisions, simply because they find themselves in similar situations. The demonstrations in the GDR in the autumn of 1989 are such a spontaneous cooperation of large numbers of citizens. How did such a coordination ensue? Let us assume an average citizen from Leipzig, who is highly motivated to express his dissatisfaction without, however, being prepared to bear the costs of governmental sanctions. This citizen is aware that for the regime even small groups gathering at certain places may constitute an act of protest and be sanctioned. He furthermore assumes that such small groups open up possibilities of voicing protest in a manner that entails low risks of governmental sanctions, for example by chanting slogans in chorus. If this is a well-known fact, gatherings will only ensue, if all these people simultaneously decide to go to the same place at the same time. This will only be the case if everybody assumes that many others will also go to a certain place. If such expectations exist, a tacit coordination of individuals' behaviour occurs (Schelling, 1960, pp. 54–8), without there being any necessity for an arrangement to meet for any organization or mobilization.

When taking such a decision, the number of persons one expects to meet at the particular place plays the following role. If one expects to meet only a few persons, there is a relatively low risk of suffering governmental sanctions, because one's presence at such a place will not be regarded as an act of protest: there are many reasons for being at a certain place at a certain time.

The larger the number of individuals, the greater the likelihood of the congregation being regarded as aiming at protest, and the lower the risk for each individual of being confronted with sanctions. In any case, on being arrested citizens can almost always claim that they were just taking a stroll through the streets.

If one wants to meet large numbers of persons in a town with a clearly defined urban centre, one will go to one of its large squares. For the citizens of Leipzig the Karl-Marx-Platz is such a meeting place, including the bordering streets and the ring road that runs nearby. The Nikolai Church is in the vicinity of this square. Leipzig citizens were well aware that since 1982 prayers for peace have been held in the Nikolai Church every Monday from 5 to 6 p.m. At least some of those attending the prayer meetings will cross the Karl-Marx-Platz after leaving the church. If a Leipzig citizen wants to express his dissatisfaction, it is an obvious choice to go to the Karl-Marx-Platz on a late Monday afternoon.

The following excerpt from a radio programme (Schneider, 1990, p. 17) illustrates this process, taking the Monday demonstrations held on 25 September and 2 October 1989 as an example:

> at 5 o'clock for prayers it [the Nikolai Church in Leipzig] is bursting at the seams as has been the case for weeks. We are waiting outside, together with hundreds of others in the churchyard and a great number in the Grimmaische Street. Something is in the air, a strange feeling of unspoken togetherness. ... The bells toll. It is 6 o'clock in the evening. The church empties. ... At about a quarter to seven the nucleus of the crowd begins to move, starts running, right into the pedestrian area of the Grimmaische Street. There is no obvious leader. Over to the Karl-Marx-Platz between the Gewandhaus and the Opera. Suddenly a few thousand have gathered. Spectators join ranks. The streets are overcrowded. Cars come to a halt. ... On the 2nd of October it was the same as the week before. Only this time the crowd had trebled. Even elderly people were present. The route and the destination was clear, as were the slogans: 'We are staying here' and for the first time: *'We are the people!'*

The 'spontaneous' nature of the Leipzig demonstrations was expressed by one of the participants as follows: 'There was no head of the revolution. The head was the Nikolai Church and the body the centre of the town. There was only one guidance: Monday 5 o'clock at the Nikolai Church'.[12] Other GDR cities also have clearly defined urban centres with large squares where one can expect to meet others, the Alexanderplatz in East Berlin being an example.

The spontaneous cooperation model does not imply that every citizen decides independently to go to the city centre. Reports by Leipzig citizens (Neues Forum Leipzig, 1990) show that to a certain extent there was a micromobilization, inasmuch as they asked friends to accompany them.

The spontaneous cooperation model is not only able to explain how the demonstrations ensued, but also why the protests gained ground in the course of time. The readiness to participate in protest increased with the rise of the incentives for protest, as shown above. A continual rise in the number who decide to go to the respective places can therefore be expected.

A further factor may perhaps have led to the protests gathering momentum: demonstrations became social events, which in turn increased the incentive to participate in further demonstrations.

6 THE VENUE OF THE REVOLUTION

It is hardly realistic to assume that at the beginning of 1989 changes in the incentives described before were the same irrespective of place or social group. It seems that the venue of the revolution was in Leipzig because the above conditions for protest are evident there to a particularly high degree.

On the one hand the regular Monday prayer meetings at commonly known venues constituted favourable structural preconditions for spontaneous co-operation that did not exist in other towns. On the other, the level of dissatisfaction among the citizens of Leipzig was particularly high (Hofmann and Rink, 1990). This was first due to several events that had occurred previously. In 1968, for example, the demolition of the university church on the Karl-Marx-Platz resulted in protests. In June 1989 police action and subsequent arrests occured as a result of a street music festival that was held in spite of it having been prohibited (Lieberwirth, 1990). These events heightened the dissatisfaction with the SED among both young and old Leipzig citizens.

Furthermore, Leipzig was the most polluted of all the large East German cities, the older buildings were in a state of decay and the supply situation or provision of goods was particularly bad. Many citizens had contact with West Germans, Leipzig being the venue of regular international trade fairs. These were not only members of the business community, but citizens who offered private accommodation due to insufficient hotel capacity. Such contact is likely to have increased relative political and economic dissatisfaction.

7 THE NON-VIOLENT CHARACTER OF THE DEMONSTRATIONS

Church members constituted a relatively high share of those participating in the protests. It was this group, in particular, who called for abstinence from acts of violence as a central precondition for any kind of opposition. The non-violent character of the demonstrations may therefore have its roots in the Christian ethics internalized by the respective church members. Although members of the church only formed a small share of the total number participating in demonstrations, they may have internalized non-violence as a norm that is also valid for demonstrations.

Even if this holds true, one has to question whether this is a sufficient explanation for the non-violent character of the demonstrations, as norms are often infringed. Such an infringement is particularly likely to occur within the framework of demonstrations, as a high degree of dissatisfaction tends to result in aggressiveness and acts of violence, especially if one is confronted with those who have been the cause of frustration for decades. Mere reference to internalized norms cannot be regarded as a sufficient explanation for the non-violent character of the demonstrations.

It seems more plausible that those involved in protests believed that they could only reach their political objectives by means of non-violent forms of action. The support of fellow citizens and the immediate social environment could be reckoned with only if the demonstrations remained non-violent, and the regime could only be made to fulfil the demands of the citizens if non-violent means were employed as, according to the official ideology, the regime had to be assumed to represent the people's interest. Furthermore, acts of violence would have given the government and the police justification to intervene and put an end to the protests and the reform movement: the SED regime would have had reason to brand the members of the opposition as hooligans and criminals. However, if the regime had placed such a stigma on non-violent demonstrations it would have lost credibility in the long run. Further, during the demonstrations the citizens were afraid that acts of violence would lead to police intervention. The non-violent character can therefore be explained as the most effective strategy towards achieving the political objectives aimed at.

The non-violent character of the protests can also be explained by the fact that prior to and during the demonstrations there were strong social incentives inhibiting acts of violence: during the prayers for peace and during the demonstrations there were repeated calls for non-violence. In addition there were physical barriers to violence: during the demonstration in Leipzig on 9 October, for example, citizens cordoned off the Stasi headquarters to protect it against any intruders or damage.

8   DISCUSSION

The explanation proposed above brings forth a number of problems. The first question is whether the suggested explanation can be empirically substantiated. Where no sources are mentioned, the respective deliberations are in line with a number of talks that I personally conducted with GDR citizens, as well as with those published by others (see especially Bohley et al., 1989; Lieberwirth, 1990; Neues Forum Leipzig, 1990). Although these data cannot be regarded as a sound testing of the proposed explanation, they nevertheless make it plausible.

One aspect that has been left out of account until now is to determine what is not explained by advanced theoretical considerations, that is the exact point in time of and the exact number of participants in the respective demonstrations. Formulating models to explain these aspects presupposes very detailed assumptions on the exact distribution of the mentioned variables among the population, as well as on the exact effects brought about by internal and external changes. Although it is highly unlikely that sufficient data will be available to test such models, their formulation is to be recommended because they provide an answer to the question of how the spontaneous cooperation of a large number of citizens emerges in authoritarian regimes in general.

The analysis presented here neglects one important question: why did the SED regime not react in a different way, for example why did it not adopt the Chinese solution? A detailed discussion of this aspect would extend beyond the scope of this chapter. Since the reaction of the SED regime could be regarded as among the indirect causes of the protests dealt with here.

NOTES

* The present chapter is part of a research project directed by the present author and Professor Peter Voss (Leipzig). This project is supported by the Deutsche Forschungsgemeinschaft (German Science Foundation). I wish to thank the Deutsche Forschungsgemeinschaft for its support and Peter Voss for valuable suggestions. This is a modified version of a paper previously published in German (Opp, 1991).

1. This was said, for example, by the previous Chancellor of the FRG Helmut Schmidt in a leader in *Die Zeit* on 10th November 1989.

2. There is no estimation of the number of participants who took part in the Monday demonstrations between 4 and 25 September.

3. See, e.g., McCarthy and Zald (1973, 1977); Oberschall (1973); Tilly (1978). For a good summary see Jenkins (1983). A critique is provided in McAdam (1982).

4. The explanation of evolutionary or 'spontaneous' cooperation is called the 'invisible hand explanation' (Ullmann-Margalit, 1978; Vanberg, 1984).

5. See, for example, Ajzen and Fishbein (1980); Ajzen (1988); Feather (1982). This model has also been applied to the explanation of protest behaviour. Cf. Klandermans (1984); Muller (1979); Opp (1986, 1989); Opp and Roehl (1990a, 1990b); Finkel et al. (1989).

6. For a more precise formulation and an empirical test of these hypotheses see Finkel et al. (1989).

7. See for example Marwell and Ames (1979); Muller (1979); Opp (1986, 1989); Riker and Ordeshook (1968, 1973).

8. Cf. e.g. Klandermans (1984); Knoke (1988); Opp (1986, 1989); Finkel et al. (1989); Mitchell (1979); Muller and Opp (1986); Tillock and Morrison (1979); Useem (1980); Walsh and Warland (1983).

9. Cf. Frohlich et al. (1971); Frohlich and Oppenheimer (1978: ch. 4); Popkin (1988); White (1988). Since political entrepreneurs only play a minor role in the revolution of the GDR, as we shall see, we will not discuss the possible role of political entrepreneurs further.
10. E.g., it was common practice to keep records of visitors in blocks of flats. Furthermore, an extensive sanction network (Stasi, police force) was there to prevent demonstrations of other public acts of protest, and if they occurred they were immediately dissolved.
11. See especially the considerations developed by Mark Granovetter (1978, 1986). See also Prosch and Abraham (1991).
12. This account is confirmed by other sources: see Schneider (1990); Döhnert and Rummel (1990); Neues Forum Leipzig (1990); Tetzner (1990).

REFERENCES

Ajzen, I. (1988), *Attitudes, Personality, and Behaviour*, Milton Keynes: Open University Press.
Ajzen, I. and Fishbein, M. (1980), *Understanding Attitudes and Predicting Social Behaviour*, Englewood Cliffs, NJ: Prentice-Hall.
Bohley, B., Fuchs, J., Havemann, K., Henrich, R., Hirsch, R. and Weisshuhn, R. (1989), *40 Jahre DDR. Und die Bürger melden sich zu Wort*, Berlin: Hanser, Büchergilde Gutenberg.
Döhnert, A. and Rummel, P. (1990), 'Die Leipziger Montagsdemonstrationen', in J. Grabner, Ch. Heinze and D. Pollack (eds), *Leipzig im Oktober. Kirchen und alternative Gruppen im Umbruch der DDR. Analysen zur Wende*, Berlin: Wichern Verlag, pp. 147–158.
Feather, N.T. ed. (1982), *Expectations and Actions: Expectancy-Value Models in Psychology*, Hillsdale, NJ: Lawrence Erlbaum.
Finkel, St E., Muller, E.N. and Opp, K.-D. (1989), 'Personal Influence, Collective Rationality, and Mass Political Action,' *American Political Science Review*, **83**, 885–903.
Fischer-Weltalmanach (1990), Sonderband DDR, Frankfurt: Fischer.
Frohlich, N. and Oppenheimer, J.A. (1978), *Modern Political Economy*, Englewood Cliffs, NJ: Prentice-Hall.
Frohlich, N., Oppenheimer, J.A. and Young, O.R. (1971), *Political Leadership and Collective Goods*, Princeton, NJ: Princeton University Press.
Granovetter, M. (1978), 'Threshold Models of Collective Behaviour', *American Journal of Sociology*, **83**, 1420–3.
Granovetter, M. (1986), 'Economic Action and Social Structure: The Problem of Embeddedness', *American Journal of Sociology*, **91**, 481–510.
Heinze, Ch. and Pollack, D. (1990), 'Zur Funktion der politisch alternativen Gruppen im Prozess des gesellschaftlichen Umbruchs in der DDR', in J. Grabner, Ch. Heinze and D. Pollack (eds), *Leipzig im Oktober. Kirchen und alternative Gruppen im Umbruch der DDR. Analysen zur Wende*, Berlin: Wichern Verlag, pp. 82–90.
Hirschman, A.O. (1970), *Exit, Voice, and Loyalty. Responses to Decline in Firms, Organizations, and States*, Cambridge, Ma.: Harvard University Press.
Hofmann, M. and Rink, D. (1990), 'Der Leipziger Aufbruch 1989. Zur Genesis einer Heldenstadt', in J. Grabner, Ch. Heinze and D. Pollack (eds), *Leipzig im Oktober. Kirchen und alternative Gruppen im Umbruch der DDR. Analysen zur Wende*. Berlin: Wichern Verlag, pp. 114–22.

Jenkins, J.C. (1983), 'Resource Mobilization Theory and the Study of Social Movements', *Annual Review of Sociology*, **9**, 527–53.
Jenkins, J.C. and Perrow, Ch. (1977), 'Insurgency of the Powerless: Farm Worker Movements (1946-1972)', *American Sociological Review*, **42**, 249–68.
Klandermans, B. (1984), 'Social Psychological Expansions of Resource Mobilization Theory', *American Sociological Review*, **49**, 583–600.
Knoke, D. (1988), 'Incentives in Collective Action Organizations', *American Sociological Review*, **53**, 311–29.
Lieberwirth, St. (ed.) (1990), *Wer eynen spielmann zu tode schlaegt ... Ein mittelalterliches Zeitdokument anno 1989*. Leipzig: Edition Peters, Militzke Verlag.
Marwell, G. and Ames, R.E. (1979), 'Experiments on the Provision of Public Goods. I. Resources, Interest, Groups Size, and the Free-Rider Problem', *American Journal of Sociology*, **84**, 1335–60.
McAdam, D. (1982), *Political Process and the Development of Black Insurgency 1930–1970*, Chicago and London: University of Chicago Press.
McCarthy, J.D. and Zald, M.N. (1973), *The Trend of Social Movements in America: Professionalization and Resource Mobilization*, Morristown, NJ: General Learning Corporation.
McCarthy, J.D. and Zald, M.N. (1977), 'Resource Mobilization and Social Movemements', *American Journal of Sociology*, **82**, 1212–41.
Mitchell, R.C. (1979), 'National Environmental Lobbies and the Apparent Illogic of Collective Action', in Clifford S. Russell (ed.), *Collective Decision Making. Applications from Public Choice Theory*, pp. 87–136 Baltimore and London: Johns Hopkins University Press.
Muller, E.N. (1979), *Aggressive Political Participation*, Princeton, NJ: Princeton University Press.
Muller, E.N. and Opp, K.-D. (1986), 'Rational Choice and Rebellious Collective Action', *American Political Science Review*, **80**, 471–89.
Neues Forum Leipzig (ed.) (1990), *Jetzt oder nie – Demokratie*. Leipziger Herbst '89, Leipzig and Munich: Bertelsmann, Forum.
Oberschall, A. (1973), *Social Conflict and Social Movements*, Englewood Cliffs, NJ: Prentice-Hall.
Opp, K.-D. (1986), 'Soft Incentives and Collective Action. Participation in the Anti-Nuclear Movement', *British Journal of Political Science*, **16**, 87–112.
Opp, K.-D. (1989), in collaboration with Peter and Petra Hartmann, *The Rationality of Political Protest. A Comparative Analysis of Rational Choice Theory*, Boulder, CO: Westview Press.
Opp, K.-D. (1991), 'DDR '89. Zu den Ursachen einer spontanen Revolution', *Kölner Zeitschrift für Soziologie und Sozialpsychologie*, **43**, 302–21.
Opp, K.-D. and Roehl, W. (1990a), *Der Tschernobyl Effekt. Eine Untersuchung über die Determinanten politischen Protests*, Opladen: Westdeutscher Verlag.
Opp, K.-D. and Roehl, W. (1990b), 'Repression, Micromobilization and Political Protest', *Social Forces*, **69**, 521–48.
Popkin, S. (1988), 'Political Entrepreneurs and Peasant Movements in Vietnam', in M. Taylor (ed.), *Rationality and Revolution*, Cambridge: Cambridge University Press, 9–62.
Prosch, B. and Abraham, M. (1991), 'Die Revolution in der DDR. Eine strukturell-individualistische Erklärungsskizze', *Kölner Zeitschrift für Soziologie und Sozialpsychologie*, **43**, 291–301.

Riker, W.H. and Ordeshook, P.C. (1968), 'A Theory of the Calculus of Voting', *American Political Science Review*, **65**, 25–42.

Riker, W.H. and Ordeshook, P.C. (1973), *An Introduction to Positive Political Theory*, Englewood Cliffs, NJ: Prentice-Hall.

Schelling, T.C. (1960), *The Strategy of Conflict*, Cambridge, MA.: Harvard University Press.

Schneider, W. (ed.) (1990), *Leipziger Demontagebuch*, Leipzig and Weimar: G. Kiepenheuer.

Tetzner, R. (1990), *Leipziger Ring. Aufzeichnungen eines Montagsdemonstranten Oktober 1989 bis 1. Mai 1990*, Frankfurt: Luchternhand.

Tillock, H. and Morrison, D.E. (1979), 'Group Size and Contributions to Collective Action: An Examination of Olson's Theory Using Data from Zero Population Growth Inc', *Research in Social Movements, Conflicts and Change*, **2**, 131–58.

Tilly, Ch. (1978), *From Mobilization to Revolution*, New York: Random House.

Ullmann-Margalit, E. (1978), 'Invisible-Hand Explanations', *Synthèse*, **39**, 263–91.

Useem, B. (1980), 'Solidarity Model, Breakdown Model, and the Boston Anti-Busing Movement', *American Sociological Review*, **45**, 357–69.

Vanberg, V. (1984), 'Unsichtbare-Hand Erklärung und soziale Normen', in H. Todt (ed.), *Normengeleitetes Verhalten in den Sozialwissenschaften*, Berlin: Duncker & Humblot, pp. 115–47.

Walsh, E.J. and Warland, R.H. (1983), 'Social Movement Involvement in the Wake of a Nuclear Accident: Activists and Free Riders in the TMI Area', *American Sociological Review*, **48**, 764–80.

White, J.W. (1988), 'Rational Rioters: Leaders, Followers, and Popular Protest in Early Japan', *Politics and Society*, **16**, 1–34.

Wimmer, M., Proske, Ch., Braun, S. and Michalowski, B. (1990), *Wir sind das Volk. Die DDR im Aufbruch. Eine Chronik in Dokumenten und Bildern*, Munich: Heyne.

Winkler, G. (ed.) (1990), *Sozialreport 90. Daten und Fakten zur sozialen Lage in der DDR*, Berlin: Die Wirtschaft.

Zimmerling, Z. and Zimmerling, S. (eds) (1990), *Neue Chronik der DDR*. Vols 1–5, Berlin: Tribüne.

2. Introduction of New Institutional Conditions and Legal Regulations into Former Centrally Run Economies: The Case of East Germany

Eva Kigyóssy-Schmidt*

To struggle for freedom was easier than to cope with it.

(Andrzej Wajda, film producer)

INTRODUCTION

Two years after the euphoria at the end of 1989 the harsh daily reality began to dominate the process of transformation in the former centrally run economies. Political change in Central and Eastern Europe opened up the possibility for the creation of democratic institutions and market relations. But contrary to earlier expectations the abolition of a central control did not result in a spontaneous development of the Western-type market system and did not come up with the hoped-for improvement in the economic situation. The very opposite happened: the economic and social situation in Central and Eastern Europe deteriorated perceptibly. The volume of industrial production, of capital investment, the rate of inflation, employment or the real income in the central and eastern regions of Europe has worsened (see also Gabrisch et al., 1991, pp. 1–6). The manifest crisis situation in the countries exposed to transformation has again raised the question of the possibility of accelerating development into a Western-type industrial state and of how and to what extent this could be reached within a given stage in the process of transformation.[1] While initially the main obstacle was that knowledge and experience were insufficiently available for the tasks to be solved, the present development is now revealing, step by step, the underlying mechanism of transformation processes. Based on newly gained experience, some contradictions in transformation processes will be outlined below.

In addition, the question is raised of the controllability of transformation processes. To provide a more detailed explanation, a working definition of

31

institutional and legal conditions is desirable. 'Adaptability' is used to describe the process of the newly introduced or essentially modified institutional and legal conditions becoming effective and resulting in reaction from the target group. The scope for controlling transformation processes is understood to lie mainly in the following fields: in moulding the content of the more or less newly created institutional conditions and legal regulations; in influencing the organizational implementation of each individual measure, and in supporting the adaptability of the changed condition by addressing, in the first instance, the level of enterprise.

The chapter aims to emphasize specific aspects of the transformation processes in Germany's five new federal states. In accordance with the subject of the research itself, the treatment of the issue has assumed a workshop character.

1 CONTRADICTIONS BETWEEN INITIAL CONDITIONS AND TASKS TO BE SOLVED IN FORMER CENTRALLY RUN ECONOMIES

In Central and Eastern Europe the following is one of the crucial contradictions in the wake of transformation: there is a decrease in funds available as internal sources for the solution of transformation require ever-increasing financial means and due to bad creditworthiness the possibilities of external funding have become worse and worse.[2] Parallel to the deteriorating economic situation, the growing social need calls for an instant and effective solution to transformation. The need for action is dictated not only by the worsening economic situation faced by broad strata of the population; political uncertainties arising from the vacuum caused by change and the unforeseeable future are apt to sow frustration. This is also the ground where, as shown by history, the seeds were sown that later produced national conflict. The civil war in Yugoslavia serves as a tragic example.

But it is not only the lack of or the misguided motivation of the population that could prove to be an inhibiting factor for transformation. If the governing party fails to create a mass basis it will be compelled in the interest of survival to try to establish a different power structure. This could be provided for example by means of state property. Thus political instability could act as a decisive brake on privatization and, accordingly, might slow down the progress of transformation.

In transforming a centrally run economic system into a Western-type 'mixed economy' the operation of the state is also not free of contradictions. In the former socialist countries the bulk of economic potential was known to be state property and the system of central control and management was predominant. Now the basis for the reform of the economy is provided by the reorganization of property relations. The privatization of former state enterprises is, in the first place, the concern of the state. It is assumed that in the future a sizeable part of former state-run property will also be administered by the state. Such state-authorized executive organs as the Trustee Agency are likely to be overtaxed in their abilities if they are expected to carry out market-conformable privatization and, at the same time, to exert control over the viable structures of future state property.[3] Similarly, the task conferred on national privatization agencies, demanding that market-conformable privatization should be coupled with a high rate of social compatibility, implies a nearly insoluble contradiction. Even if funds are initially made available for a socially compatible transition in a country, like the former GDR, which is under transformation, the period to be covered by the funds is left open in the same way as the long-term influence of labour-policy measures on the development of market relations.

The totality of change appears to be another reason for contradictions underlying the process of transformation. Generally, the old system has to give way to a completely different one. But a vacuum is emerging with the liquidation of the old system. It does not matter whether shock therapy or gradual transition is indicated – at any rate it will take some time until a new operative system emerges. Obviously, the economy fails to function smoothly during this period of transition.[4] The losses arising are slowing down the process of transformation at a time when an acceleration of transformation is required.

Considerable time is also required to acquire the experiences that have to be gained in handling strategies of transformation. It should be stressed that the economies to be transformed are not primitive ones. These are intensely interrelated economic systems and structures with an ascertainable degree of industrialization. The proper functioning of such economic systems requires the existence of adequate complex communicative structures (see Dietz, 1991, p. 33). As can be seen from the example of the new federal states of Germany, the emergence of such comprehensive structures and their adaptation will, even in the most favourable case with the availability of know-how, take a considerable time.

In an extremely simplified form, the formula underlying the vicious circle of the transformation processes in Central and Eastern Europe can be summarized as follows. Due to the inherited and deteriorating economic situation there is an urgent demand for action in the post-communist economies in order to create the foremost requirements for a properly functioning economy. As suggested, the task of implementation is substantially inhibited by the political instability following the change in power, by increasing difficulties in the external and internal funding of transition, by lack of experience with the Western-type economic model aspired to, by inexperience in expounding a transformation strategy and by the objective need for time in the process of transformation. The delay in the transformation process caused by subjective and objective obstacles does not guarantee a rapid and general improvement of the economic situation. It is only that the moment of the coveted economic upturn is put off, that the social incompatibility of transition is increasing and that, as a result, the crisis is deepening. The above assumptions give rise to several questions. A fundamental question seems to be how far the already unfavourable starting conditions for transformations in Central and Eastern Europe will be allowed to deteriorate until a perceptible improvement in the economic situation is reached. What are the consequences of a deepening of the economic crisis inside the countries and abroad? But the primary and essential question remains: how to break the vicious circle created by the transformation process? What possibilities for the control of the transformation processes exist in Central and Eastern Europe?

2   INSTITUTIONAL AND LEGAL CONDITIONS FOR TRANSFORMATIONS AND THEIR CONTROLLABILITY

There exists no generally acceptable theory on transformation, but there are a great number of concepts and recommendations concerning its nature and the coordination in time of tasks to be resolved, and on additional possibilities for control of transformations.[5] From an outline of the contradictions of transformation it becomes obvious that transformations require control. One of the requirements for control is the presence and the active role of the state.[6] Below, the general definition of macroeconomic institutional and legal conditions in transformation re-emphasizes the demand for a kind of control over the processes of transformation.

In a vacuum created between the command economy and the upcoming market economy, the following are viewed as institutional and legal conditions:

A. Existence of starting conditions
    – change of political power;
    – economic and social heritage after the 'turn'; and
B. Institutional and legal conditions of transformation to be created, such as
    – safeguarding of political stability;
    – safeguarding monetary stability;
    – creation of legal and institutional requirements;

- financial safeguarding in the interest of the transformation measures to be put through;
- extension and modernization of infrastructure;
- development of business services;
- development of adequate political instruments for the labour market.

Obviously, there are correlations between the starting conditions and the institutional and legal conditions of transformation to be created. In decisions to be taken about the choice of institutional and legal conditions, the starting conditions cannot be disregarded. Furthermore, the implementation of institutional and legal conditions is decisively dependent on the starting conditions. In the process of adaptation these correlations are crucial in the development of the desired market economy relations.

Principally in the interest of exerting influence under given conditions, a number of strategies are available. The content, scope and coordination in time of each individual measure cause a number of reactions on the side of addressees.[7] In case of the existence of possible target criteria (e.g. level of privatization, movements and balance on the labour market, investment behaviour, competitiveness, development of payments balances, or retrenchment of subsidies) the preparedness for adaptation becomes verifiable. The strategy of creating means and meaures can be modified according to the signals of adaptation preparedness.

The very fact that there is no ready-made recipe for the shaping of the transitional phase in Central and Eastern Europe, and that every attempt at control gives rise to interference, both in economic interrelations and in dynamics, results in the need for instant evaluation of the above-indicated signals caused by the process of adaptation. Further, the modification of the transformation strategy does not exclusively imply a change in control for macroeconomic conditions to be created. On the level of adaptation there are also areas which can be influenced. These include, for instance, the old burden of thinking. Thus a consensus reached between the population and the government which is based on a conclusive strategy of transformation can be viewed as a factor in promoting the transformation. If the prospects are considered advantageous for a promising establishment of the new macroeconomic conditions there is a real chance of an acceleration of the indicated social consensus. In my view, the situation in Germany's new federal states might serve as a case in point to prove this thesis.

3 IMPOSITION OF NEW INSTITUTIONAL AND LEGAL CONDITIONS IN EAST GERMANY

The process of adaptation in the transition from a former centrally run economy to a Western-type market economy system can be described as follows. The development of the desired economic model will require completely new or modified macroeconomic conditions (see also Albach, 1990; Kigyóssy-Schmidt, 1991; OECD, 1991; Riese, 1990; Schmieding and Kopp, 1991 and Treuhandanstalt, 1991). The institutional and legal conditions created are liable to cause desired and undesired reactions on the side of addressees, including enterprises. This reaction is called 'adaptability'. In a more general sense, the sequence of correlations between the introduction of macroeconomic conditions and the level of adaptation is viewed as the process of adaptation.

But in this respect the new federal states, when compared with the other East European countries, show the following differences. As for the start of transformation in East Germany, it was the unstoppable rate of political change in the GDR that led to the unification of both German states. As a result of free elections the East German population opted for the renunciation of its state sovereignty and for the imposition of the West German social and economic system. Thus, it was clear from the beginning that the strategy of shock therapy would be applied to the transformation process in East Germany. Although the misuse of statistics in East Germany as an instrument to gloss over economic deficiencies is now becoming more and more obvious, it has to be assumed that the former GDR could pride itself on the most developed national economy of the East that was brought as a heritage into the process of transformation.[8] Another component of the social legacy in East Germany is the crass intolerance of its political system that was prevailing until its very collapse.[9]

Given that the shock therapy is a historical necessity for the former GDR, the margin of choice for strategies of transformation will be narrowed down. In return, however, German unification gave the East Germans many benefits in contrast to the other peoples of Central and Eastern Europe. These benefits include in the first line the political and monetary stability achieved in a united Germany. In addition, the new federal states, in contrast to other post-communist states, have the advantage of being able to display their capabilities within the legal regulations and institutions provided by a highly developed industrial state.[10] Moreover, western Germany is putting up financial safeguards to cushion the hardships of collapse. The new federal states are expanding and modernizing their infrastructure and, in five to ten years, will have built the most sophisticated infrastructure. For expanding such business services as management consultation and services, it is possible to resort to the experiences of the old federal states. Similarly the political experiences with the labour market available in the old federal states can be utilized in the wake of transformation. Thus East Germany's transformation can be viewed as a model case in those instances when a former centrally run economic system is abruptly provided with the institutional and legal conditions needed for the development of market relations. The difficulties faced by other states of Central and Eastern Europe suggest the scope of tasks faced and the limited possibilities for their solution. Several years are still needed for these countries to change their legislation and to create their own institutional conditions; understandably, the former GDR appears to be the envy of the others. Nevertheless, the question is why there is still sluggish growth under, admittedly, favourable conditions in the new federal states? What are the obstacles to transformation? To what extent and over what time is it possible to accelerate the process of transformation in order to overcome the barriers to transformation in favour of a well-functioning market economy? It becomes obvious from the learning-type nature of these transformation activities that the question raised can now only be partially answered in terms of an empirical and theoretical analysis. Below, reference is made to the objective and subjective time required for the creation of the macroeconomic conditions needed for the transition from a centrally run to a market economy system. Several factors will be outlined that could affect the subjective time needed for transition.

By the term 'objective time required for the introduction and expansion of West German institutional and legal conditions in the five new federal states' is meant the amount of time required, for technical, technological and organizational reasons, for the implementation of given conditions (see also the working definition of the macroeconomic conditions of transformation). Consider, for example, the objective time required for the introduction and expansion of institutional and legal conditions in transition. In the case of the privatization of former state-owned enterprises, the creation of a well-run administration as well as clarification of the ownership situation may take several years.

It will also take several years, for technical reasons, to modernize the infrastructure. The introduction of labour market measures into the new federal states is another example. Even if the West German instruments of labour policy are incapable of completely coping with the threat posed by mass unemployment in East Germany they nevertheless offer an initial solution to the social compatibility of the situation. For sheer technical and organizational reasons a certain time is needed for the effective operation of the labour market instruments on account of the East German experiences.[11]

The subjective time required for the introduction of institutional and legal conditions for market economy is dependent on the fact that transformation has the character of a learning process. Parallel to the liquidation of the centrally run economic system it is necessary to establish substantially modified or completely new institutional and legal conditions for the new construction. Due to lack of experience, pressure of time and the limited funds available, the new institutional and legal conditions, as a rule, cannot be regarded as final. They give rise to desired and undesired reactions on the side of the addressees, primarily on the level of enterprises. But the signals released could be used as a basis of information for modifying the strategy of transformation. By the term 'subjective time required for the effective operation of institutional and legal conditions for market economy' is meant the amount of time which, pending the establishment of the desired economic system, is still needed for the correction of the strategy of transformation.

The constraints on the process of transformation in the five new federal states largely determine the objective time needed for the creation of the institutional conditions. Thus, in East Germany, the margin of influence on the time required for transformation lies above all in the learning process required for shaping the strategy of transformation, that is in the subjective time needed for the development of market relations. Reference should be made to the human factor.

As suggested above, a social consensus between people and government could promote transformation. But the emergence of a consensus would require a consistent and successful strategy of transformation. Worldwide, experts have agreed that the reconstruction of the economy in the new federal states will be only a question of time. Thus in spite of all the hardships to be endured in the new federal states during this transitional phase, this forecast underlines the possibility of a social consensus. The control of adaptability will shorten the difficult process of transformation. Obviously it is human resources which are most relevant in the process of adaptation. For this reason the labour market situation in East Germany is used below to serve as an example in revealing the ability of adaptation that has emerged in the new federal states.

An almost complete readjustment both in everyday life and in professional life is one of the consequences of the inevitable shock therapy administered in East Germany. At the end of 1991 the advantages and disadvantages of this dramatic change could not be sufficiently assessed. In present-day publications it has frequently been pointed out that the daily standards of West Germany cannot immediately be introduced and adopted by the eastern half of Germany (see Hickel and Priewe, 1991). On the other hand, it remains questionable whether the so-called 'old burdens' of thought in East Germany contained only negative elements.[12] However great the advances of the process of rethinking in East Germany, it can be safely assumed that the shock therapy gave rise to a great deal of uncertainty in the new federal states. This phenomenon is reflected in the labour-market of autumn 1991 (see Figure 2.1). However, the completeness of statistical data available can justifiably be questioned on account of the present transformation. The data in Figure 2.1 show the great instability of the East German labour market. This instability is likely to increase when it is considered that about two-thirds of the 6.5 million presently employed are confronted with the threat of unemployment, making one in four of them redundant by the end of 1992.

Figure 2.1:   Labour Market Situation in the New Federal States 1989 and Autumn 1991

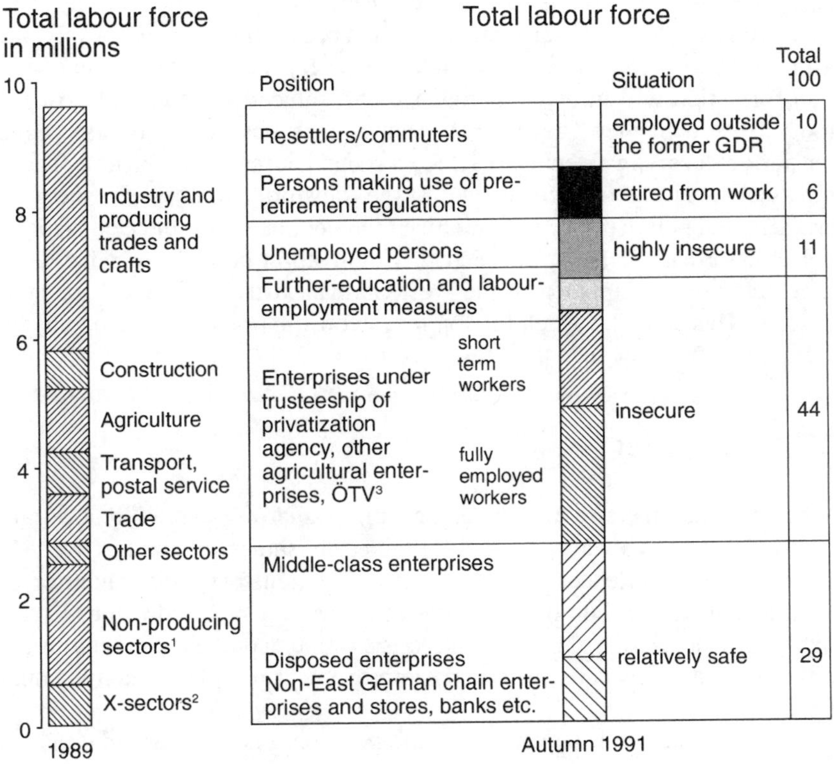

Total labour force in millions

Total labour force

Position		Situation	Total 100
Resettlers/commuters		employed outside the former GDR	10
Persons making use of pre-retirement regulations		retired from work	6
Unemployed persons		highly insecure	11
Further-education and labour-employment measures			
Enterprises under trusteeship of privatization agency, other agricultural enter-prises, ÖTV³	short term workers / fully employed workers	insecure	44
Middle-class enterprises			
Disposed enterprises Non-East German chain enter-prises and stores, banks etc.		relatively safe	29

1989 — Industry and producing trades and crafts / Construction / Agriculture / Transport, postal service / Trade / Other sectors / Non-producing sectors¹ / X-sectors²

Autumn 1991

1.   Science, education, health and social system as well as other services.
2.   Until 1990 unpublished data on army, police, state security etc.
3.   Public service, transport, traffic.
Source: Author's research based on the *Statistical Yearbook of the GDR 1990*, p. 125, as well as selected reports and interviews.

The labour market situation arising in East Germany is likely to escalate into a dreaded source of social tensions. Violence against foreigners, starting in 1991, showed that this fear is fully justified. With the material aspect of social compatibility of transformation being largely safeguarded in the new federal states, its non-financial aspect could be substantially upgraded by the social consensus between people and government, as mentioned above. Thus, in my view, the slide of the East German economy could be moderated. However, the success of the social consensus depends upon whether or not a fundamental understanding of the ongoing changes can be instilled in the minds of the public. When the Berlin Wall was torn down the East German population unmistakably demonstrated that it did not want to be treated as a child. Now it is advisable to convince these people that their newly won freedom is a platform for an open discussion of all difficulties. Certainly, the aspirations to communicate information at every step in the course of the transformation will meet with objective and subjective limits in Germany, too. In my own view, however, it seems to be possible to defuse social tensions to a certain extent by reaching a social consensus on the time factor, the assessment and the perspectives of the transformation between the government and population, and to motivate the population for the next steps of the transformation. It appears that this motivation could be conducive to accelerating the adaptation of the West German institutional and legal conditions. This would be helpful for the reconstruction of the economy in Germany's five new federal states.

4 CONCLUSIONS

Whether shock therapy (instant capitalism) or a slower evolution, a certain amount of time is always required for the establishment of an effective new system. The experiences gained so far in the transformation countries of Central and Eastern Europe have shown that the time required will be longer than expected. At the same time the crisis-prone economic situation in the post-socialist states calls for a rapid improvement in their economic situation.

In order to place the new system into operation it is necessary to establish adequate institutional conditions and legal regulations in the post-socialist states. But even in the favourable instance of the East German transformation, with the major part of institutional conditions available, the new system will not arise spontaneously. So the existence of institutional and legal conditions for transformation is a necessary, but not a sufficient condition for the emergence of an effective economic system.

The institutional conditions available have to be adopted by the target group, above all on the level of the enterprises. Controllability of the process of adaptation is primarily addressed to the shaping of the measures of transformation as well as to the human resources involved. As for Germany's new federal states, the basic requirements are provided for a more intensive utilization of human resources in the interest of accelerating the transformation from planned to market economy.

NOTES

* Here I would like to express my appreciation to Dr Lothar Römer. Serving as a real friend in this complicated period of East German history, he translated my paper into English.

1. It should be left open whether the objectives of former centrally run economies, fraught with illusions, often covered only the positive sides of market relations, such as relative prosperity. The negative consequences, such as a possible deterioration in the labour market situation, were often suppressed.

2. Thus the volume of credits of Western banks, which in 1989 increased by about US $7 billion (i.e. 1,000 million) in Central and Eastern Europe, fell by about the same amount in 1990 (Laski, 1991 pp. 2–3).

3. The experience of Western countries has shown that even under the current market economy relations the privatization of state property is problematical. In Great Britain, e.g. in carrying through a privatization drive by the Thatcher government from 1979 to 1989, the share of public enterprises in the gross domestic product declined from 10.5 to about 5 per cent (Schnabel, 1990, p. 149 and 164; also Fröhlich and Schnabel, 1990; Leipold, 1990, p. 137).

4. In general, a shop can be reconstructed and, even in the event of difficulties, selling can be continued. But if a sales department is to be completely reconstructed, selling operations are restricted. The sign 'Business as usual' does not solve the problem.

5. In analysing the processes of transformation it has become common practice to consider the institutional infrastructure, macroeconomic and monetary stabilization and the real adaptation on the microlevel to be mutually dependent tasks of the needed reforms (see also Edwards, 1989; Siebert, 1991). There was intense discussion of the temporal sequence of transformation. Kornai (1990), for example, pleaded for a shock therapy. According to his deliberations a temporally coordinated and comprehensive liberalization of the conditions of existence of private property should be put into practice together with the macroeconomic stabilization and the political requirements for social and economic transformation. In order to secure macroeconomic stability, a halt to inflation, the restoration of budgetary balance, the control of total demands, use of rational prices and the elimination of the shortage economy are demanded as conditions that are to be reached at the same time. As political supporting conditions required for the 'shock therapy' Kornai also mentioned the popularization of the programme, open discussion of its advantages and disadvantages and the existence of a capable and powerful government. As for the correlation between macroeconomic stabilization and deregulation of domestic economy, a similar view was taken by Sokil and King (1989), Bofinger (1990) and Kloten (1990). By contrast, Murell (1990) advocated an evolutionary approach. Laski (1991) and Levcik (1991), in analysing the experiences of transformation, also called into question the practicability of shock therapy. In the discussion a prominent role was assigned to the financial policies of the transitional phase. As is known, without a consistently enforced financial and fiscal concept, microeconomic steps towards reform can cause an increased surplus of money or trigger runaway inflation with

flexible prices. Based on experiences gained in former attempts at reform in the once-socialist states, several authors have argued that in this way the information value of prices can be essentially affected (Aslund, 1990; Lipton and Sachs, 1990, Wolf, 1990).

6. For the sake of simplicity, the leverage of the state is only referred to in the control of transformations. But the leverage of the state should not be understood as the only possible or next higher possibility of control (see also Kigyóssy, 1990). The development of institutional conditions and their adaptability is the result of the consensus of all involved. In choosing the strategy of transformation in Germany's new federal states it is the Federal Bank and the political parties that play a decisive role. International institutions, such as the International Monetary Fund and the World Bank, are also known to control the transformation in Central and Eastern Europe. Their crediting policies requiring liberal measures is critically discussed by experts (see also Laski, 1991, pp. 6–7 as well as Levcik, 1991, pp. 8–9).

7. Observation of this reaction is partly possible with the conventional instruments of statistics. On the one side, traditional statistics will collapse in the vacuum between centrally run economy and market economy. On the other hand, the imminent social and economic uncertainties will cause a lack of transparency of the available statistical data. Thus it is known that only a fraction of the registered joint ventures actually carry out appreciable economic activity. For this reason the consultation of experts plays a considerable role in the analysis of adaptation.

8. How the economic potential of East Germany was almost completely destroyed by the inevitable shock therapy and the collapse of Eastern trade is not discussed here in detail. To illustrate the extent of collapse we refer to an estimate according to which by the end of 1991 only some 15 per cent of the still existing former state-run enterprises in the new federal states turned out to be profitable (see author's interview with experts at the State Property Agency; Treuhand in References).

9. Only Romania competed with the former GDR in this respect. The discussion of the role of the human factor refers to additional characteristics of the East German social heritage.

10. Another question is that the adaptation of West German institutional and legal conditions in the new federal states is more time-consuming than anticipated and that this process is obviously not spontaneous. One of the reasons is that the valid institutional and legal conditions have emerged over a longer period in line with the specific requirements existing in the old federal states. This is why in the initial stage of transformation the conditions cannot be adopted without a certain degree of modification by the new federal states (see also Helmstädter, 1990; Schüller, 1990).

11. Mention should be made of labour exchange institutions, the introduction of unemployment benefits and the organization of labour-employment measures among others.

12. In the days of political 'turn' by the end of 1989 the people in the GDR were appalled at learning that the summer retreat of the former GDR prime minister accommodated a dozen chest-type deep freezers. It is thus understandable that the term 'dishonestly acquired property' in the minds of the East German population can today also be applied to property speculations and other offences.

REFERENCES

Albach, H. (1990), 'The Economics of Transformation, Economic Aspects of German Unification', The Tore Browaldh-Lecture held at the University of Gothenburg, 9 November.

Aslund, A. (1990), *Changes in Soviet Economic Policy-Making in 1989 and 1990*, Stockholm Institute of Soviet and East European Economics, Working Paper 14.

Bofinger, P. (1990), *The Role of Monetary Policy in the Process of Economic Re-*

form in Eastern Europe, London: Centre for Economic Policy Research, Discussion Paper 457.

Dietz, R. (1991), 'From Command to Exchange Economies', in Havlik (1991), pp. 31–40.

Edwards, S. (1989), *On the Sequencing of Structural Reforms*, Paris: OECD, Department of Economics and Statistics, Working Paper 70.

Fröhlich, H.-R. and Schnabel, C. (1990), *Das Thatcher-Jahrzehnt: Eine wirtschaftliche Bilanz*, Köln.

Gabrisch, H. et al. (1991), 'System Transformation under Severe External and Internal Shocks. The Economic Situation in Early 1991 and Outlook 1991', *Forschungsberichte des Wiener Institutes für Internationale Wirtschaftsvergleiche*, **173**, June.

Havlik, P. (ed.) (1991), 'Dismantling the Command Economy in Eastern Europe', in *Vienna Institute for Comparative Economic Studies, Yearbook III*, Boulder, San Francisco and Oxford: Westview Press.

Helmstädter, E. (1990), 'Zur Ordnungspolitik der Kapitalwirtschaft', in *Ordnungspolitik beim Übergang der DDR-Wirtschaft zur Marktwirtschaft*, Institute of Economics, Berlin, pp. 150–68.

Hickel, R. and Priewe, J. (1991), 'Der ewige Ost–West-Konflikt, mit alten Denkmustern lässt sich die Jahrhundertaufgabe nicht bewältigen', *Die Zeit*, **46**, 8. November, 28–9.

'Im Niemandsland zwischen Plan und Markt, Der Westen und die Wirtschaftsreformen im Osten – auf der Suche nach Auswegen aus der Krise' (1991). Forumsdiskussion mit J. Bognar, J. Kleer, A. Leysen, J. Sachs, G. Bucerius, M. Gräfin Dönhoff, H. Schmidt, Th. Sommer und R. de Weck, *Die Zeit*, **45**, 1 November, 41–6.

Kigyóssy, E. (1990), 'Some Aspects of Macroeconomic Control in the Federal Republic of Germany' in J. Kovács and B. Dallago (eds.), *Economic Planning in Transition. Socioeconomic Development and Planning in Post-Socialist and Capitalist Societies*, Brookfield: Dartmouth, pp. 156–72.

Kigyóssy-Schmidt, E. (1991), 'Business Services in the Transition of Former Centrally Planned Economies. The Case of Hungary', paper presented at The Seventh Annual Seminar on the Service Economy, 13–14 May, Paris.

Kloten, N. (1990), 'Zur Transformation von Wirtschaftssystemen', *Ordo*, **40**, 99–127.

Kornai, J. (1990), *The Road to a free Economy. Shifting from a Socialist System: The Example of Hungary*, New York: W.W. Norton.

Laski, K. (1991), 'Die Wirtschaftslage der ehemaligen RGW-Länder im Jahr 1990', paper presented at the Ordentliche Generalversammlung des Wiener Institutes für Internationale Wirtschaftsvergleiche für das Jahr 1990, 4 April, Vienna.

Leipold, H. (1990), 'Die Politik der Privatisierung und Deregulierung: Lehren für die Wirtschaftsreformen im Sozialismus,' in A. Schüller (ed.), *Zur Transformation von Wirtschaftssystemen*, Marburg, pp. 133–58.

Levcik, F. (1991),'Zentral- und Osteuropa auf dem Wege zur Marktwirtschaft, Bisherige Ergebnisse und kritische Bemerkungen zur eingeschlagenen Strategie', paper presented at International Symposium of the Austrian-French Centre, 21 and 22 May, Palais Luxembourg.

Lipton, D. and Sachs, J. (1990), 'Creating a Market Economy in Eastern Europe: The Case of Poland', *Brookings Papers on Economic Activity*, **1**, pp. 75–147.

Murell, P. (1990), 'Bing Bang versus Evolution: East European Economic Reforms in the Light of Recent Economic History', *Plan Econ Report*, **6** (26), Washington, pp. 1-11.

OECD Wirtschaftsberichte, Deutschland (1991). Paris: OECD.

Riese, H. (1990), 'Das Wirtschaftssystem in seiner Bedeutung für das Wirtschaftswachstum', paper presented at the Seminar for Economics, Ottobeuren, 25–29 September.

Schmidt, K.-D. (1991), 'Die Rückkehr Mittel- und Osteuropas in die Weltwirtschaft: Voraussetzungen und Chancen', *Aussenwirtschaftspolitik*, Stuttgart, pp. 161–72.

Schmieding, H. and Kopp, J.M. (1991), *Privatisierung in Mittel- und Osteuropa: Konzepte für den Hindernislauf zur Marktwirtschaft*, Institute of World Economics, Kiel, Discussion Paper, 165.

Schnabel, C. (1990), 'Privatisierung und Deregulierung in Grossbritannien', *List Forum*, **16** (2), 148–66.

Schüller, A. (1990), 'Angleichungsprozess in ordnungspolitischer und wohlfahrtsstaatlicher Sicht', in *Ordnungspolitik beim Übergang der DDR-Wirtschaft zur Marktwirtschaft*, Institute of Economics, Berlin, pp. 17–23.

Siebert, H. (1991), *The Transformation of Eastern Europe*, Institute of World Economics, Kiel, Discussion Paper, 163.

Sokil, C. and King, T. (1989), 'Financial Reform in Socialist Economies: Workshop Overview', in Ch. Kessides, Ch. et al. (eds), *Financial Reform in Socialist Economies,* Washington, pp. 1–27.

Treuhandanstalt, Zentrales Controlling (1991), *Privatisierung*, Stand am 31 August.

Wolf, Th.A. (1990), 'Reform, Inflation und Anpassung in Planwirtschaften', *Finanzierung und Entwicklung*, **27** (March), 2–5.

PART II

Political, Constitutional and Social Psychological Aspects of German Unification

3. German Unification: Political and Constitutional Aspects

Ulrich K. Preuss

1 INTRODUCTION

The demise of the communist regimes in Central and Eastern Europe together with efforts in those countries simultaneously to establish a market economy and a constitutional-democratic political system have exposed those societies to unprecedented social and economic experimentation. Although there is good reason to assume that the economic and the political transformations are closely connected, it cannot be taken for granted that they are always mutually reinforcing. In fact, they can become hostile to one another. Individual and collective democratic rights – for instance the right to strike or the right of national and ethnic minorities to form political organizations – can be and have been used as efficient weapons against the inevitable hardships of policies which aim at marketizing the economy. However, the most dramatic case – Yugoslavia – demonstrates that political conflicts do not necessarily originate in the economic sphere. In almost all the East and Central European countries, the collapse of authoritarian communist rule has released national, ethnic, religious and cultural conflicts which cannot be solved by purely economic policies. The most promising instrument for coping with the genuinely political difficulties of social integration seems to be a constitution. The constitutional state is supposed to foster political cooperation among diverse and conflicting pluralist social groups and to tame their centrifugal and destructive potential. Undoubtedly, constitutionalism has proven a powerful force of sociopolitical integration. Unfortunately, it seems to be less vigorous when faced with the problem of national cleavages or multinationalism. When the constitutional state was developed in North America and in France in the last decades of the eighteenth century, it was built on the foundation of the unitary nation state. It was not supposed to solve the problem of nation-building but rather the issues of an already established nation state. Many of the post-communist countries of East and Central Europe, being bi- or multinational states, lack the national homogen-

eity which at least facilitates the creation of a constitutional state. Hence
they face a threefold difficulty in managing their simultaneous transition to a
market economy and to a constitutional democracy: the genuine economic
devastations wrought by the communist regimes, the transformation of the
social and economic classes of the command economy into the social and
economic classes of a capitalist economy and, finally, the creation of a
constitutional structure for political entities that lack the undisputed integrity
of a nation state.

In the face of such difficulties, the people of East Germany – the former
German Democratic Republic (GDR) – seemed to be particularly lucky.
From an economic perspective, unification with one of the wealthiest countries and integration into one of the most productive economies gives the
former GDR an insurmountable advantage over the other European post-
communist economies in the competition for foreign investors. As to the
political aspects, unification (which was paralleled by the definitive German
renunciation of any claims to territories of the former German 'Reich' that
had been transferred to Poland and the Soviet Union after the Second World
War) created a German nation state with virtually no national or ethnic
minorities within its essentially undisputed boundaries. Finally, there seemed
to be no need to create a new constitution for the united Germany because
the political leaders of the post-communist GDR had decided to join the
Federal Republic by accession and, as a consequence, to have its Basic Law
extended over what had been their territory.

In discussing the political and constitutional aspects of German unification, I want to examine briefly three problems: (1) the tension, alleged or
real, between the Basic Law's simultaneous commitment to supranational
integration and to the German nation state; (2) the relationship between the
nation and the constitution as two different modes of political integration;
and (3) the issue of 'backward justice' as one of the most haunting problems
of all post-communist societies.

2   THE QUEST FOR NATIONAL REUNIFICATION AND THE COMMITMENT TO SUPRANATIONAL INTEGRATION

The Basic Law of the Federal Republic of Germany has become a much
praised bequest of the founders of the West German state. After over forty
years, the Basic Law has been the most long-lived constitution in all of
German history. It is, or for that matter it used to be one of the two para-
mount symbols of West Germany's political and social stability – the other
one being the Deutschmark. Ironically, the framers of the Basic Law by no

means intended to create a durable constitution. The Basic Law was supposed to be the temporary constitution of an incomplete and transitory state – that is why it was called 'Basic Law' rather than 'Constitution'. Its life span was expected to be short: no more than a few years until unification came about with the Eastern parts of the country then controlled by the Soviet Union and its German communist affiliates. This was the main reason why the founders refrained from two elements that they themselves actually thought necessary for a fully-fledged constitution and which therefore they put off for the definitive constitution of a reunited Germany. First, they eschewed the design of a basic structure of the social and economic order (as laid down in all 'Länder', or state, constitutions which were created after 1945 and prior to the Basic Law) and, secondly, they made no effort to sanction the Basic Law by a plebiscite.

After forty years of West Germany's continual progress to becoming a major economic power, a viable democratic society and a respected member of the international community of nations, almost everybody inside and outside West Germany was convinced that time had made permanent the once self-proclaimed temporary and transitory character of the state and its Basic Law. Though lip-service was paid to the official state goal of reunification, there emerged a more or less tacit understanding that the Federal Republic was a fully-fledged state with a fully-fledged constitution that did not deserve any longer to be regarded and treated as a transitional phenomenon. But history is capricious and loves surprises: as if it begrudged the West Germans their peace with the final outcomes of the post-Second World War order and their own newly achieved West German identity, history in a further ironic twist donated them national unification on a silver platter and exposed them to new uncertainties.

At first glance there was, or at least there seemed to be, a potentially explosive tension. On the one hand the Basic Law was unequivocally devoted to Germany's reunification, solemnly spelled out in the preamble. But, on the other hand, the Basic Law contained an innovative and, at that time, unique commitment to participation in the creation of supranational institutions and the transfer of sovereign powers to them (article 24). In order to emphasize the seriousness of this commitment and to ease its implementation, the requirement for constitutional amendment of it (two-thirds in the Federal Parliament, the Bundestag, and in the Federal Council, the Bundesrat) was lowered to a simple legislative majority. This tension between the goal of national unity and the goal of international integration provided the main issue of West German politics in the 1950s. During those years Adenauer pushed towards the latter against the vigorous resistance of considerable parts of the population, represented politically by the Social Democratic Party (SPD). The Social Democrats presumed that international integration would necessarily endanger or definitively frustrate national reunification. Even after the Social Democrats had finally come to accept West Germany's international integration into NATO, the EEC and other European supranational institutions, it was still widely held that national unification and international integration were ultimately incompatible under the given circumstances of the Cold War. Nobody could imagine that the Soviet Union would be prepared to offer unification without demanding in return that a united Germany abandon its integration into the different Western inter- and supranational organizations.

While it appeared that in the 1950s the majority of West Germans were still ready to pay a price of this sort for their national unity, it became evident in the 1970s that such a majority no longer existed. The generation born after 1949 in particular could hardly imagine that there could be a potential tension in those alternative political options. In other words, among the three principal potential paths of West Germany's politics – national unification at the expense of international integration into the West; inter-national integration into the West at the expense of national reunification; and national unification and at the same time international integration – only the second seemed realistic and, given the circumstances, also desirable. The first was disagreeable on several grounds: it could pose considerable danger to the political and military stability of Europe and, moreover, if pursued, would probably provoke the resistance of the three Western allies. The third alternative seemed ideal for many, but hopelessly unavailable. And yet, in the end, it was just this alternative, which nobody except some political dreamers had anticipated, that materialized and finally resolved the tension between these two main goals of the West German constitution.

It is worth mentioning here that the political front lines of the 1950s had entirely changed by the beginning of the 1990s. Although the majority of the Social Democrats and their candidate Oskar Lafontaine did not flatly oppose German unification, in 1990 they did argue for slowing down the process. Such caution was necessary because they unequivocally gave priority to West Germany's roots in and commitments to the West European collective organi-zations. Given Chancellor Kohl's and the Christian Democratic Party's cred-ibility in their fidelity to Germany's integration in the West and Kohl's simul-taneous successful push towards unification, the Social Democrats' position, asserting that these two claims were incompatible or that there was at least a serious tension between them, appeared a bit outdated to many German voters. Consequently the SPD lost the first all-German elections in December 1990 by a wide margin. Obviously, or so the majority of Germans thought, history itself had disproved yet another Social Democratic assumption.

All this sounds very much like the happy end to a story. However, being a dialectical nation, the Germans know that when there is a solution of problems then almost immediately the problems of the solution arise. Obviously, many Western governments, the EEC and the international economic community at large are concerned that Germany will shift both its economic resources and its political attention to the reconstruction of its eastern states. As a consequence, Germany could become more unable and more reluctant to further the process of economic and political integration of (Western) Europe. This, then, would mean a re-emergence of the seemingly vanquished alternative between national goals and international commitments. Indeed, on the political level Chancellor Kohl proved to be justified in pursuing what in spring and summer 1990 seemed to be a highly unlikely assumption: that Germany could be unified without being forced to cut or at least to weaken its ties with the West European communities and with Nato. Unwisely, however, he made the same contention with regard to the economic dimension of German unification, and here he appears to have encountered significant difficulties in fulfilling his promise that neither West German taxpayers nor the EEC would suffer from his drive to immediate German unification. It may be that national unification could be achieved only because political leaders simply neglected its economic implications. Given the more than 12 billion Deutschmarks which had to be paid to the Soviet Union in order to buy the approval of its leaders, and given the enormous amount of money and resources that will be necessary for the creation of approximately equal economic and social conditions in the old and the new 'Länder', it is not surprising to observe that the German economy is under enormous strain. Hence it will be extremely difficult to escape the economic and, in the long run also political, implications of this double-bind situation of Germany, one that remains a legacy of the postwar order. I leave this dilemma to the economic experts and instead address another problem which is lurking behind the seemingly perfect solution to Germany's predicament.

3   POLITICAL INTEGRATION VIA NATIONHOOD OR BY CONSTITUTION?

As I observed, German unification was accomplished by the accession of the former GDR to the Federal Republic. As a consequence, the Basic Law was put into force in the territory of the former GDR immediately after the accession became effective on 3 October 1990. The accession of the GDR to the FRG was formally a purely unilateral act of the Volkskammer, the parliament of the then GDR; it made use of article 23 of the Basic Law which stipulates that it shall be put into force 'in other parts of Germany... on their accession'. According to article 23 neither the government nor the people of the Federal Republic were allowed to participate in this decision, much less to reject the accession. The situation was seemingly paradoxical: whereas the West Germans had no say in the decision of the East Germans if they wanted to form a common state with the West Germans, using this route the East Germans had no say in the determination of the conditions under which they would live together with the West Germans. Once the Easterners declared their accession to the Federal Republic, then the quasi-self-operating extension of the Basic Law over their country would be the immediate consequence. In other words, this mode of unification did not imply the foundation of a new joint polity and its authentication through a new constitution. To put it somewhat differently: within the process of unification according to article 23, the joining part – the GDR – was doomed to disappear legally, whereas the Federal Republic survived. There was no basis for assuming that both the Federal Republic and the GDR would cease to exist and together be replaced by a new political entity.

Whereas this outcome seems to be a mere technicality of constitutional law, upon closer scrutiny it is clear that the outcome is of political significance and by no means foreordained or merely technical. By this I refer to the other alternative, the road not taken, namely the final article of the Basic Law – article 146. To the best of my knowledge, article 146 is truly unique among all present constitutions of the world. In its original version, valid until 1990, this article stipulated that the Basic Law shall cease to be in force on the day on which a constitution adopted by a free decision of the German people comes into force. The underlying idea is evident: given the expectation of the framers in 1949 that a united German nation state would soon be re-established, the Basic Law was to be replaced by a fully-fledged constitution sanctioned by the whole German people. It should be emphasized that this article 146 is not an amendment rule, that is, a rule which stipulates how to change the Basic Law. Constitutions can be revised fundamentally, but the revisions are subject to the rules of the constitution itself. In contrast, no constitution can contain rules which allow its abolition altogether and entirely. That would mean the sanctioning of revolution, whereas it is the very meaning of constitutions to avoid revolutions and to make them unnecessary. Political revolutions change political institutions in ways that those institutions mean to prohibit, whereas constitutional amendments change political institutions in ways which the constitution authorizes.

Article 146 is a paradoxical combination of these two opposites. It allows the people to annul the Basic Law and to replace it with a completely new constitution without binding the people beforehand to any procedural or substantive rules. Thereby the people can abolish the constituted powers and claim their unrestrained constituent power without running the risks of a revolution. This amounts to constitutional permission to make a revolution. As proved to be the case in 1990, this is not a purely theoretical conclusion.

After the East Germans had overthrown the communist regime, and after they had unequivocally opted for unification with West Germany, the question was raised in the political debates as to whether article 146 might not now govern developments. Had not the very situation materialized that the framers had envisioned and that endowed the whole German people with its original constituent power to create a new polity? If so, the implications could be enormous, because this constituent power was unrestricted by any superior rule including the Basic Law itself. Thus, all the constitutional and extra-constitutional achievements of the West German state, particularly its integration into the inter- and supranational organizations of the West, could have been at the disposal of the German people to re-examine and possibly revoke. Given the desperate desire of the vast majority of East Germans to accept the West German model of society almost unconditionally, a constitutional upheaval seemed to be a purely theoretical concern. However, it could not be totally excluded that, once the constituent power of the people was released, the process could assume a dynamics resulting in highly unpredictable outcomes. In the meantime, many East Germans have recently become more sceptical of the economic and social implications of the West German model. Though there is hardly any inclination to abandon economic and political ties to West European institutions, other radical changes in the constitutional framework of the Basic Law are conceivable. For instance, the inclusion of so-called social rights into the constitution, such as the rights to a dwelling or to labour, is conceivable. That is why West German constitutional lawyers in particular were extremely dissatisfied that article 146 was not repealed after the unification. They argued that this article had after all become obsolete once German unification took place under article 23. Instead, however, article 146 was amended and disconnected from its original connection to unification, and changed into a general provision for the adoption of a totally new constitution.

Again, it is entirely possible that German unification through accession of the former GDR has solved one problem only by creating new ones which in the long run may outweigh the benefits of the solution itself. New problems may, for example, emerge from the congenital defect of the unification process itself and the resulting political unity. The new Germany was launched on behalf of the principle of the nation state while another alternative was eschewed, namely founding a united, coherent country on principles and procedures of constitutional democracy. Because essential legitimation of unification was the principle of nationhood, Germany's unification lacked a thorough and deliberative democratic process that could have become the midwife of political unity and the cradle for an enlightened understanding of the complex conditions of citizenship and constitutional democracy. Surprisingly, we encounter a leitmotif of Germany's history in the nineteenth century

– the alternative between nationalism and liberal democracy. This choice may also touch upon the complicated issue of German identity, which I will here abjure; but it has more practical implications as well.

As empirical research demonstrates, democratic constitutions tend to be the more stable the more their 'authority pattern is congruent with the other authority patterns of the society of which [they are] a part' (Eckstein, 1966, p. 234). To be sure, one will hardly ever find a congruence in the strict sense of identity, but what is required is 'a pattern of graduated resemblances' which allows mutual responsiveness between the formal authority patterns of state and civil society within a country. It is not possible to elaborate on this hypothesis here, but I believe that the implantation of a particular constitution into a society lacking experience in its operation and, even more important, lacking corresponding and responsive institutions and value orientations, is likely to produce conflicts and crises rather than to satisfy that society's political needs. It is not unrealistic to assume that many structural elements produced by 40 years of communist rule (not to mention the impact of the preceding 12 years of Nazism and their subsequent one-sided processing) will persist still for quite a while. Nobody is born democrat, least of all in Germany and least of all in the late twentieth century. Democracy has to be learnt, individually and collectively, and one important step for the Germans could have been a broad and comprehensive process of constitution-making, involving both the East and the West Germans. After all, the need to learn, to reflect one's interests and values, to refine one's preferences, to redefine one's relations to 'others' is of course not only an obligation of the East Germans.

The mutual alienation of West and East Germans that clearly exists behind and beneath the enthusiasm generated in the first weeks and months after the fall of the communist regime cannot be eliminated altogether. But the alienation and hostility could have been mitigated by a process aiming at the creation of a common basis for their common political body. Of course, the Basic Law was not authoritatively imposed on the East Germans; it was self-imposed, so to speak. Moreover, unification on equal terms of both the Germanies was certainly impossible on manifold grounds. But neither submission nor voluntary self-submission is likely to engender the social and political coherence which is a necessary condition for a stable democracy.

Anticipating a possible counter-argument, I readily agree that the success story of the Basic Law also rests in part on its imposition on the West Germans in 1949 when a small indigenous political elite, in a mixture of conflict and cooperation with the Western allies, created a constitution for the West German population. I do not insist on a world of difference between the situation at that time and the present condition of the East Germans: I do not doubt that they, too, would be able to adopt a Basic Law and make use of its democratic potentials in a gradual, sometimes erratic learning process. After all, West Germans needed almost 20 years before they, really and fully, accepted it. The problem is rather the coincidence of two different political cultures within the same polity, and this may well entail cleavages that endanger the whole society.

4 THE ISSUE OF 'BACKWARD JUSTICE'

The issues discussed so far pertain to the national dimension of unification and its constitutional implications. Germany now also faces serious problems relating to more general aspects of unification, especially to the economic and social consequences of the transition to democracy and a market economy. The Eastern Germans share these problems with the other post-communist societies of Eastern and Central Europe, but they enjoy the unique advantage of not having to take them on all by themselves. However, some of these problems may have been aggravated rather than mitigated by the fact that overcoming the heritage of communist rule has to be managed within the framework of national unification. This applies particularly to two issues: the privatization of a vast amount of state property; and the punishment of the elites of the old regime and their collaborators within the extremes of 'self-purification' and 'collective amnesia'. Both issues are inherently connected, because both are concerned with justice.

The privatization of state-owned property, both real estate and businesses, presents one of the most serious difficulties in the post-communist countries. The problem is not only one of developing adequate procedures for the transfer of huge assets to private owners. Rather, protecting the acquirers against claims from former owners, or, to put the problem the other way round, satisfying the claims of former owners without deterring potential investors – this is a thorny problem. In the German case, the Unity Treaty made the important distinction between expropriations that had been conducted between 1945 and 1949, i.e. before the existence of the GDR and hence under the control of the Soviet Union, and expropriations under the aegis of the GDR. The former are considered permanent, that is, they must not be undone. During the unification negotiations this was one of the essentials urged by the Prime Minister of the former GDR, strongly supported by the Soviet Union. Interestingly, the Joint Declaration of the two German governments on the Regulation of Open Property Questions, states that the Soviet Union and the GDR see no possibility of revising the measures taken between 1945 and 1949, while the Federal government limited itself to the statement that 'it takes note of this result in light of the historical development'. The immunity of this category of expropriations from restitutions is now protected by an amendment which incorporated their irreversibility into the constitution (Quint, 1992). In April 1991 the Federal Constitutional Court acknowledged this amendment as constitutional; but the court nevertheless insisted that within this framework some kind of compensation has to be provided.[1]

In contrast, expropriations by the formerly sovereign authorities of the GDR must be undone. Only if a return of the former property is not possible – for example if the property has been assigned to public functions or dissolved into larger business units – may compensation be substituted for restitution. There have thus been cases where the heirs of a factory, for instance, were urgently besought to repossess their property, which was in the worst conceivable shape, and to invest in it in order to save the jobs at stake. Likewise, some heirs to decrepit real estate have renounced their claims. But in general, and particularly in real estate, claims to the restitution of property are being made – according to recent news more than a million to date – and this has entailed a degree of uncertainty that has dissuaded potential investors from commiting themselves. Still, the Unity Treaty tries to mitigate the negative consequences of the restitution principle by envisioning legislation which allows compensation rather than restitution when the property is urgently needed for investment. But the burden of proof for the potential investor is rather heavy, and until now private investments in the former GDR have remained modest.

The underlying constitutional problem in this area resides in the imperfect connection between property and justice. The economic function of private property does not necessarily coincide with those principles of justice embedded in the principle of restitution. In a dynamic capitalist economy property is best allocated to those who will make the most efficient use of it in the future, that is, to those who invest. In contrast, the principle of restitution is devoted to the goal of justice; property is assigned to those who deserve it because they or their families suffered injustice in the past. If the rectification of past injustice enjoys priority over the principle of allocation to likely investors, economic efficiency is likely to be severely restricted. It is one of the characteristics of all the East and Central European revolutions that they aimed simultaneously to achieve justice and to introduce a market economy. Now they must deal with the reality that the implementation of both principles simultaneously is not possible. Again, what at a first glance seemed to be a particular advantage enjoyed by the East Germans in comparison with the other post-communist countries – namely their accession to the Federal Republic and their incorporation into an established economic, legal and political order – may make their problems all the more difficult. The East Germans no longer have the possibility of arriving at a pragmatic solution to the problem of restitution, because those who would be hurt by pragmatism – West Germans – are able to force the Easterners to adhere to those constitutional standards that embody a rigorous and conventional concept of property. After all, in the first place it is the Westerners' Basic Law, and, moreover, they have the majority in political bodies and the predominant influence over public opinion.

Despite the strong normative colouring of the property claims of former owners, it was the economic dimension that prevailed. This becomes manifest when we compare the politics of property restitution with the compensations conceived for the victims of injustice who did lose not property but immaterial goods like freedom, health, the opportunity for a higher education, and so on. The Unity Treaty announces the legal regulation of the rehabilitation of those individuals who under the communist regime had become victims of arbitrary court decisions. This is a rather restrictive concept of rehabilitation, because victimization was not carried out primarily by the courts. Although the law in question has not yet been enacted, we may expect that more justice will be done for former owners of property than for those who suffered serious violations of, for example, their rights of habeas corpus.

A final observation may be in order on the problem of self-purification and collective amnesia. It is beyond the aim of this chapter to side with either of these alternatives. Given the pervasive system of communist surveillance and social control, which involved millions of people, only very few can claim 'pure hands'. As the examples of the other post-communist countries show, social peace seems to be attainable with neither of the two strategies in pure form. In Germany things are again more complicated. The West Germans can claim the 'mercy of geography'; they happened to live west of the River Elbe when Germany was divided; they are innocent. But every East German is indiscriminately exposed to the suspicion that he or she might have been a collaborator of the Stasi. Collaboration with the Stasi disqualifies one from employment in the civil service, and private businesses are also entitled to bar people from employment on this ground. The East Germans have opted for unification and for the Basic Law, but it is doubtful that they have already acquired with it full and equal citizenship.

5   CONCLUSION

German unification has been a uniquely huge social experiment. In contrast to scientific experiments, its effects cannot be confined to a laboratory. The transition from an authoritarian political regime and its concomitant command economy to a liberal democracy and a capitalist economy is as unprecedented as the short-term integration of two extremely different societies – one liberal-capitalist, one authoritarian-socialist – into one nation state. There is no constitutional pattern for either of these processes, much less so for the management of both simultaneously. Of course, in a way every historical situation is unparalleled, and it would be naive to expect any concrete conjuncture to fit into our traditional, accumulated wisdom. However, modern societies have developed a method for coping actively with the unforeseen emergence of new experiences: namely, the creation of constitutions. Constitutions symbolize the foundation or birth of a new polity; they contain the founding generation's reflection of new social and spiritual experiences; and it is through constitutions that the distinctiveness of a historical situation is transmitted to succeeding generations. From this perspective, the constitutional aspects of German unification reveal a failure of nerve and the political conservatism of the German people which diverge conspicuously from the exciting singularity of the events themselves.

NOTE

1. The decision is published in Europäische Grundrechte Zeitschrift, 1991, pp. 121–132.

REFERENCES

Eckstein, H. (1966), *Division and Cohesion in Democracy. A Study of Norway*, Princeton: Princeton University Press.
Quint, P.E. (1992), 'The Constitutional Law of German Unification', *University of Maryland Law Review*, forthcoming

4. The Unification of Germany from the Standpoint of a Social Psychologist

Dieter Frey

The problems of the unification of Germany, as well as the problems of the East European countries after the breakdown of communism, are mostly seen from a juridical, economical, political and social point of view. In this chapter a social psychological standpoint is taken and the questions are asked why the systems were able to survive for so long, what the social psychological problems are nowadays, and how these problems can be solved from the standpoint of social psychology.

1 THE FUNCTIONING OF TOTALITARIAN SYSTEMS AND THE RESULTING MENTAL DEFICITS

Totalitarian regimes can survive for a long time if they perfectly apply psychological instruments of reward and punishment and when they have the specific suppression infrastructure. The regimes of Hitler, Stalin, Saddam Hussein and Pol Pot (Red Khmer), as well as most totalitarian systems of Eastern Europe provide examples of this. Totalitarian regimes can be characterized in terms of the following aspects:

- an ideology which gives a definition of the situation and produces an interpretation of the world, i.e. a theory about the causes and the resolutions of the most important problems (e.g., Marxism, National Socialism). The ideology is very often quite simple and can be understood by the population. Very often it also contains a certain concept of the enemy (e.g., the Jew, the capitalist). The state/person must protect it/him/herself against these enemies;
- a monopoly party which rejects all kind of pluralism;
- a rewarding of conformists and privileges for those who hold the most important positions within the totalitarian system;
- punishment of nonconformists and elimination of the opposition;

- daily observation and a perfect inner surveillance system for observing the regime's population (informers, telephones that are tapped, spies, etc.) to watch for potential deviants;
- activation of killer groups which systematically eliminate or cut off potential deviants;
- a personality cult with a leader who is taken to be omniscient;
- a scapegoat, who is inside or outside the in-group and who increases the solidarity of the in-group (in-group favouritism and out-group devaluation);
- mass propaganda which daily indoctrinates the population;
- a global homogeneous educational system supporting the monopolistic party (children's songs, schoolbooks, etc.).

Most people in such systems suffer a chronic loss of control and helplessness – they can neither influence nor predict important aspects of their own lives concerning profession, politics, culture, or science. The East European countries have had very long-lasting totalitarian regimes. What type of person is a consequence of such a long-lasting regime?

Prominent social psychological theories, such as the theory of cognitive control (cf. Osnabrügge et al., 1985; Thompson, 1981; Taylor et al., 1984; Glass and Singer, 1972), as well as the theory of learned helplessness (cf. Osnabrügge et al., 1985; Seligman, 1975) predict that this produces deficits in the fields of motivation, affect-emotion and cognitions (for an overview of social psychological theories see Frey and Irle, 1984, 1985a, 1984b).

The *motivational deficits* are apathy, obesity, conformity to the existing norms, as well as low readiness for private initiative and self-responsibility. There is a general attitude that new problems are not seen as a challenge. The resulting passivity and apathy in many fields is functional in a totalitarian regime; it helps towards personal survival, as well as the (short-run) survival of the system as a whole.

To the *affective-emotional* deficits belong chronic anxieties, strong future pessimism, low self-esteem, depression, low frustration tolerance, hopelessness and emotional instability. The consequences of these affective-emotional deficits are, among others, high suicide rates, high divorce rates, a high degree of alcoholism, drug abuse and a strong degree of disturbance in private relationships. (Of course a lot of these problems, like alcoholism and drug abuse, are not only a consequence of totalitarian regimes, but also represent a serious problem in many European countries and the United States as well.)

The *cognitive deficits* include the following aspects: negative states are attributed constantly instead of variably, independent of whether there is a possibility of change or not. The cognitive deficits produce disturbances in learning to react to changing environments. The world is interpreted in terms of helplessness cognitions instead of control or mastery cognitions.[1]

The product of such a totalitarian system is a human being who can be characterized by a high degree of passiveness in many fields, and by anxiety, as well as inability to take personal responsibility and initiative. The consequences of a loss of control are described in the literature and they are confirmed empirically (cf. Osnabrügge et al., 1985; Seligman, 1975; Thompson, 1981).

Of course, there are two different groups in totalitarian states: the first is the passive group described above and the second is that one which carries the functionalist position and has the power (and probably the conviction of control). Totalitarian countries are typical two-class societies, especially because those who have political functions are privileged. In the last group the characteristics mentioned above are less pronounced. Despite this, the problem is that in totalitarian states not only do the great majority of normal people have these above-mentioned deficits, but also the small class of potential innovators within the society.

Research on innovation has shown that no society can exist successfully without a small group of inventors. Even though it is generally true that most of the totalitarian systems suppressed creativity and innovation, a lot of improvisation was still necessary and possible which was, in turn, responsible for the fact that creativity could still flourish. Nevertheless, in the long run there is a stagnation in the field of economics and in the social and cultural fields when real innovators are suppressed. The problem was that those who had the task of economic and scientific innovation were not necessarily the most competent persons, since they were mostly preferred or supported because of political reasons only. The lack of qualified people to occupy these positions greatly helped to cause the breakdown. Totalitarian societies, therefore, are always in danger of becoming rigid. The consequences are that they fall behind scientifically, technically, culturally and economically in comparison to systems which have autonomy, pluralism and responsibility.

The breakdown of totalitarian systems in Eastern Europe shows this regularity: the potential of creativity and innovativeness of people, especially in the group of innovators, was suppressed and the political as well as the economic system became rigid. If glasnost (openness) and perestroika (new structuring) are missing, the whole system will sooner or later break down. The over-engagement of the military, which happened in most regimes in Eastern Europe, reinforced this effect. In this respect Karl Marx was right in emphasizing that the state of the economic system is eventually decisive for the development of a state. Probably, the political leaders of such systems are completely aware that in the long run their system produces deficits in the emotional, cognitive and motivational fields. However, conformity, obedience and passivity of the majority is, for such a regime, more functional than disobedience, activity, civil courage or private initiative, because these factors would increase the instability of such a system. Of course, the conformity of the population to the ideology is sometimes identical with the individual's self-resignation.

2   THE IDENTITY OF THE GDR BEFORE UNIFICATION

The political elite of the GDR tried to elaborate a social identity for that country. In accordance with the Polish-English social psychologist, Tajfel's theory of social identity (1978, 1981, 1982), they first tried to elaborate a clear social categorization by differentiating between in-group and out-group. Contact with the out-group (West Germany) should be minimized in order to increase the solidarity of the in-group. Social comparisons were only made when the in-group was better; however, when the in-group was worse such comparisons were avoided. This strategy of specific social comparisons was the only means of achieving a positive distinctiveness and a positive identity for the GDR.

–   The people of the GDR were taught to be proud that they were number one in sports and many other fields.
–   The GDR was the leading economic power in the East. The politicians were always emphasizing to other states in the East that they had the best socialism. (It is known that Brezhnev was angry and bothered by the fact that Ulbricht and Honecker were proud of belonging to the 'best' socialist society; they complained that the fulfilment of socialism in the other socialist brother states was not as good.)
–   Most politicians in the East could achieve a positive distinctiveness towards the West by emphasizing the social success (social welfare, no unemployment, a perfect kindergarten system, and the low amount of egoism) which was supposedly non-existent in the West. There was also an official version of equal rights.
–   The state emphasized the aggressiveness of the West. The ideology was that capitalism suppresses the inhabitants of other countries, exploits them, and thus prevents the spreading of socialism (concept of the enemy).

Despite the search for positive distinctiveness which was supported by the mass media, there was a loss of control and a feeling of inferiority, especially to the West. The consequences of this feeling could be limited, however, by the low amount of contact with the West and because of the favourable comparison with the East European countries.

An additional explanation for why, despite massive propaganda, there was no success in convincing the people of East Germany about the negative aspects of the West must have recourse to other comparison dimensions that were more important to the population, for example freedom, human rights, democracy and materialistic values for each individual person. These values were largely exhibited on Western TV, which could also be received in most parts of the GDR.

3   IDENTITY IN THE FRG BEFORE UNIFICATION

During the last 40 years the development of social identity in the FRG has been structurally very similiar to that in the GDR. The West Germans distinguished themselves from the East Germans and compared themselves with others only in those dimensions in which they were superior so that there was a very positive picture.

- They exhibited a readiness for risks.
- They were number 1 or number 2 in exporting their products.
- They had a strong currency (DM).
- They were world soccer champions.
- They had a stable democratic system.
- They had a high degree of social welfare, individual freedom and individual responsibility.
- They were materially well off.
- They were free to travel.

Despite this positive distinctiveness, there was no national pride. There is still a certain ambivalence concerning the expectations that Germans have towards themselves (almost schizoid). The question is whether they should behave according to their political or their economic dimension. This situation can be compared with a young person who is uncertain whether he or she should look at him- or herself as a child or as an adult. The role conflict produces problems not only for Germans but also for foreign countries that had conflicting expectations towards the FRG.

The cause of this ambivalence can been seen in Germany's past since the Second World War, during which time national pride was largely eliminated: from the educational systems at schools and universities, as well as from the networks of political parties, churches, trade unions, and so on. The consequence was that Germans adapted the ideals of such neutral countries as Switzerland and Sweden. The inhabitants of West Germany have perhaps a lower patriotism than people in other European countries, but nonetheless they are very proud of their world export position – especially since after the Second World War, the Germans (as well as the Japanese) have been dedicated to postwar reconstruction.

4 GERMANY AS SEEN INTERNALLY AND EXTERNALLY DURING AND SHORTLY AFTER UNIFICATION

Despite the different pasts and different forms of achieving social distinctiveness, both German states tried by their specific comparison to get a positive distinctiveness (see Tajfel, 1982). The consequence was that foreign countries had mistrust and anxiety towards both. First of all, West Germany as well as East Germany had a relatively strong economy. But even more so, the mistrust can be explained because of historical reasons, and the reactions were clearly documented during the Gulf War in 1991.

The increase of nationalism and right-wing radicalism connected with xenophobia, since unification increased mistrust throughout the world. Mistrust also increased because of the fact that during the whole unification phase Germany was mainly concerned with itself. Especially since old structures within the USSR, Yugoslavia, Turkey, Iraq and Kurdistan were crumbling and old cultural differences between the nations were being revived, there was an increase in mistrust of what the strong 'old' Germany was up to.

After unification, it was expected that the differences between the East and West, especially concerning living standards, could be overcome quickly. Both sides found a new lease of life which was also transferred to Gorbachev (there was a real Gorbi-fever), which could not be understood throughout the rest of the world, especially in the US and England.[2] The happiness that flourished at the beginning of unification – especially among the population of East Germany – could also be explained in terms of acquired self-control in many areas, for example freedom of the press, of communication and of opinions.

5 THE NEW LOSS OF CONTROL IN EAST GERMANY

As mentioned above, the totalitarian state produced for a large proportion of the population a loss of control over the last decades. The consequences of this were passivity and a firm expectation that all problems are to be solved by the government (those with authority, the political parties, etc.) without the participation of the individual. The breakdown was primarily the consequence of this passive behaviour. However, the breakdown of the regime produced a new completely unexpected experience of control which, in turn, produced a short-run euphoria of control. However, this didn't last very long because the transfer to a market society produced new roots for the second loss of control: for the new freedom there were no rules as to how to behave, nobody knew how to use control. Freedom also means more self-responsibility and private initiative, as well as readiness to take risks. There was a new loss of control because people had to learn to deal with the new possibilities of control. From the transference of a planned economy to a market economy especially, the danger of paralysis is great because there are extreme changes in social, political, cultural and economic areas. This produces a new, unexpected amount of loss of control. Some of these areas are the following.

- The increasing unemployment (in some areas more than 50 per cent) and the breakdown of the ideological system and traditional values produce disillusion and future pessimism.
- Many people not only lose their work but also their privileges.
- Old party functionaries lose their jobs.
- A lot of people tend to think that they are second-class citizens.
- There is an increase in criminality, chaos, etc.
- Nearly all groups of the population suffer from this new loss of control, including social workers, merchants, teachers and state workers.
- The farmers feel powerless, because people prefer Western products.
- There is also discrimination against women.
- Corruption, protectionism, sabotage and criminality, as well as the dubious transactions of the Treuhand AG[3] and the market economy in general make the view of reality even worse.

This second loss of control (after unification) grew very quickly with respect to life events: on the one side, the mentality was still dominant that problem-solving is the business of those who govern, so a power was looked for in the FRG that could implement this. The West German government parties used skilful tactics during the elections by exactly supporting this expectation formation: 'We give you money, we are rich, we care for you.' The opposition, however, primarily pointed to problems that could only be solved by each individual's support, and thus lost the election in the East. Despite the predictions, the then existing loss of control produced a second loss of control and passivity. In addition, new demands for self-initiative were produced.

6   FACTORS INCREASING LOSS OF CONTROL AFTER UNIFICATION

The new loss of control is still more frustrating because of the following aspects.

Change of reference groups   The comparison is no longer with East European countries, which would produce relative gratification, but with the West, producing a sense of relative deprivation and also the feeling of being disadvantaged. The comparison is not the country's own past with its present, but with the state of the citizens in West Germany (cf. Festinger, 1954; Frey et al., forthcoming).

Direct confrontation with the West   The people recognized that the differences and their grievances were much more extreme than expected. So, for example, more of the environment has been destroyed than expected. The Western system (regardless of its weaknesses), with its products and services is more admired. There exists a contrast effect: the living standards in the East, in comparison to the West, are lower than previously expected.

High expectation because of promises from the parties   The promises of the coalition government caused expectations to increase to a high level, so that the gap in reality also increased. There was a breach of confidence in the government because the costs of unification remained unclear, which in turn produced a strong loss of control.

German virtues   The perception of loss of control is reinforced by typical German virtues such as striving for certainty, order, control and perfectionism. Because of these virtues, Germans see the problems of transition as being much worse than people from other countries see them (see Frey, forthcoming).

No elimination of early elites   Loss of control increases because a lot of people have the feeling that the old elites are still in power. They decide to keep their old jobs, to continue to suppress the East Germans, etc. This produces a lack of motivation and resignation.

7   THE BARRIERS OF THE MIND

The loss of control produced by the totalitarian regime gets stronger in times of transition towards a market economy, and thus produces new insecurities.

One of the consequences is that most citizens of East Germany feel inferior to West Germans. According to the opinion polls of 1990–91 (cf. *Spiegel*, 1991), this is true for 90 per cent of the population; on the other hand, about 90 per cent of West Germans feel superior to East Germans. From the standpoint of East Germans, West Germans are more reliable, more mature, disciplined, perfect, creative, independent, able to make better decisions, more open, flexible, tolerant, have better ideas and are busier. However, there are also negative aspects: they are perceived as more egoistic, arrogant, are know-it-alls, place too much value upon money, have more mistrust and don't love children. In general, Honecker and Ulbricht have ensured that the self-confidence of a whole society in its own ability is minimized.

The problems that arise during the process of transition to a market system produce 'enemy' pictures of the other side. So in the West, old prejudices are activated that people in the East are too passive, submissive and unable to help themselves. Here in particular it can be seen that social or human unification is not yet fulfilled. The result is mistrust, and especially a perceived superiority on the one side and inferiority on the other side that produces problems of communication.

Because of this economic crisis, there is and will be an increase in old categorizations concerning in- and out-groups. The West is perceived as being populated by know-alls; the East is perceived as incompetent. In addition, in the East we see an increase in scapegoating behaviour, and a radicalization. This radicalization is especially directed towards coloured people, Poles and other refugees. Neo-Nazi groups get stronger and intolerance of minorities increases (also in the West). In the West it is emphasized that the equity principle should be applied, i.e., that everybody gets as much as they deserve, whereas in the East there is the equality principle, i.e. that resources should be distributed equally. A lot of Western people do not accept the fact (which they consider unjustified) that their money should be sent to Eastern people.

8 THE POLITICAL CONTRIBUTION

The problem is that the politics of Helmut Kohl's coalition government induced a lot of high expectations. Unification was made more or less without any idea of personal responsibility for the people in both the West and the East – the main fault being that the population was convinced that unification could be financed without an increase in taxes. Lafontaine (the Social Democratic candidate during the 1990 elections) as well as many experts were sceptical, but because of the official politics of the government no identification with the problems of unification was achieved. By a foot-in-the-door strategy of tax increases, partly due to causes which had nothing to do with the unification, e.g. the Gulf War, there was frustration and anger towards the government and towards the East during 1991. If the government had explained to the people from the beginning that because of outstanding events everybody would have to suffer for several years, there would have been a much greater readiness to help. But now there is great resistance and the people have developed a mental blockage. This process will probably increase during the next few years.

9   WHAT CONTRIBUTION CAN PSYCHOLOGY OFFER?

Certainly, an improvement in the infrastructure is necessary, that is, information and communication channels. It is also necessary to have a much less bureaucratic administration and a simplification of the law. It is also important that a number of investment rewards be offered to make the economic behaviour of people in the West more attractive to the East (tax exemptions, etc.). However, from the standpoint of organizational and social psychology, other aspects are important that should be emphasized.

In my opinion, social psychology and organizational psychology can help to overcome the negative state of affairs (both in East Germany and in Eastern Europe). German unification has been seen up to now more or less as posing economical, juridical and political science problems. However, this perspective is too narrow. The mentality of most GDR citizens is similar to the mentality of industrial workers in the West who have given up psychologically, are demotivated, and have become resigned. The reason for this, as mentioned above, is the perceived loss of control experienced via the totalitarian system and via the problems of unification.

It would be a good idea for social and organizational psychology to use its strategies for management training to train the working people to become more engaged, critical, constructive and creative. Peters and Waterman (1982) have emphasized in their book on the search for excellence how firms with excellent results differ from firms that are mediocre or bad. The analytical conclusion is that a high degree of individual responsibility, decentralization, clarity and information are necessary for effective working conditions and that management has the task of inspiring their fellow workers. It is argued that a number of such principles which are applied daily in the best enterprises to achieve and engage responsible workers can also be applied to many firms throughout the whole GDR economy. A few suggestions will now be given.

1. Massive information campaigns to teach skills: it is really astonishing that there are no massive information campaigns on radio and TV. These could be carried out around the clock. Of course the transmission of missing skills should not be accomplished by force, but by giving people options, such as languages, computer programs, administration knowledge, knowledge about the functioning of market economies, etc. In these information campaigns scenarios about the most important weaknesses and problems of the present and the old systems should be presented in order to convince the people why a dramatic change is necessary. It is important to present positive or successful models which have succeeded because of their initiative, responsibility and readiness for risks, but also because of their specific way of looking for and processing information (see Frey, 1986). It is also necessary to establish offices where specific problems can be solved. Such scenarios about the how, when, where and why of strategies are necessary (cf. Gollwitzer, 1990). The teaching of such knowledge and abilities is important because most people do not know how to act effectively.

2. Besides information campaigns it is important to change the attitude of the people in important ways. Goodwill is not enough; the know-how is missing, but it can be acquired with the help of organizational and social psychological principles. It is important that a cognitive and affective map be constructed which produces a willingness to take over responsibility, initiative, and a readiness to take risks. Scenarios should be shown of why and under which conditions a positive economic developmental perspective can be seen, for example for small business owners. A high degree of clarity about the causes of problems and how these problems can be solved should be presented. People must be given constructive feedback about their strengths and weaknesses. This work should be carried out via the mass media, but also by the social networks of the churches, universities, schools, trade unions, political parties and so on. It is important to consider the specific mentality of East German people and to carry out this work with a high degree of sensitivity. Here it is important to take into consideration the support of positive thinking and self-responsibility. This can be done by emphasizing models in the GDR that have previously been proven successful.

3. Another very important principle is the transmission of human respect and esteem. It is important to understand people's needs, interests and emotions and also to give them future perspectives. People from the West have to listen and have to ask questions without already having the answers or even a patent remedy. It is helpful when people can make their own suggestions for solving the problems. Application of such principles would produce fewer people with inner withdrawal. This is the same on the macro-level of an economy as on the micro-level of a specific firm.

4.   Change in attitude is necessary at all levels of management. Most managers who have occupied top positions within the communist system during recent years are not at all prepared for the new market systems. They lack sufficient knowledge of modern buying, marketing, advertising, distribution and controlling; the necessary attitude and understanding is non-existent. It is necessary for a lot of younger, still untrained talents from the East to come to the West and learn as quickly as possible the necessary know-how, and for Western experts to go to the East for a certain time in order to exemplify modern models of decision-making. These top positions should probably be filled by Western managers for a short time only, to decrease envy and the impression that the West will take all the important positions. There are many possibilities in East Germany that give a lot of incentives to West Germans, but these should be made more explicit, and more initial aid should be provided.

5.   It is now time to start discussions concerning how each individual person or single institution (in both the West and the East) can help on their own. One possibility, for example, would be to introduce sponsorship of churches, parties, soccer and other sports clubs, trade unions, schools, universities and so on. A lot of changes in attitude can be achieved by better personal exchange, personal communication and direct contact. It would be conceivable that a number of sponsorships and consulting centres (made up of elderly West Germans, who are retired and thus already have a great deal of life experience and enormous professional know-how) could advise individual East Germans (e.g. employers, companies or organizations).

6.   In particular it must be made clear to the people in the East and the West that the problems cannot be solved in a short time. The differences in language and mentality are too great. So it is also important to provide a social network in order to decrease the danger of tension, especially of radicalism. If the larger problems were divided up into smaller projects and models it would make the situation more controllable and encouraging – the smaller the details, the more possibilities for action.

7.   Mutual understanding without prejudice, as well as openness, are necessary. It is important to introduce an infrastructure, but it is also important to decrease the deficits in the affective, cognitive and motivational fields. The ignorance and arrogance of Western economics and politics hardly allow these deficits to be understood. A high degree of frustration tolerance, mutual learning, listening and understanding are necessary. The know-how of modern organizational psychology should be used much more than it has been up to now.

The human aspect is the most important factor for innovation and creativity and all strategies which increase these potentialities have, in the short run, consequences on the macro-system of an economy. Modern psychology, therefore, should supply the theories and results needed to overcome the mental barriers between the two German societies and to help the citizens of East Germany to adapt better to their new situation.

It should be emphasized that there is a high probability of future positive economic development in East Germany. Realistic optimism is needed if behaviour is to change so that East Germany can belong to one of the most prosperous regions of Europe within the next ten years.

NOTES

1. Of course one should differentiate between formal (state) norms and informal norms (social sub-groups): for example groups that could have some control in accordance with the law consisted of members of the state security (Stasi) or there were a lot of so-called 'organizers' (i.e. black marketeers). However, the majority of the GDR inhabitants still had only passive strategies.
2. But the reason for this Gorbi-fever was especially the specific situation of the 40-year-old Cold War which, for geographical reasons, affected Germany more.
3. The Treuhand AG is a holding company which initiates the privatization of state-owned industry.

REFERENCES

Festinger, L. (1954), 'A Theory of Social Comparison Processes', *Human Relations*, **7**, 117–40.

Frey, D. (1986), 'Recent research on selective exposure to information', in L. Berkowitz (ed.), *Advances in Experimental Social Psychology*, Vol. 19, New York: Academic Press, pp. 41–80.

Frey, D. (forthcoming), *How was the Holocaust and the Second World War Possible? A Social-Psychological Analysis*.

Frey, D. and Irle, M. (eds) (1984), *Theorien der Sozialpsychologie: Band I. Kognitiven Theorien* (2nd edn of D. Frey (ed.) (1978), *Kognitive Theorien der Sozialpsychologie*), Bern: Huber.

Frey, D. and Irle, M. eds. (1985a), *Theorien der Sozialpsychologie: Band II. Gruppen- und Lerntheorien*, Bern: Huber.

Frey, D. and Irle, M. (eds) (1985b), *Theorien der Sozialpsychologie: Band III. Motivations- und Informationsverarbeitungstheorien*, Bern: Huber.

Frey, D., Dauenheimer, D., Parge, O. and Haisch, J. (forthcoming), 'Die Theorie der sozialen Vergleichsprozesse', in D. Frey and M. Irle (eds), *Kognitive Theorien der Sozialpsychologie*. 2. vollständige überarbeitete Auflage, Bern: Huber.

Glass, D.G. and Singer, J.E. (1972), 'Behavioral Aftereffects of Unpredictable and Uncontrollable Aversive Events', *American Scientist*, **60**, 457–65.

Gollwitzer, P.M. (1990), 'Action Phases and Mind-sets', in E.T. Higgins and R.M. Sorrentino (eds), *Handbook of Motivation and Cognition: Foundations of Social Behavior*, Vol. 2, New York: Guilford Press, pp. 53–92.

Osnabrügge, G., Stahlberg, D. and Frey, D. (1985), 'Die Theorie der kognizierten

Kontrolle'. In D. Frey and M. Irle (eds), *Theorien der Sozialpsychologie: Band III. Motivations- und Informationsverarbeitungstheorien*, Bern: Huber, pp. 127–72.

Peters, Th.J. and Waterman, R.H. Jr (1982), *In Search of Excellence*, New York: Harper & Row; (1984), *Auf der Suche nach Spitzenleistungen*, 10th edition,. Landsberg/Lech: Verlag moderne Industrie.

Seligman, M.E.P. (1975), *Helplessness*, San Francisco: Freeman.

Spiegel (1991), *Psychogramm der Deutschen*, special issue, Hamburg: Spiegel.

Tajfel, H. (1978), *Differentiation between Social Groups: Studies in the Social Psychology of Intergroup Relations*, London: Academic Press.

Tajfel, H. (1981), *Human Groups and Social Categories: Studies in Social Psychology*, Cambridge: Cambridge University Press.

Tajfel, H. (1982), 'Social Psychology of Intergroup Relations,' *Annual Review of Psychology*, **33**, 1–30.

Taylor, D.H., Lichtman, R.R. and Wood, J.V. (1984), 'Attributions, Beliefs about Control, and Adjustment to Breast Cancer,' *Journal of Personality and Social Psychology*, **46**, 489–502.

Thompson, S.C. (1981), 'Will It Hurt Less If I Can Control It? A Complex Answer to a Simple Question,' *Psychological Bulletin*, **90**, 89–101.

5. European Integration, German Unification and the Economics of *Ostpolitik*

Hélène Seppain

The Bonn–Moscow relationship is a crucial factor in the construction of the New Europe. In this context, it is appropriate to ask what a united Germany will mean for the future of *Ostpolitik*. In political and security terms, the creation of a united Germany within the NATO military alliance marks a dramatic change in German–Soviet relations. German unification and the disappearance of the GDR mark an entirely new phase in these aspects of *Ostpolitik*. But what of the impact of unification on another fundamental aspect of *Ostpolitik* – Germany's economic relations with the USSR?

I will argue that, viewed in a long-term perspective, unification will, paradoxically, lead to very little change in Germany's economic relations with the (former) Soviet Union. The political-economic role that Germany plays in the New Europe will be based on Germany's traditional and, as it has turned out, highly successful, trade policy toward the East. Indeed, it will be based on the same parameters that have determined Germany's economic approach to the Soviet Union since the revolution. This policy has been shaped by Germany's geographical position between East and West. After the Second World War, it was affected by the division of Germany and by the problem of Berlin. Today, Germany is once again looking towards both the East and the West.

1 BUYING PEACE

Germany's traditional trade policy with the USSR has been conditioned by a belief in 'buying peace', that is a belief in the long-term political gains to be obtained by the unconditional pursuit of closer economic contacts between Germany and the Soviet Union. 'Buying peace' means the unconditional pursuit of trade, as well as the provision of aid and credits. Germany has been and remains the former Soviet Union's most important Western sup-

73

plier of industrial technology. The persistent Soviet need to import new technology from the West has provided the foundation for the German strategy of buying peace. It is the qualitative importance of this trade which has proved crucial, not its quantitative importance. In 1990, for instance, the Soviet Union accounted for only 1.6 per cent of the former FRG's external trade; the highest level (2.8 per cent) was reached in 1983. In the late 1980s, 4 to 5 per cent of Soviet trade was conducted with the former FRG.

'Buying peace' is the main theme of this chapter. It is the key to understanding the economic content of *Ostpolitik*. And it is also an important element shaping the position of Germany within the Western Alliance.

2   AMERICAN INFLUENCE ON GERMAN POSTWAR TRADE

With the start of the Cold War, West German trade with the East became a controversial political issue.

A major postwar policy objective of the US was the successful economic and military integration of West Germany into the West European community. When the first US–FRG treaty (which was concerned with Marshall Plan arrangements) was signed on 15 December 1949, it confirmed the commitment by the new West German Federal government to a Western orientation in German trade policy and to an export-led economic strategy. In return for Marshall aid, the West Germans had to promise to cooperate in the US embargo policy against the Soviet bloc. This was formulated as a promise to prevent the diversion of a specific set of commodities 'to illegal or irregular markets or channels of trade'.[1] In practice this meant an embargo on iron and steel products from the Ruhr. These were essential for a rapid rehabilitation of the East German economy.

The official West German implementation of this promise accelerated the economic division of Germany. On the occasion of his visit to Washington in April 1953, Konrad Adenauer was given a further warning by US Secretary of State John Foster Dulles to the effect that all US aid to West Germany would be cancelled if the FRG breached portions of the US programme drawn up for East–West trade (Adenauer, 1965, p. 576). Since that time West German governments have tended to play down the role of trade with the USSR because such trade has been identified with disloyalty to the US.

3 THE REASSERTION OF GERMAN INTERESTS

That is, up to very recently. But now the position has changed quite radically. The new position was reflected clearly in the independent line which Helmut Kohl took at the G7 summit in Houston in July 1990. Controversy at the summit centred on the issue of whether to grant unconditional economic assistance to the Soviet Union.

On the one hand, President Bush (supported by Prime Minister Thatcher) favoured linking economic aid to the achievement of long-term progress toward a market economy and to Soviet arms reductions. Economic assistance would be conditional upon Soviet political change.

On the other hand, Chancellor Kohl (supported by President Mitterand) argued for an immediate open-ended $15 billion-plus package for the Soviet Union.[2] Kohl displayed the traditional German belief in the long-term political gains which can be derived from closer economic contacts with what used to be the Soviet bloc.

Gorbachev saw that Germany could act as a 'bridge' to secure economic and technological aid for the Soviet Union.[3] This would further his goal of perestroika to mobilize the full 'potential' of the Soviet people and would smoothe Soviet entry into the world economy.[4] In 1990 Chancellor Kohl saw that he could win Soviet recognition for one Germany in NATO in exchange for FRG concessions to Soviet economic and security concerns.[5] Within the framework of the West German long-term strategy of buying peace, he bought German unity. In domestic terms, the price is proving far higher than was expected. In May 1991 Germany started to resist pressure from Moscow to contribute a further DM 30 billion over and above the DM 25 billion pledged in 1990 for various purposes, including the withdrawal and relocation of Soviet troops from East Germany before the 1994 deadline.[6] In international terms, the main problem for the Germans, as well as for anyone wishing to do business with the USSR, is not knowing with which level of Soviet government to negotiate – a state of affairs which is bound to persist until the political situation is clarified by the adoption of a federal system, by the establishment of independent states, or by some other alignment.

4 BUYING PEACE AFTER THE WALL

Prior to the building of the Wall in 1961, political stability between the two parts of Germany required raising living standards in the GDR to levels approximating those in the FRG. The alternative was mass migration. President Kennedy addressed the issue of the link between peace and standards of living in his speech at the Free University of Berlin in 1963. When Kennedy called for an attempt to end the Cold War, he urged that the difference in living standards between Eastern and Western Europe should be eliminated – by levelling up, not down.

In 1989 the ideological defeat of communism – exemplified by the continuous flow of refugees from East into West Germany – exacerbated the contrast between the rich and the poor halves of Europe. West German policy in Eastern Europe was now focused on controlling the refugee problem. In October 1989 Egon Bahr argued that if the tide of refugees from East Germany didn't stop, it would mean destabilization for West Germany rather than East Germany.[7] The West German aim was to stimulate a reform process in the East and thereby remove the very reasons for massive emigration flows to the West. Prior to the opening of the Berlin Wall, Chancellor Kohl hinted that his government was ready to offer the GDR economic aid in return for greater democracy.

With the dismantling of the Wall in November 1989, immediate economic aid for the GDR was no longer on offer. The West German government had a more ambitious agenda. In February 1990, instead of aid Chancellor Kohl proposed a currency union linked to sweeping economic reforms in the East. All sides were under pressure of events. Moscow denounced Bonn's rejection of the GDR's proposals to cooperate in the economic stabilization of the GDR with West German credits amounting to DM 10–15 million. According to *Pravda* (16 February 1990), Bonn's position was determined by the desire to do nothing that could stabilize the Modrow (communist) government. Official Bonn policy was seen by *Pravda* as reminiscent of Adenauer's 'policy of strength' – not, in this case, a policy of military strength, but a policy of economic strength. Yet, in mid-February 1990, during the Kohl-Genscher visit to Moscow, Gorbachev promised not to stand in the way of German unification.[8]

Germany was again looking both ways, East and West. But what was less obvious to many was that Germany also *needs* to look both ways. Indeed, since the Second World War *Ostpolitik* has been conducted on the basis not only of the military strength that West Germany derives from its position within the Alliance, but also from the economic strength it has built in the West.

In mid-1988 Egon Bahr argued that West German participation in an increasingly integrated European Community undermined once and for all the FRG's pledge to seek reunification with East Germany. The internal EC market would bind the FRG 'irreversibly' to the West.[9] Bahr's argument was clearly historically wrong since a united Germany became a reality in December 1990, at the same time as the role of Germany within the EC had grown stronger. But it was also analytically wrong. As the Berlin Wall crumbled, West Germans did not need to choose between unification with East Germany and progress toward the Single Market within the European

Community. They needed one to achieve the other. They needed the strength they derive from the EC to bring about unification and further *Ostpolitik*.

5   TRADITIONAL WESTERN FEARS

But Germany's need to seek economic strength in the West to conduct its policy in the East has persistently encountered the fears and suspicions of its Western allies. These suspicions have, perhaps, been temporarily allayed by the economic difficulties created by political unification. But as recently as 1989 Germany's allies were obsessed with growing German power. This concern was not only about German economic dominance within the EC; it was also linked to Germany's position between East and West. Germany's important economic, political and military position in Europe created a 'what if' anxiety among Bonn's Western allies. What if Gorbachev's reforms succeed and West Germany's economic might is harnessed to the Soviet Union's vast natural resources and cheap labour? What if the reforms fail and the USSR lurches backward after skimming as much skill and technology as it can from its German trading partner?[10] This nervousness persisted at the time of the two-plus-four negotiations to restore Germany's full sovereignty. British newspaper headlines proclaimed that Bonn was getting too close to Moscow.[11]

After the collapse of the Berlin Wall in November 1989, there were two main issues on the agenda of the EC December 1989 summit in Strasbourg. First, the drive towards economic and monetary union, and secondly, the declaration endorsing German unity. The relationship between the two issues was vital, but never clear. What was fundamentally at stake was the future shape and nature of the EC. Was the 'deepening' (closer integration) so vigorously advocated by France and Italy intended as a device to prevent German unity? If so, none of the supporters for closer integration dared say so publicly. Yet clearly their sense of urgency was heightened by an instinctive unease on the German question.[12]

6   THE HISTORICAL BACKGROUND TO BUYING PEACE

Such unease on the part of Germany's Western allies is not only a consequence of the experience of the Second World War. Underlying any German–Soviet *rapprochement* is fear of the Rapallo syndrome.

The Rapallo treaty was concluded on 16 April 1922 during the World Economic Conference at Genoa. It determined Germany's policy toward the

Soviet Union in the 1920s. The treaty, which was largely commercial, marked the resumption of full economic and political relations between Germany and Soviet Russia. With the Rapallo treaty, the Germans gained some room for manoeuvre in their reparations policy. It strengthened German conviction that they could only conduct foreign policy through their position as a dominant economic power.[13]

The Rapallo agreement shattered the conference on European reconstruction at Genoa and confirmed the worst fears of the French about German–Russian retaliation against Versailles.[14]

Following Rapallo, the Germans extended government-backed credits to the Russians in the 1920s and 1930s. This contrasted with American practice. Under the Johnson Act (1934), Americans were prevented from extending credits to the Soviets because the Soviets had not cleared pre-1917 debts.

7   ADENAUER AS AN EXCEPTION

An important exception to the German policy of 'doing business' with the East occurred during the 1950s and 1960s. At that time Chancellor Adenauer adhered strictly to the US embargo policy. The period marked a major discontinuity in official West German trade policy. Economic power was to be an offensive weapon in the armoury of official policy, used to achieve progress on the German question and on Berlin.

Inter-German trade was central to the reunification issue and the status of Berlin. But there was a direct conflict between Adenauer's strict adherence to the US embargo policy against the Soviet bloc as part of his 'policy of strength', and the role of inter-German trade as a means of sustaining communications with West Berlin and avoiding a total break with East Germany. Despite the official line, there was certainly no West German political consensus on the appropriate trade policy toward the Soviet bloc.

The shortcomings of Adenauer's policy were most acutely revealed after the construction of the Berlin Wall in August 1961, when West Germany's allies refused to impose trade sanctions against East Germany. Instead West Germany's economic competitors sought to extend trade with the GDR and with the USSR. By the mid-1960s both the USSR and the GDR had been able to diversify their trade with the West to the detriment of West Germany.

After the second Berlin crisis (1958–61) and the building of the Berlin Wall, the failure of Adenauer's attempt to use trade as a bargaining tool to gain concessions on Berlin forced a conciliatory reappraisal of West Germany's trade policy towards the Soviet bloc. There was a rehabilitation of the old policy of 'buying peace' within the context of a revised *Deutschlandpolitik*. From the mid-1960s the government of West Germany hoped to promote trade with the Soviet Union in order to create a basis which, in the long run, would make it possible to discuss the division of Germany.[15] Inter-German trade was henceforth seen as facilitating 'humanization of separation' (*Humanisierung der Teilung*) of the two Germanies. Economic relations with the GDR and with the Soviet bloc in general were seen as a means of improving political relations.

Adenauer's 'Americanization' of German policy had failed. At the same time, West Germany's integration into Western Europe under Adenauer's chancellorship was a success. It enabled West Germany to become the economic giant of Western Europe. So that in 1968 West Germany could for the first time pursue an economic policy defined in terms of its own interests and not the interests of its allies. In that year West Germany resisted American, British and French pressure to revalue the Deutschmark. For West Germany's allies this unprecedented West German *'Nein'* raised the possibility of a new German threat.[16]

8 THE NEW OSTPOLITIK

For Willy Brandt, it was precisely West Germany's close ties with the US which made it strong enough to pursue a new *Ostpolitik*.[17] Under Brandt as Chancellor, this meant a more self-reliant foreign policy than that pursued under Adenauer. Brandt's *Ostpolitik* aroused the suspicion of many Americans about West Germany's continuing and sincere support for NATO. They also feared that West Germany was turning towards neutrality. The West German government rejected these accusations. It pointed out that *Ostpolitik* strengthened the goal of stability and reconciliation in Europe, and it reduced Soviet incentives for military action outside the Warsaw Pact area. It thereby helped to solve German military security problems at their political roots (Feld, 1989, p. 394). For a time, even the German question lost much of its emotional and political impact. The general perception was that because Germany's fate was so closely tied to that of Europe, the division of Germany could be overcome only if the rift in Europe was healed first.

9 DEMISE OF *DÉTENTE* AND RE-EMERGENCE OF THE GERMAN QUESTION

Chancellor Helmut Schmidt liked to repeat Immanuel Kant's view that a continuous process of economic integration was important for peace. Schmidt stressed that this was the motive of the Social Democrats in developing trade with the Soviet Union.[18]

'Buying peace' within the context of the new *Ostpolitik* meant that by 1980 West Germany had increased its trade with the East faster than any other OECD country and was by far the largest Western trading partner of the Soviet Union and its CMEA (Council for Mutual Economic Assistance) partners. Between 1970 and 1983 West German trade with the Soviet Union alone increased by four and a half times in real terms.

Meanwhile East–West relations had worsened appreciably since the Soviet intervention in Afghanistan in December 1979. The general deterioration was an important factor in the re-emergence of the specifically German question in the 1980s. But now the issue was not Berlin and what seemed then to be the long-term prospect of reunification. The issue was inter-German *détente* and what this implied for European security.

The system of security based on deterrence had, in the eyes of many Europeans, become distinctly less secure with the sudden acceleration of the arms race, chiefly in the area of nuclear weapons in Europe (see Fritsch-Bournazel, 1989, p. 35). The controversy over deploying nuclear missiles on German soil in 1983 posed the urgent question of Germany's role in Europe. Here the most widespread argument was that a war between East and West in Europe would pose particular danger to the German people. The consciousness of a special vulnerability was the backbone of the peace movement (see Fritsch-Bournazel, 1989, p. 36).

10 BUYING PEACE UNDER GORBACHEV

On 11 March 1985 Mikhail Gorbachev was elected general secretary of the CPSU. At first, Europe played a subsidiary role in Soviet *Westpolitik*, as it had done under his immediate predecessors. Soviet relations with West Germany continued to suffer from the West German decision to deploy cruise missiles and support for the US-led Strategic Defense Initiative (SDI) research programme.

Following the Reykjavik summit (October 1986), Soviet–West German relations evolved in the light of *détente* between the superpowers, Gorbachev's reform drive, and doubts about America's military role in Western Europe. According to Foreign Minister Genscher these changes gave Bonn the chance to overcome the division of Europe.[19] Improved trade relations with the Soviet Union became a major West German preoccupation.

With the declaration of the Single European Act in 1985 (signed in 1987), the EC had emerged from earlier 'Eurosclerosis' and was becoming an economic power on the world stage, an event which did not go unnoticed in Moscow. Genscher's visit to Moscow in July 1986 signalled a shift away from the postwar bilateral superpower focus. The change in Moscow's perception was motivated by an increasing divergence of interests between the US, its West European allies and Japan (Yakovlev, 1986), and by the Soviet recognition of the strength of the EC in which West Germany had become the dominant economic power. During Shevardnadze's visit to Bonn in January 1988, the Russians appealed for German help in perestroika (an appeal which Gorbachev repeated in his interview with *Der Spiegel* of 25 March 1991).

The prospect of the completion of the EC Single Market in 1993 heightened the Soviet perception of its own continued economic backwardness as well as that of its Comecon partners. The Soviet Union feared that EC integration would create a growing gulf between Western Europe and the USSR. The Soviets repeatedly stressed that for the success of perestroika they needed a new world characterized by mutually beneficial cooperation in politics, economics, science and culture alike.[20] In the economic field, the signing of the EC–Comecon accord in Moscow in June 1988 signalled a first step toward a new world: a new *modus vivendi* in Europe.

The West German government responded early to Gorbachev's reforms. In the aftermath of the INF (Intermediate Nuclear Forces) treaty, West Germany became the leading Western advocate of disarmament and closer political and economic cooperation with the USSR. West Germany also called for an easing of restrictions on technology transfer to the USSR.[21]

Following the Washington and Moscow superpower summits in 1987 and 1988, differences between Washington and Bonn over the role of East–West trade emerged. The West Germans stressed the importance attached in Bonn to building fresh economic links with the Soviet Union and Eastern Europe during the current *détente*. Chancellor Kohl dismissed as 'a philosophy from the Cold War' the notion that support for Gorbachev would make Moscow a more dangerous threat.[22] West German industry was pushing hard to gain advantage over other competing Western countries in investing in the Soviet economy. By late 1988, companies from non-communist countries had invested some $440 million in Soviet joint ventures, the biggest stake (15 per cent) coming from West Germany.

In security terms, Gorbachev's historic speech to the UN Assembly in December 1988 also signalled a major step toward a new world. Shevardnadze had earlier stated that the Soviet Union sought a world in which peace was ensured 'exclusively' by the UN and its Security Council.[23] Now it was evident that the Soviet Union really meant to make progress towards a reduction of its conventional arms superiority in Europe – a crucial step in the evolution of Soviet policy on Germany and the withdrawal of Soviet troops from East Germany (see Adomeit, 1990, p. 7).

The March 1989 crisis over NATO modernization of short-range nuclear forces marked the logical revolt of the West German government against

Cold War thinking. At the Bonn summit in June 1989, President Gorbachev referred repeatedly to the two nations as equal partners, and to the special nature of the Soviet–West German relationship. The Soviet–West German Joint Declaration endorsed the right of peoples to self-determination. This in effect gave *carte blanche* to the holding of free elections in East Germany, which were the precondition for the re-establishment of German unity (Adomeit, 1990, p. 5).

In 1989 a record trade surplus put West German trade performance ahead of Japan. The postwar limits on national sovereignty were now unacceptable to a West Germany which had become *the* economic power base in Europe. When Hans Dietrich Genscher returned from Moscow in February 1990 with the Soviet promise not to stand in the way of reunification, he reported that one of the main grounds for Mr Gorbachev's support was the belief that the economic dynamism of a reunited Germany could act as a motor for the whole Eastern Bloc.[24] Germany was now expected to buy peace by underwriting the reconstruction of the East.

11   THE MOTOR FOR THE NEW EUROPE

In 1989–90 the newly democratized East European governments looked to the West for trade and financial support, rather than to the Soviet Union, which itself was in deep economic crisis. So far, aid promised to Eastern Europe from the EC and the US is falling far short of budgetary need. In mid-April 1991 President Mitterand said the creation of the European Bank for Reconstruction and Development was a step towards the development of a 'Great Europe'.[25] However, despite sweeping promises to 'bring back together the two halves of Europe',[26] there has been a noticeable backpedalling by the EC as the full costs of German unity and of East European reconstruction have also become apparent. Moreover, Western commercial banks have privately expressed reluctance to extend new loans to the region for any purpose except specific project finance.[27] Governments are in flux. Markets are volatile. The root problem, especially for the less advanced East European countries, is their former dependence on the Soviet Union as their main customer.

Among the former CMEA members, East Germany stands apart because of its incorporation into the FRG. Political unification will necessitate transfers which ensure that standards of living in the Eastern Länder approach levels in the West. The powerful expansion of the West German economy in 1989 and 1990 provided the financial impetus behind unification. However, by forcing the pace towards monetary union with East Germany on 1 July 1990, and by throwing open East German industry to the pressures of international competition, the West German 'policy of economic strength'[28] has become increasingly controversial, from both the German and the EC perspective. The Eastern Länder have lost their markets at home and abroad, and this, together with a strong upward pressure on real wages, has plunged them into deep recession. Aid and investment from the West is, as yet, making little impact. Ironically, an important obstacle to economic recovery is the virtual collapse of trade with the Soviet Union and CMEA since the switch to dollar trading from January 1991. The East German experience raises new doubts about the cost, dimension and progress towards a 'wider Europe' incorporating the newly democratized countries of Eastern Europe.

Nevertheless, it is in the eastern part of Germany that West German big business feels *morally* obliged not to disappoint. For some companies like Zeiss, Maxhütte and Osram, cooperation means putting back together what more than four decades of division have kept apart. As for trade with the USSR, German business is used to taking the long view. This view is that 'the world is changing, the Soviet empire is breaking up – and who isn't in on the act now will miss the boat'.[29] The Soviet Union was the former GDR's largest trading partner, absorbing about half of its exports and supplying 40 per cent of its imports in 1990. In early 1991 Bonn provided DM 9 billion to ensure delivery of goods to the USSR to help firms in the former GDR maintain their Soviet markets.

At the same time, recent efforts to promote German–Soviet relations have been underpinned by several major treaties. In March 1991, the two-plus-four treaty, which paved the way for German unity, was ratified by the Soviet parliament. A far-reaching economic and scientific cooperation agreement was also signed in November 1990.

12 BUYING PEACE IN THE NEW EUROPE

At the time of the signing of the Moscow–EC accord in December 1989, Shevardnadze called it 'a major economic building block in the foundation of a common European Home'.[30] Then, as now, this prediction seemed ridiculously over-optimistic.

In the long term, German economic union will, in all probability, lead to a united German economic 'miracle'.[31] This prospect – rather than the EC–Moscow accord – signals what Shevardnadze called a major economic building block in the foundation of a common European home. Germany is set to remain the chief Western supplier of industrial technology to the former USSR and Eastern Europe. It holds the 'technological key' to a greater Europe incorporating the new democracies in Eastern Europe.

Despite recent German economic setbacks, it is clear that German companies are better placed than companies in other member states to take advantage of the opportunities in the EC's post-1992 Single Market. Even in 1991 – when Germany was growing at over 3 per cent, France and Italy were only growing at 2 per cent, and Britain was in deep recession – the German current account was roughly in balance. Given the differentials in growth rates, even a small deficit would be a remarkable achievement. And Germany is still the biggest exporter of manufactured goods in the world.

What is most uncertain is whether the Soviet Union will make progress towards political pluralism and a market economy. It is, however, likely that progress – or the lack of progress – will be accompanied by major political and social upheavals. So Germany still needs to buy peace. This is necessary to sustain economic progress in Eastern Europe and the former Soviet Union, and to ensure the establishment of a new secure European order. In this sense, a German policy of 'buying peace' is closely linked to the success of West European integration. In steering through a new phase of *Ostpolitik*, Germany needs the economic strength that it derives from its position in the EC; it needs this to advance the cause of democracy and market economics in the East.

The failed coup in August 1991 – and the accelerating collapse of the Soviet economy – accentuated the need to link material progress (or at least material stability) with progress towards democracy. Germany has advocated direct economic assistance to avert economic collapse. In fact, German calls for 'burden sharing' among the G7 were a recurrent theme throughout 1990–91, when Germany found itself under financial pressure due to the costs of unification. Chancellor Kohl has stated that as chairman of the G7 for 1992 he will press the case for increased aid to Eastern Europe and greater burden sharing within the G7. Among Western nations, it is Germany which most fears loss of credibility if assistance is delayed. It is once again to become a 'bridge' between East and West. This process will inevitably be accompanied by traditional Western suspicions.

In the mid-1980s there was speculation over the re-emergence of the German doctrine of *Mitteleuropa* as a separate economic entity dominated by Germany. However, it is clear that the new democracies in Eastern Europe are far happier with the prospect of associate status, and later membership of the EC, than with a neo-colonialism of a drifting, ambivalent Germany. In any case Germany is fully aware that it can sustain economic superpower status only as part of the EC.

NOTES

1. *New York Times* (*NYT*) 15 December 1949, p. 10.
2. Ten months later, in May 1991, Kohl and Mitterand, after a long period of hesitation, and in the face of US and British resistance to the idea, urged that President Gorbachev

be invited to meet the leaders of the Western world at the G7 London summit, scheduled for July 1991 (*Financial Times [FT]*, 31 May 1991). Gorbachev had meanwhile appealed for Western aid to sustain economic reforms in the Soviet Union.

3. Gorbachev on West German television, quoted in *FT*, 17 July 1990.

4. See Gorbachev's statement at the press conference following the Arkhyz accord, quoted in *Frankfurter Allgemeine Zeitung*, 17 July 1990.

5. The main security conditions of Soviet acceptance of a united Germany in NATO were spelled out in the accord between Kohl and Gorbachev at the Caucasian spa of Zheleznovodsk (16 July 1990). They were: a close interrelationship among the 'two-plus-four' talks on Germany, the CFE negotiations in Vienna, confirmation of the Oder–Neisse line as the permanent border between Germany and Poland, transformation of the Warsaw Pact and NATO, and the creation of permanent institutions under CSCE (Conference on Security and Cooperation in Europe) auspices. See Adomeit (1990). Moreover the two German armies would become an All-German army of 370 000 troops; a united Germany must not possess atomic, biological or chemical weapons.

6. The *Guardian* (London), 23 May 1991.

7. *Le Monde*, 3 October 1989.

8. See Kohl's statement of 10 February 1990, as quoted in *Süddeutsche Zeitung*, 12 February 1990.

9. *FT*, 5 August 1988.

10. See *NYT*, 13 June 1989.

11. The *Guardian*, 7 September 1990.

12. See *FT*, 5 December and 9/10 December 1989.

13. The argument of this paragraph is presented in full in Seppain (1992, chapter 2).

14. Hiden (1974, p 28). The Berlin treaty of 1926 was in direct continuity with the Rapallo treaty but it contained in addition a mutual neutrality pledge in the event of unprovoked aggression by a third country. It was extended on 5 May 1933. It was a prelude to the Ribbentrop–Molotov non-aggression pact of 23 August 1939. On 13 September 1990 the FRG and the USSR initialled a treaty in Moscow on 'Good Neighbourliness, Partnership and Co-operation'. It was intended as a further development to the 1970 Moscow treaty between the FRG and the USSR which had opened the way to expanding co-operation and *détente*. The 1990 treaty provided the Soviet Union with additional security guarantees. It included a mutual non-aggression pledge, which, in formal terms at least, contradicts part of Germany's collective security commitment within NATO.

15. Kurt Birrenbach, leading CDU spokesman, 'Lockt der rote Handel?', *Die Zeit*, 27 November 1964, p. 30.

16. *International Herald Tribune*, 25 November 1968. In October 1969, the new Brandt-Genscher government under pressure from the money markets revalued the DM by 8.5 per cent.

17. *NYT*, 29 October 1969 and 7 August 1970.

18. See 'Political Action Aimed at Fostering Understanding: Speech to the Congress on "Kant in Our Time"' (12 March 1982) in Hanrieder (1982, p. 193).

19. *FT*, 9 November 1988.

20. Vladimir Petrovsky, Deputy Minister, Foreign Affairs, *Moscow News*, August 1988, p. 3.

21. *FT*, 22 July 1988.

22. Ibid.

23. TASS International Service in Russian, 23 September 1987, quoted in Sestanovich (1988).

24. *FT*, 16 March 1990. According to *Der Spiegel* (11 June 1990), on the occasion of CSCE meetings in Geneva (23 May 1990) and Copenhagen (5 June 1990), Shevardnadze had indicated to Genscher that Moscow was prepared to accept membership of a united Germany in NATO in return for Western economic aid.

25. *FT*, 16 April 1991

26. Jacques Attali, President of the EBRD, quoted in The *Guardian*, London, 15 April 1991.

27. *FT*, 6 January 1990.

28. See *Pravda*, 16 February 1990.
29. VW chief Carl Hahn, *Die Zeit*, 23 February 1990.
30. The *Guardian*, 19 December 1989.
31. The reasons for cautious medium to long-term optimism are as follows: first, the demands of reconstruction will sustain a high rate of growth in the West which, because of Germany's position within the exchange rate mechanism (ERM) is unlikely to lead to unsustainable rates of inflation; secondly, the incorporation of the Eastern labour force within the FRG solves the problem of the demographic gap which threatened West Germany, and still hangs over the other northern members of the EC; thirdly, although there are bound to be transitional difficulties the basic quality of the Eastern labour force is high.

REFERENCES

Adenauer, K. (1965), *Erinnerungen, Vol. I: 1945–53*, Stuttgart: Verlagsanstalt.

Adomeit, H. (1990), 'Gorbachev and German Unification', *Problems of Communism*, **39** (4), July–August, pp. 1–23.

Feld, W.J. (1989), 'The Role of the Federal Republic of Germany in NATO', in P. Merkl (ed.), *The Federal Republic of Germany at Forty*, New York: New York University Press.

Fritsch-Bournazel, R. (1989), 'The Changing Nature of the German Question', in Larrabee F.S. (ed.), *The Two German States and European Security*, London: Macmillan.

Hanrieder, W.F. (ed.) (1982), *Helmut Schmidt: Perspectives on Politics*, Boulder, Co: Westview Press.

Hiden, J. (1974), *The Weimar Republic*, London: Longman.

Seppain, H. (1992), *Contrasting US and German Attitudes to Soviet Trade, 1917–1991*, London: Macmillan.

Sestanovich, S. (1988), 'Gorbachev's Foreign Policy: a Diplomacy of Decline?', *Problems of Communism*, **37** (1), Jan–Feb., 1–15.

Yakovlev, A. (1986), 'Mezhimperialisticheskiie protivorechiia – sovreminnyi kontekst' [Inter-imperialistic Contradictions in the Contemporary Context], *Kommunist*, **17**, (November), 3–17.

PART III

Economic Perspectives of the New Germany

6. On Some Macroeconomic Consequences of German Unification

Harald Hagemann*

1 INTRODUCTION

While many foreigners worry about a too-mighty Germany gaining un-matched influence over the vulnerable states in Eastern Europe, Germans themselves are shaken by new economic blows and bills. These include record public budget deficits, a higher rate of inflation, which exceeds that of the French for the first time since the existence of the European Monetary System, a dramatic swing in the balance of payments on current account from surplus to deficit, more than 3 million unemployed in January 1992 and aggravating distributional and social conflicts. This was clearly not the sort of economic development the Germans expected that unity would bring.

But the root of this year's problems was also the cause of the boom that preceded it: German unification. German economic, monetary and social union (GEMSU), which became effective on 1 July 1990, released pent-up demand from long-deprived consumers in East Germany, thus giving a fur-ther boost to West German enterprises already producing on the verge of full capacity utilization. On the other hand, GEMSU caused a collapse of the East German economy on a scale that even the pessimists underestimated. Cushioning the shock has required enormous transfer payments from the western to the eastern Länder. The German government not only underesti-mated the bill for unification, left wasteful subsidies in Western Germany nearly untouched, over-borrowed and raised taxes too late, it also failed to build a consensus on how the greater tax burden should be distributed.

Income data recently published by the German Federal Bureau of Statistics show that despite an average increase in gross income of employed persons in Western Germany of between 5.1 per cent for blue-collar workers and 6.1 per cent for white-collar employees in the period between October 1990 and October 1991, the resulting growth rate of real net earnings was in fact minus 1.1 per cent for four-person households and minus 2.7 per cent for singles – due to a higher inflation rate, higher taxes and increased social insurance payments. The trade unions' attempt to recover this lost after-tax income through higher wage claims in 1992 and later years clearly cannot work. During the 1990s the former West Germans will have to pay for unification with an absolute and/or relative decline in their real income depending on the policies pursued and the length of the transition period of the former socialist economy in Eastern Germany. German unity is a good example of the fact that greatness as such doesn't make you richer. An immediate outcome of GEMSU is that the per capita income of united Germany decreased from 100 (index for the level of former West Germany in 1989) to about 86 per cent, due to the integration of the inefficient and technologically backward former socialist economy of Eastern Germany.[1] The simultaneous attempt to catapult East German wages to the world's top level within five years is another sign that a social consensus alternative in Germany which is adequate to the changed conditions has not yet materialized.

With unification the Federal Republic of Germany has gained relatively far more labour than capital. So in the medium run it is inevitable that the time path of West Germans' real wages will be noticeably below the level on the reference path that would have been pursued without unification. Naturally Western trade unions have no interest in a policy of low wage levels in the East which would endanger the real income position and jobs of their own members. No wonder the relatively regulated West German labour market finds unification more difficult to cope with than free-market textbooks suggest. But until last summer the Kohl government was also unwilling even to acknowledge that the great financial burden of unification could not be solved by over-borrowing and without increasing taxes.

The Bundesbank, which is currently facing a severe test of its anti-inflationary credibility, has stepped into this political vacuum. The decision to raise the key discount and Lombard rates by a full half-point to 8 per cent and 9.75 per cent respectively shortly after the Maastricht summit in December 1991 was intended to send a tough message to several addressees in Europe, but especially within Germany. In particular the Bundesbank intended to send warning signals to employers and unions to agree on less inflationary wage settlements, and to the government to curb its spending. What really worries the members of the policy-making council is that the German economy, in the current phase of the transition process of knitting two divergent parts together, could be trapped in a vicious circle. Continual pressure for more goodies (such as increased wages and shorter working hours) from strong unions, and the inflationary dangers of a weak fiscal policy including the recent decision to raise the VAT rate to 15 per cent in 1993, puts upward pressure on wages (and thereby further increases that part of government spending which is wage-related) and may force the Bundesbank to continue its current policy, thus keeping interest rates high for the foreseeable future. This may impose a path that could become economically costly, slowing the economy and hence swelling the budget deficit by even more and pushing wages down once high interest rates have reduced investment and raised unemployment. If the West German economy catches a cold, this is bad news for the rest of Europe as well.

The dominant prediction for the post-GEMSU development of the East Germany economy might best be represented by the J-curve idea, according to which there is a sharp contrast between the short run and the long run (see, e.g., Siebert, 1990). That is industrial output and employment fall in the first phase of the transition process from a centrally planned to a market economy, bringing to light the inefficiencies and hidden distortions of the former socialist economy. Existing firms cannot compete for a number of reasons, and it will be a time-consuming and costly adjustment process before new and renewed firms have built up profitable productive capacities so that output and employment can increase in the medium and longer run after the 'valley of tears' has been crossed. Despite the soaring costs of unity which currently are pushing up prices and interest rates, unity implies huge business opportunities as well, especially for West German firms which can expand their markets easily. According to a well-known Schumpeterian scenario of new frontiers and the associated opportunities for innovators and investors, the East German economy will emerge as the showcase of Germany at the end of the transition process, when a new and highly modern capital stock will have been built up. This view is strongly at odds with the present gloom and the rival pessimistic scenario of a vicious circle, according to which Germany will get in the east her equivalent of Italy's Mezzogiorno.

In section 2 we will examine the free fall of the East German economy after it became an open economy endowed with a convertible currency in July 1990. Section 3 compares the East German situation with the starting point and the development of the West German economy after the currency reform of June 1948. Special emphasis will be laid on factor endowments, the development of wages in relation to productivity, and the extent and structure of the capital stock. A discussion of the process of structural change and some long-run perspectives of the East German economy will follow in section 4. Section 5 is dedicated to the analysis of important international macroeconomic consequences of German unification.

2 THE SHORT-RUN EFFECTS OF MONETARY UNION ON THE EAST GERMAN ECONOMY

Post-GEMSU economic development in Germany was characterized by a sharp division; there was an enormous contraction of economic activity in the East and a boom in the West, caused not least by the additional spending by East Germans. Since then, the West German economy has grown faster than in the 15 years before, while the East German economy underwent a shock therapy with a virtual collapse of industrial output. The index of industrial production plummeted from 109.3 in March to 96.2 in June, and to 62.6 in July, the first month after the monetary reform, and to 50.9 in December.[2] Such a massive decline, which affected every sector, is unparalleled in Germany, even exceeding that following the First World War in 1919 and the Great Depression between 1928 and 1932. The collapse of old production structures continued in 1991, although with growing differentiation. As had been expected, the reverse has occurred first in the construction industry due to growing public and increasingly also private demand.

Such a breakdown in economic activity naturally is reflected in labour market data, although only to a lesser extent. Unemployment increased from 272 000 in July 1990 to 642 000 in December 1990, and to 992 000 as the yearly average in 1991. After Treuhand ceased to guarantee credit for working capital, the number of unemployed increased by 306 000 to 1.343 million in January 1992, which implies an unemployment rate of 16.5 per cent.[3] At the same time the number of short-time workers, which had reached a peak of more than 2 million in April 1991 went down further by one-half to 520 000. This means that the 'effective' unemployment rate which comprises also the short-time workers according to their average loss of working-time has stayed roughly constant at about 20 per cent. Although once-hidden unemployment is more and more obvious, this figure is below the yearly average of 1991 and far below the range between 30 per cent and 40 per cent which was earlier predicted for the end of 1991.

There are three main factors which explain that the decline of gainfully employed persons in the former GDR by more than 3 million over the last two years is only imperfectly reflected in the development of unemployment and short-time work. First there are special rules for early retirement, which was claimed by 705 000 people at the end of December 1991 (compared to 254 000 at the beginning of the year). Secondly, the instruments of active labour market policy, like relief work, vocational rehabilitation and training measures, have been widely used. According to the data presented by the Federal Bureau of Labour (Bundesanstalt für Arbeit) in Nuremberg 390 000 people were employed on relief work (compared to only 20 000 at the beginning of the year) and 365 000 (plus 70 000 short-time workers) were supported by measures of vocational rehabilitation and training at the end of 1991 (see ANBA, 1992, pp. 35–9). Thirdly, and very importantly, a large increase in the number of commuters from East to West Germany (far more than have actually migrated to the west) has dampened the predicted increase in the level of unemployment. The German Institute of Economic

Research (DIW in Berlin) estimates that this group comprises about 600 000 in January 1992, among them more than 100 000 who commute to West Berlin from nearby communities. The increasing role of commuters is also reflected in the remarkable different development of gross *domestic* product (GDP) and gross *national* product (GNP) in East Germany during 1991 (see *Table 6.1*). The decline in GDP by more than 30 per cent turned out to be far greater than had been predicted a year ago. With 154 billion DM, the East German economy contributed less than 6 per cent to total GDP in Germany of 2 678 billion DM.

Table 6.1: Development of GDP and GNP in East Germany, 1990 and 1991 (quarterly figures)[1]

	1990				1991			
	I	II	III	IV	I	II	III	IV
GDP	68.9	68.6	50.2	48.2	39.0	37.4	38.7	38.7
g(%)[1]	−2.7	−4.5	−29.7	−32.4	−43.4	−45.4	−23.0	−19.7
GNP	67.0	64.7	48.0	51.0	43.1	43.7	48.7	57.6
g(%)[1]	−2.5	−7.1	−30.7	−26.3	−35.7	−32.5	1.4	13.0

Source: Deutsches Institut für Wirtschaftsforschung, DIW (1992, pp. 78–9).
1.   Changes in % compared to the preceding year (in constant prices of the second half of 1990, billion DM).

What has happened and why? There can be no doubt that the East German economy after GEMSU had a disappointing start, which even the greatest pessimists had underestimated. It was clear that a painful process of restructuring would take place as soon as East Germany became an open economy with a convertible currency. More than 40 years of socialism and central planning had left the economy with an industry not competitive with the West. Capital stock was largely obsolete, the infrastructure was rotten, land and water heavily polluted, the administration inefficient and people's experience with private property and individual entrepreneurial activities fell into oblivion. Due to the autarky tendencies within the former Council for Mutual Economic Assistance (CMEA), the East European counterpart of the EC, the pattern of specialization developed by the East German economy over the last four decades differed significantly from that which would have been developed if the former GDR had taken part in the worldwide division of labour.

Nevertheless some major faults can be detected which have contributed to the valley of tears becoming deeper and longer than had been expected two years ago. There is fairly widespread agreement among German economists that at least *three big mistakes of German unification policy* can be identified.[4]

1. The solution of the property rights issue is a necessary precondition for a successful restructuring of the East German economy to take place. The decision to incorporate the principle of *restitution* of old property rights in the Unification treaty has turned out to be a major barrier for investment since property rights in too many cases are still unclear. The restitution edict has caused a major delay in the rebuilding of the East German economy, a major fault against the background that the most important problem of the new Länder is the temporary mismatch between the sudden breakdown of production and the necessarily time-consuming and expensive renewal of the capital stock.

2. The organizational restructuring of the firms, which for the greater part are not competitive, is linked to the issue of privatization. According to the Unification treaty it is the task of the Treuhand, a government trust, 'to promote the structural adjustment of the economy to the requirements of the market' (article 2) and 'to restructure – under competitive conditions – and privatize the previous state-owned firms' (article 25). Treuhand was scheduled to have a limited existence and to eventually return the financial wealth obtained from selling about two-thirds of the East German economy either to the government or to the East German people. The original Treuhand goal of realizing proceeds of about DM 600 billion from privatization of firms was revised repeatedly. According to recent estimates of the German Ministry of Finance, it is expected that the debts of the Treuhand agency will amount to DM 250 billion at the end of 1993 *vis-à-vis* a remaining wealth of only DM 50 billion. Together with the additional debt of the Kreditabwicklungsfonds – covering the liabilities of the former state-owned firms – which will amount to a further DM 100 billion, these debts have to be taken over by the government sector in 1994.

Something must have gone wrong. On the macroeconomic level there is a fundamental problem which results from the attempt to sell the East German assets, a *stock* variable, against the West German *flow* of savings; the more so at a time when public budget deficits reach new record highs. No wonder that due to the limited absorption capacity of the market for wealth investments, the great number of firms supplied for sale has led to a decline in prices. The Treuhand, knowing that the more it sells the lower will be the price, therefore has an incentive to slow down the privatization process. This endangers the necessary speed of the transition process and also stretches the eventual disappearance of the Treuhand institution. On the microeconomic level credit constraints are very important, i.e. privately owned firms in

Germany[5] have difficulty getting enough equity funds in the financial markets (which is also due to the high risk of many Treuhand assets). Credit rationing thus implies a major barrier to Treuhand's sales policy.

3. Unlike most of the rest of Eastern Europe, wages in East Germany have exploded since June 1990 and have run far ahead of productivity. As a result, the competitive position of East German industry has deteriorated and employment problems have been aggravated. By the end of 1991 wages had risen to around 50 to 60 per cent of West German levels. The course for a nearly complete elimination of wage differentials within the next three years is already set. As a consequence, the East German economy will not have a temporary comparative advantage in labour-intensive industries and will attract fewer financial resources for investment in real capital, thereby lengthening the necessary time span for improving the situation on the labour market.

3   WEST GERMANY AFTER 1948 AND EAST GERMANY AFTER 1990: ANALOGIES AND DIFFERENCES

An analogy is often drawn between the East German situation after June 1990 and the development of the West German economy after the currency reform of June 1948, when central administration was eliminated and prices for most but not all commodities were set free. Both cases seem to be characterized by an abundance of qualified labour and a shortage of capital. As in West Germany, where the labour force grew by millions of eastern refugees after the Second World War, there is a rich pool of qualified labour in today's East Germany although some retraining of many workers in the use of modern Western technology is necessary. The collapse of industrial production in West Germany in 1945 and the years after was widely seen as the consequence of the considerable destruction of private plant and equipment as well as public infrastructure like bridges and railways following Allied bombing during the war and the subsequent dismantling. From a Western perspective the technologies used in the former GDR are outdated, the capital stock is also obsolete in ecological terms and the infrastructure is a shambles. With GEMSU converting all prices at par, and the subsequent policy of high wages, the East German capital stock got its final blow and to a large extent became economically obsolete overnight. Starting with an obsolete capital stock and at a very low level of productivity, it is nevertheless widely expected that with the creation of new firms and the transfer of capital and technology the East German economy can quickly catch up.

Although there are good arguments for the favourable *long*-run prospects of the new Länder, a closer look at the two starting points reveals some important differences. First of all, the indexes of industrial production went in totally different directions. While the index collapsed in East Germany after the 1990 monetary union, in West Germany just the opposite had happened. The index of industrial production went up by 50 per cent in the first five months after the monetary reform in 1948, from 54 in June to 81 in November (1936=100).[6] It must be emphasized that industrial production had already partly recovered before the currency reform, and the index in the first half of 1948 was nearly twice as high as two years before. Despite the considerable increase in production immediately after the currency reform there was still plenty of room for further increases due to a great underutilization of existing productive capacity.

This points to another important difference. Contrary to the widespread view referred to above and despite all the destruction caused by bombing and dismantling, the real capital stock in West German industry at the end of the war in May 1945 was greater than at the outbreak of war in September 1939.[7] Nor were the existing plant and equipment obsolete from a technological point of view.[8] Due to high rates of investment, industrial capacity on the territory of West Germany in 1948 exceeded the capacity at the beginning of 1936 by no less than 47 per cent. Net investment became negative only from summer 1944 until the currency reform in June 1948. Even then the capital stock was as great as in the year 1939.

Whereas East Germany in 1990 brought an economically obsolete capital stock of firms and a largely rotten infrastructure into united Germany, West Germany's capital stock in 1948 was remarkably modern. In the period between 1924 and 1936 the productive capacity of West German industry stayed roughly constant. After the end of the Great Depression, with its high rates of scrapping of old plant, a vigorous recovery in investment took place until 1943. This process was further enhanced when investment increased after the currency reform of June 1948 so that in the period between the second half of 1948 and 1960 only 23 per cent of gross investments were allotted to the replacement of depreciated machinery and 77 per cent to increase capacity. According to vintage theories, the favourable age structure of the capital stock led to a structural growth in the productivity of capital in industry during that period.

Furthermore, engineers and workers coming back from the war had not lost the technological knowledge they had previously acquired in the production process. Learning is the product of experience. From Arrow (1962) we have gained the fundamental insight that investment itself leads to the growth of knowledge and so makes further profitable investment possible, even when some of the real capital goods are destroyed or dismantled. In 1990 the situation in East Germany was totally different. During more than 40 years of socialism the economy missed its connection with modern technological development. As a consequence, only small parts of the economy are knowledge based, compared with West Germany, that is, the former GDR has been relatively weak in those productive activities which for the greater part are characterized by increasing returns thus endogenizing long-run growth. A modern capital stock therefore has to be built up from scratch. This implies an adjustment time for the transition period of 10–20 years and a financial volume of about DM 2 000 billion (i.e. 2 000 000 million) in current prices. Public investment in a well-functioning infrastructure is a necessary precondition for productivity increases and a growth process fuelled by private capital and technology transfer.

The current wage-setting process in East Germany differs very much from that in West Germany after 1948 when a rather restrained wage policy and a long-term undervaluation of the Deutschmark led to high exports, profits and investments. On the other hand, with currency union the East German economy not only lost the possibility of depreciating its exchange rate to improve the competitiveness of firms, it also imported the economic system as well as the corresponding entitlement mentality from West Germany. Due to the pressure of Western-dominated German unions to raise East German wages and the East Germans' belief that they 'deserve' West German wages, differences in wage levels have been narrowed far more quickly than the shortage of real capital could be overcome and the gap in productivity closed. Prevailing unemployment in East Germany therefore has strong *classical* features in the sense of Malinvaud (1980).

As a consequence of this 'high wage–high tech strategy' (Sinn and Sinn, 1991) most existing productive capacities have become unprofitable before new modern, highly productive plant and equipment could be built up on a broader scale. In a currency union and after the breaking down of the Berlin Wall, both capital and labour are mobile. In order to avoid greater migration, which would aggravate the housing problems already existing in West Germany, capital has to flow into the East German economy at a high speed. Western wages could be paid if the extent and structure of the capital stock corresponded to the Western level, that is, high wages are the *result* and not the *cause* of the process of capital accumulation.

Despite the current lack of profitable productive capacities (capital shortage unemployment), the depression in East Germany nevertheless also has some *Keynesian* features. The period immediately after GEMSU saw a strong decline in the demand of East Germans for East German goods, that is, a constellation of excess supply for many East German producers. Perhaps the most important characteristics of the new Länder currently is the great discrepancy between increased consumption and heavily decreased production, a difference which is only closed by West German transfer payments in the amount of three-figure billion DM numbers per year. Hitherto only a very small part of these transfers, which amounted to DM 140 billion in 1991 and are estimated to total DM 180 billion in 1992, went into investment thus contributing to the generation of future tax revenues.

4   STRUCTURAL CHANGE, PRODUCTIVITY AND EMPLOYMENT: THE LONG-RUN PERSPECTIVES OF THE EAST GERMAN ECONOMY

With the transition from a planned to a market economy which is integrated into the international division of labour, the sectoral development perspectives of the East German economy have changed drastically. The sectoral structure of the former GDR was biased in favour of manufacturing, agriculture and the public sector, and against the private service sector which had been the stepchild of the old socialist economy. Table 6.2 shows the differences in the sectoral employment structures between the East German and the West German economy in the year before unification.[9] These differences reflect various factors, of which the following can be identified as most important:

1.   The two economies were integrated into different systems of the international division of labour. The attempt of the Comecon countries to reach self-sufficiency had led to a very specialized industrial structure, different from that which would have developed if the GDR had taken part in the worldwide division of labour. Like other centrally planned economies, East Germany followed a strategy of import substitution with regard to the West. Its economic structure developed into an antiquated and less efficient replica of West Germany's.

2.   Socialist firms were guided by quantity constraints and a system of relative prices which was heavily distorted, in factor markets as well as in commodity markets. There was no capital market, energy costs were unrealistically low and external competition for the *Kombinate* (combinates) did not exist. Firms therefore had fewer incentives to innovate. As a consequence, even those which had efficiently adapted within the scope of the old conditions now face serious transition problems caused by the sudden change in prices, the emergence of product quality as a key factor, and increased international competition.

3.   Trade and services were given less attention in the former GDR because the old authorities considered them 'unproductive' for ideological reasons. Now the service sector has turned out to be the great hope for the difficult transformation process. While it is clear that it will have a high growth potential in the long run and will be able to attract a larger share of the

labour force, this future increase in employment will not suffice to compensate for the displacement of labour in all the other sectors of the East German economy.

From the foregoing considerations it becomes clear that the East German economy has to undergo a process of structural change which in parts is similar to West Germany's in the last two or three decades, albeit on a much broader scale and with far less time available for adjustment. The traverse from a centrally planned to a market economy comprises not only structural change in the traditional sense but also far-reaching changes in the institutional framework (*'Wirtschaftsordnung'*). As in the West, ailing industries have to shrink, as, for example, is currently the case in shipbuilding concentrated in the northern part of East Germany. The employment share of agriculture has already nearly adapted downwards to the West German level over the last two years. Most important, the changes in institutional arrangements imply a restructuring of firms on the microeconomic level, that is the establishment of new and small firms as well as a successful restructuring of existing firms, which have to adapt to the new system of factor prices and commodity prices. Furthermore, due to the increased role of individual preferences, i.e. the demand side, firms now have to produce goods that *do* match people's wants.

All these factors require enormous changes on the supply side of the East German economy, in the allocation of resources, the composition of production, the location of firms and the pattern of trade. Above all, the core

Table 6.2: Employment by Sectors, 1989 (shares in %)

	East Germany	West Germany
Agriculture, forestry and fishing	10.4	3.7
Energy and mining	3.0	1.7
Manufacturing	36.7	31.5
Construction	7.7	6.6
Trade and transport	17.6	18.7
Services	6.6	18.0
State	17.8[1]	15.5
Private households	0.2	4.3
Total	100.0	100.0

Sources: GDR, Rudolph (1990) own calculations; FRG, SVR (1990) own calculations.
1. State excl. the *x-sector*.

problem of a low productivity level, which is inseparably linked to the obsolete capital stock (see, e.g., Görzig and Gornig, 1991), can only be solved by a time-intensive and expensive process of capital accumulation. This is underlined by the fact that in the short run the change in labour productivity has moved in the wrong direction in the last two years. Since employment was partly stabilized for political reasons, labour productivity, measured in real GDP per employee, decreased significantly by 7.9 per cent in 1990 and 20.6 per cent in 1991 (see Erber and Pischner, 1992, p. 2). A more revealing picture is given if one considers the development of productivity per man hour. In 1989 East Germany's effective yearly working time of 1 761 hours exceeded West Germany's 1 665 hours. In 1991 the picture was completely reversed: 1 344 hours in East Germany and 1 618 hours in West Germany. The statistical result of the negative growth rate of 6.2 per cent in 1990 and 18.6 per cent in 1991 is that *productivity per man hour* in the East German economy decreased by only 1.8 per cent in 1990 and 2.5 per cent in 1991[10], still not a basis from which the wage increases could have been paid. The development of labour productivity in East Germany in the last two years therefore is heavily distorted. The fact remains that labour productivity can only be raised by new capital (gross investment) embodying new technological knowledge.

5   SOME INTERNATIONAL CONSEQUENCES OF GERMAN UNIFICATION

Finally, let us turn to some macroeconomic implications of German unification for other countries. There are two countervailing tendencies which have to be emphasized. On the one hand, German trade partners benefited from rapidly rising imports and the swing in the balance of payments on current account. On the other hand, unified Germany has contributed to the global shortage of capital since 1990. Without doubt higher interest rates in Germany slow down growth elsewhere. Especially in EMS countries trying to keep their exchange rates stable against the DM, investment is affected negatively because they are forced to follow the German example. In the following I shall briefly discuss the 'locomotive' versus the 'brakesman' argument.

During the second half of the 1980s, the West German balance of payments on current account year after year reached new record surpluses up to DM 107.6 billion in 1989. This surplus was already reduced by DM 30.2 billion in 1990, and then the German current account (which since July 1990 has included the five new Eastern Länder) went into a deficit of DM 34.2 billion in 1991. A remarkable swing of more than DM 100 billion within one year led to the fact that the current account became negative for the first time after the OPEC II period 1979–81. The fundamental change in the international position of the German economy in the wake of unification is shown in Table 6.3.

Table 6.3:   *Balance of Payments, Federal Republic of Germany, 1988–91 (million DM)*

Year	Current account	Capital account
1988	+ 88 749	−127 589
1989	+107 619	−136 165
1990	+ 77 431	− 94 479
1991	− 34 200	+ 19 148

Source: Deutsche Bundesbank.
1. Since July 1990 incl. East Germany.

Clearly this dramatic swing in the current balance has put Germany into the role of an international locomotive, causing an increase in production and employment in other countries which have significantly raised their exports to Germany. A more detailed analysis reveals that this mainly holds for the EC countries but also applies to other European countries and the United States. What were the reasons for last year's dramatic swing in the Federal Republic of Germany's current account from a surplus to a deficit? How long will this change of sign from plus to minus last? The following causes can be identified.

1. A closer look at the data shows that the swing was not caused by a massive reduction of exports (reflecting a deterioration in the international competitiveness of German firms) but by rapidly rising imports. Since the realization of currency union the accumulated excess demand in East Germany could be cut down via markets. The additional boost of demand from East Germany came at a time when most West German firms were already producing at a high degree of capacity utilization. Moreover, demand by East Germans shifted in favour of Western products, and industrial production in East Germany was collapsing. Thus the additional demand could be satisfied only by a marked increase in imports, i.e. a growing absorption quota of the economy of unified Germany. European and other trade partners benefited from this boom, as did Germany from the increase in imports in so far as the additional supply from international markets dampened Germany's inflation rate.

2. Since the fall of the Berlin Wall the West German economy was in an exceptional position. While growth in other European countries and the United States was rather weak, the West German economy boomed. The stagnation of exports over the last two years had its major cause in recessionary tendencies in many of West Germany's major trading partners. The German economy with its high share of investment goods in exports is relatively dependent on cyclical fluctuations in the world economy because demand for investment goods exhibits strong procyclical variations. With the closing of the economic gap between Germany and its major trading partners, that is an end of the German *Sonderkonjunktur*, German exports to other countries will be on the increase again and the growth rate of German imports will flatten. There are growing signs that the German trade and current balance will improve, although a fundamental reversal to new record surpluses in the medium run is rather unlikely.

3. There were some exceptional factors responsible for the fact that the traditionally negative German transfer balance ended with a new record deficit of DM 58.1 billion in 1991 (compared to DM 35.6 billion in 1990). Whereas the German contribution to the costs of the Gulf War of DM 11 billion was a one-off event, transfer payments to East European countries will probably continue, as will most other transfer payments. Since it is very likely that the most important subcategory, Germany's net payments to the European Community, will continue to rise, the current balance will improve only slightly from this side.

4. Due to the collapse of trade among the Comecon countries East German industry lost its major export markets without gaining new ones in the West. As long as East German industry does not considerably improve its international competitiveness, high import requirements will prevail without being matched by exports of an equivalent amount. Matters will probably not improve in the short and medium run as long as wages continue to run ahead of productivity. Things could become different in the long run if the optimistic scenario does materialize and the German economy should realize new record surpluses after a highly modern capital stock has been built up in East Germany.

Although Germany's development after unification is quite exceptional, there are some important ways in which the current situation resembles the situation around 1980: an increasing rate of inflation, enormous budget deficits, pressure from trade unions for higher wages, deficits in the current account and high interest rates with an inverse structure, i.e. short-term rates higher than long-term rates. In its permanent fight for price stability the Bundesbank again wants to counter inflationary dangers with a restrictive monetary policy. It was unprecedented for the Bundesbank, in the pursuit of this policy in July 1991, subsequently to revise its money supply target for the expansion of M3 in 1991 from 4–6 per cent down to 3–5 per cent (see Spahn, 1992). Against the background of the high capital requirements of the government sector this restrictive policy led to higher interest rates, especially at the short end of the market. The nominal long-term interest rate on government bonds increased from 6 per cent in 1988 to 7 per cent in summer 1989 and to about 9 per cent in the last three quarters of 1990. Since then it fell to a level of approximately 8 per cent at the beginning of 1992. The real long-term interest rate rose from under 4 per cent in mid-1989 to a historic maximum of 6.2 per cent in 1990 and dropped again to around 4 per cent at the beginning of 1992. The representatives of the Bundesbank are never tired of emphasizing that the correction of the increase in long-term interest rates is the consequence of their successful restoration of its anti-inflationary credibility.[11]

Interest rate policy has to pursue a difficult tightrope walk between the stability objective and the goals of real economic growth and full employment. It is true that monetary policy can directly affect only the level of short-term interest rates. The different development of long-term interest rates after the Bundesbank's decision to raise the discount and Lombard rates in December 1991 clearly shows that these long-term rates are influenced by additional factors such as expectations of inflation and exchange rates. Nevertheless, higher interest rates have now started to take their toll in Germany. This holds especially for West Germany, where investment is more interest-elastic than in East Germany since investors there, in general, do not have to pay market rates of interest to finance their investment due to various programmes to stimulate capital accumulation via investment grants, tax deductions and so on.

The fact that long-term interest rates today are no higher than they were two years ago is very much due to another dramatic swing: a swing in the capital balance as indicated in Table 6.3. During the 1980s West Germany was a major long-term exporter of capital, which has significantly increased Germany's foreign assets (including external reserves). For the first time since 1981–82 the capital balance changed signs in 1991; the united Germany mutated from a net exporter to a net importer of capital. With unification the absorption of private saving by private investment and especially government spending increased to such an extent that there were no capital funds left for export. On the contrary, in 1991 a net import of capital was necessary to finance the increased absorption of resources in Germany.

The large capital requirements for the restructuring of the East German economy have generated upward pressure on nominal and real interest rate levels in Germany thus stimulating demand for the Deutschmark on the foreign exchange markets and causing upward pressure on it. Provided that the Bundesbank keeps its anti-inflationary credibility, foreign capital will continue to flow into Germany. Lending capital to Germany implies relatively higher returns for international capital owners. During 1991 this influx of capital into Germany was associated with a decrease in long-term interest rates, which are so important for investment decisions, a development only possible because of the international trend of decreasing interest rates. There can be no doubt that Germany has contributed to the global shortage of capital since 1990, thus forcing other countries to keep their interest rates higher than they would otherwise.

Although one should not overemphasize analogies, there are remarkable parallels between the current situation in Germany and the situation in the United States after 1982 and its impact on other countries. With the Bundesbank as well as the Federal Reserve aiming at the maintenance of non-inflationary growth, the economic policy mix creates a conflict between an expansionary fiscal policy and a restrictive monetary policy. American Federal budget deficits contributed to the drain on world savings and an associated increase in interest rates, thus playing the role of the brakesman for investment in other countries via an international crowding-out effect. The German level of interest rates immediately after unification resembles the American real interest rate maximum in 1984. On the other hand, deficits in the US current balance and (contrary to Germany in 1991) also in the trade balance stimulated production and employment in other countries. Whether this 'locomotive' effect or the countervailing 'brakesman' effect via the interest rate mechanism dominates on balance depends very much on the specific position of other countries. Countries with a higher degree of international competitiveness will benefit more from the locomotive effect than countries with low external competitiveness. On the other hand, countries with a high foreign or government debt like Italy will suffer more from the brakesman effect. While it can be expected that the positive spillovers of German economic and monetary union for the world economy will dominate in the longer run, this can also be expected for the short and medium run the more the German government is able to reduce the budget deficits, the more wage increases are in line with productivity increases and the less pressure there is on the Bundesbank to pursue an overly restrictive monetary policy that is both economically costly and politically damaging for unified Germany as well as for other countries, especially Germany's EC partners.

NOTES

* I should like to thank Stephan Seiter for valuable discussions of the issues involved and Heinz Kurz and Christine Rider for their comments on an earlier version. This chapter includes data that were available up to February 1992.

1. As a consequence, Germany was demoted from the second to the fourth position within the European Community.
2. 1985 = 100. For greater details see the recent report of the German Council of Economic Advisers (Sachverständigenrat, 1991, p. 63) and Hagemann and Seiter (1991).
3. The number of unemployed women was 827 783 or 61.6 per cent of registered unemployed. While in June 1990 the unemployment rates for men and women were exactly equal, after GEMSU the rates increasingly diverge over time from 1.8 per cent at the end of 1990 to 5.8 per cent at the end of 1991 (14.7 per cent for women compared to 8.9 per cent for men). This clearly signals that the participation rate of women which in the former GDR was one of the highest in the world (see DIW, 1991c) is in the middle of being 'harmonized' down to the West German level, which in international comparison is rather low.
4. For a more detailed discussion see Sinn and Sinn (1991).
5. So far only a very small percentage of the firms sold by Treuhand have been bought by foreigners.
6. For a more recent and most thorough investigation of the recovering process of the West German industry after 1945 see Ritschl (1985).
7. *'Investments in Germany during the war years had been so high that they exceeded the serious war damage and the replacement value of the plant discarded during the war for reasons of obsolescence'* Krengel (1963, p. 122).
8. For a more detailed analysis see the results of the United States Strategic Bombing Survey (1945), Krengel's pathbreaking 1958 study and recently Schmieding (1990, 1991).
9. The comparison of the sectoral structures of the East German and the West German economy involves many problems. Due to differences in the statistical systems of the states, different values can be found in different studies. The sectoral structure of East Germany, for example, shows one speciality, namely the so called *x-sector*. In the former GDR there was no publication of the data of this sector which includes military activities, Stasi, secret services, customs, political parties, etc. Heinze et al. (1991) estimate that the inclusion of the x-sector increases the employment share of the state sector by about 5 per cent.
10. Another paradoxical result is that in both years the growth rate of both labour productivities in Germany as a whole exceeded the West German ones despite the negative growth rates in East Germany. This is the consequence of the structural effect caused by the shrinking of the East German economy. See Erber and Pischner (1992).
11. See, e.g., Schlesinger (1992, p. 3): 'With our last increase at the short end of the market, we have obviously increased the market's confidence in the D-Mark. The long-term interest rates are today no higher than they were two years ago. ... The markets are counting on a stable Deutsche Mark, at least in a longer-term perspective.'

REFERENCES

Akerlof, G.A., Rose, A.K., Yellen, J.L. and Hessenius, H. (1991), 'East Germany in from the Cold: The Economic Aftermath of Currency Union', *Brookings Papers on Economic Activity*, **1**, 1–105.

ANBA (1992), 'Die Entwicklung des Arbeitsmarktes im Dezember 1991 und im Jahr 1991', *Amtliche Nachrichten der Bundesanstalt für Arbeit*, **1**, 31–9 (Nuremberg).

Arrow, K.J. (1962), 'The Economic Implications of Learning by Doing', *Review of Economic Studies*, **29**, 155–73.

Collier, I.L. and Siebert H. (1991), 'The Economic Integration of Post-Wall Germany', *American Economic Review*, Papers and Proceedings, **81**, 196–201.

Deutsches Institut für Wirtschaftsforschung (DIW) (1991a), 'Gesamtwirtschaftliche und unternehmerische Anpassungsprozesse in Ostdeutschland', 1. Bericht, *DIW-Wochenbericht*, **12**, 123–43.

Deutsches Institut für Wirtschaftsforschung (DIW) (1991b), 'Gesamtwirtschaftliche und unternehmerische Anpassungsprozesse in Ostdeutschland', 2. Bericht, *DIW-Wochenbericht*, **24**, 323–46.

Deutsches Institut für Wirtschaftsforschung (DIW) (1991c), 'Frauenpolitische Aspekte der Arbeitsmarktentwicklung in Ost- und Westdeutschland', *DIW-Wochenbericht*, **30**, 421–26.

Deutsches Institut für Wirtschaftsforschung (DIW) (1992), 'Ergebnisse der vierteljährlichen volkswirtschaftlichen Gesamtrechnung', *DIW-Wochenbericht*, **7**, 73–9.

Erber, G. and Pischner, R. (1992). 'Wir brauchen einen Sozialpakt. Welchen Sinn machen Modellrechnungen zur Anpassung der Arbeitsproduktivitäten in Ost- und Westdeutschland?' Manuscript, DIW, Berlin.

Görzig, B. and Gornig, M. (1991), *Produktivität und Wettbewerbsfähigkeit der Wirtschaft der DDR*. Deutsches Institut für Wirtschaftsforschung, Beiträge zur Strukturforschung, **121**, Berlin.

Hagemann, H. and Seiter, S. (1991), 'Structural Change, Productivity and Employment: Perspectives from a Unified Germany', in I. Rima (ed.), *The Political Economy of Global Restructuring, Volume I*, Aldershot: Edward Elgar.

Hankel, W. (1991), 'Eine Mark und ein Markt für Deutschland. Ordnungspolitische Aspekte der deutschen Währungsunion', in A. Westphal et al. (eds), *Wirtschaftspolitische Konsequenzen der deutschen Vereinigung*, Frankfurt/New York: Campus, pp. 28–45.

Heinze, A. et al. (1991), 'Erwerbstätigenstruktur und Produktivitätsgefälle im Vergleich zwischen Ost- und Westdeutschland – Ausgewählte Probleme', in K. Vogler-Ludwig (ed.), *Perspektiven für den Arbeitsmarkt in den neuen Bundesländern*, ifo-studien zur Arbeitsmarktforschung 7, Munich, pp. 69–89.

Krengel, R. (1958), *Anlagevermögen, Produktion und Beschäftigung der Industrie im Gebiet der Bundesrepublik von 1924 bis 1956*, Berlin.

Krengel, R. (1963), 'Some Reasons for the Rapid Economic Growth of the German Federal Republic,' in: *Banca Nationale del Lavoro Quarterly Review*, **64**, (3) 121–44.

Malinvaud, E. (1980), *Profitability and Unemployment*, Cambridge: Cambridge University Press.

Ritschl, A. (1985), 'Die Währungsreform von 1948 und der Wiederaufstieg der westdeutschen Industrie', *Vierteljahreshefte für Zeitgeschichte*, **33**, 136–65.

Rudolph, H. (1990), 'Beschäftigungsstrukturen in der DDR vor der Wende. Eine Typisierung von Kreisen und Arbeitsämtern', *Mitteilungen aus der Arbeitsmarkt- und Berufsforschung*, **23**, (4) 474–503.

Sachverständigenrat zur Begutachtung der gesamtwirtschaftlichen Entwicklung (SVR) (1990), *Jahresgutachten 1990/91*, Bundestagsdrucksache 11/8472, Bonn.

Sachverständigenrat zur Begutachtung der gesamtwirtschaftlichen Entwicklung (1991), *Jahresgutachten 1991/92. Die wirtschaftliche Integration in Deutschland. Perspektiven – Wege – Risiken*, Bundestagsdrucksache 12/1618, Bonn.

Schlesinger, H. (1992), 'Current issues of German economic and monetary policy', in Deutsche Bundesbank (ed.), *Auszüge aus Presseartikeln*, 5, (20 January), Frankfurt.

Schmieding, H. (1990), 'Der Übergang zur Marktwirtschaft: Gemeinsamkeiten und

Unterschiede zwischen Westdeutschland 1948 und Mittel- und Osteuropa heute', *Die Weltwirtschaft*, 2, 149–60.

Schmieding, H. (1991), 'Die ostdeutsche Wirtschaftskrise: Ursachen und Lösungsstrategien, Anmerkungen im Lichte der westdeutschen Erfahrungen von 1948 und des polnischen Beispiels von 1990', *Institut für Weltwirtschaft, Working Papers No. 461*, Kiel.

Siebert, H. (1990), 'The Economic Integration of Germany – An Update', *Kieler Diskussionsbeiträge 160a*, Institut für Weltwirtschaft, Kiel, September.

Siebert, H. (1991), 'German Unification: the Economics of Transition,' *Economic Policy*, **13**, 289–328.

Sinn, G. and Sinn, H.-W. (1991), *Kaltstart. Volkswirtschaftliche Aspekte der deutschen Vereinigung*, Tübingen: Mohr.

Spahn, H.-P. (1991), 'Das erste und das zweite deutsche Wirtschaftswunder', *Wirtschaftsdienst*, 2, 73–9.

Spahn, H.-P. (1992), 'Geldmengenpolitik in der Bundesrepublik. Theoretische Grundlagen, empirische Erfahrungen und neue Probleme', in C. Rühl (ed.), *Die ökonomische und institutionelle Integration der neuen Länder*. Konsolidierung des Binnenmarktes in den neuen Ländern, Vol. 2, Marburg: Metropolis.

United States Strategic Bombing Survey Overall Economic Effects Division (1945), *The Effects of Strategic Bombing on the German War Economy.*

7. Economic Adjustment Processes in East Germany after Unification

Bernd Görzig

The German Institute of Economic Research (DIW) is situated in Berlin, amidst the former GDR and now practically part of the eastern region of Germany. It is engaged with high priority in research on the adjustment process of the former planned economy of the GDR to a market economy. This chapter is an extract of the published results of a research project which has been conducted by the DIW (DIW, 1991a, 1991b) together with the Institute of World Economics (IfW). In addition, it contains some results of the newest economic outlook on East Germany made by the five leading economic research institutes in Germany. The chapter describes the economic situation in East Germany as seen in spring 1991 (DIW 1991c, 1991d). It is the result of a joint effort of all the members of the group that has been working on this project.

The system of statistical reporting in East Germany is like anything else in the process of fundamental restructuring: the old system has been scrapped, but the new structure is not yet in operation. Official statistics provide only very limited data and can be misleading, partly due to the fact that methodological problems linked to the transition to the new economic order have yet to be solved, and partly because of changes in the institutions providing the required data. Therefore this chapter cannot be a coherent presentation of the economic situation. It is the conclusive result of conducted surveys, questionnaires, evaluated non-official data sources and estimates by the institutes. Its focus is on the economy as a whole with special consideration of the manufacturing sector.

In spring 1991 there was no sign of a recovery from the collapse of output and employment in East Germany which followed economic and monetary union with the Federal Republic of Germany. The crisis deepened in the first months of 1991 and a number of signs pointed to a further worsening of the situation at least for the first half of that year. This is a result not only of internal factors: the global economic context has become distinctly more unfavourable for economic development in East Germany.

The system of organized trade set up between the Central and East European countries after the end of the Second World War has collapsed. While all the countries have experienced a dramatic economic decline, the hopes for economic stabilization in the near future will only be realized in some. Thus the East German economy is faced with the loss of its traditional sales markets.

On top of this comes the weakening of the growth dynamics in the Western industrialized countries, with recession hitting the United States and Great Britain and stagnation in a number of West European countries. Although this development has now come to an end, the West German economy was expected now to grow only 3 per cent in 1991, more slowly than in 1990. This was due to a weakening of the domestic expansionary forces which until then had been behind higher rates of growth in the Federal Republic.

All in all, the global economic context for the East German economy in spring 1991 was considerably less favourable than in mid-1990 when monetary and economic union between the two German states came into being. Economic policy-makers were thus faced with a more difficult task than expected. The state of manufacturing industry in East Germany is alarming. On official statistics the level of production in manufacturing industry in East Germany was 30 per cent lower in 1990 than in 1989. The fall in demand was already making itself felt in the first half of 1990 – before economic union started and official exchange rates were 1 DM for 2 or 3 East German marks. But it was monetary union, the introduction of the Deutschmark as legal tender in the former GDR, which marked the widespread collapse of markets there.

Industrial contraction has been most pronounced in the consumer goods sector, particularly textiles, food and light industry (Table 7.1). This is due to the shift towards Western consumer goods by East German households. Output also declined sharply in the iron and other metal processing industries. This is also largely the result of the collapse of the domestic consumer market. Contributory factors are the difficulties experienced by other branches which used to purchase semi-finished inputs and the dramatic fall in traditional exports to Eastern Europe.

The fall in output was less dramatic in the pharmaceutical sector, which accounts for 12 per cent of total industrial output, machinery and automobiles and electrical engineering. These sectors, dominated by large industrial conglomerates, have continued to fulfil existing large-scale contracts, with the result that the fall in output has been less spectacular. However, a fall in production must also be expected in these branches, since production until the end of 1990 was sold at subsidized prices, especially to Eastern markets.

Table 7.1:   Industrial Goods Production in the GDR, 1986–90

	Structure July 1990 in %	Percentage change on previous year[1]				
		1986	1987	1988	1989	1990
Industrial sector total	100	3.0	2.9	3.0	2.2	−28.0
Energy and fuel industry	11	2.3	1.3	0.7	−0.1	−24.3
Chemical industry	12	2.2	1.5	3.4	2.4	−30.0
Metallurgy	6	3.7	3.1	−0.5	−0.2	−38.0
Building material industry	4	3.0	1.9	3.3	0.7	32.2
Water industry	2	2.3	−0.1	1.6	2.8	−0.6
Engineering and automobiles	31	4.5	3.3	4.3	3.7	−18.9
Electrical engineering/electronics	10	7.2	10.6	9.0	8.0	−24.1
Light industry	9	3.2	3.2	4.9	2.0	−31.0
Textile industry	3	3.4	3.0	2.4	3.0	−33.5
Food industry	13	2.6	0.5	0.8	1.1	−34.6

Sources: Statistical Office of the GDR and Federal Statistical Office.
1.   The figures for 1989 and 1990 are not directly comparable.

Variations in the level of output in different branches are reflected in the branch-specific growth of short-time working. In industry as a whole, in January 1991 one-third of the workforce was on short-time working. The figures are most striking for the metal production and processing, the textile and clothing and the chemical industries. There more than half of the employees are working short time.

The process of restructuring through investment in new plant and new products has barely got off the ground. This is hardly surprising given the desolate state of most East German enterprises. Firms have, however, made efforts to reduce costs: in many cases facilities external to actual production, such as health-care provision, nurseries, holiday homes, canteens and libraries, have been abandoned. Some of them have been taken over by local authorities. This process has affected about 10–20 per cent of the workforce. Job cuts of a similar order of magnitude have been made in in-firm departments such as haulage, construction brigades and repair and maintenance workshops: in some cases these have continued to exist as independent private firms.

Restructuring programmes have often resulted in a significant narrowing of product ranges, the aim being to ensure survival with a limited number of products. Assembly operations have frequently been separated from larger companies, in some cases to be taken over by West German firms as 'extended workbenches'. The incentives for such purchases are capacity constraints in West German enterprises and the lower wage costs in East Germany.

*Table 7.2:   Proportion of Workforce on Short-time Working in Selected
              Industries, January 1991*

	% of workforce[1]
Metallurgy	55
Engineering	33
Automobile industry	30
Electrical engineering	39
Textiles, clothing	52
Metal goods	33
Mining	36
Wood	32
Construction	17
Chemical industry	54

Source: DIW calculations
1. The above percentages understate the extent of short-time working as the figures for branch workforce levels refer to 1989, those for the number of short-time workers to 1991.

In the enterprises surveyed, privatization was followed by a reduction in staffing levels of up to two thirds.

But the central challenge remains unmet in almost all sectors – to develop new products, for instance on the basis of renewed R&D and marketing activity, and investment in fixed and human capital. Moreover, with a view to stabilizing employment levels, many sectors are continuing to produce goods for which there is no demand. The government-owned holding of all former socialized firms, the Treuhandanstalt, provides bridging loans, which, however, are merely used to maintain wage incomes.

Firms are trying to cut their variable costs, often opting for the so-called 'zero-hour' short-time working regime. Workers are not fired, but set to zero-hour short-time. In this case the federal labour insurance system pays some fraction of the former wage. Fixed costs are not covered by production but from the sale of real estate and property rental. In some cases domestic liabilities are not being met, while payments for exported goods are still being received.

It remains difficult to judge the growth prospects of individual branches of East German industry, though information gleaned from interviews with experts and other sources does shed some light on possible trends. Compared with the industrial sector as a whole, the following branches are set to develop favourably (Görzig and Gornig 1991):

— branches dependent on the construction industry, such as quarrying; these can expect to see an increase in output to the extent that the need for construction and reconstruction, particularly in the public sector, is matched by real effective demand and actual output in the construction industry. The same is true of parts of the telecommunications sector and steel construction.

— firms operating in regional markets, such as handicraft and trade enterprises, printers and certain sections of the food, drink and tobacco sector.

— firms which had specialized in meeting foreign demand on world markets before the borders were opened – certain specialized engineering branches and the precision mechanics and optics sector. These have good chances of survival provided they increase their productivity significantly.

Many firms, particularly those in the engineering industry and automobile and other vehicles industry, will be heavily dependent on cooperation with Western companies. Two strategies seem possible: to cut staffing levels and carry out subcontracted work for Western firms or to exploit sales opportunities in Eastern Europe.

In many cases the engineering industry will have to come to terms with a structural problem: productive plants are in most cases oriented towards large-scale, long production runs, a form of production which is no longer competitive. In these cases an increase in overall efficiency cannot be achieved by restricting production to highly productive units.

The prospects for the following branches, on the other hand, appear to be relatively bad:

— industries producing standardized products in large batches and subject to wage-cost competition, such as textiles and clothing, footwear and toys:

— the chemical industry, which produces scarcely any products that could compete on markets and in which productive plant is obsolete;

— large sections of the electrical engineering industry which have failed to reach the standard required for survival in the face of world market competition despite the great efforts made even before the opening of the border;

— the shipbuilding industry, which was heavily oriented towards the East European market and is now facing a sharp fall in demand with no sign of alternative markets opening in the short term;

— the steel industry, which can only be modernized and rendered competitive with the help of investors from the West. In view of persistent excess steel-producing capacity worldwide this does not appear a likely development.

A number of restructuring strategies are of questionable value: concepts aimed solely at streamlining the product range or subcontracted assembly work represent strategies which are only sustainable in the short run, particularly in view of the rapid rise in wages in East Germany which will soon wipe out wage-cost advantages. Only firms that also manage to modernize their products and production processes will be assured of survival. A further condition is the development of new distribution networks. In most cases this will only be possible with the help of Western know-how and investment.

Incentives for Western firms to invest in East Germany consist primarily in the plentiful supply of well-qualified labour and the prospect of gaining access to new regional markets. An often mentioned, but rather rare factor is the buying out of competitors. Nonetheless, the scale of investment by Western firms has as yet been very limited. The privatization of formerly state-owned enterprises shows very different results. About a thousand of the former 9 000 firms have so far been sold. But most of these firms are very small, like pharmacies, restaurants and shops. More important is that all of the big hotels and all newspapers have been sold. It is very difficult, however, to sell big industrial firms. The barriers to investment are numerous:

- The infrastructure required for modern production processes is totally lacking.
- The legal problem of 'property restitution versus compensation' in the case of wrangles over property ownership in the former GDR has still not been completely resolved.
- Administrative decision-making processes are too time consuming.
- Western firms are unwilling to take on large plants because buildings and equipment stocks are too large for their needs, and staffing levels are too high.
- There have been delays in the privatization programme. The Treuhandanstalt has to build up an organizational structure itself, a process which is not yet finished. With 2 000 people employed, on average one employee is responsible for 4–5 firms. In addition, the book-keeping of one of the biggest holdings of the world is presently done on eight personal computers. In spring 1991 the Treuhandanstalt had only very few initial balances in Deutschmarks of its firms. And lastly from the policy side there are too many conflicting demands on the Treuhandanstalt.

A further problem is the gloomy prospect for trade with the former trading partners of the GDR in Eastern Europe in the current year. Many observers fear that the Soviet market may collapse completely. In the case of consumer goods and consumer-oriented investment goods – for example textiles, clothing products, furniture, machinery for the textile industry – orders from the Soviet Union are running at an absolute minimum, despite the catastrophic supply situation there.

A telephone survey conducted in mid-February 1991 regarding the state of exports to the Soviet Union concluded that three-quarters of the enterprises interviewed expect exports to this region to fall by at least two-thirds. The future course of exports to Eastern Europe is, in the opinion of the experts interviewed, primarily a question of lack of foreign exchange in this region. Export guarantees under the West German government-backed Hermes insurance system have been taken up very slowly at first since the Soviet foreign trade bank refused to offer a reimbursement guarantee.

In view of the overall situation, and even assuming that exports to Eastern Europe can be stabilized at DM 10 billion, industrial output in East Germany in 1991 will reach little more than one-third of the value for 1989. The level of employment will also fall sharply. It is possible that, even given supportive economic policies, by the end of 1991 employment in East German mining and manufacturing industry would total little more than 2 million persons, compared with over 3.5 million at the beginning of 1989 (Table 7.3).

This sounds very dramatic, but it has to be taken into consideration that the proportion of people employed in the industrial sector was extremely high in the former GDR compared with the structure of employment in West Germany. Calculations made by the DIW before unification expected that in the long run about 2.3 million people would be employed in the industrial sector under market conditions instead of 3.6 million in 1989 (DIW 1990a, 1990b).

Since, however, short-time working will also remain at a high level in 1991, the industrial labour volume will clearly fall below the long-term expectations. Taking a look at areas of employment outside the industrial sector it must be concluded that hopes that services together with the construction industry would become the pacemaker for a sustained upturn in the East German economy have yet to be fulfilled. The reasons for this failure are varied, and originate partly on the supply side. Here again the problems of property rights, administrative restrictions and the lack of infrastructure have to be mentioned. But in spring 1991 there are some signs that in the second half of 1991 production in these sectors will start to grow. However, growth will not be strong enough to relieve the labour market. Productivity improvements will lead to further reduction of employment even in these sectors (Table 7.4).

Table 7.3:   *GDP and Working Population in East Germany by Sector,*
            1989–91

	1989	1990	1991	1990	1991
Gross value-added of economic sectors (in current prices)	DM billions			% change on previous year	
Agriculture and forestry	10.97	7.28	5.85	−33.6	−19.7
Goods sector	173.87	127.78	85.57	−26.5	−33.0
Mining and manufacturing	152.56	107.99	64.65	−29.2	−40.1
Construction	21.32	19.79	20.91	−7.2	5.7
Trade and transport	40.93	31.07	26.06	−24.1	−16.1
Trade	16.73	13.72	11.90	−17.9	−13.3
Transport	24.20	17.35	14.15	−28.3	−18.4
Services and public sector	59.87	63.61	69.29	6.2	8.9
Services	36.30	37.73	38.83	3.9	2.9
Public sector	20.08	21.91	25.78	9.1	17.7
Private non-profit orgns	3.49	3.97	4.68	13.7	17.9
Gross domestic product	285.65	229.75	186.77	−19.6	−18.7
Income from nationals abroad	0.00	2.32	10.25		
Gross national product	285.65	232.07	197.02	−18.8	−15.1
Working population	000 persons			Differences on previous year	
Agriculture and forestry	960	809	578	−151	−231
Goods sector	4.253	3.682	2.439	−571	−1.243
Mining and manufacturing	3.655	3.194	2.071	−461	−1.123
Construction	598	487	368	−111	−119
Trade and transport	1.408	1.306	1.033	−102	−273
Trade	732	664	530	−68	−134
Transport	677	642	503	−35	−139
Services and public sector	3.019	2.939	2.469	−80	−470
Services	1.086	1.091	1.003	5	−88
Public sector	1.746	1.678	1.325	−68	−353
Private non-profit orgns	187	171	141	−16	−30
Total	9.640	8.736	6.518	−904	−2.218

Source: DIW prognosis on the basis of the results of an empirically based model calculation for 1989 and 1990.

Table 7.4: The East German Labour Market, 1990 and 1991, in thousands

	1990	1991
Working population	8.735	6.520
Unemployed	230	1.500
Cross-border commuters	−75	−315
Emigrants (to West Germany)	−300	−210
Early retirement	100	295
Occupational pensioners	100	0
Other[1]	100	400
Additional information		
Short-time workers	760	1.665
Civil servants in *Wartestand*	60	210

Source: DIW calculations.
1. Additional pensioners, non-registered unemployed, full-time further training etc.

In addition the number of civil servants in the public sector will decrease considerably. A number of public services will be transferred to private business. However, it is important to remember that the number of civil servants was extremely high in the former GDR. According to a special provision for the state sector, East German civil servants who in the course of restructuring would normally be made redundant do not register as unemployed but enter the so-called *Wartestand*, a sort of intermediate status, which in the medium term will result in formal redundancy for almost all the workers involved.

Due to their difficult budgetary position, local authorities are often not in a position to undertake vitally important projects – the construction and refurbishing of commercial premises, the extension of urban road networks, the restoration of public facilities, of the housing stock and commercial buildings. Burdens have been placed on local authorities in East Germany which exceed their financial capabilities. First, they have been assigned the entire public housing stock. This at first makes them poorer, not richer: rent income is currently inadequate even to meet running costs. Secondly, until the matter is finally decided they are responsible for medical services. Due to the inadequate financial contributions paid by health insurance companies, polyclinics and patient-care facilities will require substantial subsidies from local government.

Taking the results obtained for the various sectors of the East German economy together it must be concluded that in spring 1991 there is no sign

Table 7.5: East German Key National Accounts Data, 1990–91

Years	1990	1991	Forecast for 1991 % Change on previous year			
			1990 1st half	1990 2nd half	1991 1st half	1991 2nd half
Components of GNP						
Employed labour force	–10.3	–23.0	–5.8	–14.7	–22.5	–23.5
Hours worked per working day	–5.8	–22.0	0.0	–11.8	–25.0	–19.0
Working days	–0.6	–0.5	–0.3	–1.0	–1.0	0.5
Labour volume (by calendar month)	–16.0	–40.5	–6.1	–25.6	–42.5	–38.0
Productivity (1)	3.0	34.0	5.6	–0.4	21.5	50.0
Gross domestic product at 1985 prices	–13.4	–20.0	–0.9	–25.9	–30.0	–7.0
GNP by type of expenditure at current prices						
Private consumption	10.0	5.5	10.2	9.8	3.0	7.5
Government consumption	5.4	13.5	2.1	8.5	12.0	15.0
Fixed capital formation	–3.5	26.0	–1.9	–5.2	10.0	42.5
Machinery and equipment	1.4	33.0	7.6	–4.6	17.5	49.5
Construction	–6.7	21.0	–7.9	–5.5	4.5	37.5
Exports	12.9	–20.0	6.8	18.8	–13.0	–26.0
Imports	70.2	49.0	21.1	113.3	119.5	14.0
Gross national product	–15.9	–1.5	–5.3	–26.4	–18.5	20.5
GNP by type of expenditure at 1990 prices						
Private consumption	15.0	–5.0	14.1	15.8	–3.5	–6.5
Government consumption	0.0	–4.5	–0.4	0.5	0.0	–9.0
Fixed capital formation	–5.7	16.5	–3.8	–7.6	3.5	30.0
Machinery and equipment	0.4	29.5	6.9	–5.9	14.5	45.0
Construction	–9.5	7.5	–10.4	–8.7	–4.5	19.5
Exports	19.0	–20.0	9.4	28.1	–10.0	–28.5
Imports	66.9	46.5	18.9	109.1	117.0	11.0
Gross national product	–12.7	–17.5	–0.6	–24.7	–27.5	–4.0
Factor incomes in GNP						
Income from employment	3.9	–5.5	10.1	–2.6	–16.0	7.5
Gross wages and salaries	4.9	–6.5	10.2	–0.7	–16.5	5.0
Net wages and salaries	4.9	–11.0	9.8	–0.4	–20.0	–1.0
memo item:						
Gross wages and salary per employee	18.0	22.0	17.8	18.0	8.5	38.0
Entrepreneurial and property income, gross	–20.1	8.5	–10.7	–28.0	–9.0	26.5
Net national product at factor cost	–3.3	–2.0	4.4	–10.8	–14.5	12.5
Depreciation	1.4	3.0	1.1	1.7	2.5	3.5
Gross national product	–15.9	–1.5	–5.3	–26.4	–18.5	20.5

Sources: 1990 calculations by the Federal Statistical Office for the second half of 1990 and empirically based model calculations by the DIW. 1991 forecast by the 'Five Institutes'. Forecast absolute figures and rate of change rounded to 0.0 and 0.5 respectively.
1. Gross domestic product at 1980 prices per hour worked.

of a broadly based economic upturn in East Germany for 1991; economic growth is restricted to a small number of sectors. The positive impulse for the East German economy as a whole will not be sufficient to lead to sustained improvement on the macro-level, since the growing sectors account only for a relatively small proportion of overall output.

According to the forecast of the five leading economic institutes, the average level of real product for 1991 will again be about a fifth below the previous year's level (Table 7.5). This further collapse of production will mean that on average at least 3 million people will be unemployed or on short-time working during the year. The volume of working hours will fall even more sharply than the number in employment. Average working hours will fall due to short-time working and collectively negotiated reductions in working time. The level of employment is calculated to fall by about one-quarter in the course of the year, having already declined by a sixth in the previous year. The fall in the number in employment is not transmitted directly into a corresponding increase in unemployment. The number affected by unemployment is much higher than the level of registered unemployed. There will, however, be some relief for the East German labour market by commuters to West Germany and by people taking early retirement or undertaking educational programmes.

REFERENCES

DIW (1990a), 'Quantitative Aspekte einer Reform von Wirtschaft und Finanzen in der DDR,' *Wochenbericht des DIW*, **14**.

DIW (1990b), 'Quantitative Aspects of Economic and Financial Reform in the GDR,' *Economic Bulletin*, **5** (27), 1 (Aldershot: Gower).

DIW (1991a), 'Gesamtwirtschaftliche und unternehmerische Anpassungsprozesse in Ostdeutschland,' Erster Bericht, *Wochenbericht des DIW*, **12**, p. 123.

DIW (1991b), 'Micro and Macroeconomic Adjustment Processes in East Germany,' *Economic Bulletin*, **4** (28), 1 (Aldershot: Gower).

DIW (1991c), 'Die Lage der Wirtschaft und der westdeutschen Wirtschaft im Frühjahr 1990,' *Wochenbericht des DIW*, **15**.

DIW (1991d), 'The "Five Institutes" Forecast: The German Economy', *Economic Bulletin*, **5** (28), 4 (Aldershot: Gower).

Görzig, B. and Gornig, M. (1991), 'Produktivität und Wettbewerbsfähigkeit der DDR-Wirtschaft,' *DIW Beiträge zur Strukturforschung*, **121**, Berlin: Duncker und Humblot.

8. On Alternative Strategies of Wage Policy in Eastern Germany

Peter Kalmbach

1 THE INITIAL POSITION

Prior to economic and currency union there was a controversial debate about the conversion rate of the Ostmark of the German Democratic Republic. The black market exchange rates that emerged shortly after the opening of the Wall did not play any role in this discussion, because they would have meant inconceivably large income differences within the unified economic territory on the target day, 1 July. The final choice was between a conversion rate of 2:1 or 1:1. The German Bundesbank supported a conversion rate of 2 Ostmarks: 1 Deutschmark. The Bundesbank argued that with regard to the productivity of the GDR economy a more favourable conversion rate would have extremely negative consequences in terms of production and employment on the territory of the GDR. The German government eventually arrived at the decision to adjust flows at a relation of 1:1. This primarily meant that wages, as valid at the end of June 1990 in Ostmarks, were paid in Deutschmarks beginning on 1 July.

Although during the months before economic and currency union was introduced wages in the GDR had risen remarkably, the difference between wages East and wages West was significant, even at a conversion rate of 1:1. Supplying clear and reliable data is problematic for a number of reasons (for example treatment of the additional payments, which are not monthly based). If I were forced, nonetheless, to provide an estimate, my results would be as follows. When economic and currency union came into being, the average monthly wage before tax of a fully employed citizen in the West amounted to 3 200 Deutschmarks, whereas a fully employed citizen in the East earned 1 150 Ostmarks on average. The level of wages in the East thus reached only 36 per cent of the level of the wages in the West.[1]

Of course, these numbers cannot unreservedly be used as welfare indicators. The difference between net wages is much smaller because of the lower tax burden in the East. As a lot of commodities for private consumption were, and still are, subsidized in the East the difference between real wages is even smaller. Regarding the incomes of households it has to be taken into consideration that female employment in the former GDR was higher. Comparing household incomes, the difference is thus smaller. A recently published study by the DIW (1991d) arrives at the remarkable result that at the beginning of 1991 the average real income of a worker's household in the East reached 80 per cent of the corresponding income in the West. However, this estimate is probably not representative of the average situation in 1991 because it depends highly on the very low rents at that time which have risen significantly since then.

If we stick to the more reliable wages before tax, it is a fact that in the unified economic territory, and since October 1990 in the unified Germany, the income differences between East and West are much larger than those between prosperous and poor regions in the West.

2   THE PROS AND CONS OF DRASTIC WAGE INCREASES IN EASTERN GERMANY

Economists from different theoretical traditions agree that such a state of affairs cannot last long. To what extent the 'law of one price' derived from a model of pure competition is modified in reality and to what degree regional income differences will persist is judged differently, but there is agreement that differences as extreme as in the unified Germany will trigger processes of convergence. The controversy therefore is not about this point. It is, rather, derived from opposing points of view as to the appropriate speed of convergence in order to avoid major economic problems in East and West Germany. To be more precise: the debate is over whether large increases of nominal wages in the East, independent of the development of labour productivity, are possible and indeed desirable, or whether an attempt to accelerate the convergence of incomes would be a heavy burden for production and employment as well as for the intended economic catching-up process.

The arguments on both sides will only be discussed briefly here. Proposals for moderate and productivity-based wage increases[2] seem to be supported by the argument that the introduction of the Deutschmark in East Germany has had the effect of a gigantic currency revaluation – according to some estimates by 300 per cent. There are only a few enterprises in the former FRG that could easily digest such revaluation; for the enterprises in the former GDR the consequences had to be disastrous. Producer prices were bound to fall greatly, and indeed they have. High costs, which have increased further due to rising wages, mean that only a small and decreasing number of firms show at least a positive margin between price and unit variable costs. Only these firms have been able to stay in the market, at least in the short run, without federal aid. With regard to firms that have not been driven into a hopeless situation by the conditions generated by currency union, it seems realistic to assume that each further wage rise, without corresponding productivity growth, will force additional firms to give up, provided that the state or the Treuhandanstalt (privatization agency) does not secure the necessary liquidity of these firms.

While this argument is mainly able to explain the fate of existing firms, a similar one is more concerned with the incentives to invest, that is, the conditions necessary for the creation of new jobs. A relevant number of the jobs that existed before economic and currency union will inevitably vanish under the new conditions, so the prevention of a dramatic rise in unemployment requires preconditions favourable to the creation of new jobs. However, such preconditons are not at all favourable. The heritage of the former GDR consists of an underdeveloped infrastructure, an administration unable to deal with the immediate tasks, and tremendous ecological problems. These obstacles to investment are reinforced by unclear property rights. Taking all this together, investors have had good reason for not wanting to move into East Germany. According to its proponents a moderate wage policy should compensate for the factors which are hindering investment. A low wage level is meant to serve as an incentive to invest.

This plea for a moderate and productivity-based wage policy faces counter-arguments, the following of which deserve mention. On the one hand, there is the argument of fairness. How can it be justified that an engine driver driving from Leipzig to Hamburg only receives one-third of the income of his colleague who starts from Hamburg?

However, fairness or justice are not the main questions with which the economist is occupied. To accept a rapid convergence of wages the economist, being rather reserved about normative questions, asks for arguments with economic substance. Furthermore, economic reasoning is not unconditionally opposed to a rapid convergence of wages. An important argument that has been presented to support a rapid adjustment of wages is that in the long run a substantial wage differential will inevitably cause massive migration from the East to the West. Certain lobbyists may be worried by this statement, which is in accordance with conventional economic theory, but most economists will not consider it a serious problem. Indeed, they generally approve of a high degree of mobility. In the special case of East Germany it must be feared that, in particular, young and skilled workers will seek a better-paid job in the West. If this is true, economic development in East Germany could be influenced negatively. The envisaged catching-up process would take place at a slower pace, or not at all.

Large and slowly disappearing wage differentials will cause another problem. They may have the consequence that only labour-intensive production processes will be established in Eastern Germany. In the short run this seems to be desirable, because of higher employment possibilities. It would mean, however, that East Germany would be exposed to competition from southern Europe and Asia, which would limit bigger wage hikes. Furthermore, the economic structures in the east and west of the unified Germany would become completely different: a problem which differs from Italy's only so far as the directions between industrialized and underdeveloped regions are concerned (i.e. an east–west as opposed to a north–south divide).

3   CAUSES AND IMPLICATIONS OF HIGH WAGE RISES

After these more theoretical speculations we will now deal with the real development that has taken place since the beginning of economic and currency union. Many expected that production would drop in East Germany. However, few anticipated the extent and duration of the collapse: only three months after the introduction of the Deutschmark, industrial production had come down by 50 per cent. Various and hardly predictable factors, such as the loss of demand caused by the economic catastrophe in the Soviet Union and the almost compulsive preference for Western products in East Germany, have contributed to this negative development. Political misjudgement has added to the problem. Too much confidence in market forces has prevented the political authorities from introducing appropriate measures to make the market work. The communities have not had, and still do not have, enough resources at their disposal to invest and stimulate private investment.

All of these are relevant factors. But the main reason for the collapse derives from a simple economic fact: the former GDR economy had suddenly been transformed from a protected economy secured by bilateral contracts into an economy that had to compete on internal and external markets with competitors that were superior in many respects. The disadvantages deriving from quality deficits were intensified by the *de facto* revaluation corresponding to the adopted conversion rate. A lot of firms suffered hopeless disadvantages, for they were confronted with prices set by the world market and unit costs determined by backward domestic productivity.

Wage policy does not take account of these facts. We have already reviewed some of the arguments supporting a rapid convergence of wages. Whether the remarkable wage rises in Eastern Germany, in spite of the disastrous economic development, are due to the persuasive power of these arguments seems rather doubtful. A more realistic explanation would be that the unions have had far better preconditions and far more compelling reasons to push through massive wage rises than the employers have had for resisting them. The unions have had a better footing in the wage bargaining, one reason for this being that West Germany's unions started very early to transfer their organizational structures to the East and to support the Eastern unions materially and personally. Understandably, employers' associations in the West had no reason to aid Eastern management in the same way, because to a large part this management was still the one that was established under the rule of the communist party, the SED, and in some cases was suspected of being involved in the East German intelligence service, the Stasi.

These asymmetric preconditions for wage negotiations were intensified by a constellation that made the demand for high wage rises look rational and easy to realize. Many union officials held the view that a massive increase in unemployment was inevitable – independent of high or moderate wage increases. Consequently, the bargaining situation became what can be described as an end game (see Akerlof et al., 1991). It seemed rational to aim for the highest possible wage rises, because the amount of unemployment benefits depends on the latest net wage. If the same reasoning also prevails on the employers' side because managers expect to become unemployed, too, the result is pre-programmed.

Other factors leading to high wage demands and favouring their accomplishment can be added. I will mention these briefly:

1. In contrast to the former FRG, unions have not had to fear that high wage rises would be succeeded by rising prices. This follows from the relatively small share of total demand of the former GDR. High increases in nominal wages give rise to expectations of high increases in real wages. In contrast to usual wage negotiations, nominal wage settlements could thus be expected to be real wage settlements – not taking into account administered prices.

2. Enterprises considered the extensive agreements on rationalization, partly agreed upon before the economic and currency union, to be the greater evil. Employers have tried to get rid of these agreements or, at least, attempted to weaken them during the first collective bargainings. In order to achieve this aim they have been prepared to agree to higher wage rises. Presumably employers assume that a rapid catching up of wages paid in the Eastern labour market cannot be prevented, even if they resisted an increase in negotiated wages. The unions also fear a divergent development of effective and negotiated wages, which is a further motive for them to opt for high increases of negotiated wages. A divergent development of effectively paid and negotiated wages would have been understood to indicate that unions' agreements are of minor importance to the actual development of wages.

Whether the above mentioned reasons are the main ones for the wage increases in Eastern Germany after economic and currency union cannot be decided here. However, it is a fact that, in spite of rising unemployment and short-time work, wage increases have been massive and not in line with the development of productivity. The latter actually fell during the first three months of economic and currency union and has only recently shown an upward trend.

Unambiguous and generally accepted data about the extent of wage increases in East Germany are not yet available. Estimates show that one year after economic and currency union a fully employed Eastern German employee earned about 45–50 per cent of his Western colleague's wage. This relative convergence – at the beginning of economic and currency union the figure was only 36 per cent – implies massive wage rises in the course of a single year: a 32.5 per cent wage rise, if the estimate of a '45 per cent Eastern wage' is realistic, 47.2 per cent if a '50 per cent Eastern wage' comes closer to reality. These high growth rates reflect, on the one hand, the catching up of Eastern Germany's wages, and on the other hand the fact that wages in West Germany also increased in that year (by about 6 per cent).[3]

It is almost self-evident that convergence of gross wages requires positive growth differentials in favour of East Germany: the larger they are, the quicker will equal wages actually be paid. Despite this fact some politicians promised quick convergence of wages during the election campaign, yet now complain about too high wage increases in East Germany. So it is perhaps of some use to look at the quantitative consequences of alternative assumptions about wage convergence. Table 8.1 shows the necessary annual growth rates of wages to achieve equal gross wages in 1995 and in 2000, respectively, given certain assumptions. Assumptions 2 and 3 take into account that high wage rises have taken place since currency union. Nevertheless, extraordinary large annual increases of nominal wages (between 24 and 33 per cent, depending on the assumption) will be needed, if convergence is to be accomplished by 1995.[4]

In Table 8.2 the way of looking at things is reversed. The share of gross wages in East Germany achieved in the years 1995 and 2000 is considered now under the – unrealistic – assumption of a productivity-based wage policy in East and West. In spite of the rather optimistic assumptions concerning the higher productivity growth obtainable in the East, the differences would still be considerable in 2000.

In a preliminary summary the following aspects deserve to be emphasized. Economic and currency union had the effect of a massive revaluation. The enterprises in the former GDR that had been protected by bilateral contracts suddenly had to compete on the world market and were forced to reduce their producer prices substantially. According to a study of Akerlof et

Table 8.1: *Annual Wage Rises in East Germany under Different Assumptions*

Assumption	Necessary annual growth rates of wages in East Germany (in %) under the following assumptions:	
	equal gross wages	
	in 1995	in 2000
1. In 1991 gross wages in East Germany amount to 40% of gross wages in West Germany		
(a) annual rise of gross wages in West Germany 6%	32.2	13.6
(b) annual rise of gross wages in West Germany 4%	30.8	12.7
2. In 1991 gross wages in East Germany amount to 45% of gross wages in West Germany		
(a) annual rise of gross wages in West Germany 6%	29.4	12.1
(b) annual rise of gross wages in West Germany 4%	27.0	11.2
3. In 1991 gross wages in East Germany amount to 50% of gross wages in West Germany		
(a) annual rise of gross wages in West Germany 6%	26.0	10.8
(b) annual rise of gross wages in West Germany 4%	23.7	9.9

Table 8.2:   *Gross Wages in East Germany as a Percentage of West Germany's under the Condition of a Productivity-based Wage Policy with Different Starting Positions*

Assumption	Relation of gross wages East to gross wages West	
	1995 (%)	2000 (%)

1.   In 1991 gross wages East amount to 40% of gross wages West
Annual productivity growth:
        West: 3%
        East: 8%
	48.3	61.3

2.   In 1991 gross wages East amount to 45% of gross wages West
Annual productivity growth:
        West: 3%
        East: 8%
	54.4	69.0

3.   In 1991 gross wages East amount to 50% of gross wages West
Annual productivity growth:
        West: 3%
        East: 8%
	60.4	76.6

al. (1991), in August 1990 producer prices, on average, amounted to only 50 per cent of the 1989 level. In the chemical and textile industries producer prices reached only 30 per cent.

In many enterprises this would have been enough to make producer prices fall below total unit costs or even below unit variable costs. Production could only be continued with losses. Pay rises without corresponding productivity growth have, inevitably, aggravated this price–cost squeeze. To supply quantitative data is problematic. The most careful – although not in every aspect fully convincing – study known to me is by the US economist Akerlof et al. (1991) – rather embarrassing for German economists. For reasons of space I must refrain from commenting on their methods of calculation and will confine my presentation to one of their results. This is quite disillusioning: in October 1990 only 8.2 per cent of all employees of former conglomerates were employed in enterprises whose prices covered at least the average variable costs. As the proportion of employment in former conglomerates to total employment is very high, this means that already in October 1990 – and even more so because of rising wages since then – only a small proportion of employees in East Germany are employed in economically viable enterprises.

4 WAGE SUBSIDIES AS A TRANSITIONAL STRATEGY?

The strategy the German government has chosen to tackle the enormous economic problems in the East is well known. After a period of *laissez-faire* that lasted far too long, it is now attempting to bring about economic recovery by means of a bundle of investment incentives. The Ministry of Trade and Commerce (*Handelsblatt*, 1991) and the Bundesbank (Deutsche Bundesbank, 1991) – otherwise not always in agreement – proclaim the same message: economic recovery of the former GDR – and the only feasible way towards rapid convergence of wages – can only take place via stimulating investment, i.e. the formation of capital. They firmly reject stopping the dramatic fall in employment by subsidizing wages.

Repeatedly, convincing arguments against subsidies have been presented: they block structural change; firms may take advantage of them; once introduced, one cannot get rid of them, and so on. But there is actually no need to discuss the avoidance of subsidies: the Federal government has developed different programmes which, in fact, are nothing but subsidies – admittedly, subsidies for capital formation instead of job creation. Is this decision in favour of investment incentives and against wage subsidies economically reasonable?

It might be argued that the financial burden for the West has reached its limit – a decision for one strategy means that the other one is no longer feasible. However, the above-mentioned study by Akerlof et al. provides estimates qualifying the problem of the financial burden. On the one hand, the self-financing aspect of subsidies has to be taken into account. Expenditure on unemployment benefits will fall and subsidized employees will pay taxes and contributions to the social security fund. A further aspect can be added. A lot of firms owned by the Treuhand cannot be sold, even at a symbolical price, because the prevailing price–cost relation and the employment guarantees demanded result in a negative value of the firm. Wage subsidies would make the firm's value rise – the Treuhand's proceeds would be a further aspect qualifying the argument that such a measure would cause an enormous financial burden.

With regard to the East German economy another argument often presented against wage subsidies is also qualified. The argument is that firms will take advantage of the employment bonus, because firms that would employ their workers in the absence of subsidies cannot be excluded. As most of the firms are owned by the Treuhand, the argument just mentioned applies for these firms. Wage subsidies also increase the value of those firms taking advantage of subsidies and should result in higher proceeds when the Treuhand sells them.

However, is it not to be feared that wage subsidies will result in higher wage rises and thus counteract the intended effect, namely higher employment? To prevent this and to ensure that wage subsidies will not last for ever, Akerlof et al. have proposed a SEFEB (Self-Eliminating Flexible Employment Bonus), calculated as

$$b = w_0 \sigma (w^* - w) / (w^* - w_0),$$

where w denotes Eastern wages per worker at time t (including additional payments for workers), w_0 denotes initial Eastern wages, w^* denotes Western wage costs at time t, and σ is the desired percentage reduction in wage costs.

It can easily be seen that according to this formula the bonus will vanish as soon as Eastern and Western wage costs are equal ($w = w^*$). In the course of time the bonus will diminish, as Eastern wages approach Western wages. According to the authors the SEFEB will serve two purposes. First, subsidies will be prevented from lasting for ever. Secondly, excessive wage demands will be controlled. High wage increases will reduce the difference ($w^* - w$) and thus the bonus. The SEFEB plan intends to make the demand for labour more elastic. To put it more directly: an automatically decreasing bonus would intensify the loss of employment usually expected to accompany rising wages. The trade-off between employment and rising wages would be aggravated. Unions would have to be more conscious than before about employment risks corresponding to massive wage rises.

So far, the SEFEB-programme seems to have some advantages. Competitive disadvantages of East German firms caused by high unit labour costs (i.e. high wages relative to the level of productivity) could be eliminated or reduced. More enterprises would be able to survive economically than in the absence of wage subsidies. Employment opportunities that otherwise would be dropped could be maintained.

In view of the obvious fact that even massive investment in Eastern Germany – which is to be expected because of the enormous subsidies – will show positive employment effects only after a considerable time lag, the necessity of an efficient transitional strategy is quite obvious. This is true, at any rate, for those who think that high and long-lasting unemployment in East Germany is not acceptable for various reasons. Even those who do not consider high levels of unemployment to be a great scandal and who prefer dealing with long-run development perspectives cannot simply overlook the corresponding problems. If long-lasting mass unemployment were accepted, this would lead to migration. The results of the surveys conducted by Akerlof et al. confirm the hypothesis that unemployment is a more important motive for migration than the West–East wage differential. A long period of high unemployment could thus turn out not merely to be a price to be paid for a rapid catching-up process, but an additional burden for economic recovery.

The transitional strategy of subsidizing wages is, however, far more problematic than it seems at first sight. To see this we have to distinguish between problems that can be solved by applying this strategy and problems that cannot. Subsidizing wages presents no solution for all the cases where collapse of production is caused by products of hopelessly inferior quality competing with Western German and international competitors' products. In these cases high unit costs are not the problem; even if falling costs brought about by means of subsidies enable firms to lower prices, it is hardly conceivable that the sale of such commodities can be stimulated.

Quality- and cost-determined sales problems are usually closely connected: inefficient organization of the work process and technically obsolete equipment result simultaneously in deficient quality and high production and transaction costs. As cost reductions resulting from wage subsidies by no means result in an automatic quality improvement – there may even be a tendency to lower the level – attempts to quantify the positive employment effects have to be treated with scepticism. They are based on a hypothesis that is problematic. This hypothesis says that the main obstacle to higher output consists of the price–cost squeeze. As the sales problems can be explained only partly by this hypothesis, the positive employment effects of wage subsidies cannot be expected to be as high as the optimistic estimates that Akerlof et al. suggest.

Moreover, the question needs to be posed whether the proposed strategy really offers advantages compared with the strategy that is already being carried out. By securing the liquidity of those firms it still owns, the Treuhand is in fact continually subsidizing them. Of course, the necessity to reduce subsidies involves a tendency to dismiss employees, because reduction in the wage bill (unaccompanied by a corresponding fall in output, which in general is possible due to the usually excessive size of the labour force) diminishes the sums necessary to maintain solvency. As the sum of bonuses goes up with the number of workers, other things being equal, this model not only favours employment but also the conservation of economic structures (DIW, 1991g), because there is only a low compulsion to modernize and to reduce high labour intensity. As wage subsidies also apply to firms not owned by the Treuhandanstalt, the same is true for them, too. In addition, the problem already mentioned of firms taking advantage of the subsidy also arises. A lesson can be learned from what is known as the Berlin support:[5] Western firms shift their (in this case especially labour-intensive) production to the East to benefit from the bonus and from lower wage costs. Hence, in the long run, the problem of different structures of production in East and West arises: technically advanced and capital-intensive production in the West, and technically backward and labour-intensive production in the East. Since, according to the SEFEB-programme, the bonus decreases when wages approach equality, a dilemma may arise: if the different structure in the East has once been established, then firms only capable of surviving because of the bonus will not be able to pay Western wages. The resulting problems of employment will exert pressure on the government not to allow the self-elimination of the subsidy. Under the pressure of economic and social conditions, a transitional strategy to fight unemployment could then become a permanent subsidy in the way already known.

Although it is necessary to think of and consider such problems, the reasonable, basic idea of this proposal should not be overlooked. It consists of searching for opportunities enabling the financing of employment rather than unemployment. According to the estimate by Akerlof et al., even a wage subsidy of 75 per cent would result in budgetary savings. This surprising result, however, is based on assumptions which must be regarded as overly optimistic. Without giving any reasons here, I consider an additional burden on the budget to be more likely. Faced with a tight budget, this may be a sufficient argument for many people not to pursue the idea of subsidizing wages any further. But such a rejection is not convincing. The additional burden for the budget is much lower than commonly expected, taking offsetting factors into account. In addition, the employment made possible by subsidies can be used to improve the infrastructure, which has to be done anyway. For the community and state governments it may be less expensive to undertake the necessary investment in the infrastructure by giving orders to low-productive enterprises with subsidized labour since the alternative is to give orders to more productive firms with higher wage costs – that is, to Western firms – and additionally to finance unemployment. It is open to debate whether, and to what extent, wage subsidies are an additional burden on the budget. A decision for or against such subsidies seems to me to be less important than the conflict deriving from the short- and the long-run consequences. Even if the above-mentioned restrictions are considered, substantial wage subsidies will improve the employment situation in East Germany – at least in so far as they are introduced as a further instrument and not as a substitute for the supportive measures already in existence.

The long-run problems facing the gains in employment have already been mentioned. To what degree they will materialize – as an unambiguous consequence of wage subsidies – cannot be forecasted by any economist. This opens the door for two opposing points of view. One consists of sticking to Keynes's statement, 'In the long run we are all dead.' Whatever the – uncertain – long-run results, they are of little importance for the necessities of today.

One objection to this view is that the problems under discussion concern periods not so distant, so that we will not all be dead before the long-run consequences materialize. On the contrary, a high proportion of the present generation will be affected by these consequences. Even if only future generations had to suffer from these problems, such a policy would hardly be legitimate.

5   CONCLUDING REMARKS

We have discussed three different types of wage policy for East Germany:

— the rapid adjustment of negotiated wages to the level of Western German wages;
— a wage policy guided by economic development – which does not necessarily imply strict adherence to productivity growth;
— a policy of subsidizing wages, which is not intended to increase wages for employees, but which aims at lowering wage costs borne by the firms relative to total wage costs.

A thoroughly conducted analysis of these options would also need to investigate their impact on Western Germany – besides considering the probable results for production, employment, structural change, and so on in East Germany. This is beyond the scope of this contribution. However, some comments on the effects of the currently dominating wage policy shall be made. As many recent union agreements show, the policy of rapid adjustment of negotiated wages has already been carried out. This has required gigantic transfers from West to East and has caused a significant extension of public expenditure and, to finance the latter, an expansion of public debt and higher taxes.

Primarily this has had the effect of a gigantic demand-increasing programme for the West, especially because the additional purchasing power in East Germany has been directed towards Western products. Relevant tendencies towards rising prices caused by the demand boom have not occurred, because bottlenecks have been avoided by increasing imports. The often criticized big trade surplus of West Germany has now turned out to be very advantageous, because it has allowed a flexibility of commodity supply that would otherwise have been impossible.

These are the short-run effects. Meanwhile the trade surplus has disappeared, the price increase has accelerated, transfer payments show a rising tendency and it is to be feared that further tax increases and/or additional borrowing may become necessary. If all of this causes doubts about the stability of the Deutschmark, the danger of capital flight and rising interest rates will appear. Rising interest rates would be disadvantageous for investment in East Germany and would in particular cause a higher burden on the budget. High transfers could not be maintained then: a consolidation policy would be inevitable.

The demand boom caused by enormous transfers might finally result in a depression. Whether this pessimistic scenario or a more optimistic one is a better description of future development depends on many factors, not at least on the speed of modernization in the East and the development of the world economy. If the main trading partners undergo an economic recovery and if competitive capacities are built up in East Germany, the optimistic scenario will be more likely. The economic problems (high unemployment in East Germany, losses of real income in West Germany) which have to be expected under less favourable conditions lead us to expect that the real endurance test of unification is still ahead.

NOTES

1. On different estimates see e.g. DIW (1991c, 1991e); Statistisches Bundesamt (1991a).
2. This does not necessarily imply a wage policy orientated towards average productivity growth. A differentiated wage policy according to sectoral and business conditions is e.g. supported by the Sachverständigenrat (SVR, 1990).
3. With a_{89} and a_{90} as the relation between the wage rates in East and West in 1989 and 1990, g_E and g_W as the respective rates of growth in wages we get $g_E = a_{90}/a_{89} (1+g_W) - 1$.
4. An obvious objection which could be put forward in respect to our simple calculations is the following: the relation between the wages in East and West reached in 1991 are higher and therefore the growth rates of Eastern wages necessary for convergence correspondingly lower. Although this is true for negotiated wages, our assumptions seem to be more in line with hourly effective wages.
5. As long as the GDR existed firms producing in West Berlin got subsidies and had some tax privileges. This induced firms from West Germany to move to Berlin. As the newly built factories often were more modern than the former ones the net employment effect for the FRG (including West Berlin) was negative. In this respect the case is different to that under discussion.

REFERENCES

Akerlof, G.A., Rose, A.K., Yellen, J.N. and Hessenius, H. (1991), 'East Germany in from the Cold: The Economic Aftermath of Currency Union,' *Brookings Papers on Economic Activity*, **1**, 1ff.

Deutsche Bundesbank (1991), 'Ein Jahr deutsche Währungs-, Wirtschafts- und Sozialunion,' *Monatsberichte der Deutschen Bundesbank*, July, 18ff.

DIW (1991a), 'Gesamtwirtschaftliche und unternehmerische Anpassungsprozesse in Ostdeutschland', Erster Bericht, *DIW-Wochenbericht*, **12**, 123ff.

DIW (1991b), 'Gesamtwirtschaftliche und unternehmerische Anpassungsprozesse in Ostdeutschland', Zweiter Bericht, *DIW-Wochenbericht*, **24**, 323ff.

DIW (1991c), 'Deutschland im Umbruch,' *DIW-Wochenbericht*, **26–27**, 365ff.

DIW (1991d), 'Einkommen und Verbrauch der privaten Haushalte in den neuen und alten Bundesländern,' *DIW-Wochenbericht*, **29**, 403ff.

DIW (1991e), 'Der Arbeitsmarkt ein Jahr nach Beginn der Währungsunion,' *DIW-Wochenbericht*, **30**, 427ff.

DIW (1991f), 'Die wirtschaftliche Entwicklung in Deutschland im zweiten Quartal 1991,' *DIW-Wochenbericht*, **33**, 463ff.

DIW (1991g), 'Allgemeine Lohnsubventionierung – kein Ausweg aus der Beschäftigungskrise in Ostdeutschland,' *DIW-Wochenbericht*, **36**, 511ff.

Handelsblatt (1991), 'Lohnsubventionen kosten viel und bringen nichts,' June, 10.

Statistisches Bundesamt (1991a), *Konjunktur aktuell,* various issues.

Statistisches Bundesamt (1991b), 'Sozialprodukt im Gebiet der ehemaligen DDR im 2. Halbjahr 1990,' *Wirtschaft und Statistik*, **5**, 305ff.

SVR (1990), Sachverständigenrat zur Begutachtung der gesamtwirtschaftlichen Entwicklung, 'Auf dem Wege zur wirtschaftlichen Einheit Deutschlands,' *Jahresgutachten*, 1990–91, Stuttgart.

9. Distributive Aspects of German Unification

Heinz D. Kurz[*]

1 PARADISE GAINED, PARADISE LOST?

When German unification became a prospective political reality in the second half of 1989, it was widely held that after many years of suffering under a totalitarian regime the East German population had finally reached the end of a long and dark tunnel. Rosy expectations about a bright future characterized by liberty, democracy and economic opulence started to burgeon.

On 1 July 1990 a monetary, economic and social union became effective between the two German states. The Deutschmark (DM) replaced the Ostmark. Legal trade barriers and barriers to capital and labour movements between the FRG and the GDR were abolished. Anticipating complete German unification, the legal, tax and social insurance system of West Germany was extended to East Germany. On 3 October 1990, in line with article 23 of the West German constitution, East Germany declared itself part of the Federal Republic of Germany. The GDR disappeared from the scene and a new and larger FRG emerged.

In less than a year after German unification the bright hopes have given way to mostly gloomy perspectives. There were bold promises by West German politicians that the majority of East Germans trusted with great naïvety. However, monetary union and German unification did not bring quick economic success, but difficulties of immense complexity and potential seriousness. After the light the East Germans discovered that there was a new tunnel ahead.

This chapter focuses on the distributive aspects of German unification. The monetary union and German unification resulted in huge conflicts over the distribution of income and wealth with consequences that are utterly detrimental to a quick economic recovery in the new Länder. These intimately intertwined conflicts concern, first, the distribution of the 'property of the people' of the former GDR; secondly, the distribution of income, in particular the question of the growth of East German hourly wages; and thirdly, the redistributive activities of the German state. While the first

134

aspect relates to the distribution of initial endowments – stocks of plant and equipment in existence, land and structures – the latter two aspects relate to flow magnitudes.

Beyond the scope of this chapter is the problem of redistribution in Europe and the world economy. Due to its huge domestic problems, united Germany will probably be unable to assume the role of former West Germany as a main financial contributor to the European community and a major capital-exporting country. It will, on the contrary, become a net capital-importing country, with negative implications for underdeveloped regions in Europe and elsewhere.

The structure of the chapter is as follows. In section 2 alternative scenarios of the restructuring of the East German economy are sketched. The argument made is that the most probable scenario is that the Eastern part will not fully catch up with the Western part. Instead there will be uneven development with marked disparities between the growth of per capita income between the old and the new Länder. Section 3 has a brief account of the distributive consequences of unification policy. Emphasis is on the depreciation of East German human capital, broadly understood, and the redistribution of the 'property of the people' away from the people as a consequence of (1) the terms of the currency conversion; and (2) the decided route to privatization. It should come as no surprise that the East Germans are keen to make good with massive wage increases and transfer payments what they lost in collective material wealth. Section 4 deals with the problem of competitiveness of the East German capital stock that holds the key to the short-run employment possibilities in the new Länder. The argument is that the rapid adjustment of East German wages to West German levels and the increase in interest rates caused by the debt financing of unification by the German government render obsolescent large parts of the East German plant and equipment and thus 'destroy' jobs, which only massive subsidies financed by West Germany can preserve. With a smaller volume of employment in East Germany total income generated will be smaller too, which in turn provides fewer resources for capital accumulation and growth and thus slows down the restructuring of the East German economy. Section 5 focuses on the medium and long run. Since unemployment benefits are proportional to terminal wages earned by workers, quickly rising East German wages imply high levels of 'unproductive consumption'; the unemployment benefits will require massive transfer payments from West to East Germany and will put a considerable strain on the West German taxpayer. Correspondingly, capacity saving will fall. Rapidly rising East German wages will thus reduce the pace of capital accumulation and the creation of new jobs. In the long run a lower rate of capital accumulation will be reflected in a lower rate of productivity growth. The final section draws some conclusions.

2   ALTERNATIVE SCENARIOS OF EAST GERMAN ECONOMIC DEVELOPMENT

We may distinguish between the following 'visions' or *scenarios* of the likely course the East German economy might take. These scenarios differ essentially with the degree of optimism involved. With increasingly bad news becoming available, many commentators adapted their expectations and switched from more to less optimistic visions. Hence the presentation of the alternative scenarios corresponds roughly with an increasing disenchantment with the observed development of the East German economy and an increasing pessimism as to its likely future. Furthermore, policy strategies are important in so far as the scenarios under consideration bear some relationship to alternative economic policies advocated.

Most people believe that in the long run the East German economy will succeed in catching up. However, the final scenario, which is perhaps the most realistic, initially received little attention because it assumes that the East German economy is on an inferior path of economic development. In this scenario the economic disparities between (parts of) East and West Germany will persist.

(a)   The 'Don't Worry, Be Happy' Scenario

As soon as German unification became a realistic political option, many West German politicians and commentators nourished the expectation among the population of East Germany that unification would bring them quick economic prosperity. Indeed, the chancellor of the FRG, Herr Kohl, maintained that after unification many East Germans would immediately be economically better and none would be worse off and that Eastern living conditions would match those of the West within three to five years. He also stood for the view that the cost of unification incurred by the West Germans would not require an increase of taxes. Most believed that the extension of a market economy to East Germany would swiftly activate dormant German entrepreneurial spirits, while attracting foreign investors who sought strategic production locations with low costs and rapidly growing markets. Only relatively small amounts of Western finance and other resources would be necessary to overcome a variety of difficulties of an essentially short-run nature. By contrast with other Central and East European countries which would have to go through a time-consuming and costly process of trial and error in the attempt to replace the old order with a new one, the integration of the former GDR into a unified Germany required little other than the adoption of the ready-made, success-proven West German blueprint. Many people counted on the coming of a new economic miracle-*Wirtschaftswunder* mark II. This strategy may be called the 'Don't worry, be happy' strategy.

(b) The 'Let's Get the Job Done' Scenario

The notoriously optimistic outlook taken by ruling politicians was partly supported by several economists, who, despite their greater sobriety and realism, advocated the view that the rich FRG could, without major difficulties, shoulder the not quite so rich GDR and carry its population within a few years to the same level of private and public opulence. They admitted, however, that the establishment of well-defined and guaranteed property rights was not enough: besides the invisible hand of the market, the visible hand of the state became necessary. In particular, substantial public investment had to improve the East German infrastructure, which is in a shambles, and to put in place in the new Länder an efficient administration. Without public investment that paves the way for and is complementary to private investment, the take-off of the East German economy would be impeded. However, given the size of the task, the politicians believed that a strong dose of solidarity with the 'brothers and sisters' in East Germany coupled with a revived spirit of the pioneer age of West German society after the Second World War would easily accomplish the task and produce another economic success story. We may call this the 'Let's get the job done' strategy.

The calculation of the necessary growth rate to be achieved by the East German economy to accomplish the catching-up process within a given time span gave the impression that the problem of economic restructuring was only moderately more demanding than the solution of the involved compound interest problem. Assume, the intellectual experiment goes, that income per head in West Germany will, on average, grow at x per cent per year; assume in addition that in the year of German unification income per head in East Germany was z per cent of the West German level. Which rates of growth of income per capita must be realized in East Germany to catch up within 10, 15 or 20 years, respectively? The answer is to be found by solving the following equation for g_e, the required East German growth rate,

$$y_0(1 + \frac{x}{100})^t = y_0\frac{z}{100}(1 + g_e)^t,$$

where y_0 is the West German income per head in the initial period, and t is the number of years required to catch up to the West German level.

Figure 9.1 illustrates the argument. The bold line gives the assumed path of income growth per head in the West German economy and the broken lines alternative paths of the catching-up process. With t, the stipulated year when

this process is assumed to be accomplished, taken as given, the required East
German rate of growth equals the slope of the corresponding line for the East
German economy intersecting the West German line at the given t.

Figure 9.1:   *The 'Let's Get the Job Done' Scenario*

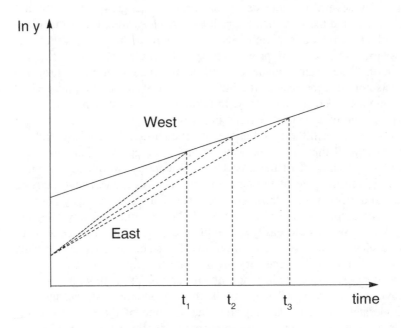

A comparison with the growth rates actually realized in West Germany in
the 1950s and 1960s, during the 'golden days' of *Wirtschaftswunder* mark I,
seemed to give credibility to the view expressed. Taking x to be 2.5 per cent
and z 50 per cent, which turned out to be too high, if t = 10, 15 or 20, then
the required growth rates g_e must be just over 9 per cent, around 7 and
around 6 per cent, respectively. W. Krelle (1990, p. 8) commented on this
result: 'These are all not impossibly high rates of growth' (see also Lipschitz
and McDonald, 1990).

While intellectual experiments of the kind entertained are not entirely
without interest, they cannot of course clear up the question whether and in
what circumstances catching up is probable, and how much time it will take.
Here it suffices to draw the attention to the following observations. First,
while catching-up processes are not uncommon in economic history, the
path they follow is normally of a sigmoid type. There are relatively high
growth rates in the backward economy at the beginning of the process, then

the rates level off as the gap between the two economies or regions narrows. There is also the possibility of an 'overshooting', that is, the backward economy overtaking the leading one. Secondly, the elimination of per capita income inequalities between different regions of the same economy will not *necessarily* happen. There is ample historical evidence that neither trade nor capital movements will, in any circumstances, counteract economic disparities between regions: the very existence of such disparities is not a sufficient reason for their disappearance. Without additional information about the two economies that merge it appears to be impossible to form an opinion of whether the integration will be beneficial to at least one of the two or both. Thirdly, calculations of the kind illustrated start from the premise that the catching-up process of the backward region does not (substantially) affect the speed and the pattern of growth of the advanced region. While this may be a valid assumption if the former economy is very small compared to the latter, it is less compelling in cases in which this is not so. The population of East Germany in 1990 accounted for roughly 20 per cent of the population of unified Germany, and its territory for just over 30 per cent. And although the contribution of the ex-GDR economy to unified Germany's GNP is at present well below 10 per cent, the economic performance in the new Länder will not leave unaffected that in the old ones.

While it is possible that the East German economy may catch up with the Western one, actual experience in the past few months has raised doubts of the probability of this. The disillusioning facts rather prompted many people to abandon the 'Let's get the job done' scenario and replace it with the 'Permanent crises do not exist' scenario.

(c)   The 'Permanent Crises Do Not Exist' Scenario

Karl Marx emphasized that 'permanent crises do not exist'. The modern economists' equivalent of this wisdom is the J-curve: a short downswing followed by a swift and lasting upswing. In other words, the East German economy has to go through a valley of tears first to embark on a journey of cheers thereafter. Many concede that the transformation process might have, for a while, some negative impact on the growth of the West German economy. This view is illustrated in Figure 9.2. As the diagram shows, there may be a tendency towards the equalization of per capita income. There are some frictions and difficulties to be overcome, perhaps substantially larger than originally anticipated, but in the medium run the East German economy will pick up and attain a living standard similar to the West German one.

There is a common idea among the three scenarios that economic integration will lead to the equalization of factor incomes and the convergence of growth rates in the different regions, which gets some support from the conventional theory of international and interregional trade.[1] Within the framework of Heckscher–Ohlin–Samuelson (HOS) types of models it can be shown that free trade in all commodities will bring about real wage rate and interest rate equalization if all the freely trading economies or regions have the same available choice of techniques, in a constant returns to scale and homogeneous labour world. Put in a dynamic setting, HOS theory predicts the convergence of national or regional economic growth rates to a uniform growth rate. If in addition to free trade there is free mobility of both capital and labour, an assumption which appears to be met as best as it can in the new Germany, then the process of factor price equalization and growth convergence is expected to be more rapid.

Figure 9.2:   The 'Permanent Crises Do Not Exist' Scenario

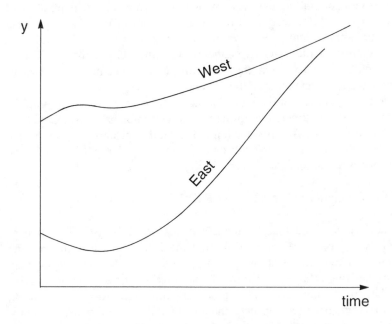

A scenario may be too optimistic or too pessimistic, it may be somewhat naive and leave out of consideration some of the complications and the retarding or accelerating moments that matter. Yet it would seem that the general view underlying the first three scenarios is basically sound.

The final scenario provides an entirely different view: there are persistent regional inequalities even when there is free trade and capital and labour mobility. The lasting economic disparity between north and south Italy is a good example. A similar disparity may persist between West and (parts of) East Germany. In other words, (parts of) East Germany may well become the equivalent of Italy's Mezzogiorno: Germany's Mezzanotte. The 'principle of circular and cumulative causation' developed by Myrdal (1957), provides an explanation of this phenomenon. For Myrdal, one region may be in a *virtuous circle*, while another may be in a *vicious circle*.

(d)   The 'Vicious Circle of Cumulative Causation' Scenario

In the 'Vicious circle of cumulative causation' scenario, the level of economic activity and income per capita in most parts of East Germany will be persistently lower than in its Western counterpart even if it recovers from the current depression (see also Kurz, 1991 and 1992). Moreover, the absolute and relative gap may widen rather than narrow in the long run. In Figure 9.3 paths A, B and C represent alternative possible trends compatible with the general scenario under consideration. Of course none of these macro developments is incompatible with rapid economic expansion in some of the East German regions and industries; those regions located closest to the West German centres of productive activity appear to be the most obvious candidates for developments that run counter to the general trend.

Figure 9.3:   The 'Vicious Circle of Cumulative Causation' Scenario

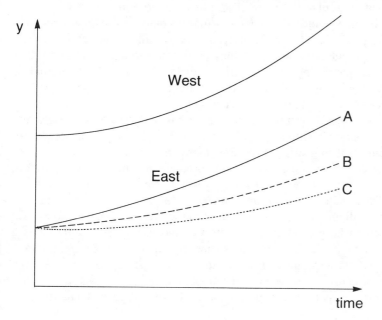

In certain circumstances interregional trade and capital mobility tend to increase rather than diminish the original inequalities. Economic policy may try to fight the emerging polarization, but it can do so only at high and possibly rising costs. It is not at all obvious that it is sensible to incur these costs. What are typical circumstances that tend to amplify existing inequalities?

A vast literature on self-perpetuating economic disparities may provide insight into the problem.[2] The root cause of uneven regional development is the presence of dynamically increasing returns: success tends to breed success and failure tends to breed failure. Within a particular country, any region that for one reason or another has become a substantial centre of industrial activity characterized by economies of scale, will exhibit higher labour productivity and, with fairly uniform wages, lower unit costs than competing industrial regions. The firms in the former region will thus be able to charge lower prices and to spend more on research and development and on marketing, which will cause their sales to increase at the expense of their competitors in the other regions. They will thus be able to expand output, further benefiting from increasing returns and competitive advantage, and so on, with migration of workers from the declining regions overcoming any labour shortages in the expanding centre. Cumulative causation explains why places that acquire an initial advantage in industrial production tend to consolidate and increase this advantage in a sort of 'virtuous circle' to the detriment of other places that are caught in a 'vicious circle'.

There are many interrelated factors that account for divergent regional growth, in particular: (1) sufficiently different initial levels of know-how and labour productivity across regions integrated through trade and factor mobility; (2) increasing returns that are external to firms but internal to regionally concentrated industries; (3) different industries exhibiting different degrees of increasing returns or economies of scale.

These conditions appear to hold true in the case of East and West Germany because of markedly different levels of economic development. Relatively large numbers of industries in the East German economy are still *resource based* (agriculture, mining, bulk-goods production) and others are highly resource intensive. These industries, however, exhibit little if any increasing returns. Those industries that are *knowledge based*, on the other hand, are relatively small and backward, compared to the West German economy. Yet they appear to be predominantly subject to increasing returns. There is a high systemic complexity in products such as computers, software, aircraft, automobiles and telecommunications equipment. While they require large initial investments in research and development, and tooling and marketing, once the product is designed production costs are relatively small and unit costs fall with the scale of output. The production of these commodities offers substantial sources of learning by doing and learning by using.

There appear to be few industries in East Germany that belong to the second group. This fact will generate negative feedbacks that hamper the future development of the economy in the five new Länder. A firm that lags behind its competitors will probably remain lagging behind, with a growing distance between it and the most advanced firms. Because of a lack of competitiveness, firms will exit their respective market(s). For the East German economy as a whole this implies that it will largely specialize in fields where it has a comparative advantage. These fields, however, are those which offer little scope for technological dynamism and may, therefore, in the long run turn out to be a dead end. Thus, because of negative and positive feedbacks the established pattern of regional concentration of industry becomes self-reinforcing: East Germany will lose many of its firms and branches operating in high-tech and even medium-tech fields. Most of these firms will go bankrupt and new firms will settle at more attractive locations, attempting to reap the benefits gained by locating near firms operating in the same markets. These firms will tend to move to West Germany. If the attractiveness exerted by the presence of other firms always rises as new firms enter the market, some region will always dominate and shut out all others. Large parts of the five new Länder appear to belong to the second kind. It seems that the East German economy, for obvious historical reasons, is 'locked' into an inferior path of economic development. On the assumption that the West German taxpayers' willingness to improve the structural deficit of the East German economy is limited, some variant of the 'vicious circle' appears to be the most probable scenario of the future economic development in the new Länder.

Why has the optimism in the sequence of scenarios deteriorated? To what extent can the economically and socially dismal state of affairs in East Germany be considered the result of particular decisions taken during unification policy? What is the role of the redistributive aspects of that policy in the present context? The following sections focus attention on some important elements in the decline of the East German economy.

3 THE DEPRECIATION AND REDISTRIBUTION OF THE WEALTH OF A 'NATION'

German unification involved a massive depreciation of received 'socialist' knowledge and moral and the associated codes of behaviour, or, in economic terms, a substantial loss of human capital. It also involved the redistribution of the material wealth of a 'nation': the so-called 'property of the people' of the former GDR. Ironically, the majority of Germans both in the East and in the West were initially unaware of this implication of the adopted policy of unification. Otherwise it would be difficult to understand why the problem of the distribution and redistribution of wealth did not play a more important role in political discussions in Germany. Indeed, in early discussions it ranked below some fervently debated issues such as preserving the East German abortion law.

(a)   Depreciation of Parts of the East German Human Capital

A lack of understanding of the important issues may explain the remarkably little interest East Germans devoted to the issue of wealth and property. Because private ownership of the means of production and the profit motive were considered despicable and odious, the East German population had difficulty in adjusting to the new social and moral norms, some of which are the exact opposite of what they used to be. A major problem of German unification and of other transformation processes in Eastern Europe seems to be the difference between the speed with which new rules are introduced and the ability to learn these rules.[3] When the surprised East Germans began to understand what had happened, it was too late for substantial modifications. This appears also to be the reason why a growing number of East Germans express the feeling of having been cheated and deceived by West German politicians. Indeed, many East Germans feel that West Germans ruthlessly exploit their lack of familiarity with the new legal system and modes of thought and behaviour. Moral hazards are prevalent on a nationwide scale. The emergence of mass unemployment and social distress have pulverized the naive conception that a change of regime would come at no cost and bring nothing but benefit to the East Germans.

For more than four decades in the GDR, private self-interested initiatives were discouraged and solutions to social problems were sought in an *étatist* way. East Germans were trapped in a position of 'learned helplessness' as they tried to adjust from this social climate to the 'revaluation of values'. There is a lack of entrepreneurial spirit and an overabundance of entitlement mentality. What is at stake is the re-education of an entire population. Compared to this the necessary retraining of large portions of the East German labour force appears a minor task.

(b)   Monetary Union

Monetary union entitled East German children under 15 years, adults under 60 years, and pensioners to exchange up to 2 000, 4 000, and 6 000 Ostmarks, respectively, on a 1:1 basis. The exchange or conversion rate applied to most other stocks of money and financial claims, including household savings and company debt, was 1:2. The conversion rate of wage and price contracts and pension claims was 1:1. The average rate of exchange of Deutschmarks for Ostmarks was approximately 1:1.8.

When monetary union became effective, many observers believed that the terms of currency conversion involved substantial gains in purchasing power by the East German population. Compared with the black market exchange rates of 1:7 before the opening of the Berlin Wall and 1:11 afterwards, the conversion rates looked extraordinarily favourable. Hence, many feared that monetary union would fail to siphon off excess money balances, a characteristic feature of any socialist economy, and that rapid inflation would ensue once the administration of prices ended. The Deutsche Bundesbank argued this point most forcefully.

The fears did not come true. Contrary to widespread opinion, currency conversion did not entail purchasing power gains but losses to the East Germans. While purchasing power comparisons between vastly different economies such as the FRG and the former GDR are difficult, there exist clear indications that the purchasing power parity between the two currencies was close to 1:1.[4] The distinction between traded and non-traded goods and the substantial subsidies put up by the East German state to keep prices of necessary goods low explains this rather astounding result. Hence all financial claims, in particular private savings, that were changed at rates of 2:1 or 3:1 implied real losses. This was the first act of expropriation that East Germans were exposed to. Because of their insufficient initial endowment with financial claims, East Germans were weak compared with West Germans and foreigners bidding for enterprises and real estates to be privatized.

(c)   The Policy of Privatization

A major problem for economies in transition is the privatization of industry and land. The unification treaty clearly distinguishes expropriations before and after 1949: those before 1949 are exempt from privatization and compensation, while those afterwards are nullified. Hence everything expropriated since the founding of the GDR is, in principle, to be returned to its legitimate owner(s). Approximately one-third of the total property that can be privatized belongs to this category. The number of applications for the return of or compensation for expropriated property exceeds one million:[5] golden days ahead for lawyers!

The actual route to reprivatization and compensation became a major obstacle to East German economic recovery. As long as property rights are unclear and costly disputes over these rights persist, potential investors will not risk engaging in business in East Germany.[6] To speed up the privatiza-

tion process the German parliament passed a law on 15 March 1991, specifying article 41 of the unification treaty which in certain circumstances
allows exceptions to the reprivatization of expropriated property to render
possible investment that is beneficial to the economy as a whole (the so-
called 'obstacle removing law'). The new law, which in principle reaffirms
the maxim 'return of property rather than compensation', allows several
exceptions to this rule in favour of employment, housing or the infrastructure until the end of 1992.

The Treuhandanstalt, a gigantic resolution trust in the Ministry of Finance, is privatizing the remaining two-thirds of industry and other property
in East Germany. Treuhandanstalt managers are responsible for the liquidation
of about 8 000 companies in East Germany. Some 20 per cent of these are
public utility companies that, as a rule, will become communal property,
whereas the remaining 80 per cent will be privatized following a procedure
in two steps. First companies will be transformed into joint-stock companies
or into other legal forms of enterprise; then they will be sold on international
capital markets. Before the end of March 1991 the Treuhandanstalt shut
about 300 of the companies and sold about 1 000 others, mostly small
enterprises.[7]

What is at issue is the gigantic problem of selling two-thirds of the
productive apparatus of an entire economy. This route to privatization exhibits serious shortcomings, the following of which deserve mention (see also
Sinn, 1990). First, it is very time-consuming. Secondly, it raises the problem
of a mismatch between effective demand and offer with the consequence of
dramatically falling asset prices. Thirdly, it is not only inefficient but also
highly problematic from the point of view of fairness and distributive justice.

The route to privatization assumes that current investment and thus savings
can buy the East German capital stock. This might be a valid assumption if
the savings activated for this purpose were international rather than essentially
national savings. However, it seems that so far only a very small percentage
of the demand for East German firms comes from foreigners, to whom
investment in the new Länder appears at present to be too risky and uncertain.
East Germans are unable to play a more important role in the acquisition of
private property, in particular productive units, because of their very limited
access to liquid funds. It is the West Germans who are getting by far the
largest slice of the cake and are about to take over East German industry and
real estate. Hence, the route to privatization comes close to a policy of
colonization – an 'expropriation' of the East German people.

The creation of an excess supply constellation is also partly responsible
for the fall in asset prices. This exaggerates the poor state of the East
German capital stock. West German saving, a flow magnitude, is insufficient

to buy that part of the East German plant and equipment that is not subject to restitution, a stock magnitude, at 'reasonable' prices. Consequently, there is downward pressure on the prices of the objects sold by the Treuhandanstalt. Two additional factors reinforce the decline in prices. First, actual and expected proceeds of firms are small because of low levels of demand for East German products and thus low degrees of capacity utilization. Secondly, the German government's reluctance to increase taxes to finance German unification entailed soaring budget deficits that put additional strain on the capital market and drove up interest rates.

It follows that both elements of privatization policy – natural restitution and the attempt to sell the remaining property on the market – are major obstacles to a quick economic recovery in East Germany. Moreover, the second contradicts distributive justice. The takeover of large parts of the 'property of the people' of the former GDR by West Germans may drive a wedge into German society that prevents unity despite unification.

The conclusions to be drawn from these observations are clear. First, to remove a major obstacle preventing private investment activity in East Germany from gaining momentum, the maxim 'return of property rather than compensation' should be replaced by the maxim 'return of property only in cases that are not controversial; compensation in all other cases'. Secondly, to speed up privatization and to avoid the unacceptable and politically dangerous distributive effects of the current policy of the Treuhandanstalt, this policy should be replaced by a scheme guaranteeing that at least the property not yet privatized is given to the people in the new Länder, e.g., in the form of shares of firms or of the entire East German capital stock, including non-private residential buildings and real estates.

The losses of financial claims, human and physical capital and land incurred by East Germans are large, and the proportion of East Germans who believe that the benefits of unification outweigh the costs is decreasing. Apparently there is a widespread feeling that losses in wealth can and should be compensated with rapid increases in wages and transfer payments: Germany is caught in a massive conflict over the distribution of income.

(d) Wages in East Germany

The state treaty on monetary union required that pre-existing wage and salary contracts be carried over with payments in Ostmark converted to Deutschmark at par. Both immediately before and after monetary union nominal wages and salaries rose substantially. The rise in East German wages continues unabated today. There are many reasons for this. West German trade unions insist on wage parity – partly in order not to undermine their political strength (there were no comparable workers' organizations in the GDR), and partly to stem what might otherwise have been unmanageable mass migration to the West. The absence of any effective counter-organization on the employers' side greatly contributed to this result, as did the general expectation of both workers and managers that they would soon become unemployed, in which case their unemployment benefits would be based primarily on their wages and salaries at the time their jobs were terminated (see Akerlof et al., 1991 and Kalmbach, Chapter 8 in the present volume).

It was particularly the wage agreement for metalworkers of 1 March 1991, negotiated by the strong West German metalworkers' union (IG Metall), which set the pace for the catching up of East German wages. According to this agreement standard wages of metalworkers in East Germany including standard fringe benefits are to match the West German level by 1995. Other wage agreements followed this example. Hence, the level of hourly wages in East Germany will reach and then overtake British and a little later US hourly wages within a few years. This is a dramatic development that probably will not be backed by a similar growth in East German (average) labour productivity. The implication is that many of the currently existing jobs in the new Länder, most of which are barely economical even in present-day conditions, will become obsolescent. Bad times ahead for workers seeking employment in East Germany!

4   CAPITAL STOCK OBSOLESCENCE AND EMPLOYMENT: A SHORT-RUN PERSPECTIVE

As was mentioned above, the absorption of the former East German economy into the Federal Republic of Germany added substantially to the latter's productive resources, at least in terms of labour and land. This concentration of potential economic power was looked upon with considerable unease by many observers, who feared that a larger German economy would dominate Europe even more decisively than had West Germany by itself. They did not foresee that unification would bring not quick economic success but difficulties of immense complexity and potential seriousness – not only for Germany's own people but possibly for all of Europe. Part of the problem lies in the disastrous underestimation of the consequences monetary union would have on the competitiveness of East German capital stock.

(a)   Plant and Equipment in East Germany

According to the East German Institut für angewandte Wirtschaftsforschung (IAW) the net value of plant and equipment (exclusive of land) in the former

GDR in 1989, estimated at an exchange rate of 1 DM for 1 Ostmark, equalled DM 1.745 billion (IAW, 1990). The capital stock in the producing sector was estimated at DM 1.25 trillion. With produced national income (exclusive of services) amounting to DM 260 billion, the output–capital ratio in the Eastern German producing sector in 1989 was 0.208, and its inverse, the capital–output ratio, 4.8. In the FRG in 1989 the net value of plant and equipment was estimated at some 6,500 billion DM, and the net social product at market prices equalled almost 2,000 billion DM. Hence, the West German output–capital ratio and its inverse, the capital–output ratio, estimated in terms of the above two magnitudes, were 0.3 and 3.3, respectively. Accordingly, the output produced per unit of capital in the GDR was much smaller than in the FRG.[8]

However, applying West German rules of accounting to the plant and equipment in the GDR, the IAW estimated that two-thirds of the East German capital stock would have to be written off because of technical and economic obsolescence, leaving a capital stock worth roughly only DM 580 billion.[9] Akerlof et al. (1991) estimated that only 8.2 per cent of the workforce in industry are employed in viable combinates (Kombinate) which often comprise whole branches of the economy. In other words, 92.8 per cent of industrial workers are employed in firms that cannot even cover short-run variable costs – a still more pessimistic result.

How can an economy, praised by both the East and West for its relatively high efficiency only a few years ago suddenly be 'unmasked' as a system with low productivity and a capital stock that is little more than a 'pile of scrap'? One of the reasons for this rather surprising finding is the economic policy the GDR carried out in the last decade or so. In this period the East German government increased consumption to appease a population which expressed ever more openly its disapproval of the oppressive conditions in the GDR. Because this required a reduction in investment, the modernization of East German industry and capital stock decelerated and larger and larger parts of it became obsolescent (see also Chapters 2 and 6, by Kigyóssy-Schmidt and Hagemann, in the present volume).

(b)   Capital Stock Obsolescence

Any attempt to assess the quality and 'quantity' of the capital stock of an economy, and thus the economy's productive capacity and competitiveness, runs into tremendous difficulties. The East German economy accentuates these difficulties because it is in a state of fundamental disarray, certain aspects of which deserve mention. First, the extant capital stock reflects former needs of the GDR and CMEA. Since the CMEA has disintegrated and the East German economy has moved to the Western trading bloc through monetary union, the composition of its capital stock is no longer appropriate: compared with the new needs its primary and manufacturing sectors and thus the respective capital stocks are too large. With often prohibitively high costs preventing the transfer of durable items of capital to other productive uses a large portion of the superfluous parts of the capital stock is rendered worthless and has to be scrapped. Secondly, many East German firms lack competitiveness because of the low quality or outmoded character of their products. In so far as these are produced by means of capital goods that are specific to their production and cannot be utilized otherwise, these capital goods will have to be wholly jettisoned. Others may be used in different lines of production if it is profitable. Thirdly, many production lines, although competitive in terms of product quality, will not survive: because of low labour productivity and a high capital–output ratio the costs of production per unit of output exceed world market product prices. The non-positive profitability of these firms is reflected in a non-positive capital value. Finally, there are firms that are able to cover production costs but that will founder because of the absence of adequate marketing and product distribution.

When investors buy a capital asset or a productive unit consisting of a given plant and equipment, they purchase the right to the series of prospective (net) yields which they expect to earn from selling its output, after deducting the expenses of producing that output, during the life of the asset or productive unit. Let the series of prospective yields be given by $Q_1, Q_2,...,$ Q_n, where t = n is the expected lifetime of the asset. The prospective yield in period t, Q_t (t = 1, 2,..., n), equals sales, S_t, i.e. quantity sold, X_t, times the price charged, p_t, minus total cost of production in that period, which consists of wage costs, $w_t L_t$, where w_t is the then going wage rate, and non-wage costs, H_t, that is,

$$Q_t = S_t - w_t L_t - H_t = p_t X_t - w_t L_t - H_t.$$

With i as the rate of interest, which is used to discount the series of expected returns, the capital or present value of the asset, PV, is given by

$$PV = \sum_t Q_t (1+i)^{-t}.$$

The lower are (expected) product prices, the lower are prospective yields Q_t; the lower are the (expected) levels of effective demand and thus the degrees of capacity ultilization, the lower are prospective yields Q_t; the higher are (expected or foreseeable) hourly wages in period t, w_t, other things being equal, the larger are prospective costs and the smaller are expected profits; the higher the rate of interest, the smaller is the present value of a given stream of prospective net proceeds. In East Germany all factors mentioned worked in the same direction, i.e. contributed to the dramatic fall in prices of firms and combinates.

After monetary union prices of tradables quickly adjusted to the going world market levels. The change from Ostmark prices to Deutschmark prices entailed remarkable changes in absolute and relative prices. While consumer prices, expressed in terms of the East German consumer price index, were fairly constant until the beginning of 1991 when subsidies on basic consumer goods such as energy and transportation were eliminated or reduced, producer prices, expressed in terms of the price index of manufactured goods, fell by almost 50 per cent in a single month. In July 1990 the East German economy was not simply opened to the world market: it was exposed to international competition on terms defined by the German monetary union, which were equivalent to a huge revaluation of its currency.

Before monetary union the East German Ministry of Trade calculated, for internal purposes, the so-called 'currency yield coefficient' (*Devisenertragskoeffizient*), which gives the number of Deutschmarks received per unit of Ostmark employed in the production of export goods. In 1989 this coefficient was 0.23, i.e. the GDR imported goods worth DM 0.23 in exchange for goods exported worth one Ostmark. Hence currency union implied a revaluation of approximately 4:1 to the previously used internal exchange rate. Since the conversion rate for wage contracts was 1:1, the wage rate in terms of export goods increased roughly 400 per cent. It should come as no surprise that East German export industries went into rapid decline. No economy that exhibits some degree of openness could absorb such a shock without serious damage.

Immediately after currency union output in East Germany fell sharply. The main reason for this was of course the swift and massive diversion of spending away from the East toward the West. Whereas in the past, trade relationships among socialist countries were essentially politically decided, the former trading partners of East German firms now have to pay for their imports in hard currency that is scarce. Because of the low quality of East German goods, the former Comecon countries will probably buy from other sources, including Western Europe, United States and the Far East. Whether effective demand for East German goods increases in the future depends, in part, on the world economic situation. With major trading partners of Germany in a recession, prospects of a quick recovery in East Germany are dim.

Taking the real rate of interest as given, the negative relationship between the value of the East German capital stock, K_e, given its traditional pattern of operation and utilization, and the level of East German real hourly wages, w_e, is illustrated in Figure 9.4. The relationship is given by KK'. At $w_e = w_e^*$, the entire capital stock would be economically obsolescent: without subsidies its 'employment capacity' would be zero. With a higher rate of interest *KK'* would be replaced by the dashed line *LL'*.

Figure 9.4:   Capital Stock Obsolescence, Real Wages and Rate of Interest

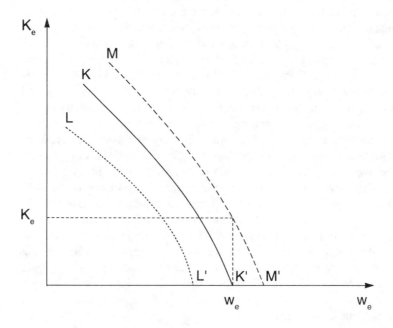

(c)   Incremental Investment

While the above argument is able to explain, in an elementary way, the economic 'destruction' of real capital and employment after monetary union, several qualifications will be added. First, the above argument assumes that the pattern of operation and utilization of plant and equipment in East Germany is constant, despite the gradual introduction of a market system and the exposure of the East German economy to international competition. This change of regime will probably also eliminate redundant labour and increase the intensity of work. In short, the process of production will probably become more efficient because of the competitive pressure firms are now exposed to.

Secondly, in some cases investment of a relatively small magnitude, or incremental investment, can markedly improve efficiency and labour productivity. Very often the task of such investment is simply to get round existing bottlenecks with the effect that productive capacity rises substantially. While there can be no doubt that the restructuring of the East German economy requires massive capital accumulation over many years, the efficiency of the existing process of production can be improved if there is some incremental investment.

Both factors tend to increase the value of the respective parts of the East German capital stock and thus may save the jobs associated with it. In Figure 9.4 the combined effect of these factors can be represented in terms of a shift of the relationship between the capital value and the real wage rate to the right: the dotted line MM^1 gives the constellation after the improvements under consideration have been carried out. Hence, while in the previous situation at $w_e = w_e^*$ the entire capital stock was obsolete, now portions of that capital stock worth K_e^o survive.

Finally, only parts of the output of the East German economy, and thus only parts of its productive apparatus, are subject to full international competition. In this context the distinction between *traded* and *non-traded* goods becomes all-important. While monetary union exposed the East German export sector to the world market, a rather large group of non-tradables were affected only indirectly by international competition. It follows that the above argument applies essentially to the capital stock employed in the production of traded goods only, whereas the capital stock employed in the production of non-traded goods is largely exempt from it.

(d) Tight Capital Markets

The magnitude of the capital stock needed in East Germany will put a substantial strain on capital markets and, with the Bundesbank following a course of tight monetary policy, raise interest rates. Currently, the tightness of the German capital markets is predominantly due to the soaring budget deficits of the Federal state and its Länder. When the German government propagated the remarkable opinion that German unification and the restructuring of the East German economy do not require substantially raising taxes, capital markets had to cope with massive increases of public credit demand to finance transfer payments to the East German population and investment in the infrastructure of the new Länder. The effect was a marked increase in the level of nominal and real interest rates (where the real interest rate is the nominal rate minus the rate of inflation). By summer 1991 the real interest rate paid on long-term public obligations in Germany was well above 6 per cent and thus substantially higher than in the United States. Given the immense demand for liquid funds to rebuild the East German economy, real interest rate differentials between Germany and its major trading partners will probably prevail: Germany, once the world's most important capital-exporting nation, may become a major capital importer.

By January 1991 the German trade balance, known to be persistently positive, showed a deficit. That is, private savings were no longer able to finance private investment and the sky-rocketing budget deficit. Negative trade balances might well become a characteristic feature of Germany's near future. The implication of this is that Germany's net foreign investment position will gradually erode. Since Germany comes second to Japan in terms of its net foreign wealth (its cumulated foreign net investments), it can easily afford to run trade deficits and import capital. While fears that Germany might become a net debtor are, of course, unwarranted in the short and medium run, they cannot be dismissed out of hand in the long run. All depends on the economic success, or lack thereof, of German unification. What is clear, however, is that the net amount of capital owned by Germans abroad, which was estimated at half a trillion DM in 1990, does not match the sum of private capital needed to rebuild the productive capacity of East Germany: depending on the amount of the capital stock in existence that is or soon will become economically obsolescent, the East German capital need might be in the range of DM 1–1.5 trillion. Hence the opinion occasionally expressed in political discussions that repatriation of German capital can accomplish the task of restructuring the East German economy is unsustainable.

5   CAPITAL ACCUMULATION AND PRODUCTIVITY GROWTH: A LONG-RUN PERSPECTIVE

A rapid adjustment of East German wages to West German levels is not only detrimental to the survival of the old capital stock; under given conditions it is also detrimental to the formation of new capital by depressing the potential for accumulation. The main reason for this is the social union, which extended the West German labour law and unemployment benefits scheme with small modifications to East Germany. Accordingly, unemployment benefits amount to 65 per cent of former net wages. With large numbers of East Germans becoming unemployed at substantially increased terminal wages, a larger proportion of the German net national income will go into consumption. Consequently, the share of capacity saving will go down and capital accumulation can be expected to decelerate.

(a)   'Unproductive' Consumption and Capacity Saving

A simple macroeonomic model can illustrate the negative impact of high real wages in East Germany on full capacity saving, i.e. saving associated with the full utilization of profitable productive resources, and thus potential investment. Let v designate the given capital–capacity ratio and a the given labour–capacity ratio, or labour coefficient; assume for simplicity that capital does not deteriorate. g gives the rate of capacity saving, or the potential rate of capital accumulation. Let w be the real wage per unit of labour, and α the percentage of the real wage paid as unemployment benefits. There is no saving out of both wages and unemployment benefits; both are consumed. In this simple economy, total output Y equals investment plus consumption,

$$gYv + C = Y. \tag{1}$$

Consumption equals consumption of workers that are employed and of workers on the dole. Hence

$$C = wL + \alpha wN \; (0 < \alpha < 1), \tag{2}$$

where L is the amount of employment and N the amount of registered unemployment. Applying a similar distinction found in the classical economists, albeit in a somewhat different context, wL is 'productive consumption' and αwN is 'unproductive consumption'. Since $L = aY$, equation (2) can be written as:

$$C = waY(1 + \alpha\theta), \text{ where } \theta = N/L. \tag{3}$$

θ gives the ratio of 'unproductive' (in the sense of not productively employed) to 'productive', i.e. employed, workers. In this model, θ is higher, the higher is the East German real wage rate because of capital and thus job obsolescence. That is,

$$\theta = f(w), \text{ where } f'(w) > 0. \tag{4}$$

Substituting equation (4) in (3) and the latter in (1), and solving for g gives

$$g = \{1 - wa[1 + \alpha f(w)]\}/v. \tag{5}$$

From equation (5) it follows that a higher level of real wages, by increasing the proportion N/L and at the same time the unemployment benefit αw, reduces the rate of capacity saving, i.e. the maximum rate of accumulation attainable. Since there is no reason to expect that under the conditions characterizing the present situation in Germany the actual rate of accumulation will move contrary to the potential or maximum rate, we may conclude that rapidly rising real wages in East Germany will retard the process of capital formation and thus the restructuring of the economy of the new Länder.

(b) Capital Accumulation and Productivity Growth

Adam Smith begins *The Wealth of Nations* (1776) by pointing out that a nation's real income per capita, and its growth, depend on two factors: 'the skill, dexterity, and judgement with which its labour is generally applied', and 'the proportion between the number of those who are employed in useful labour, and that of those who are not so employed'. While united Germany gets high marks regarding the first aspect, it performs rather poorly with regard to the second.

Let Y be net national income, P total population, F the total workforce, L the number of productive workers and N the number of 'unproductive' workers, which in our case is identified with the number of unemployed workers. Obviously,

$$\frac{Y}{P} = \frac{Y}{L}\frac{F}{P}\frac{N}{F}\frac{L}{N}.$$

With $z = Y/P$ as income per head, $y = Y/L$ as labour productivity, $p = F/P$ as the participation rate, and $b = L/F$ as the rate of employment, we have

$$z = y\, p\, b,$$

or, in terms of proportional rates of growth,

$$g_z = g_y + g_p + g_b.$$

The predominant effect of German unification has so far been a reduction in the overall rate of employment, b. The unemployment rate rose significantly faster among females in East Germany. A related effect is the reduction in the participation rate, p. Again, the female rate fell faster in East Germany; before unification it amounted to 48 per cent.[10] Further, if the rate of growth of labour productivity is positively correlated with the rate of capital accumulation, the slowdown of the latter will probably be reflected in a smaller growth of output per worker, g_y. Hence all factors contributing to the growth of income per capita in Germany are pointing downward.

6 CONCLUSION

The dramatic events in the former GDR and the 'socialist' world took most people in the West, including economists, by surprise. There was no widely accepted analytical framework to interpret what is going on and to provide governments of societies in travail with reliable policy recommendations. However, while it is true that a proper analysis of economies in transition is lacking, there do exist elements of such an analysis in various parts of economic theory. For example, a case dealt with in economic theory that comes close to the present situation in Germany is the one, investigated by Adolph Lowe in his theory of the traverse, in which the economic system has to adjust to an exogenously increased labour supply (see Lowe, 1976). What German unification implies is a massive increase in the workforce relative to the non-obsolescent parts of the extant capital stock. As Lowe stresses regarding the excess supply of workers, the 'formation of a complementary addition to real capital is the essential condition for absorption' (Lowe, 1976, p. 124). This may require the retrenchment of consumption in favour of accumulation, and, with the propensity to save out of wages smaller than the propensity to save out of other shares of income, a moderate wage policy.

Unemployment in East Germany is indeed predominantly 'classical' unemployment, that is, unemployment due to a massive shortage of plant and equipment. To overcome this shortage the quick formation of new, fresh capital is needed. Yet, as this chapter has argued, the terms of German unification entailed a huge conflict over the distribution of wealth and income that is detrimental to social cohesion in Germany as a whole and to the quick recovery and restructuring of the East German economy. A major error of unification policy was to deprive a large part of the new Länder population of the 'property of the people'. Understandably, the East Germans now try to compensate this loss with rapid wage increases and substantial transfer payments. Moreover, East German workers were supported by the West German trade unions which, for good reasons, feared that large wage differentials between West and East Germany would serve as an incentive for massive migration from the new to the old Länder. This would increase competition among workers in West Germany and exert a downward pressure on wages, thereby eroding the bargaining position and political power of the trade unions relative to the employers' associations. Yet, with East German wages rising rapidly to the West German level, ever larger parts of the East German capital stock and the jobs associated with it are rendered obsolescent.

Rising levels of unemployment in an environment characterized by the West German labour law and its relatively favourable unemployment benefits scheme involves a substantial strain on the German social budget and the diversion of resources away from investive toward consumptive purposes. Hence, in the given circumstances the process of the formation of fresh capital, desperately needed to overcome the economic malaise in the new Länder, is seriously hampered.

Unless there is a reversal of the unification policy, in particular the adopted policy of privatization, there is little hope that Germany will be economically and socially balanced and politically stable, in short: a united Germany. There is still the possibility of changing direction and minimizing damage. However, time is running out. There is no more talk of economic miracles in government circles. That sober mood may, indeed, pose the greatest risk of all. A belated awakening to the immensity of the problem and the seriousness of the errors committed might lessen the will of the German government to move ahead with resolution. The danger is that, experiencing failure on a large scale, the government will turn to retrenchment, seeking to minimize its deficits in the name of fiscal 'prudence'. That is of course likely to bring political and social restiveness as well as economic stagnation. In that case, Europe may again have a 'German problem' that would indeed spell trouble for everyone, including the Germans themselves.

NOTES

*   The present paper was originally written in summer 1991. A version was presented at a session at the Allied Social Sciences Meeting in New Orleans, 3–5 January 1992. I should like to thank the participants for helpful comments. I am particularly grateful to Mark Knell, who helped to improve the paper in many ways. It goes without saying that the responsibility for any remaining errors rests entirely with me.
1. See Samuelson (1948). For a critical discussion of the Heckscher–Ohlin–Samuelson theory of foreign trade, see Steedman (1988).
2. Besides Myrdal it was particularly Kaldor who, starting from the analysis of his teacher Allyn Young, in various publications contributed to this line of thought; see, for example, Kaldor (1970). For more recent attempts to come to grips with the phenomenon of uneven development, see Krugman (1981), Dutt (1990) and Mainwaring (1991).
3. This is also the main reason why I am sceptical that so-called 'shock therapy' is superior to a more gradual approach to the transition process, as is maintained by many commentators and quite a few Western advisers to Eastern European governments (see in particular Lipton and Sachs, 1990).
4. According to the Ifo-Institut für Wirtschaftsforschung the parity was 1 Ostmark to 0.98 DM (cf. Ifo-Schnelldienst 43, 7 May 1990, 13/1990), whereas the Deutsches Institut für Wirtschaftsforschung, using another approach, found out that the purchasing power of 1 Ostmark equalled that of even 1.20 DM (cf. DIW, *Wochenbericht* 21/1990 of 25 May 1990).
5. See *The Week in Germany* (New York) of 22 March 1991.
6. According to Sinn the privatization decision 'may have been the biggest mistake in the … unification policy of the West German government' (1990, p. 31).
7. See *The New York Times* of 5 April 1991.
8. A lower output–capital ratio need not involve a lower rate of profits (or rate of interest), given the real wage rate, since it could be associated with a higher output–labour ratio or (average) labour productivity. However, labour productivity in East Germany was estimated to be around 30 per cent of the level in West Germany only.
9. Siebert (1990) in an early attempt to assess the East German capital stock assumed that half of it has to be scrapped. See also Siebert (1991).
10. The female participation rate in West Germany was 38 per cent.

REFERENCES

Akerlof, G.A., Rose, A.K., Yellen, J.L. and Hessenius, H. (1991), 'East Germany in from the Cold: The Economic Aftermath of Currency Union', *Brookings Papers on Economic Activity*, **1**.

Deutsche Bundesbank, *Monatsberichte der Deutschen Bundesbank* (1990 and 1991), various issues: Frankfurt am Main.

Deutsches Institut für Wirtschaftsforschung (DIW), *Wochenberichte* (1990 and 1991), various issues: Berlin.

Dutt, A.K. (1990), *Growth, Distribution and Uneven Development,* Cambridge: Cambridge University Press.

Ifo Institut, *Ifo Schnelldienst* (1990 and 1991), various issues: Munich.

Institut für angewandte Wirtschaftsforschung (IAW) (1990), *Die ostdeutsche Wirtschaft 1990/1991*, 22 October.

Kaldor, N. (1970), 'The Case for Regional Policies', *Scottish Journal of Political Economy*, **17**, 337–48.

Krelle, W. (1990), 'Ost–West Wirtschaftsentwicklung im nächsten Jahrzehnt', Paper presented to Nationalökonomische Gesellschaft in Vienna, 7 June.

Krugman, P. (1981), 'Trade, Accumulation and Uneven Development', *Journal of Development Economics*, **8**, 149–61.

Kurz, H.D. (1991), 'The German Problem,' in R. Heilbroner (ed.), *Commentator: A Monthly Letter of Opinion and Policy*, **3** (3), (New York).

Kurz, H.D. (1992), 'Whatever Happened to the East German Economy', in M. Knell and Ch. Rider (eds), *Socialist Economies in Transition: Appraisals of the Market Mechanism*, Aldershot: Edward Elgar, 191–215.

Lipschitz, L. and McDonald, D. (eds.) (1990), *German Unification: Economic Issues*. Occasional Paper 75, Washington DC: International Monetary Fund.

Lipton, D. and Sachs, J. (1990), 'Creating a Market Economy in Eastern Europe: The Case of Poland', *Brookings Papers on Economic Activity*, **1**.

Lowe, A. (1976), *The Path of Economic Growth*, Cambridge: Cambridge University Press.

Mainwaring, L. (1991), *Dynamics of Uneven Development*, Aldershot: Edward Elgar.

Myrdal, G. (1957), *Economic Theory and Underdeveloped Regions*, London: Duckworth.

Samuelson, P.A. (1948), 'International Trade and the Equalization of Factor Prices', *Economic Journal*, **58**, 163–84.

Siebert, H. (1990), 'The Economic Integration of Germany,' *Kieler Diskussionsbeiträge*, 160, Kiel: Institute of World Economics.

Siebert, H. (1991), 'The Integration of Germany: Real Economic Adjustment', *European Economic Review*, **35**, 591–602.

Sinn, H.W. (1990). 'Macroeconomic Aspects of German Unification', *Münchener Wirtschaftswissenschaftliche Beiträge*, Discussion paper 90–31.

Steedman, I. (1988), 'Foreign Trade,' in J. Eatwell, M. Milgate and P. Newman (eds), *The New Palgrave: A Dictionary of Economics*, Vol. 2, London: Macmillan, pp. 406–11.

PART IV

European Integration and the New Germany

10. European Integration and the Heterogeneity of Europe

Gunther Tichy

From an American perspective the process of European integration must appear slow and wearisome: decades of negotiations over the price of milk, the tolerable crookedness of cucumbers, the maximum weight of trucks, or the reputation of exchange rates – whether adjustment has to be made by revaluation of one group of countries or by devaluation of the other! Beyond these topics of the day there are of course more basic questions which slowed down the speed of European integration. Four of them stand out markedly:

- the question of the *political form* of integration: whether Europe should plan to become an economic union, a currency union, a political union (with or without common defence) or a confederation;
- the question of the *economic system* of Europe: whether it should plan to rely on unrestricted market mechanisms, or if and to what extent (mercantilistic) industrial policy, social policy and labour market policy should be allowed;
- the question of the *optimal speed of adjustment*: whether one should quickly reduce national obstacles to a European market and quickly introduce a common currency thereby enforcing adjustment, or whether heterogeneity has to be reduced first;
- the question of the *geographical dimension* of the integrated area: the answer to this question mainly depends on the answers to the foregoing three. Proponents of an economic union propose a large area, proponents of a political union demand limited membership to alleviate decision-making. Adherents of pure market orientation or industrial policy are interested in new members but only of the same mentality, and so on. The question of the geographical dimension is strongly linked to the question of where the centre of the new Europe should be: more to the west – as it is now – or more to the east.

1   EUROPEAN HETEROGENEITY AS A RESULT OF EUROPE'S HISTORY

The main problem for unifying Europe is that the European countries are still surprisingly heterogeneous, much more than the states of the USA. And, which complicates unification even more, the countries that are not yet members of the EC tend to give different answers to the four questions above than do most of the countries which are already members: Switzerland, Sweden, Finland and Austria because they are neutral and prefer – like Norway and the EC members Great Britain and Denmark – an economic union to a political union or even a military one. Furthermore the Scandinavian countries and Austria have a long tradition in social market economy softening the impact of market forces on labour markets and income distribution. They have proved that this need not reduce growth[1] and efficiency. The potential new members opt for a deliberate path of integration, while EC members – especially France – opt for a quick transition to more ambitious goals as they fear that the potential new members would water down the political goals and that the centre of Europe would shift more towards the north-east.

To understand the importance of these questions and the sensibility of the European countries one has to look at European history and to allow for the heterogeneity still prevailing. Contrary to the US, Europe had no straightforward historical development;[2] borders and centres of power changed over and over again. Just look at the last 80 years:

- Before 1914 a large Austro-Hungarian empire, including the main part of today's Eastern Europe, bordered on the Ottoman Empire which covered the rest of Eastern Europe, Greece, Turkey and the Middle East. The German empire included half of Poland.
- The First World War changed the European landscape. It gave rise to several autonomous states: Hungary, Czechoslovakia, Yugoslavia, Albania, Romania, Bulgaria, Greece, Turkey, Finland and the Baltic republics. Poland shifted its western border westwards after the War.
- After the Second World War Poland shifted westwards even more, it lost territory in the east as a consequence of the western expansion of Russia: the Baltic republics became part of the USSR and Eastern Europe *de facto* lost its independence. In the military area, NATO and the Warsaw Pact were formed.
- In economic matters cooperation in coal and iron markets started as early as in 1951, and in 1957 the Rome treaties were signed forming the EEC. Its Eastern counterpart (Comecon) was constituted in 1949. The EEC consisted of six countries: Belgium, France, Germany, Italy, Luxembourg and the Netherlands.

- France impeded the formation of a larger European free trade area and so the industrialized rest of Europe[3] formed EFTA in 1959. Thereby the European landscape had changed another time. We find three blocks: EC, EFTA and Comecon.
- But the map has continued to change:
  1961: Finland associates with EFTA (1986 member);
  1970: Iceland becomes member of EFTA;
        Spain joins EC (1986 member);
  1972: Free trade agreement between the EC and EFTA;
  1973: Denmark, Great Britain and Ireland change from EFTA to the EC;
  1986: Portugal changes from EFTA to the EC.
  Now there is a new map again: the larger block of the EC, the rest of EFTA, willing to participate in economic but less so in political and military integration with the EC, the former Eastern European countries (after the demise of the Comecon) free of any linkage but full of problems of all sorts, and the Russian empire divorced from Eastern Europe and in full political, geographical and economic decay.

That is a lot of change within eight decades, and the consequences are serious: to economic structure, to economic relations and especially to foreign trade. The composition of Austria's foreign trade gives a good example (see Table 10.1).

Brief meditation on these data will surely convince everybody that the present map of Europe will have to change again. Austria's trade with

Table 10.1: Austria's Trade Partners (Share of foreign trade[1] in %)

	1924	1937	1947	1989
Germany/FRG	14.0	15.4	11.0	39.9
Western Europe	27.8	28.6	54.8	35.8
Eastern-middle Europe[2]	35.6	22.7	18.8	4.0
Southern Europe[3]	14.4	14.0	4.4	2.6
Russia/USSR	0.6	0.6	0.0	2.2
Rest of the world	7.6	18.5	11.1	15.5
Total	100.0	100.0	100.0	100.0

Source: Stankovsky (1990), p. 607. Differences in totals due to rounding.
1. (Exports + imports)/2.
2. Czechoslovakia, Poland, Hungary.
3. Bulgaria, Romania, Yugoslavia, Turkey.

Eastern, middle and southern Europe is much lower now than with other neighbouring countries, which can be explained by factor availability and comparative advantage. The process of European economic integration has to continue and it will have to extend eastwards. But it must take account of the heterogeneity resulting from Europe's complicated history and the excessive changes in the European map: economic integration improves wealth if it enables countries to utilize comparative advantages, economies of scale and economies of specialization or if it enables factors of production to move to the area where they are most productive in the long run. Integration may, however, even turn out to be wealth-decreasing if it diverts trade or investment, if it hinders the indigenous development of less-developed countries (in Eastern and southern Europe) or if it renders impossible custom-tailored economic policy as long as heterogeneity necessitates it.

2   PROBLEMS OF HETEROGENEOUS INTEGRATION

Integration may reduce wealth for four reasons: the danger of *trade diversion* as a result of misplaced integration is dealt with at length in the literature and need not be elaborated here. *Investment diversion*, however, is less investigated: capital may move into the integrated market to avoid duties or restrictions, even if production costs are higher there. Whether a different *stage of development* of countries participating in integration reduces wealth by hindering the development of the less advanced ones is one of the questions most heavily discussed in modern literature (see, e.g., Pearce and Sutton, 1986): according to one school, producers of technologically less advanced countries should be exposed to stiff international competition to stimulate their development and their R&D. This appears to be the view of the EC Commission implementing the south extension and of the former communist East European countries trying to rush into the EC rather than stimulating trade among themselves first. The competing school holds that the domestic producers should be protected from technologically superior competitors to give them time to close the gap. This is the reason for infant-industry protection and this view is corroborated by at least anecdotal historical evidence (Padoa-Schioppa, 1987, p. 19ff.). Clemenz (1990) demonstrated that the two schools do not necessarily contradict each other: free trade and increased competition do indeed stimulate R&D but they do this only if the technological gap is not too wide.[4] If it is too wide R&D may be discouraged in the less developed country. This result is in accordance with modern growth theory which emphasizes learning effects and accumulation of knowledge (Lucas, 1988; Romer, 1989). The integration of countries whose stage of development differs too much may give rise to polarization effects (see Tichy, 1991a) as it hinders learning effects and specialization of the poorer countries and diverts investment in skill-intensive branches towards the more developed ones. A similar stage of development may therefore be an important prerequisite of countries joining an integration area because premature integration may hinder economic development, and secondly because too wide a gap in economic development implies production of different non-competing types of goods so that integration gives rise to trade diversion, not to trade creation.

The fourth reason for potentially wealth-decreasing effects of the integration of heterogeneous countries – especially in a currency union – are the constraints on *autonomous custom tailored policy* in the presence of divergent goals, different structure and institutions, country-specific shocks and diverse country-specific reactions to common shocks.

In principle the net wealth-increasing effects of different delineations of integration areas could be estimated,[5] but in fact theory is not yet able to disentangle the complex interactions of scale economies and imperfect competition, so estimation is restricted to the ambiguous calibration of Computable General Equilibrium (CGE) models, and reliable data are not available. The questionable results of the EC Commission's attempts to measure the effects of '1992' (Emerson et al., 1988)[6] or to estimate the effects of a monetary union (Commission, 1990a) clearly demonstrate this weakness. So another approach had to be explored. In a previous study (Tichy, 1991c, 1991d) criteria were selected which indicate 'creation' and 'diversion' effects of integration, and it was investigated which groupings of countries satisfy the various criteria. The sets of criteria are of course different for different forms of integration. The most important ones, which qualify for at least some quantification, were the following:

For a *free trade area* or a customs union:
    trade intensity;
    similarity of price structure;
    high intratrade/intertrade relation;
    similarity of the structure of production and trade;
    similar stage of development;
    economies of scale and of specialization;
    low external tariffs;
    appropriate size of the area.

For a *common market* or an economic union in addition:
    similar availability of labour;
    similar level of wages.

For a *currency union* in addition:
   integration of economic policy;
   very similar rates of inflation;
   common shocks and similar effects of shocks;
   absence of exchange rate illusion;
   fiscal federalism.

Trade-creating effects will be the larger and trade-diverting ones the smaller the higher the trade intensities among the partners, the more similar the structure of production and trade which materializes in a high intratrade–intertrade relation and the more similar the stage of development. Trade diversion will be minimized furthermore by low external tariffs and an appropriate size of the area: large enough to be not too open, but small enough to remain sufficiently homogeneous, especially concerning the structure of trade with non-members.

A *common market* or an *economic union*, both of which ensure the free flow of services and factors of production in addition to the free flow of goods and afford a certain degree of harmonization of economic policy, need additional criteria for optimality: *labour availability* should not differ too much and the *level of wages* should not be too dissimilar to avoid an unmanageable degree of migration and to ensure that differences in factor availability are equalized primarily by capital flows.

For the optimal delineation of a *currency union* the *integration of economic policy* in general and very *similar rates of inflation* especially are highly important. The rates of inflation have to be very similar at least after the currency union has come into existence. Before, they can diverge to some degree, as the currency union itself may press towards stabilization: the Austrian *de facto* currency union with Germany has demonstrated this mechanism (Tichy, 1985) and France and Italy tried to utilize it in the 1980s. A further precondition for an optimal currency union is that the members are exposed not to idiosyncratic, country-specific shocks but to common ones. In addition, their structure should be such that they respond similarly to similar shocks. So changes in relative prices and exchange rates are avoided. Lack of *exchange rate illusion*, i.e. an immediate reaction of factor prices to exchange rate changes, almost demands a currency union, as it removes the chance to change real exchange rates and so leaves exchange rate policy useless. Separate currencies cannot be of any advantage under this condition and a currency union therefore cannot have any disadvantage. As a last precondition for an optimal, even for a functioning currency union some degree of *fiscal federalism* should be mentioned. In the US the consequences of local shocks are alleviated by automatic stabilizers: two-fifths of local income losses are compensated by lower Federal taxes and higher Federal transfers (Sachs and Sala-i-Martin, 1991). Besides smoothing regional busi-ness cycles, fiscal federalism redistributes income towards less prosperous regions and compensates for the loss of autonomous policy.

3   IS THE EC OR EUROPE AN OPTIMAL INTEGRATION AREA?

Applying these criteria to the OECD data clearly demonstrates the heterogen-eity even of the West European countries.[7] Using different criteria different integration areas come out as optimal. This implies that every grouping has at least some wealth-decreasing effects. Even trade intensities (normalized export quotas)[8] reveal trading blocs different from the institutional integra-tion areas of the EC and EFTA: a closely integrated Pacific bloc, a closely integrated Scandinavian bloc with Great Britain(GB)/Ireland(IR) loosely attached and continental European countries not intensively integrated with each other. Figure 10.1 shows a West European 'chain' – Portugal(P)–Spain(E)–France(F)–Belgium(B)–the Netherlands(NL) – of countries linked one by one but not among each other, a Central European 'triangle' – Germany(D)–Switzerland(CH)–Austria(A) – and a south European 'tri-angle' – Italy(I)–Greece(GR)–Yugoslavia(YU)) – which are bridged via France(F)–Italy(I) and Austria(A)–Yugoslavia(YU). The visual impression is underlined by cluster analysis and multidimensional scaling (Tichy, 1991c, 1991d). Price structure reveals a rather similar picture with the exception that the West European chain is split up: France, Belgium and the Nether-lands move to Central Europe, Spain and Portugal to south Europe. Rather low coefficients of correlation (three-quarters of them below 0.5) suggest, however, a low degree of price integration and the persistence of national markets, an observation emphasized by other authors as well (Geroski, 1989; Norman, 1990).

Trade intensities and price structure suggest that Scandinavia plus Great Britain/Ireland are quite separated from continental Europe. Trade diversion may therefore result from the inclusion of Denmark and Great Britain/Ireland into the EC and the exclusion of Switzerland and Austria. A rough intratrade index on the other hand shows very high values for Great Britain and only medium ones for Austria, thus indicating a different delineation of the groups (see Table 10.2). Production structure heavily depends on the stage of development and so separates high-income countries (Germany, Belgium, the Netherlands, Denmark, Sweden, Switzerland, Norway) from medium (France, Italy, Austria, Finland, Iceland) and low-income ones. Trade intensities, price structure, intratrade and production structure/stage of development therefore suggest different 'optimal' customs unions. Factor

Figure 10.1: Trade Intensities

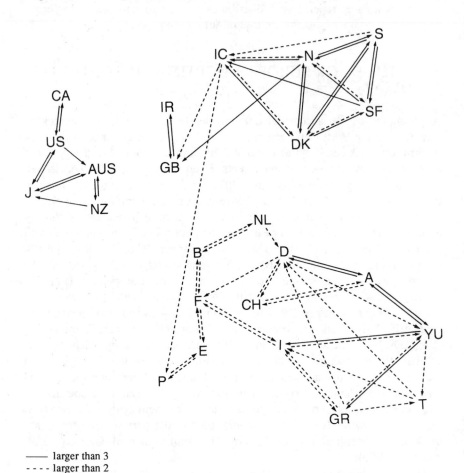

—— larger than 3
- - - - larger than 2

cost and factor availability correlate with the stage of development so that the 'optimal' economic union would be similar to the customs union proposed by this criterion.

Heterogeneity becomes even more pronounced regarding the criteria for an *optimal currency union*. As to the *similarity of policy goals* the period 1973–88 shows inflation rates ranging from 3.8 per cent in Germany to 39.2 per cent per year in Iceland and of unemployment rates from 0.5 per cent (Switzerland) to 14.4 per cent (Turkey). Countries with higher inflation rates tend to have higher rather than lower unemployment. Data for shorter

Table 10.2: *Optimal Integration Areas According to Different Indicators*

	D	F	I	B	NL	DK	GB	IR	GR	E	P	A	S	CH	N	SF	IS	YU	T
Trade intensity	3	2	4	2	2	1	(1)	(1)	4	2	2	3	1	3	1	1	1	4	(4)
Price structure	2	2	4	2	2	1	1	1	4	4	4	2	1	.	.	1	.	.	.
Intra-trade/Inter-trade	1	1	2	2	2	3	1	.	.	2	.	2	2	1	3	3	.	.	.
Production structure	1	2	2	1	1	1	3	3	3	3	3	2	1	1	1	2	2	3	3
Policy goals	1	2	2	2	1	2	2	3	3	3	3	2	2	1	2	2	3	3	3
Inflation rate	1	2	3	1	1	2	2	2	3	3	2	1	2	1	2	2	3	3	3
Common shocks	1			1	1							1							

Source: Tichy (1991c).
The members indicate the groups to which the countries belong according to the respective indicator.

periods reveal only weak tendencies of the divergencies to shrink. Per capita growth varied between 1.3 per cent per year in Switzerland and 4.8 per cent in Turkey with a tendency of the poorer countries to catch up. Current account surpluses are characteristic of the highly competitive countries Switzerland, the Netherlands and Germany, while Portugal, Iceland, Greece and Ireland are plagued by marked deficits. Cluster analysis of the four indicators (Tichy, 1991c, 1991d) distinguishes between a group of peripheral countries (Spain, Portugal, Greece and Ireland) on the one hand, the countries of high stability (Germany and the Netherlands) on the other, whereas the rest of the countries form a larger, hardly differentiated group in between. The weak ability of cluster analysis to pick out distinct groups of countries with similar policy goals must not, however, lead to the conclusion that these countries could form a currency union, as the *similarity of inflation rates* is even more important for a currency union than the similarity of the other goals. The strong economic and political position of the Deutschmark renders it impossible to create a European currency union not based on strict price stability. Therefore only those countries which have inflation under strict control will be able to participate without enormous problems. These are the very countries which form a *de facto* currency union already: Germany, the Netherlands, Switzerland, Austria and probably Belgium.

The rest of the EC countries have not come nearer to the goal of a currency union in the last decade or so. There has been no marked tendency for inflation rates to come closer together. The greater stability of exchange rates under the European exchange rate system is not caused by a convergence of inflation rates or interest rates but by capital controls (Rogoff, 1985; Artis, 1987; Thygesen, 1987, pp. 180–1). Countries like Italy, Great Britain and even more the countries of the southern periphery which devaluated at a rate of 5 per cent per year in the past and accumulated a serious overvaluation of their currencies in the most recent years could never participate in a currency union without severe structural problems and a deep stabilization crisis. Dornbusch (1988) and Williamson (1990) therefore propose a crawling peg rather than a European currency union. Williamson (1990, p. 52) suggests some sort of Tobin tax as well.

The further preconditions of a *currency union*, common shocks and *similar effects of identical shocks*, are difficult to test. Eichengreen (1989) tested for idiosyncratic shocks using real exchange rates and regional share price indices. He holds that idiosyncratic shocks are more important in Europe than in the US or in Canada and that mobility of factors of production is lower in Europe (the last point is also made by Boltho, 1989). Tichy (1991d) used three indicators to find out which groups of countries join common shocks: the correlation of time series of inflation rates over the longer period of 1970–89 and the shorter one of 1980–89, the correlation of real exchange rates over the period 1975–89, and a correlation of exchange rates and inflation in the long and the short run (1973–88 and 1986–88 respectively). Taking all things together, these attempts to distinguish groups of countries affected by common shocks have not been successful. This corresponds to the hypothesis that idiosyncratic shocks are more important in Europe than common ones, and with Eichengreen's results that idiosyncratic shocks are more important in Europe than in North America. Common shocks and/or similar effects of common shocks could at best be detected among Germany, Belgium, the Netherlands and Austria which – together with Switzerland (not sharing common shocks) – are the only countries that would be eligible for a currency union by the inflation criterion. As, however, fiscal federalism, which is an important precondition for a monetary union, does not exist in Europe at all,[9] a monetary union may create serious problems anyhow, even among the five hard-currency countries.

The empirical indicators clearly demonstrate that Europe is still very heterogeneous and they indicate that wealth-decreasing integration effects are possible – or even likely – for almost any combination of countries. Even the Cecchini report, which does not mention trade diversion in the main text, cannot avoid conceding in the appendix that the effects of the EC '92 programme will lower foreign trade of EC with non-EC by 2–3 per cent in the short run and by 10 per cent in the long run (Italianer, 1990). In particular the inclusion of Denmark and Great Britain in the EC and the exclusion of Switzerland and Austria gives rise to trade diversion, and the inclusion of less-developed Greece, Portugal and even Spain may hinder their autonomous development. One has to admit that their growth may be strengthened by integration via direct investment and transfer of footloose industries in low-tech branches in the short run. But in the long run R&D, accumulation of knowledge and of specialization will most likely be impeded, thereby eliminating the basis for increasing intratrade in the future.

A currency union among all EC members or among EC plus EFTA members eventually may turn out to be wealth-decreasing, since policy goals, especially inflation rates and institutions, differ widely, country-specific shocks seem to prevail and no fiscal federalism is available providing automatic stabilizers and a minimum degree of automatic redistribution. At least some evidence already exists to support this suspicion: comparing Portugal and Puerto Rico Eichengreen (1990, p. 144ff.) suspects that even with fiscal federalism well-developed benefits from a currency union arise only if the differences between the members are not too big. Puerto Rico's unemployment compared to the US average is much worse than Portugal's compared to the EC's average. This indicates that it was disadvantageous for Puerto Rico to renounce an autonomous custom-tailored policy. Breuss (1990, p. 66ff.) underlines the argument that a premature renunciation of policy autonomy does more harm than good: the EC was less successful in reaching its policy goals than EFTA in the shock-driven period since the mid-1970s. EC countries not only grew more slowly than the EFTA countries but the disparities increased markedly (Commission, 1990c). In addition Horne and Masson (1988, pp. 277–8) hold that inflation was reduced less and unemployment increased more in countries participating in the EC's exchange rate mechanism than in other G7 countries which were free to adjust their policy to national needs.

4   THE FUTURE OF EUROPEAN INTEGRATION

The analysis of the history of European economic integration, of the economic results achieved by the countries, and of the heterogeneity still existing allows some tentative answers to the questions posed in the introduction:

1.   Which countries should be included in European integration? The answer to this question also predetermines the answer to the second question:
2.   Should integration include political and military aspects as well as economic ones?[10]
3.   Should countries with a considerably lower stage of development be included in the integration, and if they are, what should be done to ensure their indigenous development?
4.   What is the optimal speed of adjustment?

As to the first question it is important to emphasize that the existing areas of *institutional* integration are probably not *optimal integration areas* from an economic point of view. Trade diversion reduces their potential wealth-increasing effects. The obvious solution is to exclude members who do not fit into the optimal area and to include the non-members who do fit, for obvious reasons; this solution will not work. It is impossible to exclude members for political and legal reasons, and the heterogeneity of the European countries renders this way impossible for economic reasons as well: no group of countries could be found that fits all criteria. This leaves open only one solution: to form an economic union encompassing all EC and EFTA countries. In the course of this enlargement two types of measure should be taken to avoid trade diversion: a downward adjustment of the tariffs for all goods traded by members and non-members, and continuing efforts to approximate institutions, regulations and the structure of the member countries. Such efforts have already been taken within the EC under the heading EC '92. There has been considerable progress but – contrary to the plans – border problems will still hinder European trade even in 1993.

The answer to the question of how far integration should pass from an economic to a political one implies that the European neutrals will have to participate in EC integration to avoid trade and investment diversion. The decision on the *actual extent* of integration – question 2 – has to take into account the political culture of these countries which is centuries or at least decades old. If a group of countries plans to extend integration beyond the economic to the political and/or the military sphere, separate institutions should be founded for non-economic integration to give countries the chance to participate in the one but not in the other.

The third problem is even more pressing and more difficult: how to ensure an *indigenous development of the less advanced countries* (regions). Non-neoclassical theories were always aware of the danger of polarization and neo-neoclassical growth theory is going to share that fear: polarization may arise out of the availability of specialized inputs (Romer, 1987), out of accumulation of knowledge (Lucas, 1988), learning effects or any other economies external to the firm but internal to the economy. So the danger of Mezzogiornization – being always left behind – arises for less advanced countries participating in integration with more advanced ones. They are restricted to low-tech production and to isolated manufacturing with all the higher-qualified functions (R&D, product development, marketing, and so on) concentrated at the mother company in an advanced country. Despite serious efforts no convincing success is known in overcoming this problem. A necessary but in no way sufficient solution to provide less advanced countries with the necessary means is fiscal federalism. R&D and the foundation of firms performing all entrepreneurial functions in the less advanced area should be specially promoted. In addition, some restrictions on take-overs of domestic firms in less advanced countries by foreigners could be considered.

The last question deals with the *optimal speed of integration*. Is it necessary to press very hard for an acceleration of the process? Is it advisable to introduce a currency union even prematurely to accelerate integration and make the process irreversible, in full knowledge of the fact that this may create problems for several countries? The answer to this question should take two aspects into account: that European countries are still very heterogeneous, and that the economic performance of the less integrated EFTA countries was in no way worse than that of the more highly integrated EC countries, which had the additional advantage of a larger and geographically closed market. The move towards larger and more homogeneous markets is surely important, but no evidence exists that it is so important as to dominate all other goals. The evidence that larger countries grow faster is weak,[11] and the estimated effects of integration are astonishingly low: in almost no case do they add up to more than 3–4 per cent of GDP cumulatively over a decade or so.[12] No argument exists for a rush towards faster integration, especially towards a monetary union which, in the near future, would work without problems only among four to six European countries anyhow. Restricting a currency union to such a small subgroup raises the problem of the exchange rate system with the rest of the integrated area and the problem of polarization, as the 'hard currency centre' may gain further attractiveness for holding companies and parent companies of multinationals at the disadvantage of the rest of the countries.

Adherents of an immediate introduction of a currency union (e.g. Wihlborg and Willett, 1990; Fratianni and v. Hagen, 1991) put heavy weight on credibility: only by immediately introducing a currency union can governments convince agents that they will refrain from any action incompatible with a fixed exchange rate or a common currency. And only if agents believe in absolutely fixed exchange rates will factors of production be fully mobile which – according to that theory – is the precondition for a quick equalization of wealth and quality of life. At least two elements in this line of argument need to be discussed further: first, the argument of the unlimited assimilating power of factor mobility even under the condition of marked heterogeneity: a long tradition from infant-industry protection (F. List) to neo-neoclassical growth theory (Lucas, 1988; Romer, 1987, 1989) objects to this. Secondly, the very simple construction of credibility has to be questioned: that it is regarded as credible whenever a government binds itself notwithstanding the material content of the obligation. But what will happen if a country with traditionally high inflation joins a currency union with price stability? Adjustment problems will lead to structural problems, to unemployment, and to increasing budget problems.[13] The country will no longer be in a position to counteract country-specific shocks. The committed government is most likely to be overthrown in such a situation, especially as a tradition of stable governments does not exist in many high-inflation countries.[14] Since no government can oblige its followers, a new government will quickly get rid of the commitment by leaving the currency union.[15] Agents are 'cheated' if they form the criteria of credibility so simply, but it is not the government that cheats them, it is their own naivety. One should conclude that any commitment – irrespective of its legal form – is credible only if the problems it poses are not too heavy; a net positive effect should clearly be visible to the public.

It is therefore hard to believe that a European curreny union comprising more than a very few members would add any credibility to European integration; rather the contrary – the problems originating may retard integration or even force members to leave the community. This does not imply that Europe should refrain from striving for a monetary union. But given the heterogeneity it is wise to give time to this project. The ten years the Delors plan (Commission, 1989) envisages are a reasonable though ambitious target in view. Even then a currency union will create serious problems if it is not accompanied by a minimum degree of fiscal federalism, for example in the form of EC unemployment subsidies financed by an EC income surtax.

NOTES

1. Since the beginning of the 1960s EFTA countries have grown as fast as EC countries with slower growth in the first, and faster in the second half of the period: GNP/capita US = 100 (Breuss, 1990, A 11 A)

	EC 6	EC 9	EC 12	EFTA 6
1960	74.8	76.4	67.6	93.3
1972	87.8	85.5	77.6	105.2
1987	92.5	90.1	81.0	111.5
1960/87	+23.7%	+17.9%	+19.8%	+19.5%

2. In the US it took a long time as well (some three quarters of a century) to integrate the labour market (Wright, 1986).
3. Austria, Denmark, Great Britain, Ireland, Norway, Poland, Sweden, Switzerland.
4. This result is remarkable as the model does *not* rely on learning effects.
5. For attempts see the studies cited in note 12.
6. For critical comments see Dornbusch (1989), Geroski (1989), Peck (1989) and Grossmann (1990).
7. The Eastern ones could not be included into the analysis because of lack of data. But even if Eastern Europe could have been included the analysis would not be worthwhile as the past and present structure of production and trade were heavily distorted by former plans.
8. The normalized export quota of country i to country j is the export quota of i to j divided by the export quota of all countries to j. A normalized export quota from Austria to Switzerland of 2 implies therefore that Austria's export quota to Switzerland has twice the size of the average export quota of all countries to Switzerland.
9. Only 10 per cent of EC's budget is at the disposal of the Regional Fund, 7 per cent of the Social Fund and 3 per cent of the Structural Fund (Commission, 1990b, p. 130). This sums up to 0.2 per cent of EC's GDP only. The redistributive effects are of course larger as the payments are concentrated on the backward countries: they reach from 3.5 per cent of GDP in Portugal to 0.75 per cent in Italy's south *Mezzogiorno* (Commission, 1990b, p. 134). But even these figures are a tiny fraction of those of the US, a country not renowned for excessive redistribution.
10. If countries which do belong to an optimal integration area from an economic point of view do object to political integration it will at least be unfair and economically suboptimal to set the alternative of full political integration or no (economic) integration at all.
11. The correlation between country size (population) and wealth (GDP/head at current prices and exchange rates in US $) is insignificantly positive ($r^2 = 0.11$). See also Rothschild (1963).
12. See e.g. EFTA (1972); Balassa (1974); Hamilton and Whalley (1985); Emerson et al. (1988); Breuss and Schebeck (1989) and Norman (1989).
13. Canzoneri and Rogers (1990) argued convincingly that differing rates of inflation can be optimal if the costs of tax collection differ. For Italy inflation may be an efficient way to tax the black market, which is forced to use currency instead of deposits to finance transactions.

14. Policy failures of instable governments are quite often an important cause of inflation. The pressure for monetary discipline will – under these conditions – increase the turnover of governments rather than decrease the rate of inflation.
15. The EC report on the European currency union (Commission, 1990á) clearly sees this problem. The Commission, however, suppresses this problem in its official summary of the report.

REFERENCES

Artis, M.J. (1987), 'The European Monetary System: An Evaluation', *Journal of Policy Modeling*, **9** (1), 175–98.

Balassa, B. (1974), 'Trade Creation and Trade Diversion in the European Common Market: An Appraisal of the Evidence', *Manchester School*, **XLII**, 93–135.

Boltho, A. (1989), 'European and United States Regional Differences: a Note,' *Oxford Review of Economic Policy*, **5** (2), 105–15.

Breuss, F. (1990), *Integration in Europa und gesamtwirtschaftliche Entwicklung. EG- und EFTA-Staaten im Vergleich*, Vienna: Wifo.

Breuss, F. and Schebeck, F. (1989), *Die Vollendung des EG-Binnenmarktes – Gesamtwirtschaftliche Auswirkungen für Österreich. Makroökonomische Modellsimulationen*, Vienna: Wifo.

Canzoneri, M.B. and Rogers, C.A. (1990), 'Is the European Community an Optimal Currency Area? Optimal Taxation versus the Cost of Multiple Currencies', *American Economic Review*, **80** (3), 419–33.

Clemenz, G. (1990), 'International R&D Competition and Trade Policy', *Journal of International Economics*, **28** (1/2), 93–113.

Commission of the European Communities (1989). Committee for the Study of the Economic and Monetary Union: (1) *Report on Economic and Monetary Union in the European Community*. (2) *Collection of papers Submitted to the Committee for the Study of Economic and Monetary Union (Delors Report)*. Luxembourg: EC.

Commission of the European Communities (1990a), 'One Market, One Money. An Evaluation of the Potential Benefits and Costs of Forming an Economic and Monetary Union', *European Economy*, **44** (October).

Commission of the European Communities (1990b), 'Economic and Social Cohesion in the Community,' *European Economy*, **46** (December), 121–35.

Commission of the European Communities (1990c), 'Economic Convergence in the Community', *European Economy*, **46** (December), 137–60.

Dornbusch, R. (1988), 'The European Monetary System, the Dollar, and the Yen', in F. Giavazzi, S. Micossi and M. Miller (eds), *The European Monetary System*, Cambridge: Cambridge University Press.

Dornbusch, R. (1989), 'Europe 1992: Macroeconomic Implications', *Brookings Papers on Economic Activity*, **2**, 341–62.

EFTA (1972), *The Trade Effects of EFTA and EEC, 1959–67*, Geneva: EFTA.

Eichengreen, B. (1989), 'Is Europe an Optimum Currency Area?' unpublished manuscript. Berkeley: University of California.

Eichengreen, B. (1990), 'One Money for Europe? Lessons from the US Currency Union', *Economic Policy*, **10**, 117–87.

Emerson, M. et al. (1988), 'The Economics of 1992', Commission of the European Communities, *European Economy*, **35** (March).

Fratianni, M. and v. Hagen, J. (1991), 'On the Road to EMU', paper prepared for the International Economic Conference 'Building the New Europe', Rome.

Geroski, P.A. (1989), 'European Industrial Policy and the Industrial Policy in Europe', *Oxford Review of Economic Policy*, **5** (2), 20–36.

Grossmann, G.M. (1990), Book review of Emerson et al. (1988), *Journal of International Economics*, **28**, 385–88.

Hamilton, B. and Whalley, J. (1985), 'Geographically Discriminatory Trade Arrangements', *Review of Economics and Statistics*, **67** (3), 446–55.

Horne, J. and Masson, P.R. (1988), 'Scope and Limits of International Economic Cooperation and Policy Coordination', *Staff Papers*, **35**, 259–96.

Italianer, A. (1990), 'Hype or Hope: a Review', *Economic Papers*, **77**, Commission of the European Economic Commission, Brussels.

Lucas, R.E. (1988), 'On the Mechanics of Economic Development', *Journal of Monetary Economics*, **22**, 3–42.

Norman, V.D. (1989), 'EFTA and the Internal European Market', *Economic Policy*, **9**, 424–65.

Norman, V.D. (1990), 'How Successful Has EFTA Been? "Revealed Protection" in Three Scandinavian Industries, 1965–85', Lecture given at the 30th anniversary round table: EFTA Countries in a changing Europe, Geneva, 5–6 November.

Padoa-Schioppa, T. et al. (1987), *Effizienz, Stabilität und Verteilungsgerechtigkeit. Eine Entwicklungsstrategie für das Wirtschaftssytem der Europäischen Gemeinschaft*, Wiesbaden: Gabler.

Pearce, J. and Sutton, J. (1986), *Protection and Industrial Policy in Europe*, London: Routledge & Kegan Paul.

Peck, M.J. (1989), 'Industrial Organization and the Gains from Europe 1992', *Brookings Papers on Economic Activity*, **2**, 277–99.

Rogoff, K. (1985), 'Can Exchange Rate Predictability be Achieved without Monetary Convergence? Evidence from the EMS', *European Economic Review*, **28**, 93–15.

Romer, P.M. (1987), 'Growth Based on Increasing Returns due to Specialization', *American Economic Review*, **77** (2), 56–62.

Romer, P.M. (1989), 'Capital Accumulation in the Theory of Long-run Growth', in R.J. Barro (ed.), *Modern Business Cycle Theory*, Oxford: Basil Blackwell, pp. 31–127.

Rothschild, K.W. (1963), 'Kleinstaat und Integration', *Weltwirtschaftliches Archiv*, **90**, 239–73.

Sachs, J. and Sala-i-Martin, X. (1991), *Fiscal Federalism Policy and Optimal Currency Area: Evidence from Europe and from the United States*, National Bureau of Economic Research, working paper.

Stankovsky, J. (1990), 'Neuer regionaler Analyserahmen für den österreichischen Aussenhandel', *Wifo Monatsberichte*, **63** (11), 606–7.

Thygesen, N. (1987), 'Is the European Economic Community an Optimal Currency Area?' in R.M. Levich and A. Sommariva (eds), *The ECU-Market. Current Developments and Future Prospects of the European Currency Unit*, Cambridge, Ma. and Toronto: D.C. Heath Lexington, pp. 163–85.

Tichy, G. (1985), 'Die Folgen von Wechselkursänderungen für Terms of Trade und Verteilung', in H. Hesse, E. Streissler and G. Tichy (eds), *Aussenwirtschaft bei Unsicherheit*, Tübingen: Mohr-Siebeck, pp. 213–41.

Tichy, G. (1991a), 'Wachstumstheorie und moderne Makroökonomik: (K)ein neuer Anlauf', in B. Gahlen, H. Hesse and H.J. Ramser (eds), *Wachstumstheorie und Wachstumspolitik. Ein neuer Anlauf*, Tübingen: Mohr-Siebeck, pp. 91–109.

Tichy, G. (1991b), 'EC '92 and the Outsiders' View: The European Neutrals', in S. Borner and H. Grubel (eds), *The European Community after 1992. Perspectives from the Outside*, London: Macmillan, 165–91.

Tichy, G. (1991c), 'Das optimale Integrationsgebiet: Theoretische und empirische Überlegungen', Research Memorandum 9101, Nationalökonomische Institute der Karl-Franzens-Universität Graz, Graz.

Tichy, G. (1991d), 'Theoretical and Empirical Considerations On the Dimension of an Optimum Integration Area in Europe', *Aussenwirtschaft*, **47** (1), 107–37.

Tower, E. and Willett, T.D. (1970), 'The Concept of Optimum Currency Areas and the Choice between Fixed and Flexible Rates', in N. Halm (ed.), *Approaches to Greater Flexibility of Exchange Rates*, Princeton: Princeton University Press, pp. 407–15.

Wihlborg, C.G. and Willett, Th. D. (1991), 'The Instability of Halfway Measures in the Transition to a Common Currency', manuscript.

Williamson, J. (1990), 'Britain's Role in EMU', unpublished manuscript.

Wright, G. (1986), *Old South, New South*, New York: Basic Books.

11. German Unification and European Integration: Points of Tension in Community Building

Emanuel Richter*

Throughout postwar German history, there has been a persisting ambivalence between German (re)unification and European integration. This ambivalance has been a genuine component of the West German *Staatsraison*. It also formed the basis of the yearning of the people in East and West Germany for German unification. West German politicians, interest groups and even the constitutional court have endeavoured not to exclude the one in their pursuit of the other. However, most of the people and decision-makers in the West have been thoroughly aware that the intensification of Western European integration would increasingly reduce the chances of the unification of Germany.

In the course of the violent upheavals during the late 1980s, these historical preconditions seemed to totally disappear. Both the unrestricted maintenance of European integration and the peaceful fulfilment of German unification became possible without serious constraints. The question arises, therefore, as to which political developments have facilitated or brought about this curious change. The following analysis seeks to investigate this question by classifying the relevant political developments in terms of 'community building'.

The concept of community building is an analytical instrument used to describe the formation of a political unity. This analytical concept seeks to characterize the motives and forces that lead to a new shape in political identity. It must describe the cohesive ties that form a political body, and it must explain the legitimacy of the constructed community. Due to the fact that everything seems to have changed in the historical relationship between German national unity and European integration, the issues of new political identity, cohesion and legitimacy of different political bodies are most interesting. The concept of community building represents a useful instrument for comprehending new and unexpected political developments.

An examination in terms of community building necessitates looking at five different aspects of the general problem. The historical and systematic basis for classifying recent developments derives from an examination of the different forms of community building that are demonstrated by German national unity and by European integration during the first decades of the postwar period. The curious ambivalence between the two must be described first (1). Then, special emphasis must be put on the changing forms of community building within the European Community which have persistently reduced the fundamental tensions between a demand for national unity and supranational integration (2). On the basis of this elaborate classification, a description of the current relationship between the process of German unification and the aims of European integration should be provided. It should demonstrate the increased relevance of German unification for European integration (3). This leads directly to the question of whether the enlarged and strengthened German nation state represents any threat to the European integration process, and what role the unified Germany will play in the European Community (4). Finally, a general outlook must be added that emphasizes the role of the European Community and its political cohesion for the new European order which is emerging during the 1990s (5). The view of future developments leads back to the basic analytical question. The analysis demonstrates how formerly divergent forms of community building have gradually created a broad consensus concerning the responsibilities and legitimacy of political bodies. This interesting convergence within modern industrial capitalism represents only the initial stage for critical questions about modern forms of community building in Western societies.

1   THE HISTORICAL AMBIVALENCE BETWEEN GERMAN UNIFICATION AND EUROPEAN INTEGRATION

The roots of all forms of political identity, cohesion and community building in West Germany and Western Europe have to be traced to, at least, the postwar period. The Cold War and the antagonism between East and West, which found their striking outline in the division of Germany, provided the principal preconditions for all further political developments.[1] The Western occupation of Germany, American economic engagement through the Marshall Plan, and the Organization for European Economic Cooperation (OEEC) reinforced the *Western* orientation of the later Federal Republic of Germany and replaced, at least temporarily, the prospect of national identity in a unified German territorial state. The Western political community fed on political and economic cohesion. Politically, the system of parliamentary democracy, basic civil rights, pluralism, materialism and individualism provided common, consensual values. With respect to international relations, mutual loyalty and peaceful institutional settlement of common security policy and international cooperation completed the constitutional cohesion. Economically, the capitalist market economy, a mixture of private and state ownership, integration into the world market and a basic social welfare system shaped a consensual lifestyle, and facilitated international economic organization. It could be expected that this social, economic and political cohesion would gradually replace the public desire for German national identity. It could therefore be expected that close West European cohesion, which found its representation in different forms of European integration, would compensate for the people's unfulfilled demands for national identity. This process has been described as a simultaneous 'Europeanization of the German question'.and a 'Germanization of the European question' (Hassner, 1983, p. 299).

However, the West Germans carefully cultivated a constitutional and political ambivalence between the need for national identity in a unified state and the association of the Federal Republic of Germany with the Western community. Apparently, West European cohesion could not absorb all historical demands for territorial unity and for political cohesion among all Germans. Consequently, the preamble of the German basic law states, on the one hand, that the Germans are 'determined to save their national and territorial unity and to promote world peace as an equal partner in a unified Europe'; on the other hand, it also states 'that all German people are required to fulfil in free self-determination the unity and the liberty of Germany'. In addition, article 24 expresses the willingness to transfer national political power to international institutions. The so-called 'Deutschland-Vertrag' of May 1952, which provided the Federal Republic of Germany with full sovereignty, contains similar expressions of this striking ambivalence between German unification and West European integration. The German public and many scholars have never realized that the West German government insisted an additional note to the protocol during the signing procedure of the European Rome treaties in February 1957. In that note it stated that the European treaties would have to be 'reviewed' in the event of the reunification of Germany. There was the hidden, but unmistakable, threat that Germany might leave the European Community if the prospect of German unification made it necessary (Klein, 1986, p. 69).

It demonstrates the irony of history that the corresponding revanchist political theory of 'rollback', which was formulated in those years amidst much controversy, is being proven true by the recent developments in Eastern Europe. 'Rollback' assumes the following development: the values, political orientations and economic structures of the Western community must become strong and successful; thus the general political prestige of the Western community will grow in the world. In response to the infiltration of Western values, communist ideology was questioned, socialist states in Eastern Europe were weakened, and East Germany 'surrendered' to the successful political and economic structures of Western Europe. This theory is both arrogant and contradictory at the same time: it regards the Western form of community building as the unalterable pursuit of happiness, yet it assumes contradictory political developments. In general, Western political freedom, international stability, economic progress and social security are intended to *neutralize* the demand for German national identity within the broader context of Western community orientation. However, at the same time the orientation towards German unification holds. 'Westernization' provides the only opportunity for *obtaining* the constitutional unification of both states.

Nevertheless, this political calculation seemed to work. The founding of the European Economic Community in 1957 strengthened the cooperative efforts of the Western capitalist industrial societies. The contradictions between the communist and the capitalist system were obvious and deep-rooted. Article 3 of the European foundation treaties restricted the European Community to a pure market economy. Membership of the Federal Republic of Germany enhanced the political prestige of West Germany and led, thanks to the rapid economic improvement of its economy, to a growing acceptance of the new German state and to its increasing significance within the European Community. West German politicians, interest groups and the public steadily internalized the Western community's orientation and expressed their will to promote the political progress and institutional reinforcement of European integration. Nevertheless, it could be foreseen that strengthening of the supranational elements would diminish the chances for a restoration of the prewar German national identity. A close European union would enforce the political and economic cohesion of the Western capitalist societies and would deepen the antagonism between East and West Germany in sensitive political spheres. The more a cohesive Western political identity spread over Europe, the less subordinate (i.e. 'national') forms of community building seemed to be feasible.

However, during the 1970s European integration within the European Community encountered several harsh economic and political setbacks. The general crisis of European integration, which will be discussed in the next section, weakened the expected forms of cohesion and identity, and thus disrupted the process of community building. The significance of the national 'communities' was at least economically, but to some extent politically, resurrected and led to a threatening tendency towards 'renationalization'. Nevertheless, European integration had institutionally advanced so far that no general collapse seemed possible – only, perhaps a decline in its political significance. The tensions between the divergent forms of community build-ing were re-established and politically adjusted. Thus, the ambivalence be-tween European integration and German unification maintained.

During the 1970s new steps were taken to solve the German national problem. The shift in political power in West Germany in 1969 to the Social Democrats and Liberals placed this problem on the agenda again and shaped a new motto for the general relations between Eastern and Western Europe: 'political change through convergence' (*Wandel durch Annäherung*). This formula pointed to an intensification of the pragmatic forms of cooperation between East and West Germany; the relaxation of ideological barriers; and the formation of a large European system of collective security. The new political scenario had some remarkable political consequences: the Warsaw treaty between Poland and Germany and the Moscow treaty between the Soviet Union and Germany in 1970, and the so-called 'Grundvertrag' be-tween East and West Germany in 1972. All treaties included an amendment which assumed the title 'Letter of German unity'. This letter stated that the particular treaty was not to oppose the general political orientation of the Federal Republic of Germany. So every treaty was to provide for peaceful political settlement in Europe and was not to oppose the unification of Germany in free self-determination (see the texts in Cieslar et al., 1973, p. 321). However, Social Democratic policy forced the tensions between the different forms of community building towards an ambiguous *reduction*, not towards a clear *dissolution*. The former Social Democratic chancellor Willy Brandt shaped the programmatic concept of 'two states, one nation'. The growing acceptance of the East's political system was to diminish every demand for cohesive political identity. Unfortunately, at that time the party ideology of the Social Democrats was wavering to such an extent that it could not offer any plausible alternative. The later, intermediary formula of 'constitutional patriotism' (*Verfassungspatriotismus*) was not an invention of prospective party ideologists, but of disoriented intellectuals.[2]

The new policy quickly bore fruit. In 1975 the two parts of Germany were brought together for the first time as equal, autonomous states during the final session and the settlement of the Conference on Security and Cooperation in Europe (CSCE) in Helsinki. The CSCE marked the most decisive and promising step towards a reduction of ideological and political tensions between East and West. Both superpowers participated, along with the European countries, and agreed upon provisions for disarmament, the improvement of trusteeship, and economic and cultural cooperation. In addition, the CSCE is not a traditional *institution* in international relations terms with restricted responsibilities, lim-ited competences and a well-defined membership, but instead represents a continuous, open *process* of *rapprochement*.[3] The CSCE process provoked the analytical concept of a 'Europeanization of Europe'. Antagonism appeared to diminish, cooperation and convergence seemed to grow steadily and to form a unique, but loose European community (see Bender, 1981). The demands for strong community orientation and close political identity were to be neutralized. In those formative years, the main significance of the *rapprochement* within the CSCE, of this overall European framework of negotiation and reconciliation, was not yet fully perceived. Today, in retrospect, it becomes apparent that this continuous reduction in tension and antagonism between East and West helped set the stage for the turbulent political changes of recent years. Gorbachev's perestroika and glasnost, regime changes in most of the Eastern European countries, economic cooperation between East and West and many additional political agreements would have been inconceivable without this institutionally loose, but politically effective, form of cooperation.[4]

It is not by accident that in those years the first institutional agreements between the European Community and certain Eastern countries were concluded: the ideological barriers had fallen, and European integration was no longer the principal political and economic opponent of communist regimes in Europe. It seemed no longer necessary to rebuild the bulwark of Western capitalism against the East European regimes. At the same time, it became obvious that European integration could not be the active source of community orientation needed to produce close economic and political cohesion within the 'European union'. The supranational institutions worked effectively most of the time, but they could not destroy, or markedly reduce, national political power, autonomy and political identity. According to the original aims of West European integration, the European Community was to diminish national autonomy – or the tensions between the different forms of community building would aggravate. Yet, meanwhile, European integration had experienced certain decisive developments which changed its role with respect to Western capitalist cohesion and political identity.

2 THE CHANGING FORMS OF COMMUNITY BUILDING WITHIN THE EUROPEAN COMMUNITY

At the very beginning of European integration in the postwar period, economic cooperation between the West European nation states was to gradually shape a close political community framed by the shared economic orientations and political values described above. This aim represented the general concept of 'functionalism', which was expected to initiate a process of 'spillover' from economic coherence to political identity in a West European federation. The concept partly failed due to the general tendencies of capitalist society which cannot be explained here in detail, but which will be summarized with respect to the European Community.

The European Community depends less today – in comparison to the postwar period – on political aims and more upon the efficiency of its economic system. This systemic efficiency can be described as cooperative production within the international division of capital and labour; the improvement of European economic competitiveness; and coordination in the realm of high technology. The practical performance of European integration becomes more important than the political system itself. This evolution represents a very important change in the legitimacy base of the European integration process and therefore leads to a different form of community building that was not foreseen during the initial period of European integration.

The legitimacy base of the European Community constantly shifts from political values towards economic performance. This shift is part of a general tendency in capitalist societies that becomes more significant as the framework of political organization becomes more extensive. Large and anonymous systems of decision-making extend political power automatically, while a commitment to the democratic process of political legitimization gets lost – the system becomes self-referential. Thus the European institutions, which try to imitate the Western model of parliamentarian democracy, become less important and cannot present any plausible alternative to the corresponding national political order. The European separation of power is reduced to a formal institutional structure of minor importance with respect to the output-oriented capabilities of the European Community. The process of a growing political identity and of democratization, which is closely tied to the strengthening of the European Parliament, might *institutionally* advance, but it is *substantially* devalued by the shift to the systemic legitimization of the European Community.

The European Parliament has weak legislative authority and exerts only minor influence on the executive structure of the European Community. The most serious problem of the European Parliament was, and remains, its legitimizing role. After the first direct elections in 1979 it was regarded as an institutional guarantor of the principle of representative democracy in the European Community. This might be formally correct as a description of its institutional structure, but substantively it is wrong. As has been demonstrated by all direct elections to date and by the public's attitudes to the European Parliament, European citizens have no distinct political consciousness of their legitimization function. Due to the weak 'presence' of the European Parliament in terms of legitimacy, direct elections descend to the level of 'ritual' which lacks substantial meaning (see Bülck, 1981). All direct elections seem to be test elections for national polls and are characterized by very little attention from the European public. European citizens do not accept the participatory structures of democracy and thus do not establish a cohesive political identity. The analytical category of 'Eurosclerosis', which developed during the crisis of integration in the 1970s, gives a misleading medical diagnosis: the European patient is still healthy, but on a severe diet that denies him any meaningful political nutrition.

These conclusions lead to the problem of alternative, subordinate frameworks for political identity. Remarkably, the debate on the political role of the regions and constituent states within the individual member states of the European Community has intensified during recent years. Technical harmonization and economic coordination at the European level have diminished traditional forms of autonomy at the regional level. The prospect of a European federation, which was initially meant to reduce the competition between regional self-determination and supranational power, is viewed with increasing suspicion. The systemic efficiency at the European level seems to restrict political autonomy at the regional level. However, it remains doubtful that an increase in regional autonomy – and the resulting limitations in European cohesion – would give birth to the political identity that the European Community so clearly lacks (for details see Engel, 1991 and Renzsch, 1990).

In relation to the diminished relevance of European integration to close political identity, the divergence of aims between supranational community and national identity declines. This change ultimately brings about remarkable consequences with regard to the tensions between German unification and European integration. The systemic capacity of the European Community illustrates how nation states can survive while the integration process continues. The problems of modern industrial societies have *converged* and need to be solved together. The divergent paths of economic modernization and political stability come to intersect between the different national unities in Europe (see Kastendiek, 1990). At the same time, the nation state represents the only realistic framework for democratic participation, identification and comprehensibility. The European Community is accepted as an efficient structure for solving problems of convergence, but it becomes more and more incomprehensible as a coherent political body and as a democratic system of political power. The European Single Market of 1992, which has been highly promoted in an extensive public relations campaign, thus appears in a different light. Rather than operating as a transitional stage towards democratic European union and the end of national autonomy, the European Community acts as an increasingly important vehicle for intensified economic and technical cooperation. The legitimization of the European Single Market fits into the overall importance of the systemic capacity of the European Community. The European Community acquires more political power, but does not shift towards becoming a more cohesive political community. From the perspective of democratic perception and legitimacy, the

European Community can be described as an 'invisible community' (Neunreither, 1976, p. 252).

The prospect for closer political cohesion through 'European Political Cooperation' (EPC) within the European Community does not contradict this general conclusion. EPC is an instrument of coordination at the level of the European state departments, so it lacks significance with regard to the direct democratic legitimization of the European Community. In addition, the hope that it will lead to a shared foreign policy is mainly based on the continual improvement of the security dimension of the European Community. However, due to the reduction in ideological tensions between East and West and the conclusion of numerous peaceful political settlements in Europe, common security policy has lost its significance as a framework for European political identity.[5]

The European Community only inspires a discussion about economic outcomes with regard to free movement of capital, labour and services; increasing income; and technological modernization. Even the political debate is restricted to the efficient coordination of the convergent decision-making processes. Political aims are subordinated to economic efficiency and discussions of democracy are substantially devaluated. Thus, the European Community can only be persuasive insofar as it functions as an efficient system. Yet even this systemic efficiency reveals some serious limitations. The European agricultural market, the regional difference within the European Community and the low convergence of national social achievements due to the expansion of an overall European market economy undermine any close political cohesion. Moreover, these repercussions counteract a common European community orientation in those fields where the individual's perception of political organization is concentrated: in the system's economic output, and in the transparency of political decision-making.

3 THE RELEVANCE OF THE UNIFICATION PROCESS FOR EUROPEAN INTEGRATION

Amidst such changes in the realm of community building, the political upheaval in East Germany occurred. Initially the unrest in the East did not stem from the problems afflicting West European integration. The stage was set for political change in East Germany with the appearance of political revolutions in the rest of Eastern Europe and with the emergence of a specific set of political problems in East Germany itself. With respect to community building, the motivation behind the upheavals in East Germany can be solely explained as a persisting dissatisfaction with the existing regime. First, these specific political forces should be described and then references to European integration can be explained.

Political cohesion and the formation of identity in the former German Democratic Republic have not been very successful. The principal constitutional preconceptions of the Eastern form of community building consisted of strict opposition to Fascism and the support of a general ideal of socialist society. Anti-Fascism provided a substitute for national identity in a large, unified German territorial state. The constitution of the German Democratic Republic stated: 'The German Democratic Republic has, according to the interests of the people and to its international obligations, eradicated on its territory German militarism and Nazism' (*Verfassung* der DDR, 1975, p. 11). However, the general orientation of a socialist society provided no convincing alternative source of identity. A planned economy was no feasible alternative to the economic system found in capitalist societies, and it contained many intrinsic weaknesses and obstacles to success. The socialist identity existed on the level of pure rhetoric, particularly since the socialist regime placed so many unbearable restrictions on its people: the German Democratic Republic had no free elections, no freedom of speech and press, and no freedom of movement for individuals.

These restrictions inspired the protest and unrest which led to the people's revolt. In June 1987 3 000 demonstrators in East Berlin hailed 'Gorbachev' and called for the demolition of the Berlin Wall; during a demonstration in January 1988 banners read: 'Freedom means the freedom of dissident thinking'; in January 1989 East German demonstrators demanded the freedom of speech, the freedom to hold public demonstrations, and the freedom of the press.[6] The most outstanding evidence of the seriousness of protesters' demands was the famous Monday demonstration in Leipzig. On 23 October 1989 300 000 people called for free elections and revolted against the concentration of political power in East Germany. The 'New Forum' represented the leading avant-garde among these political protesters.

The first phase of the upheaval in East Germany cannot be interpreted as a pure expression of economic dissatisfaction and desire for a Western capitalist welfare system. This misleading impression stems from the fact that the Western public did not fully realize the extent of the revolt until waves of people began leaving the country through Hungary, Czechoslovakia and the West German mission in East Berlin. Undoubtedly, the revolt went hand in hand with an expression of economic discontent and disappointment in the quality of life in the East but it cannot be reduced to a mere desire for a Western market economy. The call for political freedom intersected with economic demands that happened to coincide with the capitalist economic orientation of the West. 'Voting with the feet', which was misunderstood as a basic demand for individual participation in a capitalist welfare system, represented the East German people's disappointment at the regime's hesitation to enact necessary political reforms. Consequently, Willy Brandt's famous proclamation, 'What belongs together is growing together again', recognizes only half of the general problem of community building in East Germany. It responds to the enduring demand for national identity, yet neglects the functional economic and political framework in which such developments can take place. The process of unification cannot be carried out in a political vacuum; it is entrenched in the overall structures of a capitalist industrial system.

The first free elections in East Germany, which took place on 18 March 1990, traced the path towards a growing adoption of a Western capitalist system in East Germany, and an acceptance of the structures of West European integration. These elections represent the public acceptance of the economic and political order characteristic of Western societies and led to East Germany's absorption into the political system of West Germany (see Brückner, 1990a, p. 108). This absorption, which was urged by West German political leaders, accelerated the convergence of formerly contradictory demands for political identity. It quickly led to a currency union, which was established by 1 July 1990. At this point the Western market economy began to extend over the entire territory of Germany. The unification of Germany on 3 October 1990 represented only the East's formal adoption through constitutional means of West Germany's economic and political system, and was directed at a new common 'political' identity.

With regard to European integration, German unification fits into the overall direction of community building. The coexistence of national bodies and supranational cooperation has only gradually been expanded. Recent polls in the Eastern and Western parts of Germany demonstrate that the people do not sense a contradiction between national unification and supranational integration. In September 1990, 56 per cent of the population in the East and 47 per cent of the population in the West regarded European integration as even more important in light of the recent unification of Germany. Only 11 per cent of the population in the East and 13 per cent in the West classified European integration as less important given the recent developments in Germany (see Veen, 1991). Only a handful of German politicians – from the right as well as from the left – stated that German unification should not be subordinated to European integration and who pointed out the contradictions between these two political aims (see Langguth, 1990, p. 13).

From the viewpoint of the European neighbour states and from the viewpoint of European integration there was no scope for substantial intervention in the process of German unification. Many national statements were made by different member states of the European Community, but the supranational authorities were forced to *react* to the rapid political developments and changes. To the extent that the tensions had diminished between formerly different types of community building, the special expectations inherent in supranational integration could be ignored. Before the upheavals in the East began, the European Commission was theoretically committed to a pure trade agreement between East Germany and the European Community. This policy remained in accordance with the intentions of Western community building. The close cohesion of the Western capitalist member states, which would finally lead to European union, was to be enforced. However, at the same time, the political antagonisms between East and West were to be reduced by economic cooperation – corresponding to the motto, 'Political change through convergence'. In the course of the rapid political changes in Eastern Europe, the European Commission was forced to adapt to the new political developments. In Brussels, models for intensified economic cooperation were discussed amidst much controversy (for details see Krenzler, 1990). In December 1989, the vice-president of the commission, Andriessen, travelled to East Berlin for further negotiations. The president of the commission, Jacques Delors, declared in January 1990 that the case of the German Democratic Republic was a 'special matter' which made it possible to enforce full membership of East Germany even before the European Single Market was completed (see Langguth, 1990, p. 29). However, political developments accelerated beyond the expectations of European integration. Suddenly, the unification of Germany appeared on the spectrum of European political events, so the supranational authorities changed their positions again and began discussing appropriate models for the absorption of the Eastern parts of unified Germany into the various common policy arenas of the European Community.

This development marked the only moment during the rapid progression of events when the originally different – or even contradictory – forms of community building became politically apparent. Certain member states of the European Community expressed their fear that German unification might endanger the process of European integration. However, they referred much more to the very traditional concept of a European *balance of power* between nation states than to a sophisticated model of supranational European union. No serious resistance arose to the actual strengthening of national cohesion within one of the member states. None of the European neighbour states regarded Germany's new national identity as contradictory to supranational integration, and none of the neighbour states referred to the historical fact that European integration was originally meant to *absorb* national autonomy. Consequently, the European Council of Heads of State adopted only a short declaration on recent political development in Central and Eastern Europe. This stated in vague terms that the unification of Germany should merely be in accordance with the final agreement of the CSCE conference in 1975 and should be 'embedded into the perspective of European integration'.[7]

The tensions that had formerly existed between different forms of community building had declined. For East Germany, democratic demands in the East led to the gradual adoption of a broad capitalist market economy in which the new Germany represents only one national actor. For the European Community, the aims of supranational integration were no longer in opposition to the restructuring of national identity. The efficiency of an overall capitalist system represented a new, very loose form of collective identity for the territorially enlarged Community.

4 THE PAST AND FUTURE ROLE OF GERMANY WITHIN THE EUROPEAN COMMUNITY

The incorporation of the Federal Republic of Germany into the European integration process symbolized the restoration of a legitimate German political body after the Second World War, when Germany had lost its political credibility. In the postwar period West Germany was warmly accepted into the Western community, and demonstrated its gratitude for this welcome by its eager and enthusiastic participation in all forms of European integration.

From the very beginning, political and economic relations between East Germany and the European Community were based on a special relationship that led some observers to the conclusion that the German Democratic Republic was the 'thirteenth member state' of the Community. With the formation of the European Community and the entry of the Federal Republic of Germany, an amendment to the foundation treaties was added outlining the trade relations between the two parts of Germany ('Protokoll über den innerdeutschen Handel'). This amendment excluded any customs barriers between East and West Germany and stated that trade relations between both states were not to be classified as 'foreign trade'. Articles 82 and 92 of the European treaties conceded special grants to German regions that were economically disadvantaged by the division of Germany. Moreover, the Federal Republic of Germany contributed a statement to the European foundation treaties claiming that all people of German nationality are under the protection of the West German basic law – and article 116 of the basic law states that 'Germans' are all those who live in the area of the 'German Reich', according to the extension of 31 December 1937. The Federal Republic of Germany claimed to be the only legal successor of that old 'Reich'.

Then, with the economic crisis of the 1970s, supranational cooperation encountered new forms of national protectionism, and the pace of European integration was impeded by the sometimes harsh process of renationalization.

From the viewpoint of the European Community, the Federal Republic of Germany had – unfortunately – become politically and economically strong enough to avoid being seriously affected by the economic crisis like most of the other member states. The famous German 'economic miracle' had led to overwhelming economic stability in West Germany, demonstrated by its high rate of productivity growth, considerable currency stability, high rate of industrial investment, and positive balance of foreign trade. This economic success enhanced political reservations, suspicions and jealousy among some of Germany's neighbour states. Discussions arose about the *economic hegemony* of West Germany within Europe (see Hütter, 1978; Franzmeyer, 1981). The Federal Republic of Germany angrily responded with an intensive debate on its large financial contributions to the budget of the European Community (*Zahlmeister-Funktion*). The 'costs and benefits' of German membership in the European Community were unscrupulously weighed (May, 1982) European integration had already lost its political sanctity and had declined into a loose framework of economic benefits for the member states.

The ambiguous role of Germany within the European Community persisted until the recent developments in Eastern Europe. Germany has been regarded as an economic superpower and as the strongest member state of the Community. It has been discreetly, but repeatedly, warned not to fall into economic protectionism and political nationalism. Resentment has already developed about the role of Germany in European security policy. The two-plus-four negotiations concerning the future role of Germany within NATO caused fear and anger among European states like Poland, Italy and the Netherlands. Given these conditions, the unification of Germany was a delicate political concern to be approached with much caution. Only the altered forms of community building in the European Community and the reconciliation of European integration and national identity prevents serious reservations, tensions and unrest among the other member states. The unification of Germany aggravated already-existing problems because the Federal Republic of Germany has traditionally taken the leading role in trade relations between the European Community and Eastern Europe. For a very long time, West Germany has had the largest share of trade with the Soviet Union, Poland, Romania, Czechoslovakia, Hungary, Bulgaria and the former German Democratic Republic (Kreile, 1978). Unification of Germany will undoubtedly strengthen the leading role of Germany in East European trade and will, in the long run, improve its economic position with regard to trade relations with Eastern Europe.

Which role, then, will be preserved in the future for a unified Germany within the European Community? Despite the economic setback caused by catastrophic developments in the Eastern part of unified Germany, the new German state seems to be maintaining its former position in Europe. At the very least, expectations and commentary from abroad seem to point to that conclusion. Unified Germany has become geographically the largest member state, the most populous, and the most important economically. This superiority may not, in the long run, produce any serious reservations among Germany's neighbours, but it raises the question of 'critical size' for the German nation state. The continuing historical debate on the deviant development of Germany (*deutscher Sonderweg*) acquires a new importance focusing on its economic variables.[8] However, even political commentators from abroad plead for the acceptance of a future leading role for Germany within the European Community.[9] There arises only some 'self-admonition' on the part of Germany to remind itself not to transform its economic supremacy into political hegemony (see Geiss, 1991, p. 45). West Germany's economic miracle, which stems from the system of capitalist industrial rationality practised in Western societies, seems to be evolving into a broader economic miracle benefiting all of unified Germany (see Brückner, 1990b, p. 315).

5   PROSPECTS FOR THE NEW EUROPEAN ORDER

In Europe, the period from the 1980s to the 1990s has been characterized by far-reaching political changes throughout the continent. The European Community is itself deeply embedded in this process of changing political developments and responsibilities. The upheavals in Eastern Europe have markedly altered the international political and economic order and the institutional balance in Europe.

The original aim of the European Community was to meld the West European nation states into a political union through progressive economic integration. After two decades, the general aim has become much more modest, and today the European Community is confronted with a complex challenge: to galvanize economic aid for the weakened states of Eastern Europe; to offer various forms of integration through association or even full membership of its economic union; to promote democratization of the East European political systems; and to encourage political integration of the current member states into an institutionally cohesive European union.

Furthermore, the European Community must strengthen its general credentials as an instrument for technological modernization. Thus, it will gradually lose its significance as a political community. It must encourage the convergence of national policies, but will be excluded from the formation of a cohesive political body. Given the obstacles created by a new European order, the European Community will even have difficulty providing a strong common bond of cooperation and a reliable base for political coordination. It will become much more difficult to provide technological and political cooperation, to eliminate major economic disparities, and, in general, to guarantee universal standards of social welfare for all Europeans. German unification offers an illustrative example of how economic disparities may create at least temporary restraints on all aspects of integration.

The only medium-term solution seems to form a European Community that proceeds at different rates or in concentric circles.[10] The model of different rates reflects the fact that there are already serious economic disparities within the European Community which would be enforced by the new all-European economic cooperation. Some nations may achieve the expected standards of harmonization, others not; some may accept industrial health and safety standards, others not. However, this concept of 'step-by-step integration' produces serious constraints on the general economic and political aims expressed in the foundation treaties, and it enforces the disparities between poor and rich member states. The model of concentric circles would lead to a fragmentation of the different European forms of cohesion. The CSCE would represent the overall framework for common political values and for a common security policy; the European Community would become the 'club' of highly industrialized capitalist societies; the EFTA or the EWR (*Europäischer Wirtschaftsraum*) would remain the waiting room for countries with a growing economy or a congregation of nations with neutral political views. It is easy to imagine the serious obstacles that stand in the way of any homogeneous political cohesion within the European Community.

With respect to the demands for political identity, the *coexistence* of European integration and national unity provides an important precondition. Even for the revolutionized East European countries, the European Community has only *formal* significance as a guarantor of political stability, basic political rights and peaceful international settlement. For the realization of national identity and political union in the East, the European Community will not gain any significance as a democratic political body, but, rather, as a formal frame of reference for these countries. Recent calls in Eastern Europe for European federation originate in the belief that international stability through the European Community will enforce the formation of national identity in Eastern Europe. This is demonstrated by the movements for 'regional' autonomy in Hungary, Romania, Czechoslovakia and former Yugoslavia. The European Community will not serve as a leading agent for the *democratization* of the East, but only as an institutional framework for the protection of the *established standards* of democracy. So West European demands for democratic principles and values as a precondition for any application of membership to the European Community do necessarily point to supranational political cohesion. The basic democratic values which are being sought in East European countries and which are required of future member states are not an institutional invention of the European Community but the supranational adoption of the constitutional principles of the Western member states. The West European nation states are still the most important proponents of democracy in general, and of democratization in the East European countries in particular.[11]

In general, the realization of national identity represents a persistent political demand. The identity of *nation* and *democratic community* seems to be a necessary point of reference for the formation of a cohesive political body. However, the intensity of political demands is decreasing in relation to the proven material effectiveness of political power. 'Politics' is reduced to the capitalist promotion of welfare. The process of German unification fits completely into this general conclusion. The decreased tension between German unification and European integration offers an important example of some general trends in modern industrial societies. It demonstrates how strong democratic demands can be supplanted by a political retreat into the pursuit of welfare effectiveness.

On the 40th anniversary of the founding of the German Democratic Republic, a date representing the initial stage of the revolt in East Germany, the former Soviet president Mikhail Gorbachev made the famous statement, 'Life punishes those who come too late.' With respect to political identity and democratic cohesion throughout Germany and the European Community, it must be pointed out that most people actually came too early. Life punishes those who by forcing economic productivity limit politics to the pursuit of mere welfare gains. These individuals do not comprehend the complex challenges of democratic community building.

NOTES

*   I wish to thank Jody Friedman for her precise grammatical corrections and for her acute remarks on the content of this chapter.
1. For further details concerning the 'German question' see Richter (1987), Krell (1990).
2. Dolf Sternberger was the first to adopt the notion. Jürgen Habermas picked it up and tried to launch it towards a new password for a 'post conventional identity'; cf. Habermas (1986), p. 40.
3. The CSCE can be characterized by the category of 'agreed principles' instead of 'institutional obligations', cf. Nötzold and Rummel (1990), p. 215.
4. Cf. the prospects given by Senghaas (1990).
5. For the general aspects of European security policy see Buzan et al. (1990).
6. Cf. for the chronology of those events *Der Fischer Weltalmanach. Sonderband DDR* (1990), p. 98ff.
7. 'Wir streben die Stärkung des Zustands des Friedens in Europa an, in dem das deutsche Volk in freier Selbstbestimmung seine Einheit wiedererlangt. Dieser Prozess muss sich auf friedliche und demokratische Weise, unter Wahrung der Abkommen und Verträge sowie sämtlicher in der Schlussakte von Helsinki niedergelegten Grundsätze im Kontext des Dialogs und der Ost-West-Zusammenarbeit vollziehen. Er muss auch in die Perspektive der europäischen Integration eingebettet sein.' Tagung des Europäischen Rats (1990), p. D 14.

8. For the concept of 'Sonderweg' see Faulenbach (1981).
9. Even a British expert on European integration calls for a strong German attitude within the future European Community; cf. Wallace (1990); see also Heimann (1990), and Langguth (1991).
10. For different scenarios see Buzan et al. (1990).
11. Ungerer (1990, p. 233) states that the European Community will be an 'anchor' for Central and Eastern Europe. This conclusion seems to be overemphasized. See Schöpflin (1991).

REFERENCES

Bender, P. (1981), *Das Ende des ideologischen Zeitalters. Die Europäisierung Europas*. Berlin: Siedler.

Brückner, H. (1990a), 'Neudeutsches Wirtschaftswunder oder "Eigernordwand im Winter"', *Perspektiven des demokratischen Sozialismus*, 7, 102–9.

Brückner, H. (1990b), 'Neuer deutscher Nationalismus und die Metaphysik des Wirtschaftswunders', *Die Neue Gesellschaft/Frankfurter Hefte*, 4, 312–17.

Bülck, H. (1981), 'Der Europabürger', in I. v. Münch (ed.), *Staatsrecht – Völkerrecht – Europarecht. Festschrift für Hans-Jürgen Schlochauer zum 75. Geburtstag am 28. März 1981*, Berlin and New York: De Gruyter, pp. 777–811.

Buzan, B. et al. (1990), *The European Security Order Recast. Scenarios for the Post-Cold War Era*, London and New York: Pinter Publishers.

Cieslar, E. et al. (1973), *Der Streit um den Grundlagenvertrag. Eine Dokumentation*, Munich: Hanser.

Engel, C. (1991), 'Regionen in der Europäischen Gemeinschaft: Eine integrations-politische Rollensuche', *Integration*, 1, 9–20.

Faulenbach, B. (1981), '"Deutscher Sonderweg". Zur Geschichte und Problematik einer zentralen Kategorie des deutschen geschichtlichen Bewusstseins', *Aus Politik und Zeitgeschichte*, B 33, 3–21.

Der Fischer Weltalmanach. Sonderband DDR (1990), Frankfurt/Main: Fischer Taschenbuch.

Franzmeyer, F. (1981), 'Wirtschaftliche Dominanz als Integrationsproblem. Zur Position der Bundesrepublik Deutschland in der EG', *Europa-Archiv*, 24, 737–44.

Geiss, I. (1991), 'Europäische Perspektiven nach der deutschen Einigung', *Aus Politik und Zeitgeschichte*, B. 52–3, 41–7.

Habermas, J. (1986), 'Eine Art Schadensabwicklung. Die apologetischen Tendenzen in der deutschen Zeitgeschichtsschreibung', *Die Zeit*, 29, 40.

Hassner, P. (1983), 'Zwei deutsche Staaten in Europa. Gibt es gemeinsame Interessen in der internationalen Politik?' in W. Weidenfeld (ed.), *Die Identität der Deutschen*, Munich and Vienna: Carl Hanser Verlag, pp. 272–302.

Heimann, G. (1990), 'Die Auflösung der Blöcke und die Europäisierung Deutschlands', *Europa-Archiv*, 5, 167–72.

Hütter, J. (1978), 'Die Stellung der Bundesrepublik Deutschland in Westeuropa. Hegemonie durch wirtschaftliche Dominanz?' *Integration*, 3, 103–18.

Kastendiek, H. (1990), 'Convergence or a Persistent Diversity of National Politics?' in C. Crouch and D. Marquand (eds), *The Politics of 1992. Beyond the Single European Market*, Oxford: Basil Blackwell, pp. 68–84.

Klein, E. (1986), 'Die Deutsche Frage in der Europäischen Gemeinschaft', in D.

Blumenwitz and B. Meissner (eds), *Die Überwindung der europäischen Teilung und die deutsche Frage*, Cologne: Verlag Wissenschaft und Politik, pp. 61–74.

Kreile, M. (1978), *Osthandel und Ostpolitik*, Baden-Baden: Nomos.

Krell, G. (1990), 'Die Ostpolitik der Bundesrepublik Deutschland und die deutsche Frage. Historische Entwicklungen und politische Optionen im Ost–West-Konflikt', *Aus Politik und Zeitgeschichte*, **B 29**, 24–34.

Krenzler, H.G. (1990), 'Die Europäische Gemeinschaft und der Wandel in Mittel- und Osteuropa', *Europa-Archiv*, **3**, 89–96.

Langguth, G. (1990), 'Die deutsche Frage und die Europäische Gemeinschaft', *Aus Politik und Zeitgeschichte*, **B 29**, 13–23.

Langguth, G. (1991), 'Germany, the EC, and the Architecture of Europe. The German Question in the Context of the EC', *Aussenpolitik*, **42**, 137–46.

May, B. (1982), *Kosten und Nutzen der deutschen EG-Mitgliedschaft*, Bonn: Europa Union Verlag.

Neunreither, K. (1976), 'Legitimationsprobleme der Europäischen Gemeinschaft', *Zeitschrift für Parlamentsfragen*, **7**, 245–58.

Nötzold, J. and Rummel, R. (1990), 'On the Way to a New European Order', *Aussenpolitik*, **3**, 211–19.

Renzsch, W. (1990), 'Deutsche Länder und europäische Integration. Kompetenzverluste und neue Handlungschancen in einem "Europa der Regionen"', *Aus Politik und Zeitgeschichte*, **B 28**, 28–39.

Richter, E. (1987), 'Die Bundesrepublik Deutschland in der europäischen Integration. Zur Ambivalenz von nationaler Identität und internationaler Einbindung', in J.P. Nautz and J.F.E. Bläsing (eds), *Staatliche Intervention und gesellschaftliche Freiheit. Staat und Gesellschaft in den Niederlanden und Deutschland im 20. Jahrhundert*, Melsungen: Kasseler Schriften zur Zeitgeschichte, pp. 269–87.

Schöpflin, G. (1991), 'Post-Communism: Constructing New Democracies in Central Europe', *International Affairs*, **67**, 235–49.

Senghaas, D. (1990), 'Frieden in einem Europa demokratischer Rechtsstaaten', *Aus Politik und Zeitgeschichte*, **B 4–5**, 31–9.

Tagung des Europäischen Rats (1990), *Europa-Archiv*, **1**, D 14.

Ungerer, W. (1990), 'The Development of the EC and its Relationship to Central and Eastern Europe', *Aussenpolitik* **3**, 229–35.

Veen, H.-J. (1991), 'Die Westbindungen der Deutschen in einer Phase der Neuorientierung', *Europa-Archiv*, **2**, 31–9.

Verfassung der Deutschen Demokratischen Republik (1975), Berlin: Aufbau Verlag.

Wallace, W. (1990), 'Deutschlands zentrale Rolle. Ein Versuch, die europäische Frage neu zu definieren', *Integration*, **1**, 13–20.

12. From the EMS to European Economic and Monetary Union with German Economic and Monetary Union as a Major Sideshow

Hugo M. Kaufmann

1. INTRODUCTION

When I chose this topic, which focuses on long-run aspects of monetary integration, German Economic and Monetary Union (GEMU) or even German Economic, Monetary and Social Union (GEMSU) might have been viewed as a minor distraction. However, experience with GEMU and GEMSU and the lessons one might have to draw from them have elevated them to a topic *sui generis* that could cast a long shadow. The Christian Democratic Union (CDU) experienced a crushing defeat in the Rhineland-Palatinate, Chancellor Kohl's home state, on 21 April 1991.[1] The rapidly worsening conditions in Eastern Germany and the increasing costs of unification with the vacillation on taxes conspired against the Kohl government in the spring of 1991.

With the opening of the Berlin Wall on 9 November 1989, Germany – East and West – luxuriated in euphoria, and between November 1989 and the end of 1990 it seemed that the German unification process could not have gone better: the Wall was down, East Germany had voted to be absorbed into the Federal Republic; it was not a merger of the two countries but application of Article 23 of the Basic Law whereby the erstwhile German Democratic Republic (GDR) voted itself out of existence; the then perestroika-and-glasnost-minded Gorbachev consented to the enlarged Germany's membership of NATO; and with the massive victory of the CDU in the first free all-German elections in over 50 years the stage was set for the cloning of the prior (West) German *Wirtschaftswunder* – or was it?

What went wrong? Did the not-quite-anticipated extent of the difficulties result from unforeseeable events or from defective information and/or analysis? In other words, could or should one have foreseen that things would get

200

much more difficult before they would eventually improve in a kind of J-curve phenomenon? Current projections of Germany's economic future, which are daily making headlines and are politically exploited, have to be considered as very tentative, at best, and subject to changes without prior announcement.

The first part of my chapter outlines some of the central thinking that preceded the creation of the European Monetary System (EMS), a regional pegged-rate system for the members of the European Economic Community (EEC)[2] and other (European) countries that might wish to join, its functioning and its projected development, as the Community is on the road to an economic and monetary union (EMU) with its own European central bank (ECB). Details and the timetable may change. A broad review of the major issues is therefore of interest. With history being prologue in this instance, the discussions and negotiations in the European Community (EC)[3] concerning the stages towards the creation of a European central bank and the movement toward a European economic and monetary union (Committee 1989) remind one of the debate during the 1960s and 1970s that preceded the introduction of first the 'narrow margins arrangement' (the so-called 'snake') and later that of the EMS. The dramatis personae remained the same,[4] and their positions have not drastically changed over more than two decades.

2 DEBATE OVER A MONETARY SYSTEM FOR EUROPE

(a) General Concerns over the New Monetary Systems

The debate in the 1970s over a new European Monetary System concerned the abandonment of flexible exchange rates and the enlargement and modification of the narrow-margins arrangement that had evolved into a Deutschmark zone, with the Deutschmark as its anchor and the Deutsche Bundesbank in charge of monetary policy for the system. In the early debate over the creation of the EMS, Germany feared that a shift from an informal structure, as the 'snake' represented, to a formal one like the EMS would evolve into an inflation union. That fear was unsurprising. France, the prime mover for an EMS, had previously withdrawn from Germany's monetary discipline and by 1978 registered an inflation rate of 9.1 per cent, more than three times Germany's inflation rate of 2.7 per cent. Non-members and intermittent members of the snake differed from the permanent members in their ranking of the macroeconomic goals and their economic performance: the former group hoped to lower their unemployment rates by accepting higher inflation rates ('full employment at any cost'), whilst the snake members viewed inflation as part and not as a solution of the unemployment problem.[5]

(b) 'Monetarists' versus 'Economists'

The parties to the discussion about EC monetary integration conceded that without converging economic policies and performance, the durability of the exchange rate arrangement would be threatened if capital movements were to be freed. They have disagreed to this day, however, over the best way to achieve such a convergence.

Two major camps emerged in the 1960s: the 'monetarists',[6] advocating pegged rates in order to force convergence (the functionalist approach); and the 'economists', on the other hand, who regarded convergence as a prerequisite for the successful launching of a pegged-rate monetary zone. France took the monetarist, Germany the economist stance.

The monetarists and the economists also differed in attitude to economic policy: the monetarists favoured activist policy with administrative interventions beyond the mere smoothing of exchange rate fluctuations through major support operations, whereas the economists relied more on market forces.

The authors of the Werner report, some designers of the EMS, as well as some committee members producing the 1989 Delors report on the stages towards the creation of an EMU, sided with the monetarists when they proposed three stages of progressively narrowing the margins of permissible exchange rate fluctuations for EC currencies until after a ten-year transition period the Community would be ready for monetary union (*Bulletin*, 1970). Small exchange rate fluctuations were to effect a convergence in inflation rates, productivity and economic growth, while avoiding complications associated with voluntary policy coordination. Additionally, the EMS and the Delors Plan were to provide member countries with an alternative to the preponderance of the dollar and the Deutschmark.

According to the 'economists', convergence of economic policy and performance had to antecede exchange rate pegging. They argued that the Bretton Woods experience had generated neither disciplining constraints nor economic convergence. Rather, countries interfered in the market mechanism through exchange controls and foreign exchange markets provided so-called one-way options, whereby one could bet with little risk on exchange rate changes. According to the 'economists', mutually consistent international policy and performance convergence would *ipso facto* bring about stable exchange rates, since the fundamentals that affect demand for goods and assets would similarly affect exchange rates: stable and convergent fundamentals would produce stable exchange rates.

In the present discussion about the new monetary system for Europe, the views of the past have played an important role. However, international capital movements, which have been freed since mid-1990, have overshadowed real flows. As expectations about the future course of fundamentals significantly affect exchange rates, past and present fundamentals have lost power on theoretical grounds in the dispute over the proper sequence towards economic and monetary union (Dornbusch, 1986).

(c) Search for Symmetry in the EMS

The Bretton Woods system had two asymmetries which the EMS was to eliminate: the dollar had become the 'key' or 'n-th' currency to which other countries pegged their exchange rates. Consequently, the US could not choose independently its exchange rate *vis-à-vis* other countries but had to accept other countries' exchange rate decisions.

The second asymmetry was that the balance of payments adjustment burden fell mainly on the non-reserve-currency countries with balance of payments deficits. The surplus countries, on the other hand, were free of balance of payments constraints.

The debate over the EMS as a strategic game sometimes emphasizes monetary discipline and at other times stresses the gains from exchange rate cooperation.[7] In the former, price stability gets top priority, whereas the latter sees countries benefiting from the reduction and eventual elimination of transaction and conversion costs as well as from exchange rate uncertainty associated with exchange rate fluctuations. This is particularly significant for the smaller countries with large trade ties.

3 GERMAN ECONOMIC AND MONETARY UNION

The major issues in the 1990s concerning the transition from central planning to a market-type economy rest with the former German Democratic Republic and the other Eastern Bloc countries. Once it was agreed that the planned economies had to be converted to market economies, new questions arose as to the speed of the transition and its sequencing as well as the budgetary impact of privatization and competition (Calvo and Frenkel, 1991).

(a) Speed of Transition

In the discussion about the optimum speed for transition from the defunct system of central planning to a market-oriented system two camps emerged, one recommending high-speed transition while the other recommended a go-slow, gradualist approach. Similarly, the (systemic) question is whether the Treuhandanstalt, whose task is to privatize the government enterprises of Eastern Germany, should sell the firms as they are, that is in their various states of disrepair and uncompetitiveness, or whether it should first try to refurbish them to give some assurance of success in the market place.

Those in favour of a high-speed bullet train, racing from one system to the other, immediately embracing the market domination of demand and supply conditions, reasoned as follows: compress the inevitable costs into as short a time span as possible, get the metamorphosis behind as fast as possible and proceed on the new track. They feared that the longer the unavoidable adjustments are postponed, the more difficult and costly they will be. Moreover, the more protracted the adjustment process, the more people's patience will be taxed, with the consequence that the dislocation and distress might not be accepted and the transition to a new system might stop short of successful completion. They reasoned that an end with shock was preferable to a shock without an end. The other camp, though subscribing to the same ultimate goal, opted for a gradual transition to a market-oriented economy, fearing that the consequences of market forces and the absence or inadequacy of a safety net would make the pain intolerably and unnecessarily grave for those who fell by the wayside.

(b)   Sequencing

Sequencing refers to the progression by which the transition from a command to a market economy should proceed. At issue are, among others: the abandonment of central planning and the adoption of a market pricing mechanism; the endorsement of property rights; the introduction of competition (breaking up of the Kombinate) and privatization of government-owned and operated enterprises; the establishment of a two-tier banking system with private banking serving the needs of the public and a separate monetary authority conducting monetary policy; and the creation of financial markets, including stock exchanges. These tasks seemed much simpler in the case of Eastern Germany than for the other centrally planned economies of Eastern Europe, as the German Democratic Republic accepted Article 23, by which it adopted the political, legal and economic system and the institutions of the Federal Republic of Germany. In addition the former GDR had the backing of the Federal Republic of Germany's financial power. Consequently, sequencing and speed were determined simultaneously in the case of Eastern Germany.

(c)   Privatization and Budgets – 'Hard' and 'Soft'

Since most enterprises were state-owned and state-run, managed and run (down) by functionaries, the firms would have to be privatized. There have been and still are major obstacles to the privatization process and investment in Eastern Europe:

1. Property rights

There is the uncertain issue of property rights; who owns the land, the buildings, the equipment; what will be the claims by previous owners? There were various episodes of expropriation: first, under the Nazi regime, property owned by Jews was either confiscated outright or *de facto* expropriated through forced sales at unrealistically low prices. After the Second World War, government expropriations took place under the communist regime. As long as the issue of property rights remains unresolved, potential investors will hesitate to make new commitments.

According to a recent ruling by the Federal Constitutional Court in Karlsruhe (23 April 1991), large landowners and industrialists who were expropriated during the land reform in the Soviet occupation zone of Germany between 1945 and 1949 have no claims to restitution but only to compensation.[8]

2. Accounting principles

Accounting principles in the East bore no resemblance to those of the West. For instance, terms such as market cost and profits were alien; since firms did not operate on a cost (historic or replacement cost) and profit basis, they could very well survive even if they never covered operating costs. Firms and the large Kombinate belonged to the state ('the people'), which financed them. How is one to estimate the value of firms that have been established and have been operating in a non-market arbitrary-pricing environment? Furthermore, the equipment in most cases is antiquated, environmentally unsound and will have to be scrapped on both economic efficiency and ecological grounds. The style and quality of many products have been shoddy and acceptable only against soft currencies within the erstwhile and recently defunct Comecon. Hard currency was looking for internationally acceptable goods.

Consequently, it was clear from the beginning that the majority of enterprises might go under when forced to compete with Western products and run on a profit-making basis. Conservative estimates conjectured that only about 30 per cent of the former German Democratic Republic's industry could survive the transition to a competitive market economy; 40 per cent 'could be restructured with reasonable chances of success and 30 per cent was probably beyond redemption' (Lipschitz et al., 1990).

3. Recent speed of investment

According to economics minister Jürgen Möllemann (24 April 1991), investments in the new federal states are gaining momentum as the demand for low-interest credit has increased. As part of the regional development programme, applications have been submitted for projects amounting to DM 31 billion, of which some 30 per cent have already been approved. In addition, applications are on hand for planned investments in the Eastern German commercial infrastructure totalling DM 7 billion. A total of DM 6.6 billion in credits had been approved as part of the European Recovery Plan for modernization and business start-ups.[9]

4. Subsidization

This led to the question of whether 'temporarily' to subsidize those enterprises, the 'soft-budget' option, or whether subsidies should be ruled out, the 'hard-budget' option. Anyone with some experience of subsidies knows that they are as temporary as tax increases or import restrictions. Those who benefit from them will form a powerful lobby, particularly when the firms have prospered as a result of these interferences with the market mechanism and have gained political clout.

(d) Eastern Germany's transformation

Many thought that the process of transformation would be easiest in the case of Eastern Germany, since the richer Western Germany would absorb them and finance the revival of the Eastern industrial sector after the economic, monetary and social union, GEMSU. The Federal Republic had performed an 'economic miracle' after the Second World War, and many expected this miracle to be replicable. This belief in miracles seemed justified in the eyes of many observers since Eastern Germany was widely held to be the Eastern Bloc's industrial powerhouse, which it was. And yet, as we have already mentioned, the socialist countries' accounting principles did not permit facile comparison of economic conditions and performance in East and West. This alone should have forewarned analysts and decision-makers not to take the Eastern data at face value. Furthermore, the optimists had ignored the fact that the revival of the German economy did not start immediately after the Second World War, but only in 1948.

(e) Importance of the Exchange Rate

The choice of exchange rate between the Ostmark (M) and the West German Deutschmark (DM) was determined by the following considerations: too favourable an exchange rate for the Ostmark, say, 1 DM = 1 M would make Eastern Germany uncompetitive, would benefit Ostmark holders and reduce migration to the West. On the other hand, the Bundesbank in particular was concerned about the potentially inflationary impact of such an exchange rate, as it would instantly increase the domestic money supply by an estimated 10 per cent.

Too low a rate, on the other hand, would hurt Eastern Germans' past savings. Germany chose the first alternative up to a maximum total, graduated according to age and category of income and assets, not least in order to stem the large influx of people from the East. The basically favourable exchange rate for Eastern Germans may have slowed but could not halt migration from the East, as business failures and unemployment in the East continued to mount. A recent study has assessed the relative importance for migration of wage differentials and job availability respectively, and found that it is the latter that has the greater influence on the propensity to migrate. Consequently, the metalworkers' union, IG Metall's demand for wage parity in East and West by 1994 was misguided with respect to the migration argument (Akerlof et al., 1991).

Observers inside and outside Germany had suggested that it was impossible to calculate a 'correct' exchange rate and that the black market rate was not a good yardstick either. The black market rate had started to decline from 15–20 M to about 6–10 M for 1 DM in anticipation of the currency union, especially after an official 1:1 exchange rate had emerged as a distinct possibility. An interim floating exchange rate arrangement for the transition period, while an elegant solution in the absence of reliable indicators for an 'equilibrium' exchange rate, had never been seriously considered by policymakers. A consensus emerged in economic circles and at the Deutsche Bundesbank that a 3:1 ratio, or possibly even a 2.5:1 exchange rate, would be about appropriate under the circumstances. These figures were arrived at since productivity in Eastern Germany was estimated to amount to about one-third of West Germany's. While at one time one might have viewed an exchange rate as merely the price ratio of two currencies with little or no impact on the real sector, this was no longer the case in the 1980s, as has manifested itself in the case of German monetary unification.

On 1 July 1990 the Deutsche Bundesbank became the central bank and its currency, the Deutschmark, became the legal tender for the united Germany, which also adopted Western Germany's banking system (Lipschitz et al., 1990).

(f) The Unemployment Issue

Many observers stressed that the setting of a realistic rather than a favourable exchange rate was essential for avoiding complete uncompetitiveness of the Eastern German economy within Eastern Germany, in the rest of Germany and in foreign markets. In this new environment inferior Eastern products, for which hard currency had to be paid after monetary union, had to compete against Western goods. Second, labour productivity in East Germany was estimated at about one-third of West Germany's, and would suggest a wage and salary structure of one-third of West Germany's. Yet GEMSU would rapidly eliminate wage differentiation between Eastern and Western Germany, raise Eastern Germany's cost and price structure and reduce the chances of competing with the West. The rapid and dramatic increase in unemployment and the near-collapse of Eastern Germany's economy shocked many in the East as well as in the West, especially since it followed so swiftly on the heels of GEMSU: 'One of the worst and sharpest depressions in European history had begun' (Akerlof et al., 1991). According to the German Federal Bureau of Statistics (Wiesbaden), unemployment during the second half of 1990 rose from 1.6 per cent to 7.3 per cent.[10] By the end of May, workers on 'short work' schedule worked 50 per cent less than the normal working hours in spring 1991 as against 40 per cent of the regular workweek in November1990.[11]

While the magnitude of the unemployment problem has been staggering, some of the increase may have been a statistical quirk. Under the socialist regime, unemployment did not exist, as far as statistical records are concerned, because it was not allowed to exist. Workers would go to their workplace irrespective of whether there was work for them, that is, there must have been a high degree of what one calls in the West disguised unemployment. Even when factories ran out of raw material or intermediate products and could not produce any goods, workers would still go to their place of work, leaving their shops early. Nevertheless, workers were considered fully employed.

The existence of disguised unemployment in the previous GDR became evident when Eastern German workers moved to the West. The accepted argument was that Eastern German workers matched the West Germans in their work ethics, skill and motivation and could easily be integrated into the West German labour force. Not quite; the work ethics and habits in the two parts of Germany had become rather different. Many immigrants left their new place of work in the early afternoon as they were used to from their previous place of work. There is an important difference though: in the East they had been paid no matter what; disguised unemployment thus provided them with an economic safety net.

(g)   Taxes

Chancellor Kohl based his initial promise that Eastern Germany could and would be absorbed without new or increased taxes in West Germany on a combination of projections: first, there was a singular opportunity, an opportunity that would not present itself again, certainly not in the near future, to unify the two Germanies; nothing must be done that might spoil this unique occasion, certainly not frightening his own people with the cost they would have to shoulder. Secondly, estimates of the cost of unification were based on incomplete and overly optimistic assumptions about the growth rate of the Federal Republic of Germany and the recovery of Eastern Germany after unification. The growth rate would be sufficiently high for increased tax revenues to pay for the cost of unification. Finally, foreign investments in Eastern Germany would help finance some of Eastern Germany's investment needs.[12] In spite of these optimistic assumptions, some correctly suspected that the cost figures would have to be revised upwards and that taxes would have to increase.

4 LESSONS FROM THE THEORY OF OPTIMUM CURRENCY AREAS

The application of the theory of optimum currency areas to the German situation should have given sufficient warning against monetary union at so early a stage in the unification process. The two Germanies were far from meeting some of the prerequisites for a monetary union.

The theory of optimum currency areas (OCA) (Mundell, 1961), developed in the 1960s, has been relevant for the period preceding the EMS and GEMSU and for the current plan to create an economic and monetary union for the countries of the EEC. The OCA model distinguished between national borders with a single currency and economic regions which do not necessarily coincide with national boundaries but which may be suitable for monetary union. OCA theory postulated that an optimum currency area must be 'open' with a large percentage of its output being traded, or an economy with a high ratio of tradables to non-tradables in the output mix of the country (McKinnon, 1963). Factor mobility within an OCA must be high for correcting imbalances through the movement of factors of production; but it was precisely the mobility of labour that was to be reduced through the GEMSU. The two Germanies agreed on policy priorities and the Deutsche Bundesbank has been conducting their monetary policy; but economic performance of the two economies was and has remained disparate. Hence the fear lest Eastern Germany become Germany's *mezzogiorno*.

Was the situation more propitious for the EMS members, that is did they represent an OCA in 1979, or has the EMS reached the status of an optimum currency area as it entered stage I of the road to EMU? The answer to the first part of the question has to be negative in light of diverging policies and increasing inflation differentials shortly after the initiation of the EMS. The crucial difference between the EMS and GEMSU is that in the EMS exchange rate changes were still possible. Towards the end of the 1980s the EMS moved much closer toward being an OCA. For instance, France's inflation rate of 3.3 per cent approached Germany's of 3.1 per cent in 1989 and was lower than Germany's in 1991.

It is interesting to observe, however, that the Delors Commission planned economic and monetary union (EMU) for the entire European Community even though it does not yet qualify as an optimum currency area. However, some claim that OCA aspects nowadays are a good starting point for judging whether the EMS would be able to form an EMU, but no longer carry the same weight as in the 1960s. They postulate substantial microeconomic benefits from one money through the abolition of transaction and information costs. The latter reduces the potential for segmenting markets and thus fosters competition. Physical and financial capital mobility are much higher than in the 1960s, when exchange controls and restrictions to capital movements existed in most countries, replacing the importance of labour mobility; wage rigidity may be less than OCA theory assumed; analysts assumed that exchange rate variability was a form of price flexibility that would not impart inefficiencies upon the economy (Commission, 1990), a contention which is no longer widely accepted.

5   THE EUROPEAN SINGLE INTERNAL MARKET

A study of the future of the European Monetary System requires a look at expected monetary developments in conjunction with the completion of the European internal market set to start on 1 January 1993. Expectations range from reduced exchange rate pressures within the EMS, even as capital controls are removed, to the conviction that only with European economic and monetary union can the benefits of the Single Internal Market be reaped (Folkerts-Landau and Mathieson, 1989). Ironically, the EC appears to be making greater strides in monetary integration than in the real sector.[13]

At its 27–28 June 1988 Hanover meeting, the European Council established a committee under EC Commission president Jacques Delors 'to study and propose concrete stages leading towards economic and monetary union' (Committee, 1989) and at its December 1990 summit the European Community began the first in a series of intergovernmental conferences to negotiate the constitutional foundations of European economic and monetary union and the creation of a European central bank. These negotiations culminated in the Maastricht negotiations of 9–11 December 1991 and the signing of the Treaty on 7 February 1992.

(a)   Salient Features of the Delors Committee Report[14]

Economic and monetary union is to be reached in three stages. In stage I, which started on 1 July 1990, the EC will intensify policy coordination in order to create greater economic convergence to parallel the completion of the internal market in the real sector. Capital controls were eliminated at the beginning of July 1990, with the exception of countries 'in extreme conditions' (Greece and Portugal). All EC countries have to join the EMS and accept the narrow exchange rate band of the ERM during Stage I.[15]

In Stage II central banks would move from policy coordination to a common monetary policy. While exchange rate changes in the ERM would still be tolerated *in extremis*, other policies are also to be resorted to and official exchange rate operations involving non-member currencies are to be coordinated. It is in this stage that a new institution ought to be created – the 'European System of Central Banks' (ESCB) consisting of a European central bank (EuroFed) which would increasingly take on responsibility for EC monetary policy.

In Stage III, the final stage, exchange rates will be irrevocably fixed; a single European currency will replace national ones, and the Community will move to full EMU. The Community will have a single monetary policy through the ESCB and the Community institutions will coordinate international policy with non-Community countries.

(b)   Convergence and the Economic and Monetary Union

The Commission of the European Communities estimated recently that about half the EC countries (Germany, France, Belgium, the Netherlands, Luxembourg,[16] Denmark and Ireland) could advance to EMU without great difficulty in light of their converging inflation and cost trends. Italy, Spain and the UK could make the necessary adjustments within a few years, and only Greece and Portugal are the laggards (Commission, 1990). Accordingly, Spain, the UK and most recently Portugal have joined the ERM,[17] while Greece will join later.

(c)   The Sovereignty Issue

The current drive towards the creation of a European central bank and an economic and monetary union for the European Community raises the issue of sovereignty anew. The Deutsche Bundesbank under its previous president, Karl Otto Pöhl, and his successor, Helmut Schlesinger, had reservations about the wisdom of starting with the first stage toward a European central bank and then rushing via the second and third stages into EMU, before the countries' economies converged. Chancellor Helmut Kohl and especially his foreign minister, Hans-Dietrich Genscher, were pushing for more rapid integration, even before the unification of Germany, and with more vigour since then. In England, monetary integration has remained a major political issue to this day, though Prime Minister Major has softened the tone of opposition.

Fearing interference by the centre, that is by the Commission of the European Community, the European Council of Ministers or the European Parliament, a country might object to closer institutional integration. Denmark, in its referendum of 2 June 1992, rejected – though by the narrowest of margins – the Maastricht Treaty.

The Bundesbank's hesitancy about a European central bank is reminiscent of its stance predating the creation of the EMS. The Bundesbank was concerned that its anti-inflation policy, which had gradually been accepted by other, but not all EMS central banks[18], would be compromised if the Commission or the European Parliament involved itself in monetary policy directly or through the European central bank, since the Bundesbank's stability-oriented policy was habitually assailed within and outside of the Community, and since central bank independence of political pressure facilitates the achievement of the price stability goal.[19] For Britain's Mrs Thatcher, on the other hand, the issue that deterred her was less that of price stability – the UK's inflation rate accelerated in the late 1980s – than the prospect of undoing her policies. As she declared in her famous Bruges (Belgium) speech in September 1988: 'We have not successfully rolled back the frontiers of the state in Britain only to see them reimposed at a European level, with a European super-state exercising a new dominance.'

European Community countries, Britain included, have gradually been losing monetary sovereignty through the operation of the European Monetary System and its exchange rate mechanism (Britain's non-membership of the ERM did not guarantee her insulation from EC and EMS developments) and it will decline even further as the EC moves toward the completion of the internal market by removing the remaining barriers to the free movements in trade of goods and services, capital and that of people, the so-called 'four freedoms'. Most countries, even if their currencies were independently floating, could not exercise independent monetary policy for long. Greater interdependence has limited the time consistency of intertemporal choice between joining a pegged-rate system and somewhat greater policy independence (Guitián et al., 1988). The trade-off between exporting imbalances under fixed exchange rates, on the one hand, and choosing the speed and instruments of adjustment under flexible exchange rates has largely vanished. If independence for Community countries were still available, at least for the short run, then the issue would be one of timing with regards to joining a currency union.

Institutional differences, such as the degree of independence of national central banks, or the potential conflict between external and internal economic stability, had to be ironed out before the establishment of the EMS. They have, nevertheless, remained a source of friction on the way to the ECB. Even if national governments or their central bankers agreed on the goals, they might nevertheless pursue incompatible policies, given differences in their understanding of the workings of their economies, and the possibility that their policy mix, while correct internally, will produce undesirable results from an international perspective.

We have witnessed a gradual shift in the targets of central banks. During the Bretton Woods system and the initial stages of the EMS, countries had generally expected central banks simultaneously to pursue the four macroeconomic objectives: reasonable full employment, price stability, sustainable growth rates and balance of payments equilibrium.[20] The ranking of these goals, though, had been changing over time and differed among the various countries. Recently, monetary authorities seemed to have been concentrating on the price stability goal. Secondly, since the early 1980s the link between monetary aggregates and nominal gross national product has been weakened in most industrial countries in the wake of regulatory control changes and institutional innovations. Thirdly, closer international linkage through the freeing of capital movements has 'complicated the link between the monetary component directly controlled by the authorities (domestic credit) and monetary growth' (Folkerts-Landau and Mathieson, 1989). Fourthly, other countries besides Germany have realized that the inflation–unemployment trade-off could not be used as a policy tool for the longer run. Inflation, easily generated, did not reduce unemployment but was a part of the problem.[21]

(d)   Germany and the European Community

Members of the European Community, France in particular, expressed concern that West Germany, being preoccupied with the process and the problems of German unification, might lose interest in moving towards further European integration, slowing the process toward monetary union and the creation of a single European currency. Consequently, Delors pressed ahead with the integration process and the timetable in an effort solidly to anchor Germany in the EC camp. What these observers might have overlooked is that EC membership presented Germany with an opportunity not to have to shoulder the cost of integration alone, but to make it, at least partly, a Community responsibility.

'Europe 1992' with its four freedoms has stirred the emotions of many Europeans. But there is also fundamental misunderstanding, primarily in non-EC countries, about the significance of that date. We are not talking about a deadline by which everything has to be in place as if otherwise the European Community would break apart. Rather, 'Europe 1992' is part of an ongoing process, one that started a few years back and will continue after the date has passed. Furthermore, even though some polls seem to indicate that there are some second thoughts about the desirability of introducing a Single European Market, the polls are by now of minor importance, since business firms have started to behave as if '1992' is around the corner and will take place; investments and mergers activity, both within nations and more significantly intra-Community, has intensified over the last two years. There is no turning back, even if there are some hesitations now and then. The German economy is one of the best prepared for the single European market because of its competitiveness and relative openness ever since the German currency reform of 1948 and its export-oriented economy.

6   CONCLUSION

What, if anything, can we say about the outlook for the short and medium run in light of the disillusionment that followed the initial euphoria over German unification? It was only natural that disillusionment would follow after the exaggerated expectations. While catching up with Western Germany's standard of living, productivity and quality are not as easily upgraded as some wanted us to believe; the task will also not be as difficult as the doomsayers now argue, provided policy-makers do not make major mistakes *en route* by, for instance, reverting to more protectionist policies. Here the successful conclusion of the GATT negotiations has to play a major role. The danger is that the importance of GATT is being downplayed and that trade between blocs that could lead to economic warfare will replace multilateral trade.

It might be ironic that Germany, which took the 'economist' stance against the 'monetarist' camp in the discussions preceding the establishment of the EMS, ignored its own position and insight when it came to GEMSU. Of course, like the creation of the EMS, GEMU and GEMSU were political decisions, as is the creation of the EuroFed. However, in order not to repeat past mistakes, Pöhl recently warned the Commission of the European Communities as well as the other central bankers and ministers at the intergovernmental conference, to learn from the past, especially from the mistakes with GEMSU. And yet there probably was no realistic political or economic alternative to rapid progression toward GEMSU.

While it is as tempting to give in to the gloom of the recent discussions as it was to express euphoria last year, we may not be too far from the truth if we try to find it somewhere in the middle, especially when we are mindful of the J-curve phenomenon. But alas, economists, too, are fashion-conscious in their own way.

NOTES

1. At the beginning of June 1991 the CDU suffered its third election defeat in a row, this time in the city-state of Hamburg.
2. Belgium, Denmark, France, the Federal Republic of Germany, Ireland, Italy, Luxembourg, the Netherlands and the United Kingdom. Greece joined the EEC in 1981 and Portugal and Spain in 1986.
3. I shall use the terms 'EEC' and 'EC' interchangeably.
4. This refers to the prime actors, France and Germany, or the representatives of their institutions, the central bankers and finance ministers, rather than the persons themselves.
5. This is not the place for discussing the non-accelerating inflation rate of unemployment (NAIRU) and the shape of the long-run and short-run Phillips curves.
6. The terms 'monetarists' and 'monetarist school' in this context do not refer to the Chicago school.
7. Melitz (1988) argues that 'neither cooperation nor monetary discipline alone adequately' justify the EMS. If monetary discipline benefits the inflation-prone countries, what is Germany's benefit? The cooperative model, on the other hand, cannot explain Germany's dominance of the system.
8. For details, see, for instance, *The Week in Germany*, 26 April 1991, p. 4.
9. Ibid.
10. Ibid., p. 5.
11. Deutsche Bundesbank, *Monatsberichte*, March 1991, p. 12 and June 1991, p. 8.
12. This portion may well be jeopardized in case of internal or external developments such as the attempted Moscow 'putsch' of 18 August 1991.
13. According to a report which the Community's Executive Commission released on 22 November 1990. *The New York Times*, 24 November 1990, p. 38.
14. The following is based on the Delors report.
15. Again, Greece and Portugal were exceptions.
16. Belgium and Luxembourg have already formed a monetary union.
17. On 20 June 1989, 8 October 1990 and 4 April 1992, respectively.
18. Bundesbank President Pöhl was not convinced that all members of the ERM were firmly in favour of monetary stability. 'Bundesbankpräsident Pöhl vor der ECU Banking Association (EBA) am 26. Oktober 1990 in Berlin: Souveränitätsverzicht ist wahres Problem der Währungsunion.' *Börsen-Zeitung*, Frankfurt am Main, 26 October 1990; Deutsche Bundesbank, *Auszüge aus Presseartikeln* (26 October 1990), 1.
19. Recent studies seem to confirm that countries with the most independent central banks are also those with the lowest inflation rates.
20. The ranking was frequently determined by the goal that had become the most elusive which then had to be pursued most vigorously. This approach was prevalent in countries convinced of their ability to fine-tune their economies.
21. The Banque de France, France's central bank, declared that 'all industrial countries have nowadays accepted that price stability is the precondition of steady economic growth'. 'Europawährung?', *Zeitschrift für das gesamte Kreditwesen*, 1 May 1989; quoted in Deutsche Bundesbank, *Auszüge aus Presseartikeln*, 36 (2 May 1989), 8. Such an attitude in 1982 would have averted the major EMS crisis of March 1983.

REFERENCES

Akerlof, G.A., Rose A.K., Yellen J.L. and Hessenius H. (1991), 'East Germany in from the Cold: The Economic Aftermath of Currency Union', *Brookings Papers on Economic Activity*, **1**, 1–87.

Bulletin of the European Communities (1970), 'Report to the Council and the Commission on the Realization by Stages of "Economic and Monetary Union" in the Community', Supplement 1/70.

Calvo, G.A. and Frenkel J.A. (1991), 'From Centrally Planned to Market Economy', *International Monetary Fund*, Staff Papers, 38, 268–99.

Commission of the European Communities (1990), *European Economy*, **44**.

Committee for the Study of Economic and Monetary Union (1989), *Report on Economic and Monetary Union in the European Community*, Luxembourg (?).

Dornbusch, R. (1986), *Dollars, Debts, and Deficits*, Cambridge, MA: MIT Press.

Folkerts-Landau, D. and Mathieson D.J. (1989), *The European Monetary System in the Context of the Integration of European Financial Markets*, Occasional Paper 66, Washington, DC: International Monetary Fund, October.

Guitián, M., Russo, M. and Tullio, E. (1988), *Policy Coordination in the European Monetary System*, International Monetary Fund, Occasional Paper, 61, Washington, DC: International Monetary Fund, September.

Lipschitz, L. and McDonald, D. (eds) (1990), *German Unification. Economic Issues*, International Monetary Fund, Occasional Paper, 75. Washington, DC: International Monetary Fund.

McKinnon, R.I. (1963), 'Optimum Currency Areas', *American Economic Review*, **53**, 717–24.

Melitz, J. (1988), 'Monetary Discipline and Cooperation in the European Monetary System: A Synthesis', in F. Giavazzi, S. Micossi and M. Miller (eds), *The European System*, New York: Cambridge University Press, pp. 51–79.

Mundell, R.A. (1961), 'A Theory of Optimum Currency Areas', *American Economic Review* **51**, 657–65.

13. The Unification of Germany, the Deutschmark, and European Monetary Union

Wolf Schäfer

1 THE PROBLEM

The fact that the unification of Germany has now been completed calls for an analysis of its economic consequences. Seen from an economic point of view, the unification of Germany constitutes the integration of two national economies with different sectoral structures and a divergent level of development. In this respect, the theory of economic integration provides an adequate basis for an impact analysis of the unification. The process of integration in Germany will be characterized by the following circumstances:

1. A tremendous structural change will occur, not only in the former GDR but also to some extent in the western part of Germany. With respect to integration theory, this means that comparative advantages that are oriented towards world standards will have to emerge. In the process, considerable trade creation and trade diversion will occur.
2. Capital mobility will play an important role in the process of structural adjustment. The states in the former GDR will require large capital and technology imports in order to become locationally competitive on an international level. During the process of attaining this competitiveness, comparative locational advantages will frequently change.
3. Starting from a comparatively low level of productivity and with largely obsolete capital stock, the economy in the former GDR will presumably, after going through an initial contraction phase, develop a high rate of growth.

Against the background of this complex scenario, this chapter intends to address the special issue of how the process of integration in Germany will affect the external value of the Deutschmark. The analysis of this issue is based on the following line of reasoning. When, as a result of economic integration, considerable structural adjustments occur – especially in the new German states – the adjustments in the real sector will also have an effect on the real exchange rate of the Deutschmark. As a result of the previously misdirected structuring of production and trade in the GDR, the relationship between tradables and non-tradables will be especially subject to sectoral shifting.[1] Using internationally tradable and non-tradable goods as sectoral divisions would thus seem to provide a framework well suited to analysing the effects of integration on the external value of the Deutschmark. This well-known framework in international economics will serve as the basis of the analysis presented here.

If one uses a functional distinction between tradables and non-tradables, then goods are to be assigned to the foreign trade sector if they are directly subject to international pricing. This means that prices for tradables are determined basically by price levels on the world market, whereas the prices for non-tradables are determined by the domestic supply and demand situation. As a result of sectoral structural change concomitant to the unification of Germany, it is to be expected that there will be considerable shifts in the output and price reactions between tradables and non-tradables. The question that arises itself is therefore what effects such structural shifts could have on the real and nominal external value of the Deutschmark. To answer this question, the following considerations are necessary.

2   THE NOMINAL AND REAL RATE OF EXCHANGE

Define the nominal exchange rate in the usual manner[2] as

$$e_n = P_T - P^*_T, \tag{1}$$

where P_T (or P^*_T) is the price level of domestic tradables (or the corresponding level abroad). Further, define the real exchange rate as

$$e_r = e_n - (P - P^*), \tag{2}$$

where P (or P^*) is the general domestic price level (or the corresponding level abroad). Equations (1) and (2) yield

$$e_r = (P_T - P^*_T) - (P - P^*). \tag{3}$$

The general domestic and foreign price levels are determined as a function of the prices of tradables and non-tradables. With a linearly homogeneous relationship, the following is obtained:

$$P = aP_N + bP_T, \qquad a + b = 1; \tag{4}$$

$$P^* = a^*P^*_N + b^*P^*_T, \qquad a^* + b^* = 1; \tag{5}$$

where P_N (or P^*_N) is the price for domestic (or foreign) non-tradables, a and b (or a^* and b^*) represent the share of the individual commodity batches in the total domestic (or foreign) expenditures. Equations (3), (4) and (5) yield the real exchange rate:

$$e_r = a(P_T - P_N) - a^*(P^*_T - P^*_N). \tag{6}$$

Using (2), (4) and (5), the following is derived:

$$e_r = e_n - (aP_N + bP_T - a^*P^*_N - b^*P^*_T). \tag{7}$$

This equation allows us to recognize the determinants of the real exchange rate: with given conditions abroad, and with sector sizes remaining constant, the real exchange rate changes when the nominal rate and/or the price relationship between tradables and non-tradables change.

These considerations provide the basis for a further analysis of the effects of the unification of Germany on the exchange rate for the Deutschmark. Because of the backlog of demand in the population in the former GDR, the transfer of income to this region and the increases in factor income that will occur there in the medium and long term, the demand for tradables, and especially for non-tradables (i.e. services), will increase. This increase in demand will, in turn, increase the internal absorption. If price controls are abolished or gradually relaxed, as is already the case for the most part, such an increase in absorption will bring about an increase in prices. Whereas tradables, however, are basically subject to international price levels, which do not change, or change only slightly, as a result of absorption, prices for non-tradables will rise. Thus, apart from there being an absolute increase in the price of tradables, there is also a relative price decrease *vis-à-vis* non-tradables.

This analysis can be refined if we describe the determination of the prices for tradables and non-tradables in more detail. As is usual in open macroeconomics, we assume vertically integrated sectors which are (more or less) independent of each other. Using markup pricing, we obtain

$$P_N = g_N + w_N - \pi_N, \text{ and} \tag{8}$$

$$P_T = g_T + w_T - \pi_T, \tag{9}$$

where g is an expression for the markup on unit labour costs,[3] w is the nominal wage, and π is the labour productivity, each in the respective sectors. Based on equation (6), the real exchange rate is thus

$$e_r = a(g_T + w_T - \pi_T - g_N - w_N + \pi_N) - A, \tag{10}$$

where $A = a*(P*_T - P*_N)$ is the given conditions abroad. The relationships between changes in wages and productivity in the tradables and non-tradables sectors are thus of decisive importance for the development of the real exchange rate. Whereas wage increases in the tradables sector which exceed productivity growth cause a real devaluation, the same constellation in the non-tradable sector leads to a real upward revaluation. Whether wages (especially) in the former GDR will develop sector-specifically in line with productivity[4] is thus important to answering the question of how German unification will affect the exchange rate for the Deutschmark.

3   WAGES, PRODUCTIVITY AND THE REAL EXCHANGE RATE

A crucial problem manifests itself here, one that represents a labour market policy dilemma. Wages in the former GDR are not in line with labour productivity: they are higher and seem to be decoupling from productivity to an ever-increasing extent. This can be explained by the fact that productivity appropriate wages obviously are not compatible with the conditions preventing the migration of labour from the Eastern part of Germany to the Western part. Whereas the demand side of the labour market is calling for productivity-appropriate wages so that jobs will either be preserved or created, the supply side expects 'stay-put' wages that, from the point of view of migration incentives and the social acceptance of regional wage differentials, are not very much lower than the wages in the older part of the FRG.[5] This aspect of the problem is what is causing the pressure to adjust the nominal wages in the Eastern part of Germany to those in the Western part, a pressure that is increased by expectations in areas of employment, such as the civil service, in which wage levels are not primarily determined by market forces anyway.

While one can thus expect that the short- and medium-term development of productivity in the new states will, on average, not keep pace with wage increases, it is nevertheless to be expected that in this respect there will be sector-specific differences. In light of the international orientation of competition in the tradables sector, it would seem realistic to assume that productivity in this sector will grow faster and more intensively than in the non-tradables sector. If, however, the nominal wages do not tend to adjust to levels in Western Germany in a sector-specific manner, then the gap between wage levels and labour productivity will increase especially in the non-tradables sector – to a lesser degree, by comparison, in the tradables sector. An increase in the prices for non-tradables could then go hand in hand with a markup increase in the non-tradables sector. Since the prices for tradables, on the other hand, cannot change, or can only change marginally, due to their linkage with international price levels, productivity levels that do not keep pace with wage increases imply a reduction of profits in the tradables sector.

However, one has to take the following into consideration: whether, and to what extent, increases in productivity are realized depends greatly on the success of efforts to stimulate capital imports into the former GDR, especially private capital imports that incorporate technical know-how and modern management techniques, and can thus increase labour productivity.[6] Since the capital stock as well as production was previously oriented, for the most part, towards the requirements in the Comecon countries, the result of which was a misdirected specialization that grew out of a decade-long disregard of the basic principles of the international division of labour according to comparative cost advantages, private capital imports are just what is needed to bring about a restructuring of the capital stock appropriate to the conditions of international competition.[7] Because of its orientation towards the international market, this is especially important for the tradables sector, whose production, compared to the non-tradables sector, is (necessarily) relatively capital intensive. An inflow of capital into Germany results in a greater increase in productivity in the tradables sector than in the non-tradables sector.[8] Hence a relative increase in productivity in the tradables sector *vis-à-vis* the non-tradables sector can also be deemed realistic from a capital supply side perspective. This capital-induced increase in productivity aids in mitigating the above-mentioned wage policy dilemma of 'productivity appropriate wages versus "stay-put" wages'. To put it simply: if capital flows in, the workforce does not migrate out.

Thus, the following overall result can be derived using (10):

$$\left| \frac{\partial e_r}{\partial P_T} \right| < \left| \frac{\partial e_r}{\partial P_N} \right|, \qquad \begin{aligned} P_T &= g_T + w_T - \pi_T \\ P_N &= g_N + w_N - \pi_N, \end{aligned} \qquad (11)$$

which means that the real devaluation effect produced by the tradables sector is overcompensated by a real upward revaluation effect produced by the non-tradables sector, so that the Deutschmark on balance experiences a real upward revaluation as a result of the relative price increases for non-tradables.[9] For the medium term, it appears realistic that the unification of

Germany and the sectoral adjustments it induced (in the form of a demand shock) will bring about a real appreciation of the Deutschmark.[10]

4   EFFECTS ON THE NOMINAL EXCHANGE RATE FOR THE DEUTSCHMARK

The question is how this real appreciation trend will influence the nominal exchange rate for the Deutschmark. This question is important especially with respect to Germany's membership of the European Monetary System (EMS), as well as with respect to the process of currency integration leading up to the European Monetary Union (EMU) as envisaged and already partially implemented according to the three phases of the Delors Plan. These circumstances are important for this analysis because the EMS fixes the nominal, rather than the real, exchange rates and because the parity change proviso in the first two phases of the Delors Plan[11] is to be successively limited as early as possible, so that it will have been completely eliminated by the time the third phase is reached.

But how can a real appreciation trend for the Deutschmark be reconciled with the more rigid pegging of the nominal exchange rate for the Deutschmark that is occurring because of the process of monetary integration? The analysis presented here gives rise to the following consideration.

Equation (4) shows that absolute and relative price increases for non-tradables, which indeed cause the real upward revaluation effect, should bring about an increase in the general domestic price level. Should such a general increase actually occur, this then implies that the real upward revaluation of the exchange rate can only take place if the nominal exchange rate remains constant (see equation (2)). A real upward revaluation of the Deutschmark would go hand in hand with an increase in inflation. The fundamental precondition for such a process, however, is that it is accommodated by monetary policy. But if domestic monetary policy is oriented towards maintaining price level stability, then there is no room for monetary policy to support price increases. In this case, a relative increase in prices for non-tradables can only succeed if there is a simultaneous decrease in prices for tradables.[12] This could be brought about by a decrease in the nominal exchange rate (see equation (1)), that is, a nominal upward revaluation of the Deutschmark.[13] The nominal upward revaluation would function as an adjustment mechanism that implicitly brings about an absolute and relative reduction in the price of tradables. Hence, it is clear that the more persistent the German Bundesbank is in pursuing its stability objective, and the more it intends to maintain its reputation by doing so, the greater will be the pressure for a nominal upward revaluation of the Deutschmark that could satisfy the need for a real upward revaluation.

This monetary policy dimension leads directly from a supply-theoretic to a demand-theoretic corroboration of the hypothesis of the appreciation of the Deutschmark. The basis for this is to be found in the present and presumedly ongoing policy mix in the FRG, which in a similar form has already caused the interest rates to rise once in the past, namely in the US after 1982. This policy mix is a combination of expansive fiscal policy and a (restrictive) monetary policy oriented towards maintaining price level stability. The high capital requirements of the German public fiscus for financing the creation of a new infrastructure in the former GDR, together with the relatively strict monetary policy of the Bundesbank, are generating an upward pressure on the real and nominal interest levels in Germany. This upward trend in interest rates will tend to stimulate the demand for the Deutschmark on the foreign exchange markets, and thus will exert an upward pressure on the Deutschmark. Hence, medium-term expectations for an appreciation of the Deutschmark can be substantiated not only from a supply side but also from a demand side point of view.[14]

There is also an additional factor that could stimulate the demand for the Deutschmark and that should also be considered here. If one looks at the developments in the countries in Eastern Europe, it would seem realistic to assume that Germany will probably become Eastern Europe's most important trading partner and, at the same time, its most important lender. There are a number of indications that the East European countries will increasingly use the Deutschmark as their invoicing currency after Comecon has switched over to a convertible currency early in 1991. As long as the currency in these countries is not completely convertible, it seems to be a reasonable assumption that the Deutschmark, along with the dollar, will be used for intra-Comecon commerce. Further, it is to be expected that because of these countries' already existent interdependence with Germany, the required transfer of resources to Eastern Europe will increasingly take place to a large extent via German financial markets.

5 EFFECTS ON THE MONETARY INTEGRATION IN EUROPE

The question arises whether and how the above-mentioned consequences of German unification on exchange rate policy effect progress towards the European Monetary Union as set forth in the Delors Plan and effected in its first phase on 1 July 1990. Of special interest here are the parts of the plan that are relevant to exchange rates. Whereas parity changes, according to the EMS parity change proviso, are still possible during the first phase,[15] in the second phase the proviso only allows central rate adjustments in exceptional situations,[16] and at the same time narrows the official spread. The third and last phase of currency integration begins with the exchange rates being fixed irreversibly and ends with national currencies being replaced by a uniform European currency. According to the Maastricht agreement of December 1991, this will come into effect no later than 1999.

The nominal exchange rates are thus to be fixed as soon as possible by means of a successive limitation of the parity change proviso, that is the exchange rates as an adjustment variable are to be obsolete within the EMS at the earliest possible time. Such a strategy is clearly at odds with the tendency of the Deutschmark towards a real upward revaluation while the Bundesbank is maintaining a policy of stability, which it is doing because it sees the Deutschmark as the anchor of stability in the EMS. This must necessarily put a strain on relations among the countries in the EMS in that pressure is created for a nominal upward revaluation of the Deutschmark against the other EMS currencies. This will have the following consequences.

Should the upward revaluation of the Deutschmark not occur, the other EC countries would be forced to raise their interest rates, which would tend to cause a decline in production and employment in these countries. In other words, with fixed exchange rates, the other EC countries would carry costs of German unification by suffering a reduction in growth and employment levels. These costs would also be increased due to the floating of EMS currencies as a block against non-EC currencies, such as the dollar or the yen. The tendency of the Deutschmark towards a real upward revaluation and the increase in interest rates induced by the trend would bring about, in turn, an upward revaluation of the EMS currencies *vis-à-vis* non-EC currencies, or in other words, the Deutschmark would push up the other currencies in the EC exchange rate group. This would tend to worsen the competitiveness of these countries. On the other hand, an appreciation of the Deutschmark within the EMS could relieve them of the costs of German unification mentioned. The basic dilemma of prematurely fixed exchange rates is that those countries that are pushing forward the process of institutional monetary integration would at the same time have to be prepared to take over the costs of German reunification. And it is doubtful whether they would, or whether their doing so could even be considered a reasonable option. If they were to take over these costs, this would surely lead to their demanding compensation payments, which would reinforce the development of the intra-community transfer payment system (structure funds) already provided for in the Delors Plan. This would mean that necessary exchange rate adjustments that remained to be effected would have to be transformed into transfer payments. Such a transformation would not be allocatively optimal.[17] If the upward pressure on the Deutschmark were to lessen, then the other EC countries would tend to be able to improve their balance of payments on current account *vis-à-vis* Germany because this would stimulate their exports and reduce their imports. This adjustment via the exchange rate would be allocatively efficient and would bring about an increase in production and employment in these countries.[18]

Here we should refer to the experiences with the German Monetary Union which came into effect as a monetary shock on 1 July 1990. As legal tender the Deutschmark was introduced into the former GDR from one day to another almost without preparation or possibility of correction and – from an economic point of view – with a false, i.e. undervalued, exchange rate. In other words, the former Ostmark was swapped on an irreversibly overvalued level. As a foreseeable consequence, the former GDR economy lost its competitiveness overnight. This might not have been so aggravating if the exchange rate between the two German currencies had been allowed to function as an adjustment variable for a sufficiently long period.[19] One can be in two minds whether this option was politically realistic or not but the economic consequences of the German Monetary Union should nevertheless be deeply evaluated and might be a warning to those in Europe who insist on increasing the pace in the European monetary integration process on the basis of the Delors Plan philosophy.

One must ask whether these relationships are being given enough attention in the debate about the European Monetary Union, now that after German unification politicians are pressing forward with the creation of the union. If the second phase of the Delors Plan is to go into effect on 1 January 1994, it would appear that the politicians' time preference rates for European integration are far too high in view of the fact that the structural changes that the 'supply shock' of German unification[20] has set in motion within the EC require a more flexible application of the parity change proviso rather than a forced limitation. Steps toward irreversibly fixing the exchange rates should thus not be accelerated. On the contrary, they should be retarded.

NOTES

1. Tradables are to be understood as commodity batches consisting of exportable and importable (import-competing) goods.
2. Logarithmic notation.
3. $g = \ln(1+g')$, where g' is the markup on unit labour costs. An interesting variant of the inclusion of imported purchased materials and services is provided by Shone (1989, p. 50 ff.)
4. The reason for the emphasis in the following on the former GDR is that the relation of wage trends to productivity is the most problematic in this part of Germany. The real exchange rate of the Deutschmark is, of course, determined by wages and productivity in all of Germany, but these are in turn affected by the situation in the former GDR. In order to explicitly indicate the 'GDR effect', one could define the pricing of tradables and non-tradables in Germany as

(4-1) $P_N = \alpha^e P_N^e + \alpha^w P_N^w$, and

(4-2) $P_T = \beta^e P_T^e + \beta^w P_T^w$,

where α^e and α^w (or β^e and β^w) are the eastern German and western German shares of total expenditures for non-tradables (or tradables). Since the purpose of this chapter is to analyse trends rather than to present quantitative calculations, an explicit specification of the 'GDR effect' will not be included.

5. Hence, the dilemma is that employment in the former GDR is not solely determined by real wage levels nor by nominal wage levels. This situation ('*Mezzogiorno* problem') plainly demands that new approaches be taken by wage policy.

6. How necessary capital inflow is becomes clear in view of the fact that approximately 76 per cent of the industrial plants in the former GDR are more than five years old, approximately 55 per cent are more than ten years old, and approximately 21 per cent are more than 20 years old. See Siebert (1990, p. 12).

7. Increased capital imports require that the marginal productivity of capital, or the real interest level in Germany, is attractive for foreign investors. This means that real interest rates must rise rather than fall, which is already the case in Germany.

8. This effect has already been demonstrated by Rybczynski (1955). With a linearly homogeneous production function in the tradables and non-tradables sector, the marginal rate of substitution remains constant in the production of both commodities if the factor 'capital' is increased, but nonetheless the transformation curve for the tradables and non-tradables does shift.

9. The extent to which a relative price increase for non-tradables *vis-à-vis* the tradables can take place also depends, of course, on the income elasticity of the demand for tradables and non-tradables: the greater the relative elasticity for non-tradables, the greater the real appreciation.

10. In the long term, it is to be expected that noticeable increases in productivity will also occur in the non-tradables sector, which will then counteract the trend towards real appreciation.

11. See *Report on Economic and Monetary Union in the European Community* (1989), hereafter cited as *Report*.

12. See also Schäfer (1990b, p. 359).

13. This implicit reduction in the price of tradables via a nominal upward revaluation would take place without the otherwise necessary increases in productivity, or reductions in wages and profit markup.

14. These appreciation expectations fit into the scenario, which gives reason to expect that the trend will be towards a reduction of the balance of payments surplus on current account, which is a result of increased imports and reduced exports (because they were diverted to the former GDR).

15. Each country is to make an effort to make other adjustment mechanisms function better. See *Report* (1989, para. 52).

16. *Report* (1989, para. 57).

17. Apart from bureaucratic costs, the costs concomitant to the transfer payments imply allocative distortions, a reduction of incentives and rent-seeking costs. Altogether, they will cause transfer payments as exchange rate adjustment substitutes to bring about currency union a conditioned negative sum game. See Issing and Masuch (1991, p. 29).

18. In recent years Germany's trade surplus and balance of payments surplus on current account have become increasingly larger in relation to the other EC countries, which has caused some criticism within the EC. If, as a result of reunification, the reduction in Germany's export surplus leads to an increase in exports from other EC countries, then this export pull will, opportunely enough, come at a time when the trend in the other EC countries is towards a slowdown.

19. See Schäfer (1990a).

20. The sweeping changes in Eastern Europe will serve to intensify this shock.

REFERENCES

Issing, O. and Masuch, K. (1991), *EWS, Währungsunion und Kapitalallokation – Neue Perspektiven durch die deutsche Wiedervereinigung*, Preliminary Paper.

Report on Economic and Monetary Union in the European Community (1989), Luxembourg, Office for Official Publications of the European Community.

Rybczynski, T.M. (1955), 'Factor Endowment and Relative Commodity Prices', *Economica*, N.S. **22**, 336–41.

Schäfer, W. (1990a), 'Falsches Bindemittel', *Die Zeit*, 7 February, 27.

Schäfer, W. (1990b), 'Binnenmarkt und Wechselkurs', *Aussenwirtschaft*, **45** (3), 353–70.

Shone, R. (1989), *Open Economy Macroeconomics. Theory, Policy and Evidence*, New York, London and Toronto: Harvester Wheatsheaf.

Siebert, H. (1990), *The Economic Integration of Germany – An Update*, Kieler Diskussionsbeiträge, 160a, Kiel: Kiel Institute of World Economics.

PART V

Political and Economic Reforms in Central
and Eastern Europe

14.   Where is the Keynes of Eastern Europe?

Edward J. Nell

Once upon a time the question was widely asked in Eastern Europe, 'What is the difference between capitalism and socialism?' And the answer came, 'Capitalism is the exploitation of man by man; whereas socialism is just the opposite.' So much for lofty ideals and grand tradition, for the hopes of a society organized by the principle of cooperation and mutual assistance!

The great visionaries of socialist thought had always foreseen a popular and democratic system: no doubt socialism could not be achieved without a struggle, possibly an armed struggle, but certainly it would be overwhelmingly popular, and the idea that it might have to be maintained by a police state never occurred to any of the nineteenth-century architects of socialist ideals. Even Marx and the Marxists considered the 'dictatorship of the proletariat' not only to be temporary, but also to be a 'dictatorship' of the *majority*. But the revolutions of the twentieth century brought in their wake a new realization: that democracy, especially a manipulated democracy, left to its own devices, might choose capitalism. Socialism might require police protection. But the one-party police state, if it ever had socialist ideals, soon developed a life of its own, one that had little to do with the great traditions that had inspired the revolutions – but owed much to the politics of acquiring and maintaining power.

Yet we also forget too easily. Bad as it was, 'real world socialism' had real accomplishments to its credit. It rebuilt the war-devastated economies of Eastern Europe and the Soviet Union, without Marshall Plan aid; it provided education and medical care for whole populations that had never had either; it also supplied pensions and social services. Crime was suppressed, and civil order maintained, in parts of the world that had been in turmoil for two generations or more. The system provided full employment, no doubt with plenty of feather-bedding, but even so, there were jobs of some sort for everyone. And, until reform began, there was no inflation – or rather, inflation was successfully suppressed. A kind of austere egalitarianism was practised, imperfectly, but still evident at all levels; no better testimony can be found than the pathetic inventories of 'wealth' and 'privilege' accumulated by the former leaders, advanced as evidence of their corruption by the popular press; no fuel for the bonfire of the vanities there! Middle-level Wall Street executives have country houses in the Catskills or the Hamptons far more lavish than the fabled dachas of the Kremlin. Many state legislators, let alone Congressmen or party leaders in Chicago, do far better when it comes to corruption! Finally – its most touted achievement, its proudest accomplishment – the system industrialized and modernized backward economies at a prodigious rate in the first two decades after the war, averaging more than twice the rate of growth of capacity of the Western economies.

Lately these achievements have come under fire. The records of the former governments show that many statistics were inflated, that growth was less than claimed, that the quality of many products and services was appalling, so bad as to be unusable, leading to the conclusion that the entire history was falsified. This seems unwarranted. Critical analyses at the time, and later, do indicate that the early years were successful, even discounting the official claims. But after the first two decades the troubles became progressively more serious, until by the mid-1980s they had become unmanageable. The regimes were never popular, and it may be argued that they were never as successful as was once believed, but in the early decades their economic achievements were considerable, especially compared to the later decades. What happened?

Another story may help. After many years of waiting the East German worker was told that his name had arrived at the head of the queue and he was eligible to buy a new car. It would be delivered to the shop, and had to be picked up at once, exactly ten years from this date, to the day. Sign here. 'Morning or afternoon?', he demanded anxiously. 'What do you care, morning or afternoon, it's ten years in the future!' 'Yes, but the plumber is coming in the morning on that day, and I don't want to miss him!'

The Soviet-style economies of Eastern Europe suffered from chronic shortages during virtually the whole of the postwar era. Queues, waiting periods, empty shelves, arrogant salespeople, poor-quality goods – and black markets – were endemic throughout the Comecon during the whole period of Soviet dominance. These are often taken as evidence of a breakdown in supply, a failure of planners, or of the planning system, to organize production properly. And this breakdown was often attributed to the absence of an adequate price system. Improper prices gave the wrong signals and resulted in misallocations, which caused the shortages. But it is not that simple. 'Shortage' turns out to be a complex idea. In the first place it is a market concept, a ratio of available goods to effective demand, demand backed by money, and secondly, both the goods and the demands are generated by the system. Shortage is, therefore, not a purely bureaucratic phenomenon, though it may be a consequence of the impact of planners on markets. But it is not necessarily due to a failure or breakdown of the supply system. Nor need it have anything to do with prices. (Prices are also 'distorted' in Western economies; and very effective economies, like Singapore, also have elaborate systems of subsidies for basic consumer goods.) Shortage appears to arise, instead – and this will be our basic theme – from too generous a system of creating incomes and/or entitlements. Persistent shortage means that the system persistently recreates the imbalance in this ratio. And persistent shortages, as we shall see, whatever their initial origin, also tend to create supply problems, which, in turn, make the shortages worse (Nell, 1991, 1992b; Sawyer, 1991).

DEMAND PRESSURE AND SUPPLY SHORTAGES

A Soviet-style economy has a natural tendency to create excess demand. First, as a matter of ideology it creates a large set of entitlements – to education, to medical care, to pensions, to dwellings, to the fulfilment of citizens' basic needs generally. In many respects this is admirable – but it does create problems when entitlements exceed capacity. (Soviet-style planning aims to fulfil basic needs, but as the Budapest school has pointed out, such systems also arrogate to themselves the right to define needs, a uniquely repressive posture: Brown, 1988.) Secondly, the Soviet system tries to provide jobs for everyone – even when there is no productive work to be done. This distributes purchasing power without creating a corresponding value of goods. Thirdly, the pressures created in the planning system by these commitments – to provide everyone with jobs and a basic standard of living – tend to generate a strong push for investment. The capital base has to be expanded in order to make it possible to meet socialist commitments. No available capacity or labour should be left idle. When these three sets of pressures are combined, it is clear that the resulting system will have a tendency to generate excess demand.

This is sometimes explained, following Kornai (1986, pp. 1–52), as the consequence of 'soft budget constraints', a very misleading phrase. According to this idea, the excessive pressure to spend arises because neither firms nor government agencies nor planners are bound by hard budgets. Funds will be allocated, and projects will be approved, whether or not resources are actually available. By contrast, it is supposed, under capitalism projects will not be approved unless the hard cash is actually there.

Nothing could be further from the truth. Capitalist firms considering investment face no budget constraint at all; modern banking systems create money endogenously, in response to demand. If the balance sheet looks good, the money will be no problem, as long as the system is not in too deep a recession. What capitalist firms have to do, however, in contrast to socialist enterprises, is succeed in the market – the products have to sell at a sufficient profit to cover the expenses and turn a profit. Existing firms are 'constrained', if that is the word, by their current profits and by their unwillingness, on the one hand, to dilute equity (and jeopardize control), and on the other, by the risks associated with further leverage. Potential new firms have to strike an appropriate balance between equity control and risky leverage. In neither case is this a matter of 'budget constraints', and it certainly never comes to a question of cash in hand; the issue is the balance sheet. Good prospects will be funded; if they don't pan out they will be liquidated and others will be taken up. Capital moves restlessly and ruthlessly in search of profits. But it is never subject to strict budget constraints, nor does it have to wait to have cash in hand before acting (Nell, 1991, 1992a).

Contrary to general belief, the economic difficulties of the Comecon 'socialist' systems were not, strictly speaking, due to socialism, nor to the lack of, or interference with, markets. Markets were subject to heavy regulation and controls; there were few *free* markets, but all consumer goods and labour and some capital goods exchanged against money. Prices were frequently adjusted, especially in the later years, in an attempt to relieve the pressures of excess demand. None of these attempts at reform succeeded in any fundamental way. Most of the problems listed earlier – chronic shortages, poor-quality goods, long queues and waiting times, rudeness of salespersonnel and bureaucrats, and black markets – appeared in the US and the UK during the Second World War, when both economies, while remaining unquestionably capitalist, operated as planned systems running under the pressure of heavy excess demand, but selling all consumer goods and labour and most capital goods for money (Argyrous, 1992). In short, the economic difficulties had their origin, not in planning *per se*, nor in the lack of markets and flexible prices, but in the constant and unremitting pressure of excess demand, lasting over a period of almost half a century.

INCENTIVES

The consequences of excess demand do not seem to have been adequately appreciated to date, either by economists or by political commentators. Yet they may well be largely responsible for the breakdown and demise of the Soviet-style systems. Basically, system-wide excess demand pressure changes the nature of the incentives facing firms and retail outlets. Since demand systematically exceeds supply, selling is not a problem; hence no great effort need be devoted to it. Nor do goods always have to meet high quality standards. Even poor quality will move in a seller's market. Nor do costs have to be kept down, since there is no price competition.

By contrast, in capitalism – apart from special episodes like the Second World War – demand systematically falls short of potential supply, forcing firms to compete for sales, which they do, for example, by maintaining and improving quality, keeping costs down, and investing in marketing, packaging and retail merchandising.

The incentive changes set up by excess demand pressure can be seen to have both short-run and long-run consequences; the effects on current production are adverse, but if anything the impact on growth and technological development is even more serious. In regard to current production, both the quality of the goods turned out and productivity tend to deteriorate as workers cease to care about the way production is run and lose the desire to work with intensity and close attention. As for growth, the pressures of excess demand make it harder to turn out the right combinations of goods for investment, resulting in long delays and uncompleted projects. And they also set up adverse incentives for technological progress. These points need to be explained further.

Taking the short-run effects first: the existence of persistent excess demand means that, within limits, whatever is produced will be absorbed by the market. Hence no special effort either to improve or even to maintain quality needs to be made. Products don't have to be improved to ensure that the market will remain loyal, the market will be there anyway; the firm doesn't have to compete with other firms for a limited trade. It's not necessary to make a better mousetrap to have the world beat a path to your door – the world will come anyway, and wait in line, in the hopes of any mousetrap, however flimsy. Over the long run, then, there will be few design improvements, and a tendency to let quality gradually deteriorate.

Workers are placed in an especially strong position. The system guarantees both jobs and job security, which of course encourages feather-bedding, and this is further supported by excess demand, since there is no competitive cost-cutting. Feather-bedded workers can't be pressured into working hard – there is nothing for them to do! But if some workers are expected to do next to nothing, it is difficult to develop strong penalties for poor performance on the part of anyone, unless the shirking becomes really dramatic, or, of course, if political issues get involved. In Soviet systems an elaborate system of worker protection prevented management from imposing any penalties on those who simply did their jobs in a minimal way. Hence workers never had to take great care in seeing that defects were eliminated or corrected. Indeed, there was no special reason for them to care about costs, either; the firms were never engaged in price competition, or indeed, in any other form of competition. True, it was necessary to meet the output goals – but there was never any particular need to cut costs. If the firm failed to turn a profit nothing would happen. And investment funds would still be made available, since in view of the widespread shortages, it was imperative that capacity be expanded. Hence, in such a system, over time, costs will tend to drift upwards, and productivity will stagnate or fall.

If a firm turned in a good record, it might get a bonus so that everyone working for it would benefit. But, notoriously, the bonuses and special treatment often went to those with political clout, as much as to those who actually earned and deserved them. Cynicism tended to undermine the effectiveness of the few strong incentives to improve productivity that did exist. But even those incentives faced the 'free rider' problem. If everyone worked hard, the firm would win a bonus that everyone would share; but if everyone but you worked hard, the firm would still win the bonus, and everyone, including you, would share in it. If everyone worked hard, and the firm didn't get the bonus, everyone would be disappointed – but if you quietly slacked off, at least you wouldn't have busted yourself for nothing. In other words, for any given individual worker, slacking on the quiet is the best strategy. And of course the more apparent and widespread this becomes, the more it will spread still further. Hence, over time there will be a tendency for worker effort, and therefore productivity, to decline (Kornai, 1986; Shmelev and Popov, 1989).

TECHNOLOGY

Now consider growth and technological development. First, just as there is no particular need to improve product quality or design, there is similarly no need to introduce innovations, in the form of either new products or new processes of production. Product innovations will not be welcomed because they will be considered not needed; there are shortages of existing products, and it must seem to planners that it would be more sensible to build the capacity to remedy shortages of goods already in use than to open a whole new can of worms trying to develop something novel. In much the same way it can be argued that process innovations are not needed either. New capacity is needed, of course, and if a new method will clearly work, and can be shown to be superior, it should, of course, be tried. But if there are doubts, or problems, then it would be better, in view of the shortages and the urgent need for capacity, to build to a tried and true design, rather than mess around with something that will take years to get running, that neither workers nor management are familiar with, and which might not be that much better anyway. Innovation risks non-fulfilment of the Plan; with tried and true designs the only thing that will prevent competing the construction of new capacity will be shortages and bottlenecks, which are not the fault of the firm (Shmelev and Popov, 1989).

(By contrast, when there is a shortage of demand, competitive pressures will force firms to introduce new products and try out new processes – if the innovation works, and your competitor introduces it and you don't, you stand to lose the whole ball of wax. But if you introduce it and your competitors don't, you walk off with the trophy.)

Nevertheless, excess demand does create incentives for a kind of technical progress. When demand is scarce, the incentives encourage cost-cutting through breaking down processes and specializing. Expensive workers should not be used on simple jobs; tasks should be broken down, and simplified, so the process can be speeded up; workers should specialize to improve their skills, and do only what they are relatively best at. All these changes will cut costs and speed up production, making it more reliable, and improve quality. They make the firm more competitive. By contrast, shortages create pressures for a different kind of technical progress, the kind that will overcome bottlenecks. The firm can't get on with the job, because they lack equipment, or spare parts. The problem is to make the equipment they have do the work necessary. Can they reshape or reformat what they have to do it? Instead of breaking processes down and specializing, they have to make one kind of equipment do many jobs; it is a kind of generalizing. And it is an important form of technical progress. (It was very significant in eliminating bottlenecks in machine tools in the US in 1942, for example: see Argyrous, 1992.) The best-known example of such a product is probably the Swiss army knife, or perhaps, nowadays, the Cuisinart. What has been called 'baroque' technological development in military procurement (Kaldor, 1981) has resulted in an array of less attractive examples – the aerospace jet, for instance, and various amphibious vehicles, none of which appear to work.

But even when it works there is a cost to technical progress of this kind: a breakdown will generally affect everything that the multipurpose equipment does. If it services two or more processes, then when it breaks down, two or more processes can't run! Thus the more production becomes dependent on equipment of this sort, the more vulnerable it becomes to breakdowns – which, of course, intensifies the incentives to develop new equipment of this kind, another 'increasing returns' cycle. Over the long run, therefore, we can expect to find a growing susceptibility to breakdown (Nell, 1991, 1992).

And it is not only multipurpose equipment that is encouraged. Multi-skilled workers and multi-function departments are required. In a state of generalized shortage, equipment manufacturing firms will concentrate their efforts on the largest, most visible and most congenial jobs. 'Trifles' will be left unattended; especially small, specialized and difficult projects that arise unexpectedly – these will almost invariably be overlooked, or put to the end of the queue, unless they have been factored into the Plan, which will be unlikely, since almost by definition such problems are hard to foresee (Shmelev and Popov, 1989). Repair and maintenance problems, replacements of broken parts, specialized on-the-spot adaptations, and shaping equipment to customized uses all fall into this category. Hence workers will have to learn multiple skills; they will have to know not only how to operate their equipment, but also how to repair it and adapt it to various uses. Factories will find that they have to develop servicing departments, spare parts manufactories, storage for specialized hard-to-get inventories, and systems for producing specialized supplies. And all of this will have to be done by their normal labour force, supervised by the management and designed by their own engineers. Virtually everyone will be doing jobs for which their training has not prepared them, and which lie outside their specialization. A limited amount of this might be a welcome change, but when these activities become crucial to the running of the system the result has to be a decline in productivity.

GROWTH

Finally, demand pressure makes it virtually impossible for the system to grow at its maximal rate. Because there is excess demand, every industry must operate at full capacity (apart from bottlenecks, of course.) But if industries are operating at capacity, bottlenecks cannot be eliminated by further expansion. In a modern mass production economy, industries are interdependent; so overall growth will be constrained by that industry whose net output is the *least*, when considered in relation to the amount of it required in the aggregate (that is, by all other industries) as intermediate input. This ratio is sometimes called the 'own-rate of growth', because it expresses the amount available for investment in relation to the amount required in current production. It can be shown that the growth rate will be maximized when all the 'own-rates' of basic investment goods are equal, and it can further be shown that if any one good has an own-rate higher than this balanced rate, some other or others must have a lower rate (Pasinetti, 1977). But since every one of these goods is necessary, directly or indirectly, in the production of all goods, the lower rate will be binding on the system as a whole! (By contrast, in a capitalist economy, operating under conditions in which there is normally a good measure of slack – excess capacity – bottlenecks can easily be overcome by increasing the rate of capacity utilization of the producers of whatever is in short supply: Nell, 1992a.)

Planners, of course, will try to set targets so that a maximal growth rate can be achieved. But the process of planning and the setting of targets became highly politicized, undermining the effort to achieve a balanced rate. In addition, incentives were set to encourage overfulfilment, apparently in a complete failure to understand that overfulfilment *lowered* the growth rate! The more some industries overfulfiled their quotas, the more other industries (or, eventually, those same industries, later) would find themselves facing shortages and bottlenecks. Demand pressure, of course, would lead firms to stockpile and hoard, which again would create unexpected shortages elsewhere. For all these reasons, over time outputs would tend to move away from the balanced path, causing the growth rate to fall further and further below the maximal rate. But as growth slackens, planners and political leaders will step up the pressure to produce, and to build more capacity, thereby further intensifying the demand pressure.

WHAT ARE THE LESSONS?

There is a minor and a major lesson to be learned here. The minor, and obvious, lesson is that excess demand – suppressed inflation – has serious effects, effects which, in fact, don't disappear when prices are allowed to rise. The fact that the inflation is suppressed does not eliminate the dangers; it changes their nature. The problems of suppressed inflation arise from the pattern of incentives created by demand pressure, which tend to undermine the economy's productivity and technological development. Permitting price increases may not help, because rising incomes are likely to accompany the rising prices, and the effect may simply be to convert suppressed into open inflation – without removing the shortages!

Moreover, deregulating the prices of capital goods will not matter, since the finance for capital goods will normally be built into the Plan; higher prices will be offset by higher finance and there will therefore be no cutbacks of investment or demand pressure. But allowing consumer goods prices to rise may lead to seriously perverse results. First, the rationing or 'allocation' provided by the higher prices simply assigns scarce goods to those who can best afford them, not to those who need them most, in contradiction to socialist principles. Secondly, while sufficiently high prices could, in principle, eliminate excess consumer demand by reducing household incomes in real terms, this need not even affect the excess demand for capital goods! The demand for capital goods is determined by the Plan, as is the projected (but not the actual) supply. Consumer excess demand is essentially a by-product. The imbalance between planned investment and the actual output of capital goods is what creates the system's excess demand; it begins in the capital goods sector and spills over into consumer goods, as the attempt to grow as rapidly as possible generates incomes without a corresponding creation of effective productive capacity. Raising consumer goods prices may remove pressure on consumer goods suppliers, but it does nothing to reduce pressure or increase capacity in capital goods.

The major lesson, however, is that these problems *interact cumulatively*. Demand pressure leads to a weakening of supply incentives, which intensifies the shortages, and leads to further weakening of incentives, and so on. Shortages and productivity problems will compound. Over time, then, especially over a long period of time, if left untended these problems clearly could become very serious, even if at the outset they appeared little more than minor scratches on the smooth surface of the Plan.

And that is exactly what happened. For the Comecon economies never developed an effective set of policies for controlling shortages due to excessive demand pressure. The problem was never clearly identified, and appropriate demand management policies were never even adequately formulated, let alone implemented.

In the early years the official position tended to be that shortages were the consequence of supply problems, and would be overcome by greater effort. Hence the encouragement of 'overfulfilment'. In later years reformers tended to blame the absence of markets and 'rational', i.e. supply and demand determined, prices. If prices could be got right, and if enterprises responded to profit incentives, all would be well. Reforms tended to concentrate on these objectives, but, needless to say, since the problem had little to do with the 'correctness' or otherwise of prices, reform failed to stop the growing shortages and downward spiral of productivity. Incentive schemes were established, including attempts to set up profit incentives, but the failure to earn a profit could not be allowed to override the need for the firm to expand, in order not to worsen the shortages faced by its customers. Unprofitable firms could, therefore, still obtain funds and equipment for capital expansion, especially if they were positioned well in the bargaining process that underlay the Plan. So a lack of profit could not seriously penalize a wasteful firm. The incentives were half-hearted, at best.

Put schematically, we could say that both 'free markets' and 'free planning' lead to a systematic imbalance between capacity and aggregate demand. 'Free planning', that is, economic administration unhampered by constraints, restrictions or incentives arising from feedback from the markets, leads to excess demand, while 'free markets', acting without pressure from government regulations or intervention in response to politically expressed needs, generate excess capacity and unemployment.

The remedy for the socialist system would have been to develop a set of policies to control, in particular to reduce, the pressure of excess demand in response to the public's discomfort; such policies could also have provided at times for the development of excess capacity and competition for sales, in order to put firms to the test and improve cost controls and product quality. Such policies were never developed, and indeed the problem was never correctly identified.

CAPITALISM, BY WAY OF CONTRAST ...

The contrast with the West could hardly be sharper. Capitalism also faces a demand problem, a tendency to generate inadequate, rather than excessive, demand, but it has developed a large and sophisticated array of policies to deal with this problem in virtually any form. (Even though at present a combination of pandering to greed and reluctance to redirect markets on the part of conservative governments seems to have led capitalism into a perilous impasse.) Nevertheless, the tools do exist and they have been used with great success to attenuate the business cycle over the entire postwar era. Of course, many of these policies have multiple dimensions – besides their macroeconomic implications they benefit particular groups, contribute to the election of politicians or parties, or are the unintended outcome of political infighting, in which no one's programme succeeded, leaving the result a hodge-podge of overlapping and partly contradictory policies. Still, a quick survey reminds us of the large set of possible and frequently used options available to manage aggregate demand.

Fiscal policy covers a variety of spending programmes, transfers, subsidies and taxation instruments, which can be adjusted to provide stimulus or restraint both in the short run and the long. The GI Bill of Rights and later programmes of veterans' benefits provided support for household formation that, in turn, implied a stable basis of long-term consumer demand. Government employment and procurement for defence and other purposes can be speeded up or slowed in order to contribute to macroeconomic adjustment. *Monetary policies* include control over interest rates, direct controls over credit, and, less effectively, the 'money supply' (defined somehow), specially targeted loan programmes and subsidies or tax credits for certain kinds of interest payments. *Exports and imports* can be stimulated or restrained through licensing programmes, open or hidden subsidies and taxes, fair trade and fair pricing policies ('anti-dumping') and government advertising and promotional programmes, including tie-ins with foreign aid and international assistance. *Wages and incomes policies* include minimum wage programmes, setting wage and salary levels in government employment and government-operated or regulated industries, tax-based incomes policies (using taxes or subsidies to encourage or discourage wage or price increases), and, of course, direct controls or freezes. *Price policies* include a similar range of options, plus 'yardstick' pricing by government-owned or operated 'model' firms –

the government firms act as price leaders. *Regulations* cover a vast variety of areas, including job safety, consumer protection and product safety, regulation of advertising and claims, anti-discrimination, licensing, regulating traffic on roads, railroads and in the air, regulating communications, the construction and fire safety of housing, zoning and urban planning, underwriting scientific research, and many, many other facets of modern life. These regulations, of course, are designed to protect the public interest in specific ways, but they also very often have macroeconomic implications and can be adjusted to help in the management of demand.

Modern governments have divided these policies into two kinds: 'automatic stabilizers', such as unemployment compensation, which sustains consumption spending in a downturn, and progressive taxation, which reduces spending out of increased incomes in an inflationary boom, and 'discretionary policies', such as changes in specific spending projects, tax cuts or surcharges, and changes in interest rates. Regardless of arguments over particular cases, both have been used to good advantage in every advanced capitalist country since the Second World War. There were simply no comparable policy developments in any country of the former Eastern Bloc. There were no automatic stabilizers, institutional responses that would reduce incomes in response to additional demand pressure. Nor were there discretionary policies to ease demand pressure, or enhance supply without increasing incomes. For the most part the problem of excess demand was not even recognized.

WHY?

The economic policies of the West developed during the postwar period in the course of intense political competition between progressive and conservative political parties, centred around the issue of who could better ensure growth and prosperity while controlling inflation. The position of the governing party was always precarious; it always had to promise improvement – and its challengers were ready to debunk its claims. Policies not only had to sound good, some of them at least had to work. However crude and oversimplified the rhetoric, at bottom the issues were real and the policies mattered – if the economy did not pick up in time the election would very likely be lost.

Politics in the countries of the Eastern Bloc provided for no such competition; nor was there any way for popular discontent with economic conditions to be registered. No alternative programmes could be offered, nor did the ruling party have to prove itself in a political race. Unpopular conditions did not have to be improved; discontent did not have to be mollified. Reforms were seen to be necessary, but there was no immediate urgency about them.

Since discontent could not be registered politically, it made itself manifest in other ways, most notably at work. Discontent showed in cynicism, shirking, stealing from the enterprise or the state, and in a general attitude of distaste and contempt for the system, which translated into lower productivity, poor-quality goods and a widespread sense of malaise. In the end the system could neither function nor reform itself.

THE NEED FOR A KEYNES

Keynes was an intensely political figure; his policies were designed as a programme for the Liberal Party, and to reform the capitalist system in order to maintain it. Policies had to be devised to ensure that the system would deliver the goods. The allegiance of the working class had to be won or won back, with a programme that would control or eliminate the excesses of the system; and this had to be done in competition with socialist parties that sought to abolish or at least radically transform the system. Keynes, Keynesians and liberal democrats generally succeeded in this, and for more than a generation, capitalism delivered the goods. Again, by contrast, no such figure and no such movement ever emerged in the socialist world. The flaws in the Soviet-style systems were never the subject of a 'General Theory' and no array of policies to deal with them was ever proposed, let alone made the subject of political competition.

PROMISES OF SAUSAGES TO COME

What is happening now is acutely paradoxical. Leaders of the former communist bloc seem to have abandoned socialism altogether, and are moving to establish free markets, much 'freer' markets in some cases than have existed in the West since the 1930s, when, of course, such markets brought the system to edge of collapse. In doing so, they are provoking a strong counter-reaction, especially among the working class, who are being asked to bear the major share of the costs of the transition (Knell and Rider, 1992). The people are being offered democracy, free markets and promises of sausages to come – at the price of austerity and unemployment today. But how can it fail? Look at the fabled prosperity of the West!

Yet even as the promises are made, the (in fact, highly regulated) market system of the West has entered a period of deep recession, following, in the US and Britain, at least, a decade of slow growth, and for the first time in the postwar era, deteriorating living standards for the great majority of the population. Keynesian policies are no longer sufficient, it seems, and only a few countries, notably Japan and Germany, have successfully developed industrial policies. In the US especially, but also in the UK, poverty and urban decay have reached crisis proportions; parts of our once-great cities have literally become war zones. Moreover, the growing inequality extends to the international sphere. The division between rich and poor worldwide has become accentuated even more sharply, as development in most of the Third World has faltered. Even the comparatively slow expansion of world industry, however, is proving too much for the environment, and serious problems are developing more rapidly than the ability to deal with them.

In short, just as enthusiasts are celebrating capitalism's greatest victory, the shadows of the future portend its greatest failure. Keynesian policies enabled it to deliver the goods to the working and middle classes of the advanced nations for half a century. But Keynesian policies were never adopted worldwide, and conditions in the Third World have deteriorated alarmingly. Even worse, it now appears that Keynesian policies may no longer be sufficient even to manage the economies of the advanced nations, to say nothing of the world's environmental problems.

A FUTURE FOR SOCIALISM?

So it seems that even in the West some forms of socialism and planning may be more necessary than ever, for all the old reasons – to control and limit the inequities of markets, to take positive steps to redistribute income, limit concentrations of wealth and establish social justice, to ensure rationality in economic organization, and above all, to manage 'externalities', that is, to make rational decisions about goods and production processes that have public dimensions. Some of this will be practised under the label of 'industrial policy', but whatever it is called, it means overriding the market.

Yet the case for doing this is even stronger in the countries of the former Eastern Bloc. Some of the most serious problems are to be found in areas like agriculture, transportation and housing; but the market has always performed badly in such fields. Free markets in agriculture are unstable, while in housing and transports there are social concerns and externalities that the market cannot handle. Education requires reform, but the market will be little or no help. Communications systems will have to be updated; private enterprise is often cited for leadership here – but France Telecom, a state-owned company, has far and away outperformed the privatized British Telecom in the past decade (Costello et al., 1991). Environmental damage will have to be reversed, and further pollution controlled. Incentive systems of various kinds will help, and market pressures should be deployed. But doing so will require careful monitoring and regulation. More, not less, government supervision will be required, and better, not less, planning and bureaucracy. The market works no magic; there is no escape from Leviathan. But we can let ourselves writhe helplessly in its clutches – or we can tame it and make it work for us.

If the fundamental cause of the breakdown of the Eastern Bloc was the failure to develop policies to manage excess demand, and if that failure, in turn, stemmed from the one-party system's deafness to social and economic discontent, together with the lack of a competitive political system, then the movement to 'free markets' is not only not necessary – it may be, and apparently is, for the great working majority, a road not to serfdom, but to pauperdom.

This is made all the more intense by the insistence that austerity policies must be followed in the transition. Real wages must be cut, credit tightened, government industries shut down or sold off, and government spending curbed – especially spending on consumer subsidies and welfare and social programmes. These measures are alleged to be necessary to promote the 'transition to a market economy'. These austerity programmes have brought about a disastrous collapse in living standards throughout the former Eastern Bloc. Yet it is difficult to see why they are necessary.

No doubt real wages could be set too high, and governments can over-spend, and certainly they can spend unwisely, on social programmes. But the common people of Eastern Europe are not wallowing in a sea of luxury today. If anything, more and better social programmes are needed. Moreover it is arguable that credit should be made available, on easy terms, to enterprises that have a reasonable plan to make themselves competitive. If the balance sheet and the investment plan look good, it should not matter who owns the firm. What counts is creating market pressures to perform – to cut costs, innovate, and produce quality goods. The heavy emphasis on privatization and austerity carries a whiff of ideology.

(The development of a private sector able to compete with public enterprises may be an excellent idea. Nor should public enterprises have privileged access to funds. But private ownership, in and of itself, guarantees neither cost-consciousness nor efficiency, nor even the best use of resources. Compared to the Germans and Japanese, US firms overpay top management, plan with too short-term a horizon, and waste potential capital resources paying excessive dividends and fighting off takeovers. There is no magic in privatization, either.)

Most of all, why depress real wages? Can we really expect to make a country prosperous by impoverishing its people? Of course, real wages could be too high – but they can also be too low. Low wages help to perpetuate technologically backward industries, keep the local market small, and encourage out-migration of the adventurous and skilled. Once firms have to meet the market test and succeed or fail on the basis of their balance sheets, high real wages will have a number of desirable effects, both on the supply side and on demand. First, high wages will provide a strong stimulus to cut feather-bedding, modernize and streamline production, and generally tighten productivity standards and expectations of the labour force. Paying high wages will compensate workers for having to change work routines, re-skill themselves and reorient their efforts. It provides the carrot to accompany the stick of unemployment in breaking down worker – and management – resistance to change. Secondly, it will force the closure and liquidation of enterprises that cannot improve sufficiently. Thirdly, high wages will direct investment into high-productivity, high-technology activities, improving prospects for working people in the future. These are likely to be 'leading-edge' industries that will generate further technological advances, stimulating further growth. On the demand side, high real wages mean high per capita consumption demand. This means a market for high-quality goods, and, as employment expands with growth and recovery, a larger market overall for consumer and household goods. High per capita consumption, in turn, allows for more possibilities of household experimentation with new products; it encourages product innovation and technical progress in design, both of which interact with technical progress in production. A high wage economy encourages growth in productivity on both sides of the market – and such growth, in turn, promotes higher wages, in a favourable pattern of 'cumulative causation' (Nell, 1988, Ch. 10).

But such a high-wage high-demand policy would require careful management; it could set off inflation, and it could easily upset the balance of payments. Very likely, it would require selective controls, and managed trade (as in Singapore during the early and mid-1980s). It is risky, but it promises a far better life for the working population. However, it is not conceivable without extensive planning and careful economic management, relying on market incentives, but directed by government. If state agencies are dismantled and the government stripped of its powers, by default the economy will have to rely on 'free markets'.

AN ALTERNATIVE PATH

Rather than dismantling the entire system of planning, it needs to be rebuilt; rather than eliminating regulations, they need to be rewritten; rather than shutting down government and selling off the assets and the enterprises, they need to be reorganized. To be sure, the old system had become so rotten, so corrupt and so fixed in impossible traditions and unacceptable work habits that it had to be swept away. But not for 'free markets'. A new system has to be built, but it should not be a new capitalism of the 1930s!

Indeed, there is no reason why it should be a new capitalism at all. No socialist ideals have been called into question; the concepts are valid, but the system of planning and economic administration was flawed. Being authoritarian, it allowed for no responses by consumers. Yet there are many ways to learn what consumers want, and market-like systems can be used to reward successful firms and penalize others. The old system tended to generate persistent excess demand, and no policies to control this were ever developed. As a direct result the system resisted, rather than stimulated, technical innovation, and tended to undermine rather than promote productivity growth. Market capitalism is superior in both these respects, and when subject to democratic politics, its business cycles and tendencies to recession can be controlled. But market systems at best are hard put to handle questions of externalities, poverty, inappropriate skills in the labour force, environmental damage, and the like. Markets stimulate the development of private goods and services, and provide incentives to private decisions. Where public issues are involved, markets may actually encourage socially damaging activity. Markets are useful and important, but have to be controlled and corrected. The most serious problems facing the former communist bloc seem to be social in nature – revising education, retraining labour, restoring the environment – and where they are purely economic, as in the problems of developing adequate housing, modernizing transportation and improving agriculture, concern fields where market systems have proved inadequate. As a consequence, solutions, even where they rely on markets, will almost certainly still have to rest ultimately on planning and governmental action. A democratic socialism, guided by demand management, may be necessary to manage the problems of externalities and the environment facing the former Eastern Bloc. But this will require filling the shoes of Keynes.

REFERENCES

Argyrous, G. (1992), 'Investment, Demand and Technological Change: Transformational Growth and the State during World War II', PhD thesis, New School for Social Research, New York.

Brown, D. (1988), *Towards a Radical Democracy*, London: Unwin Hyman.

Brus, W. and Kowalik, T. (1983), 'Socialism and Development', *Cambridge Journal of Economics*, **7** (3–4).

Costello, N., Michie, J. and Milne, S. (1991), 'Industrial Restructuring and Public Intervention: Planning the Digital Economy', in J. Michie (ed.), *The Economics of Restructuring and Intervention*, Aldershot: Edward Elgar.

Dahrendorf, R. (1990), *Reflections on the Revolution in Europe*, New York: Times Books.

Davis, C. and Charemza, W. (eds) (1989), *Models of Disequilibrium and Shortage in Centrally Planned Economies*, London: Chapman & Hall.

Kaldor, M. (1981), *The Baroque Arsenal*, New York: Hill & Wang.

Kalecki, M. (1986), *Selected Essays on Economic Planning*, Cambridge: Cambridge University Press.

Knell, M. and Rider, C. (1992), *The Socialist Economy in Transition: Appraisals of the Market Mechanism*, Aldershot: Edward Elgar.

Kornai, J. (1986), *Contradictions and Dilemmas*, Cambridge, MA: MIT Press.

Kornai, J. (1990), *The Road to a Free Economy*, New York: W.W. Norton.

Lipton, D. and Sachs, J. (1990), 'Creating a Market Economy in Eastern Europe: The Case of Poland', *Brookings Papers on Economic Activity*, 1.

Nell, E. (1988), *Prosperity and Public Spending*, London: Unwin Hyman.

Nell, E. (1991), 'Capitalism, Socialism and Effective Demand', in Nell and Semmler (eds), *Nicholas Kaldor and Mainstream Economics: Confrontation or Convergence?* London: Macmillan.

Nell, E. (1992a), *Transformational Growth and Effective Demand*. London: Macmillan; New York: New York University Press.

Nell, E. (1992b), 'Demand and Capacity in Capitalism and Socialism', *Economic Record*.

Osiatynski, J. (1988), *Michal Kalecki on a Socialist Economy*, New York: St Martin's Press.

Pasinetti, L. (1977), *Lectures on the Theory of Production*, New York: Columbia University Press.

Sawyer, M. (1991), 'The Economics of Shortage: A Post-Kaleckian Approach', in J. Michie (ed.), *Economics of Restructuring and Intervention*, Aldershot: Edward Elgar.

Shmelev, N. and Popov, V. (1989), *The Turning Point: Revitalizing the Soviet Economy*, New York: Doubleday.

15. European Integration and Problems of Economic Reform

Christine Rider*

1 INTRODUCTION

Economic restructuring in the former East European socialist economies, the unification of Germany and increasing progress towards the closer integration of the European Community are not unrelated developments. While there is an additional concern in Eastern Europe with personal freedom, democracy and the rule of law, these developments all share a common economic aim: to improve economic performance and raise living standards. Even though the theoretical justification for regional economic integration differs from the theoretical justification for moving from a centrally planned to a market economy, both visualize more productive economies. There is an additional reason for focusing on this similarity, because some of the East European nations have expressed a desire to apply for membership of the EC. In order to be considered for membership, these countries must meet certain conditions, the most important of which is the abandonment of central planning and the introduction of a market economy.

It is unclear whether these economies will progress sufficiently towards the adoption of market mechanisms to make them compatible with the EC economies. There is another important implication. The EC's movement towards monetary unification marks a further step towards the goal of closer political integration. Such political ties among nations are possible only if they share similar political institutions and ideologies. While there is definitely not total agreement, the current EC members do share certain key values. (In fact, one reason for the hesitation in approving Turkey's membership was due to concern over the extent of its commitment to political democratization.) The implication for the potential Eastern and Central European applicants is that much more needs to be done in the area of political change before the same can be said of them. (Discussion of the moves towards democratization, although important, are beyond the scope of this chapter, and will not be discussed here.)

These challenges are no longer a matter of purely academic speculation; events of the last few years have provided a useful case study in the unification of Germany. This experience perhaps offers a foretaste of what is to come when two different political and economic cultures eliminate barriers between them. For this reason, the success or failure and the problems and solutions that emerge will be closely watched for the insight they give to the more general European situation.

This chapter argues that introducing changes in the price mechanism only, without the simultaneous development of other complementary institutions, will not be sufficient to produce successful 'reformed' market economies, hence may make future membership in the EC a questionable proposition. It will be organized as follows. The next section presents a set of propositions to show the linkages between economic restructuring and possible enlargement of the EC. In the third section, the reasons for the economic reforms of the formerly socialist centrally planned economies will be briefly described. The last section evaluates the possibility of successful economic restructuring from four different perspectives: microeconomic (the resource allocation-efficiency problem); macroeconomic (the demand management problem); institutional and behavioural. It will be necessary to achieve 'success' in all of these areas if the restructuring economies hope to have their applications for full EC membership approved, but the partial nature of the reforms in some countries and a failure on the part of their leadership to be realistic about the time frame gives reason for pessimism.

2 CONNECTIONS BETWEEN REFORM IN EASTERN EUROPE AND EUROPEAN INTEGRATION

Perhaps the connection between market reforms and European integration can best be established by progressing through a series of statements and questions which will make clear the similarities of the goals of the economic reformers and those of the EC member countries.

1. First, is expansion of the EC possible? From its very beginning in 1957, and as expressed in the Treaty of Rome, the European Community has never been a closed grouping confined only to the original six signatory countries. Any European country can apply for membership.
2. How has the EC grown in the past? While the original six members of the European Common Market (the predecessor of the European Community) were a relatively homogeneous group, the enlargement of membership to 12 in the 1980s dramatically reduced that homogeneity. The newer members – Spain, Portugal, Greece – are poorer and have

less in common with the more industrialized countries to their north. (See Colchester and Buchan, 1990, and Harrop, 1980, for a discussion of the EC's potential as an enlarged grouping.)

3. Where may future expansion possibilities lie? Some of the East European economies – Hungary, Czechoslovakia, Poland – have recently expressed an interest in becoming affiliated with or a full member of the EC, presumably because they perceive an advantage in doing so.

4. Is such affiliation possible? For the potential members, is restructuring away from a bureaucratically planned economy to a decentralized market economy seen as part of the preparation for affiliation or membership? For the EC, what are the advantages of further enlargement? How compatible would the East European economies be? There are two main issues that are relevant here. First, the structure of the applicant's economy should be more oriented to market mechanisms. The EC's institutions and policies are designed for a particular type of market setting and for market response mechanisms, so it must be assumed that a precondition for membership is possession of an institutional, organizational and behavioural mechanism compatible with the existing members. The second concern relates to the question of ownership. The EC countries are mixed capitalist social democracies, and although some of the East European countries are beginning a process of privatization and introducing more political openness, they can hardly be characterized as entrepreneurial economies or as secure democracies.

5. Economic restructuring and economic integration have similar goals. Economic integration is a way of improving the international allocation of resources, expanding the market to increase competition and encourage new innovative technologies which tap economies of scale; it is, in short, intended to improve economic efficiency and growth potential so as to permit increased production and a higher standard of living. The idea is to enable the members of an integration scheme to capture some of the economic advantages of a large country with a large internal market. Similarly, the economic restructuring now proposed or underway in Eastern Europe is also intended to improve efficiency, thus leading to expanded output levels and faster growth. So in its own right, economic restructuring away from the rigidities of bureaucratic central planning is intended to improve internal efficiency and the functioning of the economy. It can also be seen as a precondition for inclusion in a Europe-wide integration scheme which is itself intended to improve efficiency and economic functioning.

3   ECONOMIC PROBLEMS FACED BY THE FORMER SOCIALIST ECONOMIES

Any economic system, in one way or another, serves the material needs of the society; it is the organizing framework for the production and distribution of the goods and services needed for everyday life. There are many different ways of organizing and influencing the operation of economic behaviour. What makes most modern economies similar today is that they are industrial rather than agricultural, hence relying on longer and more indirect ways of processing naturally occurring materials into economically useful end-products.

A desire to industrialize in order to raise income levels has been characteristic of economies wishing to modernize in the nineteenth and twentieth centuries.[1] The question many faced, especially those starting an industrialization effort late, is how best to encourage it: hope that private entrepreneurs will seize the initiative, or use state-directed efforts? In all the Eastern and Central European economies, the centralized Stalinist version of administrative planning was adopted in the 1940s as part of the effort to industrialize and speed up the process of economic growth.

There were differences in the level of economic development at the time – Czechoslovakia and the German Democratic Republic were the most industrialized, Albania and Romania the least. However, the common element in the industrialization process was to give priority to building a base of heavy industry. A deliberate strategy of central decision making was adopted, with the goal of producing a modern industrial economy as quickly as possible (Asselain, 1984; Bergson, 1948; Hewett, 1988; Ofer, 1987; Zaleski, 1971).

This approach accounts for several basic characteristics of virtually all centrally planned development.

1.   Priority in the use of resources was given to building up heavy industry at the expense of both consumer industries and agriculture.
2.   A system of material balances rather than financial accounting was used to accomplish the plan's goals. This meant that enterprises were allocated resources in physical terms and given output targets to meet.
3.   Planning was taut, meaning that targets were over-optimistic in terms of resources available. The reason for this was partly to motivate the labour force and partly to fulfil the socialist commitment to maximum use of resources at all times.
4.   The role of prices was very different from that in a market economy. A system of subsidies and centrally determined prices was intended to accomplish the aims of encouraging certain types of production while discouraging others so as to speed up growth. However, because they

were rarely changed, they could reflect neither changing resource supplies nor changing consumer preferences, and hence became an element adding inflexibility to the economy.

Initially, the results of the administrative planning experiment were impressive, and growth rates of the planned economies were higher than those of the market economies (World Bank, 1981). But problems resulting from the institutionalization of rigidity began to appear in the 1950s, and various attempts to deal with them were made in the following years. These attempts tried to adjust the planning mechanism, as by the late 1960s it was becoming more apparent that its initial promise was not going to be kept. Unfortunately, simply tampering with the planning mechanism did not work, and the attempt to give a little more authority to enterprises by some limited decentralization was followed by a period of recentralization. By the late 1980s then, the stage was set for a complete rejection of administrative planning in favour of restructuring to introduce a decentralized market economy. What made this period even more memorable was the simultaneous occurrence of events with far-reaching political implications, such as the rise of Solidarity to official power in Poland, the overthrow of the Ceaucescu government in Romania, the disintegration of the Soviet Union and the tearing down of the Berlin Wall.

The problems were due partly to the original goals, partly to the operating mechanisms intended to achieve them, and partly to the paradox that the behavioural mechanisms intended to stimulate rapid growth only made the problems worse. In addition, these economies became more rigid and inflexible, less innovative, and the political input into the planning process, originally justified as adding a democratic element to decision-making,[2] became more and more an obstacle to change while maintaining privileges for a select few. Increasingly, senior decision-making positions in the enterprises and throughout the economic hierarchy went to those well established in the Communist Party hierarchy rather than those qualified solely on the basis of their managerial and decision-making skills.

A list of the problems has to include the following.

1. Intermediate inputs were underpriced, which led to inefficient and wasteful production. Originally the reason for this was to speed up industrialization by encouraging the wider use of intermediate inputs, thus enlarging the market, which would permit their producers to tap economies of scale in production. The unintended results were to discourage innovation and to result in higher intermediate input use per unit of output.
2. Related to this, and of particular relevance for the Soviet Union, was the deliberate underpricing of energy inputs. The point again was to encour-

age the use of modern energy sources, but because efficient energy use
was discouraged, these economies show less energy efficiency per unit
of output than non-planned economies.

3.   These economies exhibit a distressing lack of innovativeness. The prac-
     tice of allocating inputs and specifying outputs in physical terms was
     originally intended to encourage productive enterprises to focus on the
     technical problem of improving efficiency because they were free of the
     necessity to show short-term financial profits. Ironically this did not
     happen, mainly because lack of overall flexibility and an inappropriate
     incentive mechanism discouraged innovative activity. Enterprise man-
     agers were resistant to introducing higher productivity methods or
     methods that reduced input requirements for fear that their output targets
     would be permanently raised or their input allocations cut. Oddly enough,
     in an environment where a dependable, continuing supply of inputs was
     not assured, such an attitude was rational for the enterprise, but socially
     inefficient.

4.   The priority given to industrialization and especially to heavy industry
     resulted in several problems. First, an inefficient agricultural sector
     remains common; in many countries the agricultural sector carried the
     burden of rapid industrialization – via taxation and a lack of priority in
     access to needed resources. Secondly, all countries have an inadequate
     infrastructure – especially transportation – which exacerbates distribution
     problems. In a few cases, the problem is not so much absolute shortages
     of goods but getting them to users. Thirdly, both consumer goods output
     and output of light manufacturing industries were sacrificed to the needs
     of heavy industry, but the sacrifice never paid off and has never been
     made up. The failure of living standards to rise has also added political
     problems.

In summary, the problems faced by the socialist planned economies include
poor overall efficiency, low growth rates, shortages of consumer goods (and
a parallel phenomenon, the appearance of black markets), poor quality of
goods and the potential of social unrest. While a variety of non-market, non-
plan devices emerged in response to these problems, they served only to
deflect attention from the overall problems by permitting localized solutions.
Some of these devices, such as enterprise hoarding of labour or materials,
helped the individual enterprise, but only exacerbated the overall tendency
to shortages coexisting with bottlenecks.

Because of the way these centrally planned economies operate, they have
been described as 'resource constrained' economies (cf. Kaldor, 1985; Kornai,
1979). Rather than being constrained by a lack of effective demand as in
capitalist economies, they are limited by resource availability, and there is

excess aggregate demand occurring when the economy functions at 'normal' levels of capacity utilization. Together with the fact that they also incorporate various socialist principles, this explains both the paradoxical situation of shortages coexisting with localized bottlenecks and half-finished projects and the behavioural response which only worsens the situation. That is, given the policy decision to maintain full employment (which means that in principle there is no buffer of unemployed labour power), and given the desire to speed up economic growth, there is overinvestment. The official commitment to high investment also meets the interests of the individual enterprise, especially where competition between enterprises is not horizontal competition for market share and customers but a struggle with the central bureaucracy for preferential access to resources, a struggle in which size and political connections are important. That is, the obvious response to a shortage situation is to expand productive capacity to make good the shortage, but this puts pressure on resources and the lack of one can hold up completion of an entire project, which has ripple effects across the economy. Also, because an individual enterprise's prestige and ability to get favourable access to resources was closely correlated with size, an enterprise was also under pressure to expand – a proposal for a new investment project was rarely rejected, but again simply served to add to the pressure of excess demand.

Although efforts at reform date back to the 1950s,[3] they only tampered with the basic planning mechanism. By the late 1980s, somewhat earlier in Hungary, there was growing recognition that more than just tampering was needed. Perhaps because of the political developments that were also occurring – increasing demands for more democratic procedures, for example – serious consideration was given to introducing more decentralized market mechanisms as a feasible alternative to centralized planning.

4   EVALUATING THE REFORMS

The two key words behind the reform process are marketization and privatization. Marketization implies introducing institutions and structures that will permit the generation of and response to price signals; privatization involves permitting new forms of private and cooperative ownership.

Some of the key elements of the marketization reforms are as follows:

- Decentralization of the economy will be accomplished by reducing the authority of the planning bureaucracy.
- At the same time enterprises will become decision-making units, responsible for their own production decisions.

- Enterprises will also become financially self-sufficient, responsible for financing their own capital needs. They will be subject to a hard budget constraint, and will no longer be able to rely on unlimited access to the state treasury for funding, which had previously contributed to the overinvestment tendencies.
- The first step towards price reform will be an elimination of subsidies; the aim is that prices should reflect production costs – that is, they are to become scarcity indexes.
- Finally, because financial signals will be given more importance, certain new institutions will be introduced. These include a revamped banking system composed of (profit-seeking) commercial banks able to extend loans, and a central bank with supervisory functions; a stock exchange and stockbrokers able to facilitate the transfer of ownership shares; an accounting system able to generate and record the information needed by enterprise managers and investors; new legal institutions capable of dealing with, for example, contracts, agency relationships and the possibility of bankruptcy.

The justification for such restructuring is the presumption that the market mechanism will improve efficiency and increase output levels – that is, that it is more desirable and will result in the production of maximum output and maximum satisfaction at minimum costs. It therefore places the idea of an inefficient planned economy in opposition to the image of a well-performing market economy. On the one hand are the socialist centrally planned bureaucratic economies characterized by inefficiency, low consumer satisfaction and shortages, and on the other hand are the capitalist market economies characterized by efficiency, high consumer satisfaction, high levels of output and low costs. While some of these characteristics may appear, the dichotomy is false, although it is a mistake that is commonly made (Nell, 1992). All economies rely on bureaucratic procedures (no large organization can be run without them) and all require market exchanges (to effect transfers of ownership of goods, for example). However, if the reformers are of the opinion that restructuring will in fact have these particular results, then it is possible to formulate an appraisal. This will focus on four levels. The microeconomic level will deal with the questions raised by the price reforms, which have a particular relevance to efficiency. At the macroeconomic level, attention will turn to the problems of demand management and policy issues. Then it is necessary to appraise the institutional changes, as without the correct institutions, even a perfect design will perform poorly in practice. Finally, at the level of the individual, it is necessary to consider whether the right behaviour will be forthcoming.

To deal with the microeconomic issues first, according to the textbooks efficient resource allocation results from the operation of a flexible price mechanism working within an economic system that has certain characteristics. Ignoring for now all the other things that prices do (such as signal change, finance growth and be used to accomplish an enterprise's market strategy, for example) so as to focus on their allocative role, can the suggested price reforms achieve these goals? The problem is that even in a capitalist economy the conditions required for achieving efficient resource allocation are not met in reality. This means that, no matter how flexible the market, the actual price will not be a scarcity price which equates the marginal resource cost of the resources used to produce the last unit with the marginal satisfaction buyers gain by acquiring one more unit.[4] Because it does not produce an equality in this way, it is possible to identify other resource allocations that increase social welfare.

This failure also puts into question the unleashing of the profit motive as a stimulus to action in the restructured economy. In the textbooks, profit has a special role to play in reallocating resources in response to changing conditions; for it to do this also requires certain elements to be in place. If the equilibrium price described above is reached, all resources are being paid exactly what they are worth, which means that the owners of capital are receiving a rate of return on invested capital that is uniform and equal in all lines of production. Now if prices change for any reason – such as a change in consumer preferences or technology or resource supplies – then pure economic profits or losses appear. Capital owners respond to this by shifting capital out of areas where below-normal rates of return are being earned and into areas where above-normal returns are being earned (and in the process, restoring a tendency to uniformity of the rate of profit). This movement in response to the desire to make profits and avoid losses theoretically accomplishes many desirable ends: attention to consumer wishes, efficiency, maximization of output, economic flexibility and dynamism.

The stumbling block, of course, is that if these results are to occur, prices must be the textbook scarcity ones; if they are not, then the prices, profits and losses that are generated by the market mechanism will not truly reflect consumer wishes or the true costs of production. The conditions required for an efficient resource allocation are highly restrictive: a closed economy (no trade), perfect knowledge, perfect competition (atomistic agents with no market power), direct exchange of goods (no wholesalers or other market intermediaries), and so on (see, for example, Kaldor, 1966). Refinements which are required to demonstrate the existence and uniqueness of an equilibrium position add even more restrictiveness. They include substitutability of factors in production, linear homogeneous production functions (to rule out increasing returns to scale), no technical progress, no productivity improvements due to learning, no market power, no externalities, no uncertainty, no obsolescence and no debt-issuing government (which would 'deneutralize' money) (see, for example, Kaldor, 1972, 1979).

Of course none of these characterize a real economy, which makes it too easy to criticize the model providing a rationale for marketization. To give just a few of the most obvious discrepancies: factors are complementary (capital accumulation also increases employment); industrial processes are not independent of each other; increasing returns via technical change have been a continuing feature of post-Industrial Revolution economies; externalities and economies of scale do exist; monopoly and oligopoly markets are not the only reasons why prices are not scarcity prices; there are productivity improvements through learning; and so on.

The important consideration is that when prices are set by enterprises in a real life market setting, the outcome will not be scarcity prices reflecting opportunity costs. The way prices are established and markets work in the Western capitalist mixed market economies is different from the textbook model, and accomplishes a variety of different aims (Sawyer, 1993). Now if this is the case, then the other evaluative aspects become more important.

This is so because it is the entire functioning of these economies that results in higher output levels and so on, not just because they rely only on the price mechanism (and prices cannot be set in any modern economy along textbook lines) or have more privately owned property. It is neither the price mechanism/profit motive nor private property that is the single key to 'success'. There is, in fact, no single key. We cannot look to so-called national characteristics such as German efficiency, Japanese group loyalty or American individualism for the answer – such national stereotyping is a dangerous, and futile, undertaking. Ultimately what is important is that the 'right' opportunities and motivations exist, and the mix will differ from country to country.

What will also differ is the macroeconomic environment. Western market economies in the post-Second World War era developed a series of demand management policies which, in spite of reversals in the monetarist 1980s, still have an important impact on the macroeconomy. Ideally – and recognizing that other requirements of the capital accumulation process will modify this to some extent – an economy should operate as close to full employment as possible and avoid business cycles via countercyclical demand management policies. The achievement of this goal is recognized to require control over investment, as it is fluctuations in investment that determine fluctuations in aggregate demand and thus in the level of capacity utilization. In practice, such control has been attempted only indirectly, and a variety of so-called traditional fiscal and monetary policies developed instead to modify to some extent the level of aggregate demand. Traditional policies include, for example, taxation (a progressive income tax) and transfers (countercyclical income maintenance payments), preferential taxes (lower rates to encourage business investment), and monetary and credit policy. While taxes and interest rates existed in the centrally planned economies, they were structured differently. For example, taxes were not part of a demand management policy, central determination of both the level and structure of investment tended to result in expansion of investment over time, and the overall expansionary bias resulted in demands for investment financing being met rather than controlled.

This means that the entire structure of government involvement has to be changed to switch to a system in which deliberate macroeconomic policy-making becomes a necessity – which will hardly involve an elimination of bureaucracy. In other words, what has to be thought through carefully is how to structure a tax system to generate revenues for government operation, incorporate equity in tax burdens, and be manipulable for macromanagement purposes; how to operate monetary policy to generate just the right amount of liquidity, and so on. These are not easy functions to introduce and operate in a society unused to them; whether or not they will be successful is also connected with the third requirement, the presence of the right institutions.

Again, mixed capitalist economies work the way they do because institutions have evolved over time to fulfil certain complementary functions. Included here are the various banking and financial institutions, a legal system that protects property rights, an educational system that produces people with the right attitudes and values (as well as labour force skills), an accounting system that makes financial calculations possible, and so on.

Just to give some idea of the changes that will be required by the restructuring economies, we can mention a few. What will be needed include a central bank which has money-issuing powers as well as supervisory and control functions over (new) commercial, profit-oriented banks; changes in the bankruptcy laws (if enterprises are to be financially self-sufficient and no longer dependent on unlimited access to the state treasury, they must also be financially accountable for their mistakes); new educational and training institutions to educate enterprise managers so they are able to make their own decisions; new laws guaranteeing property rights; new institutions facilitating transfer of property; and some type of anti-monopoly policy to prevent abuses of market power.

This incomplete list indicates the immensity of the challenge. Those economies with fairly complete sets of these 'facilitating institutions' took many generations to develop them, and they are still undergoing modification and refinement to meet changing needs. Even when a high degree of sophistication and adaptability exists, as in the US economy, success is not automatic. For example, the savings and loan industry in the US is only the latest in a long line of industries (textiles, steel, consumer electronics, automobiles, semiconductors, for example) to undergo strain if not collapse in the face of a changing environment. The moral of the story is that it is difficult to design institutions that continue to work effectively over long periods of time. It will be very much harder for the post-communist economies which are at the beginning of a learning process. Some of these necessary changes are also the outcome of political pressures – for example limits on pollution or prevention of other environmental damage. The point here is that while it does not take long to introduce laws or policies or physical institutions, it takes much longer for them to be accepted and work adequately – and this time factor has not been well recognized in the restructuring economies.

Finally, and closely associated with this last point, the behavioural element must also be considered. None of the required elements in the restructuring work by themselves; all depend on the human factor. While it is true that some in Eastern Europe – mainly the already-existing entrepreneurs and others who have had links with the West such as intellectuals – can be expected to adopt appropriate behaviour patterns, the overwhelming majority have inherited a deep suspicion of capitalism. After having adapted to the behaviour patterns required for functioning in a planned socialist economy, it will not be easy to switch to those appropriate to the new environment. For example, East Germans, Hungarians and Poles have already been shocked by problems associated with unemployment and homelessness; protests over rising prices of basic consumer goods following removal of subsidies have occurred in Poland, and newly independent enterprises often seem to be wondering what to do next now that no one is telling them.

This problem has two aspects. The first, more easily solvable one, is the aspect of specific training – training managers how to run enterprises, teaching accountants the skills required for recording and analysing financial information, setting up new types of social service institutions to cope with the casualties of the restructuring, for example. The second aspect is more problematic, as it requires changing deep-seated, firmly ingrained convictions, which will require a long process of re-education. Furthermore, many of the values already in existence, such as concern for the economically weak and socially disadvantaged, are socially useful, and should not be suppressed.

In summary, too narrow a focus on price reform and privatization will lead to the neglect of certain crucial institutional and policy requirements associated with the restructuring process, and this will be a recipe for failure. In particular, the approach to price reform based on an impractical model is not useful for understanding how real life capitalist mixed economies work, and therefore does not provide a good basis for restructuring.

Unfortunately, many of the recent reform proposals imagine that there is an either–or choice between markets and bureaucratic central planning; a false dichotomy which we have seen to be illusory. Because of the characteristics of all modern economies, bureaucratic processes are essential. If too much attention is given to the introduction of market processes in the expectation that the state bureaucracy will wither away, the result will be failure. The problem for the reformers seems to come with the assumption that the abstract principles of capitalist market economies are universal and timeless. An application of these principles to the socialist economies in transition that overlooks the entire range of complementary elements that must also be in place is unlikely to be successful.

The best example so far of the dashed hopes of the market reformers has been the experience of the former East Germany since union with West Germany in 1990. Perhaps the massive decline in output and rises in unemployment should have been anticipated, but recent analysis suggests that the economic problems will persist. If this is true for what had been considered an advanced industrial economy, what can be expected for the other East European economies? While East Germany did have certain advantages in its integration with the West – such as financial support from the EC's largest and strongest economy – advantages that others cannot rely on, the magnitude of problems is far beyond what most analysts were expecting (see Kurz, 1992 for a thorough survey of the issues).

It has been estimated that a very high proportion of East German enterprises are unviable in that they cannot cover even short-run variable costs. A feature of German unification, and now of the European Community, is free movement of labour and capital. Taking just the German case first, if these unviable enterprises collapse, what happens next? A movement of labour into the most prosperous areas imposes many different types of social cost, especially in highly urbanized areas. But income transfers to prevent such movement are also costly, and the question of who pays these costs has not been adequately answered.

If new investment is to take place to provide a more dynamic future, the prospects for new investors is not good. Labour productivity in East Germany is probably no more than 30 per cent of West German levels, an estimate likely to be duplicated in the other East European economies. If transfers are made so as to control emigration from these areas, this implies rising wages (wages in East Germany are already rising towards West German levels), but this implies a reduction in the rate of return to investors.

In fact, opening up the East European economies to free trade and free movement within the EC is likely to reinforce their relative backwardness, which is not desirable. This is particularly likely to happen if more faith is placed in the ability of market mechanisms to provide answers. What is needed in this case is public involvement – but of a different nature than before. Only this will help provide a solid base on which the development of more innovative activity can start. This must include the following (which can easily incorporate government assistance from the West): infrastructure investment to help improve the poor state of the distribution network, improved communications, and investment in education and training. These are not the most glamorous of all projects associated with introducing market reforms, but they are necessary – and in combination with other socially oriented policies, can help produce a more equitable society, which should be another aim if these countries wish to retain the best aspects of their heritage.

In conclusion, it is vitally necessary that more attention be given to the macroeconomic, institutional and behavioural aspects of socioeconomic restructuring. Once real improvements become possible, the broader integration of the European economies can be considered. This should not be an integration of identical societies (which is impossible in this situation) but one based on mutual complementarity and respect in which valuable differences derived from their cultural heritage characterize each country's contribution to the effective operation of the whole.

NOTES

*   The author is grateful to Christian Gehrke, Heinz Kurz and Gary Mongiovi for their helpful comments. The usual caveats apply.
1. This is not meant to imply that industrialization is a prerequisite for high income levels and that predominantly agricultural economies are poor: the examples of Australia, Canada and New Zealand are sufficient to show that such reasoning is false. While historically industrialization, by diversifying the economy towards innovative and high value-added activities, is associated with rising income levels, sustained economic growth also depends on other factors, such as market expansion and information through trade.
2. One of the early concerns of the founders of the socialist states was to avoid the 'us–them, worker vs. owner' mentality associated with the operations of capitalist enterprises. Such a standoff, with the associated problems of resentment, work stoppages and unequal rewards from industrial operations, would be incompatible with a 'true' workers' state. Hence the establishment of workers' councils (or some equivalent) to represent workers' interests in enterprise operations. But increasingly, the practical result was for Communist Party representatives to take over this function; the party, after all, officially expressed the interests of all.
3. The image of a monolithic 'communist bloc' has never been accurate, and cracks frequently appeared. The earliest expressions of dissatisfaction, both with the results of the full central planning model and with the lack of effective democratic socialism, occurred in the German Democratic Republic and Hungary in the mid-1950s. But dissatisfaction did not automatically lead to change. Ironically, these two countries later represented two divergent approaches to planning: the increasingly liberalized, 'goulash communism' of Hungary, and the more rigid, increasingly centralized approach of the GDR.
4. Buyers in the theoretical case are rational, with complete knowledge of all they need to have knowledge of in order to make rational decisions. A discussion of these assumptions is beyond the scope of this chapter.

REFERENCES

Asselain, J.-Ch. (1984), *Planning and Profits in Socialist Countries*, London: Routledge & Kegan Paul.

Bergson, A. (1948), 'Socialist Economics', in Howard S. Ellis (ed.), *A Survey of Contemporary Economics*, Homewood, IL: Richard D. Irwin.

Colchester, N. and Buchan D. (1990), *Europe Relaunched*, London: Economist Books.

Financial Times (1990), 'The Soviet Economy', Survey, 12 March.

Harrop, J. (1989), *The Political Economy of Integration in the European Economy*, Aldershot: Edward Elgar.

Hewett, E. (1988), *Reforming the Soviet Economy*, Washington, DC: Brookings Institution.

Kaldor, N. (1966), 'Marginal Productivity and the Macro-Economic Theories of Distribution: Comment on Samuelson and Modigliani', *Review of Economic Studies*, **33** (4), 309–19.

Kaldor, N. (1972), 'The Irrelevance of Equilibrium Economics', *Economic Journal*, **82**, December.

Kaldor, N. (1979), 'Equilibrium Theory and Growth Theory', in Michael J. Boskin (ed.), *Economics and Human Welfare: Essays in Honor of Tibor Scitovsky*, New York: Academic Press.

Kaldor, N. (1985), *Economics without Equilibrium*, New York: M.E. Sharpe.

Knell, M. and Rider, Ch. (eds) (1992), *Socialist Economies in Transition: Appraisals of the Market Mechanism*, Aldershot: Edward Elgar.

Kornai, J. (1979), 'Resource-Constrained versus Demand-Constrained Systems', *Econometrica*, **47**, 801–19. Reprinted in Kornai (1986).

Kornai, J. (1986), *Contradictions and Dilemmas: Studies on the Socialist Economy and Society*, Cambridge, MA: MIT Press.

Kornai, J. (1990). 'The Affinity between Ownership Forms and Coordination Mechanisms: The Common Experience of Reform in Socialist Countries', *Journal of Economic Perspectives*, **4** (3), Summer, 131–48.

Kurz, H.D. (1992), 'Whatever Happened to East Germany', in Knell and Rider, (1992).

Lipton, D. and Sachs J. (1990), 'The Case of Poland', *Brookings Papers on Economic Activity*, Washington, DC: Brookings Institution.

Nell, E. (1992), 'The Failure of Demand Management in Socialist Economies', in Knell and Rider, (1992).

Nuti, M. (1988), 'Perestroika: Transition from Central Planning to Market Socialism', *Economic Policy*, **8**.

Ofer, G. (1987), 'Soviet Economic Growth, 1928–1985', *Journal of Economic Literature*, **25**, December, 1767–1832.

Rider, Ch. (1992), 'Justifying the Need for Reform: The Price-Theoretic Approach', in Knell and Rider (1992).

Sawyer, M. (1993), 'The Nature and Role of the Market', *Social Concepts*, **6** (1).

World Bank (1981), *World Development Report*, New York: Oxford University Press.

Zaleski, E. (1971), *Planning for Economic Growth in the Soviet Union. 1918–1932*, Chapel Hill: University of North Carolina Press.

16. Industrial Restructuring in Eastern Europe and East–West Trade Integration

Michael A. Landesmann*

INTRODUCTION

This chapter has two parts: Part One makes a number of comparisons of industrial structures and examines past experiences of structural change across East (EE) and West European (WE) economies. These show that considerable diversity exists across EE economies in the degree to which their composition of industry differs from that of WE economies and in the way they experienced structural change in the past. We also document – using a variety of indicators – the considerable 'quality' and 'price gaps' of EE exports to EC markets relative to WE competitors.

Part Two maps out a scenario of East–West European trade integration. The basic long-run scenario assumed is that export performance (and hence market shares) of EE economies converges to those of other WE economies; however, current 'quality gaps' and inherited patterns of industrial production still leave a mark – even in the long run – and affect the different economies' position in inter- and intra-industry specialization within overall European trade. Short-term projections are derived from an analysis of feasible reorientation of trade (from East–East to East–West) and the building up of new export capacities. The analysis shows that short-run export growth patterns may deviate significantly from longer-term specialization.

PART ONE: INDUSTRIAL RESTRUCTURING IN EASTERN EUROPE

Part One focuses on two aspects of economic restructuring in Eastern Europe. First it attempts to measure the composition of manufacturing industry and the extent of structural change in the different East European economies during the period 1963–89, making comparisons with West European economies. The relevance of this investigation is as follows. Economies with very little experience of structural change and with industrial structures and relative prices very dissimilar to those of market economies of similar size, location, and so on have furthest to go when embarking on a major restructuring programme. On the other hand, economies which have already undergone significant structural change in the past and whose industrial structures are closer to those of market economies are in a better position in this respect. Moreover, these economies also have a better chance of adjusting the composition and destination of their exports in the fast-changing international economic environment that all East European economies presently face.

Secondly, Part One investigates the trade performance of East European economies in EC markets during the last 10–15 years. Before the recent sweeping changes, exports of most of the East European economies were mainly directed to CMEA markets and their presence in EC markets was only marginal (Köves, 1985; Landesmann and Székely, 1991; Levcik and Stankovsky, 1985). This situation is, however, currently changing at a rapid rate. Intra-East European trade has practically collapsed and although one can reasonably expect some of the previous trade links to be restored, it is highly unlikely that (after adopting world market prices and trade in hard currency) the extent of these trade relations will be anywhere near that observed in the past. Although it is hard to foresee precisely how successful these countries will be in redirecting their exports (and imports), it can be taken for granted that they will attempt to have a much greater presence in EC markets. It is, therefore, of interest to investigate how they performed in these markets in the past and, particularly, to obtain a picture of the extent to which they are lagging behind West European producers in quality and price.

This section deals with three of the East European economies, Czechoslovakia, Hungary and Poland. These economies were the first to embark on major social and economic reforms and also the ones which are currently at the forefront of developments in these areas. Data availability, especially on industrial production, also determined this choice.[1]

1.1 Structural Change in Manufacturing

The first issue addressed is the extent of structural change in manufacturing production in the East European economies under investigation. The indicator chosen to measure it is described in the Appendix (A1) and the results are presented in the main diagonal of Table 16.1. Two aspects of structural change were explored, one referring to changes in employment structure, the other to those in value-added. While the first is clearly related to the real side

Table 16.1: Similarities/Differences in Structure, 1966 and 1988

	Czechoslovakia 66	Czechoslovakia 88	Hungary 66	Hungary 88	Poland 66	Poland 88	Austria 66	Austria 88	Germany 66	Germany 88	S. Europe[a] 66	S. Europe[a] 88	N. Europe[b] 66	N. Europe[b] 88
Weighted														
Czechoslovakia														
employment		1.19	5.67	5.72	4.86	3.63	6.20	5.69	3.52	3.86	8.21	7.68	5.35	5.35
value added		1.48	6.02	6.59	6.94	4.17	7.10	5.93	3.84	4.83	8.64	7.15	5.72	6.13
Hungary														
employment	4.69	5.08		2.85	5.19	2.52	3.37	2.25	4.13	4.81	4.47	3.34	3.18	2.38
value added	4.23	4.69		2.89	3.11	3.06	2.32	2.43	2.68	2.63	2.85	3.41	2.14	2.98
Poland														
employment	3.98	3.21	2.05	2.42	2.03		2.59	2.58	4.18	3.90	2.99	3.59	2.43	2.50
value added	6.76	3.30	3.46	2.93	3.03		3.06	3.79	4.56	3.18	2.04	4.41	3.61	3.88
Austria														
employment	4.15	4.60	2.06	2.68	2.51	2.70		2.12	3.30	4.03	3.47	3.47	1.57	1.81
value added	4.70	4.59	2.30	2.51	2.71	3.90		2.44	2.99	3.34	2.30	2.52	2.10	1.87
Germany														
employment	3.69	4.26	3.29	4.46	3.79	3.76	3.49	4.27	2.65		6.07	6.38	2.86	3.81
value added	3.24	4.20	2.59	3.00	3.62	2.30	3.40	3.80	3.24		4.66	4.89	2.53	3.84
Southern Europe														
employment	5.44	4.82	3.81	2.98	2.53	2.68	3.73	3.50	6.32	6.00		2.71	4.43	3.83
value added	4.51	4.80	2.37	3.24	1.51	5.03	2.49	2.68	4.08	4.47		3.20	3.13	2.08
Northern Europe														
employment	4.03	4.44	1.86	2.65	2.27	2.41	1.55	1.58	2.87	3.81	3.68	3.14	2.42	
value added	4.64	4.88	2.17	3.46	2.94	4.11	2.02	1.92	2.65	4.14	3.06	2.11	2.46	

Notes:

[a]Southern Europe: Greece, Ireland, Portugal, Spain, Turkey.

[b]Northern Europe: Austria, Belgium, Denmark, Finland, Netherlands, Norway, Sweden.

The indicators above measure the weighted average difference in the shares of respective (ISIC) 3-digit manufacturing industries (expressed in percentages). The shares of the country in the first column are used as weights. The smaller the value of this indicator the more similar the two structures compared. For a detailed description of the indicator and data used see Appendix (A1). The elements in the main diagonal show the degree of structural shift in one country during the period 1966–88, while the off-diagonal elements measure the degree of similarity between two economies.

of the economy, the second also entails relative price changes.[2] Amongst the three countries, Czechoslovakia stands out with her very low degree of structural change in both respects. On the other hand, Hungary and Poland are within the range of structural change measured for the market economies under investigation, lying rather at the upper end of this range. In fact, for employment, Hungary shows the highest degree of structural change during the period under investigation.

The results for structural similarities between the Eastern and Western economies (see Table 16.1, off-diagonal elements) again show Czechoslovakia to be the country which is the furthest away from any of the market economies (or any group of these). Hungary, on the other hand, appears to be quite similar to Austria and, in fact, only the group of small north European countries is more similar. In relation to the other market economies, Hungary is well within the range spanned by market economies and is more similar to Germany and the group of north European economies than is the group of south European economies. Similarly, she is more similar to the group of north European economies than is Germany.[3] The same is true for Poland as far as employment is concerned; however, this is not the case for value-added. Although information on relative prices is not available for Poland directly, we do attribute this discrepancy to relative prices.

The results in Table 16.1 present two snapshots, taken in 1966 and 1988 respectively. They show the cumulative impact of structural shifts over a longer period. Next, we examine the *dynamics* of structural change. The yearly values of the indicators measuring structural shifts in output, employment and relative prices are plotted in Figure 16.1.[4] These graphs further corroborate that Czechoslovakia had a quite distinct pattern of structural change, especially during the 1980s. (For most of the period, its graphs lie below those of the other economies, reflecting the very low degree of structural shift.) Hungary, on the other hand, with the exception of the first half of the 1980s, exhibits a pattern quite similar to that of Austria and Germany. It is also interesting to see the difference in the pattern of structural change in Austria and Germany in the 1960s and 1970s and in the 1980s. In the first period, the degree of shift in the structure of employment is well below that of output (reflecting an inelastic response of employment structure to shifts in output composition), while in the 1980s they were of a similar size, although the dynamics were quite different until 1984. Interestingly enough, a similar finding is true for Hungary: although the second period starts somewhat later, the dynamics of output and employment are very similar. The same is not true for Czechoslovakia. The degree of structural change in the Czechoslovak economy appears small not only when compared to Austria and Germany but also in comparison with Hungary. With the exception of the first half of the 1980s, a period of the Hungarian economy definitely

268   *Political and Economic Reforms*

Figure 16.1:   Structural Shift Indicators over the Period 1964–89

Czechoslovakia

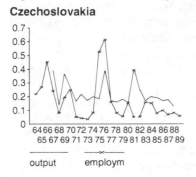

output   employm

Germany, FR

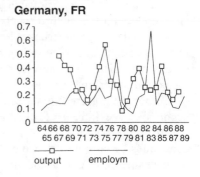

output   employm

Hungary

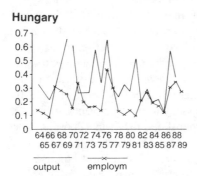

output   employm

Hungary

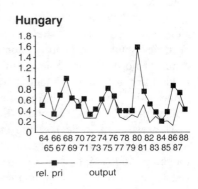

rel. pri   output

Austria

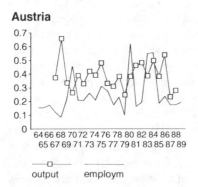

output   employm

Austria

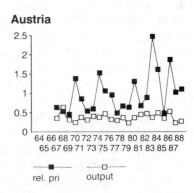

rel. pri   output

Notes:
The time series plotted above measure, year by year, the (weighted) average difference in the shares of respective (ISIC) 3-digit manufacturing industries (expressed in percentages). The shares for the more recent year are used as weights. The smaller the value of this indicator the smaller the degree of structural shifts. For a detailed description of the indicator and data used see Appendix (A1). Series denoted by *output* refer to the structure of real gross output and the ones denoted by *employm* to the structure of employment. Series denoted by *rel.pri* measure the degree of shifts in relative prices, using formula (2) in Appendix A1.

worth further investigation, structural change in Czechoslovakia in all aspects is well below the level observed for Hungary throughout the whole period under investigation. For Hungary, we can also observe a very similar dynamic pattern of relative price and output changes after 1968. Relative prices are not as volatile as, for example, in Austria but their dynamics, again with the exception of the first half of the 1980s, are remarkably similar.

1.2 Export Performance in EC Markets

In the following exercise we used a detailed trade data base from the European Statistical Office (Eurostat) to examine whether there is a gap – both in price and in product composition – between the products sold by East European producers to EC markets as compared to EC imports in general.

The types of 'quality' indicators calculated to examine the nature of intra-industry trade performance of East European producers in EC markets are summarized in Appendix (A2). Here is a short description of these indicators:

- Q_j^c measures the relative orientation of a country C industry j's export basket towards high or low value per kg items (whereby these values are calculated from total trades in EC markets).
- Q'_j^c reveals the relative *price gap* of the different commodity items in a country's commodity basket relative to the respective price leader in each commodity market; these price gaps are weighted by the respective shares of the different commodities in a country C's exports of industry j.
- QV_j^c shows the relative composition of an industry j's exports towards high or low *volume growth* items in EC's traded goods markets, and
- QS_j^c does the same as QV_j^c but with respect to high or low *value growth* items.

The additional variables QdV, QdS, dQ and dQ' represent, respectively, changes in the above indicators over the period 1977–87. They thus reflect whether compositional changes between 1977 and 1987 were in the direction of fast/slow growing traded product markets (in volume, QdV, and value, QdS, terms), or in the direction of a higher/lower representation of high price per kg items in an industry's export basket (dQ) or whether the weighted price gap to the price leader (in each commodity market) has grown or has been closed (dQ').

Parts (i) and (ii) of Table 16.2 present the values for the various indicators calculated for the years 1977 and 1987 for two broad industry groups, mechanical engineering and electrical engineering; these two industries comprised respectively 480 and 254 traded products for which volumes and values of exports and imports from and to EC countries were available. The results are quite revealing (further results concerning a number of three-digit industries are reported in Table 16.4 p. 275). They show the following.

1.   There is, according to most indicators, a considerable gap between the West European economies and the East European countries. That gap is considerable with respect to each of the indicators examined except – in some instances – with respect to QV, which is the indicator for the orienta-

Table 16.2:   Quality Indicators of East European Exports to EC Markets

(i) Mechanical enginerring (NACE 32) – 480 products

		Germany	Hungary	Poland	Czechoslovakia	Italy	Austria	RWEur
Sh(%)	1977	35.5	0.1	0.4	0.4	10.3	2.2	16.1
	1987	34.3	0.2	0.1	0.2	12.4	3.8	19.7
Q	1977	1.000	0.903	0.646	0.729	0.855	0.845	1.064
	1987	1.000	0.715	0.726	0.761	0.908	0.856	1.064
Q'	1977	1.000	0.528	0.612	0.587	0.793	0.928	1.112
	1987	1.000	0.421	0.353	0.417	0.829	0.933	1.109
QV	1987	1.000	0.877	0.802	0.612	0.940	0.952	0.775
QS	1987	1.000	0.799	0.713	0.584	1.027	0.965	0.961
QdV	77–87	1.852	1.875	1.499	1.392	1.895	1.845	2.059
QdS	77–87	1.394	1.291	1.062	1.098	1.445	1.338	1.557
dQ	77–87	2.108	1.668	2.367	2.201	2.240	2.134	2.110
dQ'	77–87	0.987	0.738	0.569	0.701	1.032	0.993	0.985

(ii) Electrical engineering (NACE 34) – 254 products

		Germany	Hungary	Poland	Czechoslovakia	Italy	Austria	RWEur
Sh(%)	1977	30.7	0.4	0.3	0.3	10.5	3.5	12.2
	1987	29.7	0.2	0.2	0.2	10.7	3.6	18.0
Q'	1977	1.000	0.319	0.422	0.327	0.794	0.925	1.076
	1987	1.000	0.591	0.480	0.497	0.825	1.050	1.103
QV	1987	1.000	0.609	1.010	1.123	2.010	0.737	0.544
QS	1987	1.000	0.444	0.531	0.601	0.952	0.874	1.261
QdV	77–87	2.276	1.509	1.511	1.528	1.858	3.264	2.123
QdS	77–87	1.633	1.062	0.982	1.190	1.312	1.512	1.851
dQ	77–87	3.052	1.228	1.048	1.752	2.400	2.845	2.417
dQ'	77–87	0.924	1.711	1.053	1.404	0.961	1.049	0.947

Source: Eurostat, Detailed Trade Data; see text for method of calculation. RWEur comprises the following economies: Denmark, Finland, Ireland, Iceland, Norway, Sweden, Switzerland. Sh (%) refers to market shares (in %) in total EC trades supplied by European producers, East and West.

tion towards high-volume growth areas in traded products; however the gap was and remains large with respect to QS, which indicates the orientation towards high growth areas in value terms.

The price gap (indicator Q') remains high although it has closed somewhat for electrical engineering products where it started from an even lower base than for mechanical engineering. The indicator Q, which refers to the product composition with respect to high/low price per kg items, reveals the particularly abysmal performance of East European electrical engineering products.

For comparative purposes, we also included in these tables information about Italy, Austria and the group of small advanced West European economies, which shows that by 1987, with respect to most indicators, Italy and Austria have in most industrial sectors by 1987 closed their gap with Germany or, where no gap existed in the first place, have maintained pace with Germany. The group of small West European economies (RWEur) have from the outset been more or less level with Germany. Furthermore, while these countries have managed to increase their market shares over the 1977–87 period, East European producers have mostly lost market shares. The market shares that East European economies occupy in EC trade are (with very few exceptions, such as Czechoslovakia's exports of glassware, Hungary's and Poland's of meat products; see Table 16.4) very small.

2.   There are considerable differences between the different East/Central European economies: in many ways Hungary has performed somewhat better than the other two East/Central European economies, especially Czechoslovakia. In some cases, Hungary started from a lower base than the other two economies, but improved more rapidly or deteriorated less. This is particularly the case when one considers the price gap (Q') indicator.

1.3   Conclusions from Part One

The two parts of our empirical investigation led us to similar conclusions. First, as far as the structure of manufacturing and export performance in EC markets are concerned, Hungary has, among the three East European economies investigated, perhaps the best starting position. Relative prices in manufacturing (to which firms have adapted their production technologies and plans) most closely resemble the relative price structure of market economies.[5] While West European economies exhibit a wide range of different structures with regard to production (output and employment), relative prices and especially changes in relative prices seem fairly uniform across them. Secondly, the Hungarian economy experienced a fairly high degree of structural change in the past and seemed reasonably responsive to internal and external shocks. The only period when it departed significantly from the pattern exhibited by the market economies we investigated was the first half of the 1980s, but later on it appeared to catch up. Thirdly, Hungary's exports to EC markets, although subject to a sizeable decline, performed slightly better in many of the industrial branches examined in comparison with the other East European economies under investigation.

On the other hand, all the results obtained in this study suggest that the Czechoslovak economy will have to undergo a tremendous restructuring before it can compete successfully on the world market. In all the aspects studied, Czechoslovakia's past performance turned out to be the most rigid and unresponsive throughout the whole period under investigation, especially during the 1980s when Western economies underwent substantial restructuring.[6] The analysis of trade performance further corroborates our general finding for Czechoslovakia.[7] Each particular indicator designed to measure quality and price gap and trade performance suggests a massive loss of competitiveness during the period under investigation. Although the major part of Czechoslovak exports was not traded on these markets but rather in CMEA markets, it is hard to believe that taking into account those products traded on non-EC markets would improve this picture. Poland seems to lie between Hungary and Czechoslovakia, perhaps nearer to Hungary than to Czechoslovakia.

In the light of these findings, the performance of these economies during the second half of 1990 and in 1991 is by no means a surprise. The relative success of Hungary in redirecting her exports towards EC markets and achieving a relatively smooth transition so far fits nicely into the picture drawn in the present chapter. The relative sluggishness of the Czechoslovak economy in reorientating its trade and restructuring its industries up to now also fits with our analysis. In spite of radical devaluations, the response of the supply side is slow in the Czechoslovak economy. This clearly shows that past experience with structural change, and attitudes and skills developed as a result of this, are indeed very important. Similarly, obsolete production capacities which are mementos of the enormous lock-in effect which intra-CMEA trade had on these economies (see Köves, 1985; van Brabant, 1987b) cannot be overcome overnight simply using the tools of demand management. It is also clear that the legacy of the past four decades cannot be overcome in a couple of years and, consequently, deserves much more attention if the impact and time scale of current reform programmes are to be assessed.

Naturally, there are various other political, social, cultural and economic factors enhancing or severely limiting the ability of the different East European countries to carry out successful restructuring of their economies. With respect to some of them, the ranking of these countries might be quite different. For example, as far as the burden of foreign debt is concerned,

Czechoslovakia and by now also Poland are, no doubt, in a much better position than Hungary (Cohen, 1991). The study above does not deny the importance of these factors but rather emphasizes other aspects of the problem related to inherited structures on the supply side. So far, these aspects seem to have had much less attention than they deserve.

APPENDIX (PART ONE)

A1

The following general measure was used, both, to analyse structural shifts in manufacturing industry and to compare industrial structures across economies:

$$S_{ij} = \sqrt{\Sigma_k (sh^i_k - sh^j_k)^2 (sh^i_k / 100)}, \qquad (1)$$

where $sh_k{}^i$ and $sh_k{}^j$ are the (employment or value added) shares of industry k in years i and j when the extent of structural change in a country over a given period is investigated, and the shares of industry k in countries i and j when the structures of two countries are compared at a given point in time. Country i (that is, the country providing the weights) is indicated in the first column of Table 16.1. When i and j refer to years, i always stands for the more recent year. The time series shown in the graphs in Figure 16.1 are the series of S_{ij} measuring the degree of structural shift from one year to the next (that is i=j+1). When S_{ij} is used to measure the degree of shift in relative prices in a given country, the following formula is used:

$$S_{ij} = \sqrt{\Sigma_k (rp^i_k - rp^j_k)^2 (sh^i_k / 100)}, \qquad (2)$$

where $rp_k{}^i$ and $rp_k{}^j$ are the relative prices of industry k (the price index for industry k over the price index for total manufacturing) in years i and j, and $sh_k{}^i$ is the share of industry k in total value added in manufacturing in year i.

The data used in the above analysis of structural change in manufacturing industries are from the UNIDO Industrial Statistics Data Base, which provides the following time series for 28 3-digit (ISIC) industries in manufacturing (ISIC codes 311, ..., 390):

employment – average number of employees (code 04)
output   – gross output in current prices (in domestic currency) (code 14)

value added – value added in current prices (in domestic currency) (code
                20)
output index – index numbers of industrial production (1980 = 100) (code
                51)

Real output series were calculated from nominal output and output index
series. The shares in the above measure were calculated by the author, taking
total manufacturing (ISIC 300) as 100 per cent. Time series cover the period
1963–89.

A2

Table 16.3:   *Quality Indicators of East European Export Performance in*
                EC Markets

(a) $Q_j^c = \sum_{i \in J} p_i^{EC} x_i^c$

(b) $Q_j^{'c} = \sum_{i \in J} rp_i^c x_i^c$

(c) $QV_j^c = \sum_{i \in J} g_i^{EC} x_i^c$

(d) $QS_j^c = \sum_{i \in J} \tilde{g}_i^{EC} x_i^c$

Q_j^c, $Q_j^{'c}$, QV_j^c, QS_j^c are all various 'quality' indicators of country c's exports in a particular industry j. Within that industry j, a (large) number of products $i \in J$ are traded.
x_i^c represents the share of product i in country c's exports to EC markets;
p_i^{EC} is the average price per kg of product i traded in EC markets; rp_i^c is the relative price of c's exports of commodity i relative to the 'price leader' (i.e. the producer charging the highest price per kg) in EC markets ($rp_i^c = p_i^c/p_i^L$ where p_i^L is the price per kg which the 'price leader' in EC markets charges for commodity i); g_i^{EC} and $\tilde{g}_i^{EC}$ are respectively the volume and value growth rates of commodity i in EC markets for traded products.

Table 16.4: *Quality Indicators (Q') of Intra-industry Exports of EC Markets*

		Germany	Italy	Austria	Hungary	Poland	Czechos	Soviet U.	RWEur
NACE 31 298 products Manufacture of metal articles									
Q'	1977	1.000	0.789	1.029	0.636	0.493	0.483	0.571	1.097
	1987	1.000	0.777	0.963	0.550	0.424	0.412	0.275	0.960
Sh%	1977	33.3	11.9	3.1	0.3	0.4	0.2	0.1	10.9
Sh%	1987	30.1	13.7	4.5	0.3	0.4	0.3	0.1	13.8
NACE 32 491 products Mechanical engineering									
Q'	1977	1.000	0.793	0.928	0.528	0.612	0.587	0.352	1.112
	1987	1.000	0.829	0.933	0.421	0.353	0.417	0.510	1.109
Sh%	1977	35.5	10.3	2.2	0.1	0.4	0.4	0.2	16.1
Sh%	1987	34.3	12.4	3.8	0.2	0.1	0.2	0.1	19.7
NACE 324 66 products Manufacture of machinery for the food, chemical etc. industries									
Q'	1977	1.000	0.786	0.915	0.342	0.599	0.895	0.323	1.187
	1987	1.000	0.790	0.814	0.406	0.436	0.354	0.397	1.079
Sh%	1977	38.2	11.4	2.8	0.0	0.1	0.0	0.1	16.6
Sh%	1987	35.3	15.7	4.7	0.1	0.1	0.0	0.0	17.7
NACE 34 264 products Electrical engineering									
Q'	1977	1.000	0.794	0.925	0.319	0.422	0.327	0.328	1.076
	1987	1.000	0.825	1.050	0.591	0.480	0.497	0.343	1.103
Sh%	1977	30.7	10.5	3.5	0.4	0.3	0.3	0.1	12.2
Sh%	1987	29.7	10.7	3.6	0.2	0.2	0.2	0.0	18.0
NACE 37 137 products Instrument engineering									
Q'	1977	1.000	0.746	1.128	0.503	0.402	0.749	0.414	1.396
	1987	1.000	0.732	1.269	0.302	0.406	0.374	0.264	1.230
Sh%	1977	28.0	6.3	3.1	0.1	0.3	0.3	0.7	21.9
Sh%	1987	28.7	5.7	3.2	0.1	0.1	0.1	0.3	18.4
NACE 247 59 products Manufacture of glass and glassware									
Q'	1977	1.000	0.788	1.220	0.432	0.443	0.610	0.572	1.194
	1987	1.000	0.924	1.420	0.628	0.724	0.640	0.736	1.359
Sh%	1977	20.1	8.4	3.9	0.8	0.8	2.8	0.5	6.0
Sh%	1987	22.6	9.8	5.9	0.4	0.4	3.5	0.2	8.1
NACE 412 114 products Slaughtering, preparing and preserving of meat									
Q'	1977	1.000	1.211	1.188	0.940	1.050	0.970	0.781	0.992
	1987	1.000	1.041	0.736	0.833	0.868	0.758	0.771	0.937
Sh%	1977	7.6	1.7	0.5	3.6	3.3	0.3	0.3	19.5
Sh%	1987	13.6	1.8	1.5	2.3	1.5	0.5	0.7	18.6
NACE 451 18 products Manufacture of mass-produced footwear									
Q'	1977	1.000	0.726	0.812	0.358	0.524	0.342	0.415	0.890
	1987	1.000	0.708	0.996	0.738	0.372	0.350	0.648	1.035
Sh%	1977	10.5	40.0	6.2	0.9	1.2	1.1	0.0	2.6
Sh%	1987	9.8	50.8	5.4	0.2	0.9	0.9	0.1	3.0
NACE 453 132 products Manufacture of ready-made clothing and accessories									
Q'	1977	1.000	0.893	0.884	0.533	0.422	0.445	0.538	0.901
	1987	1.000	1.020	1.103	0.485	0.349	0.431	0.287	0.951
Sh%	1977	21.2	20.7	2.5	0.6	0.8	0.7	0.0	5.6
Sh%	1987	21.3	26.5	4.3	0.3	0.6	0.5	0.0	6.8

Source: Eurostat, Detailed Trade Data; Q' defined in the text; RWEur comprises the following economies: Denmark, Finland, Ireland, Iceland, Norway, Sweden, Switzerland. Sh (%) are market shares (in %) in total EC trades supplied by European producers, East and West.

PART TWO: PROJECTING EAST–WEST TRADE INTEGRATION

Introduction

In this part of the chapter we project an optimistic scenario of East–West trade integration for the long run (which, for the purposes of this chapter we define as the year 2010). The main assumption behind this scenario is that the 'frontier' countries (Poland, Hungary and Czechoslovakia) will occupy market shares in EC markets which are roughly in line with those of other West European countries which are either not yet members of the European Communities or have only recently joined. We will use measures of the current 'quality gap' and 'distance measures' of industrial structure comparisons (see analysis in Part One) to allow for the fact that the 'historical legacy' will still play a role in the longer run and affect the different EE economies' positions in inter- and intra-industry specialization in European trade. We also make short-run projections of trade integration (for the period up to 1995) using a very different methodology. Here trade reorientation from East–East to East–West trade and the conversion of old, and investment into, new export capacities play the major role. The use of different methodologies for short-, medium-, and long-run projections reveals, first, the great difficulty of achieving growth rates which allow EE countries to reach market share positions similar to those of West European economies and, secondly, significant differences in shorter- and longer-term specialization patterns of EE economies in international trade.

2.1 Long-term Projections

The objective is to forecast the long-run level of exports from Eastern Europe (EE) by country and commodity into the European Community (EC) as well as imports from the European Community into Eastern Europe. A country's export success will depend on a range of factors – its level of development, size, comparative advantage (which will depend on factor endowments, skill, managerial and technological competence, infrastructure and distance from the market). Many of these are unobservable, and others will evolve in response to the market forces now beginning to be unleashed in the East. The forecasting approach taken here is pragmatic, as it must use observable data, but it is defensible. It proceeds in a series of steps, each of which takes account of one factor. This has the advantage that the relative importance of different factors can be examined and adjusted if other evidence suggests the need for such adjustment. The long-run equilibrium is assumed to be reached in the year 2010, by which time a large part of the technological catching up will be assumed to have taken place in the EE countries.

2.1.1 Naive long-term projections (step 1)

The first step is to attempt to identify the equilibrium level of exports (in the year 2010) to the EC which might be expected from countries at the level of development observed in the East. Ideally, one would estimate a model in which exports to the EC were a function of GDP per capita, size, industrial structure (as a proxy for comparative advantage), distance, contiguity, tariff levels, non-tariff barriers and so on. In practice, this is an overambitious task and we adopt the following short cut. The idea is to select a group of roughly similar countries (in terms of size, proximity to EC markets and average GDP per head), and then work out the extent to which any given EE country approximates this group. Its trade share in the EC in 2010 will then be taken as equally similar. The reference group of countries is Austria, Switzerland, Finland, Sweden, Denmark, Spain, Portugal, Greece and Turkey, and the reference year is 1986–87. These are comparable in population to the core group of EE countries (Czechoslovakia, Poland and Hungary, but we shall take Czechoslovakia as our benchmark country). They are on average richer and so might be expected to enjoy larger trade shares in the EC, but we are looking considerably ahead and taking an optimistic view.

Before taking any other factors into account we will assume that the trade shares (in the year 2010) of any given EE country in the EC are weighted averages of the trade shares of these reference countries.[8] The weights measure the degree of similarity of the given EE country to each reference country, which is in turn defined as proportional to the inverse of the 'distance' of its employment pattern to that in the reference country.[9] In turn, the distance of country c from reference country c' is given by the distance coefficient $D_{cc'}$, defined as

$$D_{cc'} = \sqrt{\frac{1}{n}\sum_{j=1}^{n}(\omega_j^c - \omega_j^{c'})^2} \tag{3}$$

where ω_j^c is the share of industry j in country c in total manufacturing employment (and similarly for the reference country c'), and n is the number of manufacturing industries in the UNIDO data base. The employment shares are for 1987 and are based on UNIDO industrial statistics. If these shares are expressed in percentage terms, we have $0 < D_{cc'} < 100$, though there is no special merit in this particular scaling (Table 16.5(a) presents these distance measures comparing employment structures in 1987.)

The actual similarity weight by which the trade share of country c' is multiplied is

$$\alpha_{cc'} = \frac{D_{cc'}^{-1}}{\sum_{k=1}^{K}D_{ck}^{-1}} \tag{4}$$

where K is the number of reference group countries (9 in this case). Table 16.5(b) gives these weights, and in the final column, the *distance* of each country from its own 'employment target structure', which is the weighted average of the employment structures of the reference countries with the $S_{cc'}$ used as weights.

These weights are then used to calculate the long-term *target market shares* for each EE country as the weighted average of the market shares of the reference group of countries. (For the market shares in EC markets of these reference countries see Table 16.5(c)) These unadjusted 'target market shares' are presented in Table 16.6 and are compared with the original market shares of each EE country in the EC markets in 1986–87. At the bottom of each country's projection are the average EC market shares for total manufacturing under the hypothetical and the original scenario. We call these *naive* (or step 1) projections since no other factor is taken into account besides the market share structure of the group of reference countries. At this stage what we have attempted to determine are the predicted market shares at the product level, taking account of the proxied level of development of the EE countries.

2.1.2   Modified long-term projections (step 2)
Two sets of further factors have been taken into account to modify the *Naive* projections.

1.   Differences across industries in the degree to which they will reach the target market shares in EC markets.
2.   Global adjustment factors such as size of the country, distance from EC markets, differences across the EE economies of how much of the final target they will reach by the year 2010, and some (subjective) adjustment for the expected degree of political instability impinging upon economic (export) performance.

2.1.2.1   Accounting for the industry-specific quality gap   Each EE country will have a different pattern of comparative advantage in products compared to other countries, and we should take account of this in forecasting product-level export shares. In the following the assumption will be made that comparative advantage is measured by *relative* product quality. If Poland is relatively better at chemical production than manufacturing as a whole, then we should expect a larger share of Polish exports to be chemicals. The 'quality' measure adopted here will be the Q' described in section 1.2. To remind the reader, 'quality gap' Q' was measured by the value per kg of the product relative to the highest value per kg observed in EC imports of that product (the market leader). The calculation of these 'quality' (or 'value') indicators is derived from detailed trade statistics supplied by Eurostat at the

Table 16.5:   *(a) Distance coefficients (Differences in employment structure)*

	Austria	Switz.	Finland	Sweden	Denmark	Spain	Portugal	Greece	Turkey	Own target
HUNGARY	1.98	2.95	2.89	3.22	2.55	2.00	3.79	3.01	3.16	1.74
POLAND	1.91	2.84	2.55	2.70	2.35	1.81	3.53	3.05	2.98	1.39
CZECH.	2.91	2.98	3.14	2.88	3.09	3.11	4.75	4.58	4.13	2.63
BULGARIA	3.16	3.89	3.63	4.00	3.64	3.22	4.29	3.96	3.90	2.89
ROMANIA	4.34	3.67	4.37	4.79	4.24	4.81	5.34	5.57	4.95	4.05
USSR	5.18	4.29	5.40	5.33	4.50	5.54	6.84	6.58	6.27	4.97
YUGOSLAVIA	1.74	3.21	2.55	3.09	2.92	1.63	2.72	2.42	2.75	1.22

Source: UNIDO 1987 industrial statistics; own calculations.

Table 16.5:   *(b) Similarity coefficients (used as weights for target export share structure)*

	Austria	Switz.	Finland	Sweden	Denmark	Spain	Portugal	Greece	Turkey
HUNGARY	0.15	0.10	0.10	0.09	0.12	0.15	0.08	0.10	0.10
POLAND	0.15	0.10	0.11	0.10	0.12	0.16	0.08	0.09	0.09
CZECH.	0.13	0.13	0.12	0.13	0.12	0.12	0.08	0.08	0.09
BULGARIA	0.13	0.11	0.11	0.10	0.11	0.13	0.10	0.10	0.11
ROMANIA	0.12	0.14	0.12	0.11	0.12	0.11	0.10	0.09	0.10
USSR	0.12	0.14	0.11	0.11	0.13	0.11	0.09	0.09	0.10
YUGOSLAVIA	0.15	0.08	0.11	0.09	0.09	0.17	0.10	0.11	0.10

Source: UNIDO 1987 industrial statistics; own calculations.

Table 16.5:   *(c) Market shares in EC markets in 1986/87 (%)*

		EEC(6)	Austria	Switz.	Finland	Sweden	Denmark	Spain	Portugal	Greece	Turkey
Met. ex.	21	10.29	0.01	0.01	0.03	5.73	0.02	0.81	0.09	0.41	0.34
Met. pr.	22	57.7	3.09	4.57	1.32	3.76	0.5	2.11	0.25	0.68	0.1
Min. ex.	23	40.94	1.48	0.45	1.43	1.63	0.78	3.1	0.85	1.64	3.74
Min. pr.	24	71.77	3.91	1.59	0.36	1.42	1.02	4.49	2	0.35	0.24
Chem.	25	69.53	1.27	5.92	0.45	1.62	0.96	1.56	0.47	0.09	0.16
Fibres	26	69.68	5.53	4.65	1.2	0.84	0.83	1.27	0.27	0.32	2.03
Met. Pd.	31	69.31	3.47	4.25	0.53	3.1	1.8	2.53	0.79	0.09	0.14
Mech. Eng.	32	64.78	2.85	8.4	0.83	4.1	1.79	1.62	0.2	0.04	0.04
Office	33	40.95	0.22	3.38	0.19	3.62	0.52	0.32	0.07	0.01	0
Elec. Eng.	34	57.95	2.37	5.31	0.51	3.21	1.6	1.52	0.34	0.15	0.03
Motor	35	75.37	1.36	0.33	0.16	3.1	0.14	3.23	0.36	0	0.01
Transp.	36	39.92	2.02	1.76	0.5	5.28	0.95	1.31	0.34	0.31	0
Instr.	37	46.69	2	8.3	0.16	0.95	0.8	0.29	0.29	0.01	0
Food	41	56.09	0.55	1.19	0.12	0.25	5.26	1.08	0.31	0.5	1.38
Drink, T.	42	66.2	0.37	0.64	0.05	0.15	2.23	2.62	1.78	0.24	0.06
Text.	43	57.31	2.92	3.64	0.24	0.64	0.63	1.65	2.48	2.98	3.11
Leath.	44	46.14	2.19	0.75	0.12	1.04	0.46	3.09	0.38	0.14	0.3
Foot./Clo.	45	44.75	2.24	1.02	0.64	0.47	0.53	2.78	3.8	2.5	4.27
Timber	46	31.47	5.35	1.08	7.62	10.63	2.55	1.88	3.16	0.02	0.03
Paper	47	47.43	3.68	2.5	7.51	9.95	0.81	2.52	2.44	0.07	0.01
Rubber	48	72.77	2.83	2.96	0.44	2	1.54	2.32	0.31	0.18	0.11
Other	49	35.52	1.59	4.59	0.21	0.37	1.04	1.59	0.21	0.06	0.03
Total Man.			2.17	3.68	0.99	2.80	1.32	2.02	0.85	0.45	0.56

Source: Eurostat, Detailed Trade Statistics.

Table 16.6: Market Share Projections – Step 1

NACE		Hungary step 1	Hungary 1986–87	Hungary diff.	Poland step 1	Poland 1986–87	Poland diff.	Czech. step 1	Czech. 1986–87	Czech. diff.
Met. ex.	21	0.75	0.00	0.75	0.81	0.12	0.69	0.93	0.04	0.89
Met. pr.	22	1.91	0.32	1.59	1.92	0.80	1.12	2.02	0.53	1.49
Min. ex.	23	1.73	0.05	1.68	1.73	0.05	1.68	1.64	0.69	0.95
Min. pr.	24	1.95	0.25	1.70	1.95	0.38	1.57	1.81	0.99	0.82
Chem.	25	1.41	0.25	1.16	1.41	0.32	1.09	1.54	0.26	1.28
Fibres	26	2.06	0.16	1.90	2.03	0.09	1.94	2.04	0.21	1.83
Met. man.	31	1.99	0.22	1.77	2.00	0.36	1.64	2.06	0.23	1.83
Mech. Eng.	32	2.25	0.13	2.12	2.25	0.11	2.14	2.50	0.19	2.31
Office	33	0.86	0.04	0.82	0.88	0.02	0.86	1.06	0.05	1.01
Elec. Eng.	34	1.73	0.14	1.59	1.73	0.15	1.58	1.88	0.14	1.74
Motor	35	1.09	0.01	1.08	1.12	0.18	0.94	1.08	0.08	1.00
Transp.	36	1.41	0.04	1.37	1.45	0.43	1.02	1.56	0.20	1.36
Instr.	37	1.24	0.68	0.56	1.39	0.05	1.34	1.60	0.09	1.51
Food	41	0.97	0.16	0.81	1.23	0.68	0.55	1.23	0.15	1.08
Drink, T.	42	2.02	0.20	1.82	0.98	0.25	0.73	0.91	0.13	0.78
Text.	43	1.12	0.30	0.82	1.98	0.20	1.78	1.95	0.39	1.56
Leath.	44	2.01	0.17	1.84	1.12	0.18	0.94	1.03	0.42	0.61
Foot/Clo.	45	3.57	0.38	3.19	1.98	0.31	1.67	1.85	0.35	1.50
Timber	46	3.22	0.07	3.15	3.69	1.11	2.58	3.92	1.25	2.67
Paper	47	1.56	0.18	1.38	3.34	0.06	3.28	3.59	0.51	3.08
Rubber	48	1.16	0.03	1.13	1.56	0.11	1.45	1.57	0.20	1.37
Other	49				1.14	0.09	1.05	1.20	0.24	0.96
Total Man.		1.66	0.21		1.67	0.33		1.74	0.30	

NACE		Bulgaria step 1	Bulgaria 1986–87	Bulgaria diff.	Romania step 1	Romania 1986–87	Romania diff.	USSR step 1	USSR 1986–87	USSR diff.
Met. ex.	21	0.79	0.00	0.79	0.79	0.00	0.79	0.82	0.09	0.73
Met. pr.	22	1.86	0.18	1.68	1.94	0.26	1.68	1.96	1.31	0.65
Min. ex.	23	1.70	0.03	1.67	1.62	0.00	1.62	1.61	0.69	0.92
Min. pr.	24	1.81	0.03	1.78	1.73	0.22	1.51	1.73	0.04	1.69
Chem.	25	1.39	0.07	1.32	1.55	0.17	1.38	1.58	0.56	1.02
Fibres	26	1.97	0.16	1.81	2.03	0.69	1.34	2.02	0.22	1.80
Met. man.	31	1.91	0.01	1.90	1.98	0.28	1.70	2.02	0.06	1.96
Mech. Eng.	32	2.22	0.04	2.18	2.46	0.04	2.42	2.51	0.09	2.42

NACE		step 1	1986–87	diff.	step 1	1986–87	diff.	step 1	1986–87	diff.
Office	33	0.89	0.13	0.76	1.01	0.00	1.01	1.04	0.00	1.04
Elec. Eng.	34	1.69	0.03	1.66	1.83	0.08	1.75	1.87	0.05	1.82
Motor	35	1.01	0.00	1.01	0.95	0.07	0.88	0.98	0.43	0.55
Transp.	36	1.39	0.00	1.39	1.42	0.01	1.41	1.46	0.13	1.33
Instr.	37	1.41	0.01	1.40	1.67	0.03	1.64	1.69	0.16	1.53
Food	41	1.20	0.03	1.17	1.24	0.07	1.17	1.30	0.25	1.05
Drink, T.	42	0.93	0.02	0.91	0.90	0.00	0.90	0.92	0.18	0.74
Text.	43	2.02	0.08	1.94	2.03	0.34	1.69	2.00	0.22	1.78
Leath.	44	1.02	0.08	0.94	0.95	0.28	0.67	0.96	0.02	0.94
Foot/Clo.	45	2.01	0.10	1.91	1.93	0.64	1.29	1.88	0.06	1.82
Timber	46	3.61	0.08	3.53	3.63	1.74	1.89	3.66	4.70	-1.04
Paper	47	3.28	0.01	3.27	3.33	0.05	3.28	3.35	0.84	2.51
Rubber	48	1.47	0.02	1.45	1.50	0.13	1.37	1.53	0.02	1.51
Other	49	1.11	0.04	1.07	1.22	0.04	1.18	1.23	4.35	-3.12
Total Man.		1.62	0.05		1.58	0.21		1.60	0.64	

Yugoslavia

NACE		step 1	1986–87	diff.
Met. ex.	21	0.73	0.11	0.62
Met. pr.	22	1.84	1.09	0.75
Min. ex.	23	1.78	0.29	1.49
Min. pr.	24	2.00	0.84	1.16
Chem.	25	1.30	0.41	0.89
Fibres	26	2.00	1.26	0.74
Met. man.	31	1.91	0.68	1.23
Mech. Eng.	32	2.06	0.28	1.78
Office	33	0.76	0.59	0.17
Elec. Eng.	34	1.60	0.65	0.95
Motor	35	1.11	0.70	0.41
Transp.	36	1.35	1.64	-0.29
Instr.	37	1.26	0.11	1.15
Food	41	1.11	0.42	0.69
Drink, T.	42	0.98	0.07	0.91
Text.	43	2.06	1.03	1.03
Leath.	44	1.14	0.97	0.17
Foot/Clo.	45	2.13	2.03	0.10
Timber	46	3.52	2.09	1.43
Paper	47	3.19	0.43	2.76
Rubber	48	1.50	0.64	0.86
Other	49	1.08	0.11	0.97
Total Man.		1.48	0.70	

6-digit NIMEXE level.[10] For an industry such as mechanical engineering (NACE 32) this allows 480 commodities to be distinguished, so the hope is that products are sufficiently narrowly defined to be comparable on the basis of weight. For each of these commodities i belonging to an industry j the price per kg (p_i) has been calculated for each of the competitor countries trading in EC markets (i.e. EE, EC and other non-EC economies). The price per kg of competitor c, p_i^c, has then been divided by the price per kg of the price leader, p_i^l, that is by the price of the competitor with the highest price per kg for this commodity item.

The ratios p_i^c/p_i^l have then been weighted by the share which commodity i has in industry j's total exports to EC markets, and the 'quality indicator' Q_j^c is the sum of the weighted price per kg ratios across commodities $i\varepsilon J$ (where $i\varepsilon J$ is the set of all commodities traded by industry j in EC markets):

$$Q_j^c = \sum_{i \in J} \left(\frac{p_i^c}{p_i^l}\right) \chi_i^c, \qquad (5)$$

where χ_i^c is the share of exports of commodity i in c's total exports in industry j to EC markets.

The Q_j^c are then scaled by dividing by the Q_j^{EC} achieved by the EC six (Germany, France, Italy, UK, Netherlands, Belgium) to give the ratios Q'$_j$ = Q_j^c/Q_j^{EC}, shown in Table 16.7(a).

The first modification to the *naive* projections is to correct for these proxies for industry-level comparative advantage, in turn measured for industry j as Q'$_j$/$\bar{Q}$ where $\bar{Q}$ is the average value of the Q'$_j$. The values of $\bar{Q}$ for the different countries are reported in the last row of Table 16.7(a).[11] The matrix in Table 16.7(b) reports the ratios Q'$_j$/$\bar{Q}$, that is, the range of quality by industry around the country mean, $\bar{Q}$. These ratios have been used as simple multiplicative factors to adjust the *naive* projections of industrial-level export shares in order to account for the differential qualities of the different industries, though they will not affect the country's overall share of manufactured exports in the EC.

Thus if the *naive* projections where χ_j^c, we obtain the modified shares as

$$\bar{\chi}_j^c = \chi_j^c \cdot \left(\frac{Q_j^c}{\bar{Q}^c}\right). \qquad (6)$$

This adjustment means that if industry j had a quality gap of, say, 40 per cent below the average quality gap for country c's total manufacturing exports in EC markets, it will also obtain 40 per cent less of its long-run target market share calculated under the *naive* projections. If the quality gap is lower than the average for total manufacturing it will overachieve the target market shares. These modified (step 2) projections are presented in Table 16.8 and they are compared to the *naive* (step 1) projections.

2.1.2.2 Accounting for size, distance, over-all catching up and political instability (steps 3 to 5) The next correction recognizes the importance of the countries' relative size and of their relative distance from EC markets.

DISTANCE FROM EC MARKETS

Adjustments for relative distance to EC markets will be derived from gravity model estimates which the Kiel group of regional economists obtained by NACE industries. Two effects have been found to be important in regional models:

— distance (in 000km) from the market in question; it is obvious that such distance matters more for some commodities (such as heavy pipes) than for others;
— neighbourhood effects: if countries share a common border the trade intensity is increased in addition to the distance effect. We will introduce both these factors into our final estimates.

SIZE

As proxy for size we use total export capacity of the different EE economies as revealed by their total exports in 1987. (We could have taken an average over a number of years.) In order to obtain data for total exports (rather than just exports to the EC) we had to have recourse to another data-set provided by the United Nations Economic Commission for Europe (UN-ECE): these provide trade flows (in US$) divided into rouble (SU (Soviet Union) and EE6 (the remaining six East European countries excluding Albania)) and non-rouble (EC, other developed, developing) areas. Since the rouble-dollar rates applied by the different EE economies to measure their tradable flows into rouble areas are widely different they have been recalculated applying the 1987 Hungarian rouble-dollar rates to all the other East European economies' trade flows.

The resulting trade flows (and trade shares of export markets) as well as the total (non-fuel) export capacity (in US$) are given in Table 16.9. From these figures our size adjustment coefficients have been derived with Czechoslovakia's (non-fuel) export capacity used as numeraire. Alternative scaling factors might be constructed by attempting to predict total exports as a function of level of development and population, using the methodology of Chenery and Syrquin (1975), but this has not been attempted.

Table 16.7: Quality Measures

(a) Compared to EC(6) – Q'

Q'j		EC(6)	Poland	Czechosl	Hungary	Romania	Bulgaria	Yugosl.	USSR
Met. ex.	21	1	0.68	0.593	1.461	0	0.439	0.984	0.799
Met. pr.	22	1	0.951	0.809	0.859	0.89	0.914	0.836	0.934
Min. ex.	23	1	0.841	0.681	0.822	0.589	0.707	0.782	0.747
Min. pr.	24	1	0.754	0.57	0.778	0.505	0.706	0.619	0.732
Chem.	25	1	1.431	0.848	0.981	0.91	0.842	1.043	0.96
Fibres	26	1	0.478	0.616	0.64	0.61	0.689	0.681	0.625
Met. man.	31	1	0.496	0.486	0.643	0.51	0.469	0.622	0.326
Mech. Eng.	32	1	0.434	0.539	0.624	0.486	0.437	0.661	0.604
Office	33	1	0.585	0.289	0.278	0.176	0.72	0.682	0.604
Elec. Eng.	34	1	0.596	0.611	0.754	0.317	0.446	0.62	0.39
Motor	35	1	0.421	0.387	0.651	0.539	0.374	0.964	0.396
Transp.	36	1	0.488	0.305	0.795	0.247	0.136	0.463	0.647
Instr.	37	1	0.332	0.419	0.338	0.213	0.454	0.542	0.281
Food	41	1	0.832	1.092	0.881	0.651	0.684	0.821	0.862
Drink. T.	42	1	0.893	0.676	0.916	0.697	2.256	0.814	0.700
Text.	43	1	0.477	0.496	0.646	0.565	0.556	0.752	0.578
Leath.	44	1	0.602	0.542	0.88	0.6	0.234	0.711	0.385
Foot./Cl.	45	1	0.466	0.503	0.894	0.413	0.394	0.78	0.747
Timber	46	1	0.604	0.584	0.594	0.442	0.413	0.616	0.861
Paper	47	1	0.967	0.809	0.438	0.716	0.84	0.63	0.925
Rubber	48	1	0.606	0.579	0.703	0.459	0.481	0.641	0.5
Other	49	1	1.167	0.943	0.632	0.479	0.389	1.243	0.377
Average (Qbar)		1	0.841	0.681	0.822	0.589	0.707	0.782	0.747

(b) Compared to country's total manufacturing – Q'j/Qbar

		EC(6)	Poland	Czechosl	Hungary	Romania	Bulgaria	Yugosl.	USSR
Met. ex.	21		0.809	0.871	1.778	0.000	0.621	1.258	1.070
Met. pr.	22		1.131	1.188	1.045	1.511	1.292	1.069	1.250
Min. ex.	23		1.000	1.000	1.000	1.000	1.000	1.000	1.000
Min. pr.	24		0.897	0.837	0.947	0.857	0.998	0.792	0.980
Chem.	25		1.702	1.246	1.194	1.545	1.191	1.334	1.285
Fibres	26		0.568	0.905	0.779	1.036	0.974	0.871	0.837

284

Met. man.	31	0.590	0.714	0.782	0.866	0.663	0.795	0.436
Mech. Eng.	32	0.516	0.792	0.759	0.825	0.618	0.845	0.809
Office	33	0.696	0.424	0.338	0.299	1.018	0.872	0.809
Elec. Eng.	34	0.709	0.897	0.917	0.538	0.631	0.793	0.522
Motor	35	0.501	0.568	0.792	0.915	0.529	1.233	0.530
Transp.	36	0.580	0.448	0.967	0.419	0.192	0.592	0.866
Instr.	37	0.395	0.615	0.411	0.362	0.642	0.693	0.376
Food	41	0.989	1.604	1.072	1.105	0.967	1.050	1.154
Drink, T.	42	1.062	0.993	1.114	1.183	3.190	1.041	0.938
Text.	43	0.567	0.729	0.786	0.959	0.786	0.962	0.774
Leath.	44	0.716	0.796	1.071	1.019	0.331	0.909	0.515
Foot./Cl.	45	0.554	0.739	1.088	0.701	0.557	0.998	1.000
Timber	46	0.718	0.858	0.723	0.750	0.584	0.788	1.153
Paper	47	1.150	1.188	0.533	1.216	1.188	0.806	1.238
Rubber	48	0.721	0.850	0.855	0.779	0.680	0.820	0.669
Other	49	1.388	1.385	0.769	0.813	0.550	1.590	0.504

(c) Compared to EEFSU average for each industry

								EEFSU
Met. ex.	21	0.82	0.72	1.77	0.00	0.53	1.19	0.97	1.0
Met. pr.	22	1.07	0.91	0.97	1.01	1.03	0.94	1.06	1.0
Min. ex.	23	1.14	0.92	1.11	0.80	0.96	1.06	1.01	1.0
Min. pr.	24	1.13	0.86	1.17	0.76	1.06	0.93	1.10	1.0
Chem.	25	1.43	0.85	0.98	0.91	0.84	1.04	0.96	1.0
Fibres	26	0.77	0.99	1.03	0.98	1.11	1.10	1.01	1.0
Met. man.	31	0.98	0.96	1.27	1.01	0.92	1.23	0.64	1.0
Mech. Eng.	32	0.80	1.00	1.15	0.90	0.81	1.22	1.12	1.0
Office	33	1.05	0.52	0.50	0.32	1.30	1.23	1.09	1.0
Elec. Eng.	34	1.12	1.15	1.41	0.59	0.84	1.16	0.73	1.0
Motor	35	0.79	0.73	1.22	1.01	0.70	1.81	0.74	1.0
Transp.	36	1.11	0.69	1.81	0.56	0.31	1.05	1.47	1.0
Instr.	37	0.90	1.14	0.92	0.58	1.23	1.47	0.76	1.0
Food	41	1.00	1.31	1.06	0.78	0.82	0.99	1.04	1.0
Drink, T.	42	0.90	0.68	0.92	0.70	2.27	0.82	0.71	1.0
Text.	43	0.82	0.85	1.11	0.97	0.96	1.29	0.99	1.0
Leath.	44	1.07	0.96	1.56	1.06	0.41	1.26	0.68	1.0
Foot./Cl.	45	0.78	0.84	1.49	0.69	0.66	1.30	1.25	1.0
Timber	46	1.03	0.99	1.01	0.75	0.70	1.05	1.46	1.0
Paper	47	1.27	1.06	0.58	0.94	1.10	0.83	1.22	1.0
Rubber	48	1.07	1.02	1.24	0.81	0.85	1.13	0.88	1.0
Other	49	1.56	1.26	0.85	0.64	0.52	1.66	0.50	1.0

285

Table 16.8: Market Shares Projections – Step 2

NACE		Hungary step 1	step 2	(2)–(1)	Poland step 1	step 2	(2)–(1)	Czech. step 1	step 2	(2)–(1)
Met. ex.	21	0.75	1.33	0.58	0.81	0.65	-0.15	0.93	0.81	-0.12
Met. pr.	22	1.91	1.99	0.09	1.92	2.17	0.25	2.02	2.41	0.38
Min. ex.	23	1.73	1.73	0.00	1.73	1.73	0.00	1.64	1.64	0.00
Min. pr.	24	1.95	1.85	-0.10	1.95	1.75	-0.20	1.81	1.51	-0.29
Chem.	25	1.41	1.69	0.27	1.41	2.39	0.99	1.54	1.92	0.38
Fibres	26	2.06	1.61	-0.46	2.03	1.15	-0.88	2.04	1.85	-0.19
Met. man.	31	1.99	1.56	-0.43	2.00	1.18	-0.82	2.06	1.47	-0.59
Mech. Eng.	32	2.25	1.71	-0.54	2.25	1.16	-1.09	2.50	1.98	-0.52
Office	33	0.86	0.29	-0.57	0.88	0.61	-0.27	1.06	0.45	-0.61
Elec. Eng.	34	1.73	1.58	-0.14	1.73	1.23	-0.50	1.88	1.68	-0.19
Motor	35	1.09	0.86	-0.23	1.12	0.56	-0.56	1.08	0.61	-0.47
Transp.	36	1.41	1.36	-0.05	1.45	0.84	-0.61	1.56	0.70	-0.86
Instr.	37	1.42	0.59	-0.84	1.39	0.55	-0.84	1.60	0.99	-0.62
Food	41	1.24	1.33	0.09	1.23	1.22	-0.01	1.23	1.97	0.74
Drink, T.	42	0.97	1.09	0.11	0.98	1.04	0.06	0.91	0.90	-0.01
Text.	43	2.02	1.59	-0.43	1.98	1.12	-0.86	1.95	1.42	-0.53
Leath.	44	1.12	1.20	0.08	1.12	0.80	-0.32	1.03	0.82	-0.21
Foot./Cl.	45	2.01	2.18	0.18	1.98	1.10	-0.88	1.85	1.37	-0.48
Timber	46	3.57	2.58	-0.99	3.69	2.65	-1.04	3.92	3.36	-0.56
Paper	47	3.22	1.72	-1.50	3.34	3.84	0.50	3.59	4.27	0.68
Rubber	48	1.56	1.33	-0.23	1.56	1.12	-0.44	1.57	1.33	-0.23
Other	49	1.16	0.89	-0.27	1.14	1.59	0.44	1.20	1.66	0.46

NACE		Bulgaria step 1	step 2	(2)–(1)	Romania step 1	step 2	(2)–(1)	USSR step 1	step 2	(2)–(1)
Met. ex.	21	0.79	0.49	-0.30	0.79	0.00	-0.79	0.82	0.88	0.06
Met. pr.	22	1.86	2.40	0.54	1.94	2.93	0.99	1.96	2.46	0.49
Min. ex.	23	1.70	1.70	0.00	1.62	1.62	0.00	1.61	1.61	0.00
Min. pr.	24	1.81	1.81	-0.00	1.73	1.48	-0.25	1.73	1.70	-0.03
Chem.	25	1.39	1.66	0.27	1.55	2.40	0.85	1.58	2.02	0.45
Fibres	26	1.97	1.92	-0.05	2.03	2.10	0.07	2.02	1.69	-0.33
Met. man.	31	1.91	1.27	-0.64	1.98	1.72	-0.27	2.02	0.88	-1.14
Mech. Eng.	32	2.22	1.37	-0.85	2.46	2.03	-0.43	2.51	2.03	-0.48
Office	33	0.89	0.91	0.02	1.01	0.30	-0.71	1.04	0.84	-0.20

				(2)−(1)							
Elec. Eng.	34	1.69	1.06	−0.62	1.83	0.98	−0.84	1.87	0.97	−0.89
Motor	35	1.01	0.54	−0.48	0.95	0.87	−0.08	0.98	0.52	−0.46
Transp.	36	1.39	0.27	−1.12	1.42	0.60	−0.83	1.46	1.27	−0.20
Instr.	37	1.41	0.91	−0.51	1.67	0.60	−1.07	1.69	0.64	−1.05
Food	41	1.20	1.16	−0.04	1.24	1.37	0.13	1.30	1.50	0.20
Drink, T.	42	0.93	2.96	2.03	0.90	1.07	0.17	0.92	0.87	−0.06
Text.	43	2.02	1.59	−0.43	2.03	1.95	−0.08	2.00	1.55	−0.45
Leath.	44	1.02	0.34	−0.68	0.95	0.97	0.02	0.96	0.50	−0.47
Foot./Cl.	45	2.01	1.12	−0.89	1.93	1.35	−0.58	1.88	1.88	0.00
Timber	46	3.61	2.11	−1.50	3.63	2.72	−0.91	3.66	4.21	0.56
Paper	47	3.28	3.90	0.62	3.33	4.05	0.72	3.35	4.14	0.80
Rubber	48	1.47	1.00	−0.47	1.50	1.17	−0.33	1.53	1.03	−0.51
Other	49	1.11	0.61	−0.50	1.22	0.99	−0.23	1.23	0.62	−0.61

Yugoslavia

NACE		step 1	step 2	(2)−(1)
Met. ex.	21	0.73	0.92	0.19
Met. pr.	22	1.84	1.97	0.13
Min. ex.	23	1.78	1.78	0.00
Min. pr.	24	2.00	1.58	−0.42
Chem.	25	1.30	1.74	0.44
Fibres	26	2.00	1.74	−0.26
Met. man.	31	1.91	1.52	−0.39
Mech. Eng.	32	2.06	1.74	−0.32
Office	33	0.76	0.67	−0.10
Elec. Eng.	34	1.60	1.27	−0.33
Motor	35	1.11	1.37	0.26
Transp.	36	1.35	0.80	−0.55
Instr.	37	1.26	0.87	−0.39
Food	41	1.11	1.16	0.06
Drink, T.	42	0.98	1.02	0.04
Text.	43	2.06	1.98	−0.08
Leath.	44	1.14	1.04	−0.10
Foot./Cl.	45	2.13	2.12	−0.01
Timber	46	3.52	2.78	−0.75
Paper	47	3.19	2.57	−0.62
Rubber	48	1.50	1.23	−0.27
Other	49	1.08	1.71	0.64

Table 16.9: Calculation of Export Capacity in 1987 (at official and adjusted $ exchange rates)

	World	Socialist	Non-soc.	Exch.adj.	World adj.	Soc. adj.	% fuel soc.	% fuel non-soc.	Non-fuel exports	Index
Hungary	9 584	5 259	4 324	1.0000	9 584	5 259	0.5	7.4	9 237	0.79
Czechoslovakia	13 632	8 871	4 761	0.8561	12 355	7 595	2.0	9.4	11 756	1.0
Poland	12 210	5 921	6 288	1.3183	14 095	7 806	7.8	14.5	12 574	1.07
Bulgaria	15 855	13 090	2 766	0.3877	7 840	5 075	0.4	22.2	3 352	0.29
Romania	10 491	4 748	5 743	0.7540	9 323	3 580	1.8	22.4	5 516	0.47
Yugoslavia	12 549	3 711	8 838	0.8561	12 015	3 177	2.0	9.4	11 121	0.95
USSR	107 623	69 808	37 814	0.3666	63 408	25 594	47.9	43.9	34 548	2.94

ACCOUNTING FOR GLOBAL DIFFERENCES IN OVERALL CATCHING UP

So far we have assumed that on average (for total manufacturing) the countries will reach their target market share, although the different industries will under or overperform relative to this target. This effectively assumes that the EE countries will achieve the same average quality level as the reference countries by 2010, but while this may be reasonable for the more advanced of the EE countries, i.e. Czechoslovakia, Poland and Hungary, it is less plausible for the remainder.[12] For the remaining countries, that is, Romania, Bulgaria, Yugoslavia and Russia, we assume that they will only achieve a fraction of the equilibrium market share by 2010, where the fraction is equal to their current ratio of average quality to that of the 'frontier countries'. Thus we multiply their target market share by the ratio $\bar{Q}^c/\bar{Q}^{PO}$, where PO is the abbreviation for Poland, as a proxy for their difference in technological ability to export to EC markets. Since Poland has the highest measured $\bar{Q}$ in 1987, the market shares of the 'lagging' Eastern European countries (i.e. Ro, Bu, Yu, SU) are adjusted downwards by that ratio.[13]

Table 16.10 summarizes all the global adjustment factors, and shows that the size variable is the most important variable in this set of global adjustment factors. Since these different adjustment factors are used as simple multiplicative terms (to adjust the market shares for all industries of each country) the total impact of these combined global adjustment factors can be easily calculated (see last row of Table 16.10).

Table 16.10:   Global Adjustment Factors

	Poland	Czech.	Hungary	Romania	Bulgaria	Yugosl.	USSR
Qav/QPoland	1	1	1	0.700	0.841	0.930	0.888
Distance from EC	1	1	1	0.9	0.9	0.95	0.8
Political instability	1	1	1	0.9	0.9	0.85	0.85
Export capacity	1.07	1.00	0.79	0.47	0.29	0.95	2.94
Total Adj.	1.070	1	0.786	0.266	0.194	0.710	1.775

The additional impact of these global adjustments (steps 3 to 5) is shown in Table 16.11 together with the difference between it and the previous modified projections (step 2) which took account of industry-specific quality gaps. The results are summarized in Table 16.12, which shows the original market shares in 1986–87, the market shares arrived at in the *naive* (step 1)

Table 16.11: Market Share Projections – Accounting for Global Factors (Steps 3 to 5)

NACE		Hungary			Poland			Czech.		
		Step 5	Step 2	diff.	Step 5	Step 2	diff.	Step 5	Step 2	diff.
Met. ex.	21	1.33	1.43	0.09	0.65	0.70	0.05	0.81	0.81	0.00
Met. pr.	22	1.99	2.13	0.14	2.17	2.32	0.15	2.41	2.41	0.00
Min. ex.	23	1.73	1.85	0.12	1.73	1.85	0.12	1.64	1.64	0.00
Min. pr.	24	1.85	1.97	0.13	1.75	1.87	0.12	1.51	1.51	0.00
Chem.	25	1.69	1.80	0.12	2.39	2.56	0.17	1.92	1.92	0.00
Fibres	26	1.61	1.72	0.11	1.15	1.23	0.08	1.85	1.85	0.00
Met. man.	31	1.56	1.67	0.11	1.18	1.26	0.08	1.47	1.47	0.00
Mech. Eng.	32	1.71	1.83	0.12	1.16	1.24	0.08	1.98	1.98	0.00
Office	33	0.29	0.31	0.02	0.61	0.66	0.04	0.45	0.45	0.00
Elec. Eng.	34	1.58	1.69	0.11	1.23	1.31	0.09	1.68	1.68	0.00
Motor	35	0.86	0.92	0.06	0.56	0.60	0.04	0.61	0.61	0.00
Transp.	36	1.36	1.46	0.09	0.84	0.90	0.06	0.70	0.70	0.00
Instr.	37	0.59	0.63	0.04	0.55	0.59	0.04	0.99	0.99	0.00
Food	41	1.33	1.42	0.09	1.22	1.31	0.08	1.97	1.97	0.00
Drink, T.	42	1.09	1.16	0.08	1.04	1.11	0.07	0.90	0.90	0.00
Text.	43	1.59	1.70	0.11	1.12	1.20	0.08	1.42	1.42	0.00
Leath.	44	1.20	1.28	0.08	0.80	0.86	0.06	0.82	0.82	0.00
Foot./Cl.	45	2.18	2.33	0.15	1.10	1.17	0.08	1.37	1.37	0.00
Timber	46	2.58	2.76	0.18	2.65	2.83	0.18	3.36	3.36	0.00
Paper	47	1.72	1.84	0.12	3.84	4.11	0.27	4.27	4.27	0.00
Rubber	48	1.33	1.42	0.09	1.12	1.20	0.08	1.33	1.33	0.00
Other	49	0.89	0.95	0.06	1.59	1.70	0.11	1.66	1.66	0.00
Total Man.		1.50	1.61		1.53	1.64		1.66	1.66	0.00

NACE		Bulgaria			Romania			USSR		
		Step 5	Step 2	diff.	Step 5	Step 2	diff.	Step 5	Step 2	diff.
Met. ex.	21	0.49	0.10	-0.39	0.00	0.00	0.00	0.88	1.56	0.68
Met. pr.	22	2.40	0.47	-1.93	2.93	0.78	-2.15	2.46	4.36	1.90
Min. ex.	23	1.70	0.33	-1.37	1.62	0.43	-1.19	1.61	2.85	1.24
Min. pr.	24	1.81	0.35	-1.46	1.48	0.39	-1.09	1.70	3.02	1.32
Chem.	25	1.66	0.32	-1.33	2.40	0.64	-1.76	2.02	3.59	1.57
Fibres	26	1.92	0.37	-1.54	2.10	0.56	-1.54	1.69	3.00	1.31
Met. Man.	31	1.27	0.25	-1.02	1.72	0.46	-1.26	0.88	1.56	0.68
Mech. Eng.	32	1.37	0.27	-1.10	2.03	0.54	-1.49	2.03	3.60	1.57

	Step 5	Step 2	diff.	Step 5	Step 2	diff.	Step 5	Step 2	diff.
Office 33	0.91	0.18	-0.73	0.30	0.08	-0.22	0.84	1.50	0.65
Elec. Eng. 34	1.06	0.21	-0.86	0.98	0.26	-0.72	0.97	1.73	0.76
Motor 35	0.54	0.10	-0.43	0.87	0.23	-0.64	0.52	0.92	0.40
Transp. 36	0.27	0.05	-0.22	0.60	0.16	-0.44	1.27	2.25	0.98
Instr. 37	0.91	0.18	-0.73	0.60	0.16	-0.44	0.64	1.13	0.49
Food 41	1.16	0.23	-0.93	1.37	0.37	-1.01	1.50	2.66	1.16
Drink. T. 42	2.96	0.57	-2.38	1.07	0.28	-0.78	0.87	1.54	0.67
Text. 43	1.59	0.31	-1.28	1.95	0.52	-1.43	1.55	2.75	1.20
Leath. 44	0.34	0.07	-0.27	0.97	0.26	-0.71	0.50	0.88	0.38
Foot./Cl. 45	1.12	0.22	-0.90	1.35	0.36	-0.99	1.88	3.33	1.45
Timber 46	2.11	0.41	-1.70	2.72	0.72	-2.00	4.21	7.48	3.27
Paper 47	3.90	0.76	-3.14	4.05	1.08	-2.97	4.14	7.36	3.21
Rubber 48	1.00	0.19	-0.81	1.17	0.31	-0.86	1.03	1.82	0.80
Other 49	0.61	0.12	-0.49	0.99	0.26	-0.73	0.62	1.10	0.48
Total Man.	1.40	0.27		1.78	0.47		1.61	2.86	

Yugoslavia

NACE	Step 5	Step 2	diff.
Met. ex. 21	0.92	0.65	-0.27
Met. pr. 22	1.97	1.40	-0.57
Min. ex. 23	1.78	1.27	-0.52
Min. pr. 24	1.58	1.13	-0.46
Chem. 25	1.74	1.24	-0.50
Fibres 26	1.74	1.24	-0.50
Met. Man. 31	1.52	1.08	-0.44
Mech. Eng. 32	1.74	1.24	-0.50
Office 33	0.67	0.47	-0.19
Elec. Eng. 34	1.27	0.90	-0.37
Motor 35	1.37	0.97	-0.40
Transp. 36	0.80	0.57	-0.23
Instr. 37	0.87	0.62	-0.25
Food 41	1.16	0.83	-0.34
Drink. T. 42	1.02	0.72	-0.30
Text. 43	1.98	1.40	-0.57
Leath. 44	1.04	0.74	-0.30
Foot./Cl. 45	2.12	1.51	-0.61
Timber 46	2.78	1.97	-0.80
Paper 47	2.57	1.83	-0.74
Rubber 48	1.23	0.87	-0.36
Other 49	1.71	1.22	-0.50
Total Man.	1.63	1.16	

Table 16.12:   *Shares in EC Markets, Total Manufacturing – 1986/87 and*
                   Projections for the Year 2010

	Poland	Czech.	Hungary	Romania	Bulgaria	Yugoslav.	USSR	East Eur.
Actual 86–87	0.33	0.30	0.21	0.21	0.05	0.70	0.64	2.42
Step 1	1.67	1.74	1.66	1.58	1.62	1.48	1.60	11.35
Step 2	1.53	1.66	1.50	1.78	1.40	1.63	1.61	11.12
Step 5	1.64	1.66	1.61	0.47	0.27	1.16	2.86	9.67
Step 6	1.47	1.48	1.43	0.42	0.24	1.04	2.56	8.64

projections, and the two additional sets of modifications for total manufacturing. Using the final long-term projections (step 5) we can calculate the
total increase in market shares of the whole group of Eastern European
economies (for total manufacturing see again Table 16.12) and we can come
to our last question linked to the market shares projections for the year 2010:

2.1.3.   At whose cost will increases in market shares by Eastern
European economies in EC markets occur? (Step 6)

We used a very simple method to calculate the future market shares (by the
years 2000/2010) of the other trading groups in EC markets. We assume that
their market shares would continue to expand or contract relatively at half
the annual rates they experienced over the period 1977–78 to 1986–87 from
1987 to 2000, and thereafter remain constant. (See Figure 16.2).

Figure 16.2   Market Share Increases of Other (non EE) Trading Groups

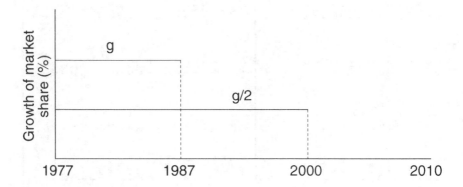

From these projections for the non-EE trading groups plus the EE projections derived under 2.1.1 and 2.1.2 above we obtained initial market shares for the year 2010 which add up to more than 100 per cent. The market shares of EE and non-EE economies were scaled down to add up to exactly 100 per cent. Table 16.13 shows the results and derives the increases/decreases in market shares of the different trading countries by the year 2010 as well as percentage differences from the original 1986–87 market shares.

This completes our long-term projections apart from some modifications, made to highly natural resource-based industries (minerals and furs) which are treated differently (see Appendix B1 for their separate projections).

2.2 Short-term Projections

The projections of exports up to 1995 are done separately from the long-term projections using a different methodology. (At one point, however, the long-term projections do play a role and this will be pointed out below.) We take two factors as determining the growth in export volumes from EE to EC markets:

1. The conversion of export capacities which were – in the past (i.e. in 1987) – oriented towards East European markets (including the Soviet Union).
2. The building up of new export capacities designed to capture an increasing share of EC markets.

To analyse these two factors we used a data base supplied by UNCTAD in Geneva which was on an SITC (revision 2) classification basis – and not on a NIMEXE basis as the Eurostat trade statistics used so far. The data for East European countries as reporting countries included only Czechoslovakia, Hungary and Poland. The figures for the remaining countries (Bulgaria, Romania, Yugoslavia and the Soviet Union) were calculated from global trade figures supplied by the UN Economic Commission for Europe (see Table 16.9) supplemented by the industrial structural information contained in the statistics for Czechoslovakia, Hungary and Poland. (For details concerning these calculations see Appendix B2.)

Since we are interested in conversion of capacities previously oriented towards East European markets we had to obtain information on past export flows to rouble and non-rouble areas and so it was essential to complement our Eurostat statistics by the UN statistics. This implied that we also had to put considerable effort into mapping the SITC based data into a NIMEXE/NACE classification.[14] This was done at a 3-digit SITC and 2-digit NACE level.[15] The result of this conversion of SITC trade flows into NACE indus-

Table 16.13: Market Shares in EC Markets

(a) Actual in 1986–87

		Eastern Europe Proj. Step 5	EEC (6)	Rest EC	Rest WE	East Eur.	Japan	Rest OECD	NICs	RoW
Met. ex.	21	5.24	10.29	3.06	7.83	0.36	0.01	17.29	0.04	61.12
Met. pr.	22	13.86	57.7	3.92	15.75	4.48	0.63	3.02	0.39	14.11
Min. ex.	23	10.22	40.94	11.22	7.96	1.8	0.06	10.01	0.03	27.99
Min. pr.	24	10.25	71.77	9.15	7.59	2.75	2.5	2.92	2.23	1.1
Chem.	25	12.07	69.53	4.62	10.07	2.05	2.69	6.9	0.46	3.67
Fibres	26	9.97	69.68	7.9	12.24	2.8	1.56	3.86	0.59	1.36
Met. man.	31	7.75	69.31	6.82	11.98	1.85	2.09	2.77	3.99	1.19
Mech. Eng.	32	10.69	64.78	4.22	16.69	0.88	5.46	6.41	0.81	0.77
Office	33	3.64	40.95	1.44	7.63	0.85	29	9.51	9.28	1.35
Elec. Eng.	34	7.79	57.95	5.42	11.91	1.23	7.84	10.51	3.67	1.48
Motor	35	4.36	75.37	3.81	5.08	1.46	12.99	0.47	0.16	0.66
Transp.	36	6.08	39.92	3.02	12.1	2.46	25.38	7.77	5.56	3.79
Instr.	37	4.29	46.69	2.01	11.6	0.48	25.84	8.16	4.37	0.85
Food	41	8.78	56.09	12.22	2.55	2.28	0.29	7.38	0.3	18.88
Food/Drink	42	6.30	66.2	8.73	1.28	0.81	0.08	2.58	0.07	20.23
Text.	43	9.30	57.31	11.78	7.58	2.46	2.42	1.14	5.94	11.37
Leath.	44	4.90	46.14	4.73	4.28	2.24	1.02	1.38	11.66	28.55
Foot./Cl.	45	10.29	44.75	14.8	4.44	3.66	0.58	0.83	16.86	14.08
Timber	46	19.54	31.47	8.05	25.24	11.34	0.1	8.62	2.08	13.11
Paper	47	21.23	47.43	6.53	25.2	1.97	0.74	14.99	0.67	2.47
Rubber	48	7.16	72.77	5.91	8.74	1.3	2.9	4.16	2.51	1.71
Other	49	7.02	35.52	3.86	6.86	4.89	2.92	6.12	11.11	28.72

(b) Projections for 2010

NACE	EEC (6)	Rest EC	Rest WE	East Eur.	Japan	Rest OECD	NICs	RoW
210	13.53	2.88	5.66	5.04	0.01	16.64	0.01	56.23
220	52.62	4.91	17.50	12.24	0.28	1.64	0.62	10.17
230	38.83	15.15	7.11	8.69	0.02	5.08	0.02	25.11
240	62.38	12.42	6.92	9.37	2.18	2.68	2.72	1.32
250	60.81	5.68	9.58	10.76	3.65	4.84	0.91	3.77
260	59.90	11.27	11.43	9.03	1.50	2.75	2.03	2.10
310	63.58	7.37	12.08	7.24	1.61	1.96	5.13	1.03
320	55.67	4.16	15.94	9.45	8.04	4.44	1.49	0.80
330	35.07	0.93	6.77	3.42	31.10	8.33	11.62	2.76

	EEC (6)	Rest EC	Rest WE	East Eur.	Japan	Rest OECD	NICs	RoW
340	49.97	6.63	11.29	7.16	9.39	9.38	4.35	1.83
350	65.84	4.58	6.54	4.09	17.82	0.22	0.91	0.00
360	38.60	2.70	5.27	4.80	19.08	11.01	11.45	7.09
370	43.39	2.19	8.80	4.06	27.85	7.98	4.87	0.86
410	57.40	11.63	2.09	8.04	0.17	5.76	0.14	14.78
420	68.17	8.04	0.73	5.81	0.09	2.40	0.06	14.70
430	48.09	15.99	7.37	8.40	3.59	0.56	6.00	10.00
440	43.40	4.89	5.14	4.71	0.64	1.14	13.17	26.91
450	34.59	23.45	3.64	9.03	0.49	0.49	14.37	13.94
460	28.22	9.95	22.00	17.55	0.03	7.57	1.25	13.43
470	42.25	7.09	18.12	17.48	0.85	10.59	0.70	2.91
480	65.12	5.87	8.59	6.65	4.32	3.43	3.67	2.35
490	34.34	4.00	4.62	6.52	3.24	4.94	17.57	24.77
Total Man.	56.37	7.33	9.61	8.64	6.61	3.83	2.71	4.90

(c) *Changes in Market Shares from 1987 to 2010*

NACE	EEC (6)	Rest EC	Rest WE	East Eur.	Japan	Rest OECD	NICs	RoW
210	3.27	-0.17	-2.16	4.50	-0.00	-0.62	-0.03	-4.78
220	-5.08	0.99	1.75	7.76	-0.35	-1.38	0.23	-3.94
230	-2.11	3.93	-0.85	6.89	-0.04	-4.93	-0.01	-2.88
240	-9.39	3.27	-0.67	6.62	-0.32	-0.24	0.49	0.22
250	-8.72	1.06	-0.49	8.71	0.96	-2.06	0.45	0.10
260	-9.78	3.37	-0.81	6.23	-0.06	-1.11	1.44	0.74
310	-5.73	0.55	0.10	5.39	-0.48	-0.81	1.14	-0.16
320	-9.11	-0.06	-0.75	8.57	2.58	-1.97	0.68	0.03
330	-5.88	-0.51	-0.86	2.57	2.10	-1.18	2.34	1.41
340	-7.98	1.21	-0.62	5.93	1.55	-1.13	0.68	0.35
350	-9.53	0.77	1.46	2.63	4.83	-0.25	0.75	-0.66
360	-1.32	-0.32	-6.83	2.34	-6.30	3.24	5.89	3.30
370	-3.30	0.18	-2.80	3.58	2.01	-0.18	0.50	0.01
410	1.31	-0.59	-0.46	5.76	-0.12	-1.62	-0.16	-4.10
420	1.97	-0.69	-0.55	5.00	0.01	-0.18	-0.01	-5.53
430	-9.22	4.21	-0.21	5.94	1.17	-0.58	0.06	-1.37
440	-2.74	0.16	0.86	2.47	-0.38	-0.24	1.51	-1.64
450	-10.16	8.65	-0.80	5.37	-0.09	-0.34	-2.49	-0.14
460	-3.25	1.90	-3.24	6.21	-0.07	-1.05	-0.83	0.32
470	-5.18	0.56	-7.08	15.51	0.11	-4.40	0.03	0.44
480	-7.65	-0.04	-0.15	5.35	1.42	-0.73	1.16	0.64
490	-1.18	0.14	-2.24	1.63	0.32	-1.18	6.46	-3.95
Total Man.	-7.60	1.29	-0.44	6.59	1.56	-1.30	0.44	-0.53

295

Table 16.14: *Short-run Projections – Capacity Conversion and Export Growth, 1987–95*

Czechoslovakia

		(1) EE (6)	(2) USSR	(3) Other Europe	(4) Other Devpd	(5) EC share 11/(3+4+11)	(6) EEFSU share (1+2)/ (1+2+3+4+11)	(7) EEFSU factor
Metal Pr.	22	351 376	314 059	271 235	14 385	48.86	54.37	0.59
Miner Ex.	23	23 514	0	15 251	0	58.24	39.17	0.71
Miner Pr.	24	211 838	170 147	27 984	24 237	70.70	68.19	0.49
Chemicals	25	432 587	343 218	185 348	13 727	58.33	61.89	0.54
Fibres	26	41 839	18 068	3 804	0	74.97	79.77	0.40
Metal Pds.	31	130 572	76 153	10 214	557	74.64	82.96	0.38
Mech Eng.	32	1 413 959	2 434 944	144 719	200 620	28.77	88.81	0.33
Office Eq.	33	97 209	193 286	10 496	0	0.00	96.51	0.28
Elec Eng.	34	518 143	430 132	49 305	5 858	53.64	88.85	0.33
Motor Veh.	35	726 326	705 599	22 683	2 412	76.23	93.13	0.30
Other Tran.	36	212 792	818 665	42 536	10 998	13.35	94.35	0.29
Instr Eng.	37	127 088	102 183	2 903	152	41.17	97.79	0.27
Food, Dri.	41/42	50 996	72 841	84 174	19 377	56.51	34.22	0.74
Textiles	43	116 348	169 287	111 365	35 302	48.94	49.86	0.63
Leather	44	1 833	0	2 208	564	24.59	33.27	0.75
Ft., Cloth.	45	93 783	786 674	47 327	26 878	60.29	82.49	0.38
Timb., Furn.	46	37 919	200 074	87 873	3 648	65.68	47.16	0.65
Paper	47	55 716	25 079	64 204	807	65.98	29.71	0.78
Rub., Plast.	48	68 209	37 673	7 275	4 861	71.08	71.61	0.46
Oth. Man.	49	105 610	137 959	23 528	21 651	71.92	60.22	0.55

NACE		(8) USSR share 2/(1+2)	(9) USSR factor	(10) Convers. rate	(11) EC 1987	(12) EC 95	(13) Convers. gr. rate	(14) Q'	(15) new inv. gr. rate	(16) overall gr. rate
Metal Pr.	22	47.20	0.92	0.54	272 901	449 447	2.71	0.809	5.70	8.41
Miner Ex.	23	44.54	0.93	0.66	21 272	30 294	1.92	0.671	4.76	6.68
Miner Pr.	24	44.54	0.93	0.46	126 005	249 084	3.70	0.57	4.08	7.78
Chemicals	25	44.24	0.93	0.50	278 656	505 262	3.23	0.848	5.97	9.20
Fibres	26	30.16	1.02	0.41	11 393	29 780	5.22	0.616	4.39	9.60
Metal Pds.	31	36.84	0.98	0.37	31 703	88 777	5.59	0.486	3.50	9.09
Mech Eng.	32	63.26	0.82	0.27	139 458	442 759	6.27	0.539	3.87	10.14
Office Eq.	33	66.54	0.80	0.22	0	0	6.75	0.289	2.17	8.91
Elec Eng.	34	45.36	0.93	0.31	63 814	221 249	6.75	0.611	4.35	11.10
Motor Veh.	35	49.28	0.90	0.27	80 464	378 066	8.40	0.387	2.83	11.23
Other Tran.	36	79.37	0.72	0.21	8 251	37 401	8.20	0.305	2.27	10.48
Instr Eng.	37	44.57	0.93	0.25	2 138	25 608	13.48	0.419	3.05	16.53
Food	41	58.82	0.85	0.63	134 544	178 610	1.54	1.092	7.63	9.16
Food, Dri.	42						1.54	0.676	4.80	6.34
Textiles	43	59.27	0.84	0.53	140 589	214 491	2.29	0.496	3.57	5.87
Leather	44	59.27	0.84	0.63	904	1 190	1.49	0.542	3.89	5.38
Ft., Cloth.	45	89.35	0.66	0.25	112 648	247 020	4.26	0.503	3.62	7.88
Timb., Furn.	46	84.07	0.70	0.45	175 166	245 444	1.83	0.584	4.17	6.00
Paper	47	31.04	1.01	0.79	126 112	168 114	1.56	0.809	5.70	7.26
Rub., Plast.	48	35.58	0.99	0.46	29 834	64 204	4.16	0.579	4.14	8.30
Oth. Man.	49	56.64	0.86	0.47	115 716	198 340	2.93	0.943	6.61	9.54

Note:

Data in cols (1–4 and 11) come from UNCTAD trade statistics; trade flows to EE6 and USSR have been recalculated at Hungarian transferable Rouble/ECU exchange rates for all Eastern European economies. The data are in 000 ECU and differ somewhat from the Eurostat figures presented in Table 16.15 below.

Hungary

		(1) EE (6)	(2) USSR	(3) Other Europe	(4) Other Devpd	(5) EC share 11/(3+4+11)	(6) EEFSU share (1+2)/ (1+2+3+4+11)	(7) EEFSU factor
Metal Pr.	22	78 409	102 004	92 283	48 618	47.68	40.12	0.70
Miner Ex.	23	1 802	234	3 759		25.87	28.65	0.79
Miner Pr.	24	16 878	14 380	20 928	9 902	57.18	30.27	0.77
Chemicals	25	147 059	258 936	157 025	54 298	55.98	45.82	0.66
Fibres	26					41.12	35.93	0.73
Metal Pds.	31	29 776	46 236	14 095.8	2 868.997	72.93	54.81	0.59
Mech Eng.	32	243 756	358 362	18 885.65	3 875.999	76.36	86.22	0.35
Office Eq.	33					16.64	96.34	0.28
Elec Eng.	34	26 818	10 904	8 512.795	78.9972	55.77	66.01	0.50
Motor Veh.	35	5 738	6 843	951.7953	69.9972	68.72	79.39	0.40
Other Tran.	36	5 738	6 843	951.7953	69.9972	68.72	79.39	0.40
Instr Eng.	37					76.36	86.22	0.35
Food, Dri.	41/42	154 541	452 616	154 642.5	60 385.5	62.59	51.37	0.61
Textiles	43	29 293	61 711	65 023	30 521	41.12	35.93	0.73
Leather	44	8 433	6 610	9 424	4 135	66.03	27.37	0.79
Ft., Cloth.	45	38 032	209 233	35 499	58 888	65.16	47.72	0.64
Timb., Furn.	46	12 314	14 764	29 053	8676	66.09	19.57	0.85
Paper	47	8 349	12 113	15 816.88	1 015.75	44.28	40.38	0.70
Rub., Plast.	48	19 754	21 072	13 572.88	9 342.75	53.07	45.54	0.66
Oth. Man.	49	24 396	38 245	12 282.25	6629.5	61.28	56.19	0.58

NACE		(8) USSR share 2/(1+2)	(9) USSR factor	(10) Convers. rate	(11) EC 1987	(12) EC 95	(13) Convers. gr. rate	(14) Q'	(15) new inv. gr. rate	(16) overall gr. rate
Metal Pr.	22	56.54	0.86	0.60	128 399	180 163	1.84	0.859	6.04	7.88
Miner Ex.	23	11.49	1.13	0.89	1 312	1 780	1.66	0.807	5.69	7.34
Miner Pr.	24	46.00	0.92	0.71	41 169	53 934	1.47	0.778	5.49	6.96
Chemicals	25	63.78	0.82	0.54	268 694	390 605	2.03	0.981	6.87	8.90
Fibres	26	67.81	0.79			0.58	2.16	0.64	4.55	6.71
Metal Pds.	31	60.83	0.84	0.49	45 703	72 964	2.54	0.643	4.57	7.11
Mech Eng.	32	59.52	0.84	0.30	73 504	210 447	5.71	0.624	4.44	10.15
Office Eq.	33	66.48	0.80			0.22	3.78	0.278	2.09	5.87
Elec Eng.	34	28.91	1.03	0.52	10 832	21 736	3.78	0.754	5.33	9.11
Motor Veh.	35	54.39	0.87	0.35	2 244	5 300	4.66	0.651	4.63	9.29
Other Man.	36	54.39	0.87	0.35	2 244	5 300	4.66	0.795	5.61	10.27
Instr Eng.	37	59.52	0.84			0.30	5.71	0.338	2.50	8.21
Food	41	74.55	0.75	0.46	359 686	535 507	2.16	0.881	6.19	8.35
Food, Dri.	42						2.16	0.916	6.43	8.59
Textiles	43	67.81	0.79	0.58	66 727	88 409	1.53	0.646	4.59	6.12
Leather	44	43.94	0.94	0.74	26 360	33 752	1.34	0.88	6.18	7.53
Ft., Cloth.	45	84.62	0.69	0.44	176 492	248 105	1.85	0.894	6.28	8.13
Timb., Furn.	46	54.52	0.87	0.74	73 547	86 875	0.90	0.594	4.24	5.14
Paper	47	59.20	0.84	0.59	13 378	18 715	1.82	0.438	3.18	5.00
Rub., Plast.	48	51.61	0.89	0.59	25 909	38 609	2.17	0.703	4.98	7.15
Oth. Man.	49	61.05	0.83	0.48	29 929	48 444	2.61	0.632	4.50	7.11

Poland

		(1)	(2)	(3) Other	(4) Other	(5) EC	(6) EEFSU	(7) EEFSU
		EE (6)	USSR	Europe	Devpd	share 11/(3+4+11)	share (1+2)/ (1+2+3+4+11)	factor
Metal Pr.	22	120 942	150 387	135 603	37 954	73.20	29.53	0.78
Miner Ex.	23	67 043	59 874	33 472		72.69	50.87	0.62
Miner Pr.	24	27 657	8 402	26 739	16 094	53.84	27.99	0.79
Chemicals	25	77 956	367 546	154 628	28 310	53.33	53.20	0.60
Fibres	26	5 488	654	2 026	17	32.64	66.94	0.50
Metal Pds.	31	88 012	105 764	43 938	16 653	55.15	58.92	0.56
Mech Eng.	32	565 304	546 233	51 862	31 421	60.89	83.92	0.37
Office Eq.	33	81 643	161 553	4 977	1 505	33.28	96.16	0.28
Elec Eng.	34	215 787	341 153	74 679	9 672	53.56	75.41	0.43
Motor Veh.	35	136 789	158 405	40 480	5 370	69.68	66.13	0.50
Other Tran.	36	118 021	384 355	163 251	30 148	20.13	67.48	0.49
Instr Eng.	37	63 144	57 747	5 810	2 223	57.30	86.53	0.35
Food, Dri.	41/42	30 249	87 060	89 465	152 759	54.01	18.21	0.86
Textiles	43	30 438	38 961	61 220	29 310	46.17	29.21	0.78
Leather	44	0		4 909	554	46.17	29.21	0.78
Ft., Cloth.	45	23 516	222 798	35 480	49 492	73.27	43.66	0.67
Timb., Furn.	46	6 760	48 176	38 809	8 739	79.50	19.15	0.86
Paper	47	5 755	7 557	17 203	867	66.34	19.87	0.85
Rub., Plast.	48	11 070	14 084	8 526	272	63.14	51.31	0.62
Oth. Man.	49	19 530	22 225	12 686	4 502	65.84	45.35	0.66

NACE		(8) USSR share 2/(1+2)	(9) USSR factor	(10) Convers. rate	(11) EC 1987	(12) EC 95	(13) Convers. gr. rate	(14) Q'	(15) new inv. gr. rate	(16) overall gr. rate
Metal Pr.	22	55.43	0.87	0.68	473 983	608 108	1.35	0.951	6.67	8.02
Miner Ex.	23	47.18	0.92	0.57	89 082	141 397	2.51	0.841	5.10	7.60
Miner Pr.	24	23.30	1.06	0.84	49 956	66 218	1.53	0.754	5.33	6.86
Chemicals	25	82.50	0.70	0.42	209 035	309 703	2.13	1.066	7.45	9.58
Fibres	26	10.65	1.14	0.57	990	2 124	4.14	0.478	3.45	7.59
Metal Pds.	31	54.58	0.87	0.49	74 500	126 536	2.88	0.496	3.57	6.45
Mech Eng.	32	49.14	0.91	0.34	129 642	356 647	5.49	0.434	3.15	8.64
Office Eq.	33	66.43	0.80	0.22	3 233	21 317	10.24	0.585	4.18	14.42
Elec Eng.	34	61.25	0.83	0.36	97 289	205 176	4.05	0.596	4.25	8.30
Motor Veh.	35	53.66	0.88	0.44	105 355	196 383	3.38	0.421	3.06	6.44
Other Tran.	36	76.51	0.74	0.37	48 733	85 737	3.07	0.488	3.52	6.59
Instr Eng.	37	47.77	0.91	0.32	10 779	32 986	6.07	0.332	2.46	8.53
Food	41	74.21	0.75	0.65	284 520	325 809	0.74	0.832	5.86	6.59
Food, Dri.	42						0.74	0.893	6.27	7.01
Textiles	43	56.14	0.86	0.67	77 637	99 233	1.33	0.477	3.44	4.78
Leather	44	56.14	0.86	0.67			1.33	0.602	4.29	5.63
Ft., Cloth.	45	90.45	0.66	0.44	232 935	312 720	1.60	0.466	3.37	4.97
Timb., Furn.	46	87.69	0.67	0.58	184 417	209 621	0.70	0.604	4.31	5.00
Paper	47	56.77	0.86	0.73	35 619	42 077	0.90	0.967	6.78	7.68
Rub., Plast.	48	55.99	0.86	0.53	15 069	23 510	2.41	0.606	4.32	6.74
Oth. Man.	49	53.23	0.88	0.58	33 135	49 112	2.14	1.167	8.14	10.27

Sources:
Cols (1–4 and 11): UNCTAD Trade Statistics (ISTC classification: own reclassifications).

try exports is reported in Table 16.14 (columns 1–4). We again recalculated rouble trade flows of each country using the Hungarian rouble/dollar exchange rate in 1987.

The methodology applied to calculate conversion rates (i.e. which proportions of export capacity previously orientated towards East European markets will be converted into trade with the West) was the following:

First we calculated the shares of exports of each of the three countries (CZ, HU, PO) to EE (including the SU) in total exports (column 5). We made the following assumption: if an industry's exports went entirely to EE markets (i.e. none to the Western markets) in 1987 only 25 per cent of those exports could be converted into trade to Western markets, but if a fraction t went to the West, the fraction reallocated to Western markets would be 0.25 + 0.75t, as shown in Figure 16.3.

Figure 16.3:   Derivation of Export Capacity Conversion Rates

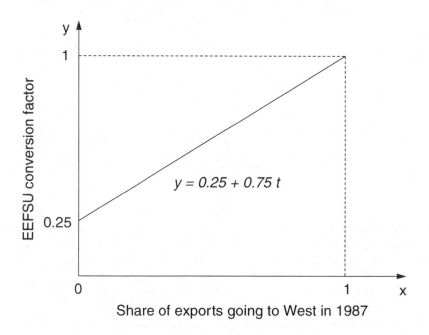

Share of exports going to West in 1987

These calculated conversion rates for the different industries were further modified to account for the proportion of exports to the Soviet Union in total exports to Eastern Europe in 1987 (column 8 of Table 16.14). That is, if a high proportion of total exports to Eastern Europe went to the Soviet Union, then the previously calculated conversion rates would be further modified by multiplication with the ratios derived from the following linear relationship: $y = 1.2 - 0.6x$, where x is the ratio of exports to the SU in 1987 divided by total exports to EE, and y is the multiplicative factor (see Figure 16.4).

*Figure 16.4:   Derivation of USSR Modification Factors in Export
                 Capacity Conversion*

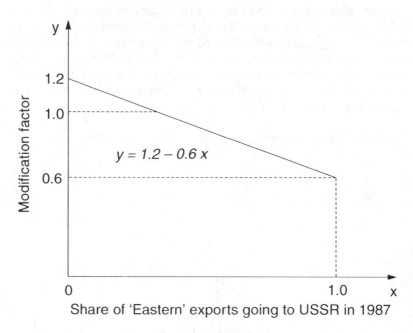

Share of 'Eastern' exports going to USSR in 1987

The derived conversion rates (to Western markets) of capacities previously orientated towards exports to Eastern Europe are given in Tables 16.14 (column 10). The shares of these converted capacities (by 1995) going to the EC as compared to other Western markets has been assumed to remain a fixed ratio (the same as in 1987). The implied annual growth rates of exports to EC (at 1987 prices) until 1995 which result from this conversion of capacities are given in column (13) of Table 16.14.

In addition to this conversion of capacities previously orientated towards EE markets we have to take account of the *building up of new export capacities* to the West. Here we assume the following: If there were no *quality gap* (i.e. $Q'_j = 1.0$) the growth rate of new export capacity to the EC would be equal to 7 per cent p.a. (This translates into an average growth rate for the core EE countries of about 5 per cent p.a., which could be scaled up if thought appropriate.) Different industries which had a different starting position in terms of the quality gap in their exports to EC markets would – in the period up to 1995 – then build up their new export capacities at differential rates given by the relationship: $g_j = 0.2 + 6.8Q_j$, shown in Figure 16.6.

The resulting annual growth rates of new export capacity to EC markets (starting with their levels in 1987 are in column (15) of Table 16.14. The overall growth rates – i.e. the combined growth rates derived from the conversion of capacities previously orientated towards East European markets and from the assumption about the building up of new export capacities oriented towards EC markets – are in column (16) of Table 16.14. The methodology used to arrive at short-term forcasts for Bulgaria, Romania, Yugoslavia and the Soviet Union for which comprehensive trade statistics at a comparable level of disaggregation are not available in the UNCTAD data base, is described in Appendix B2.

Figure 16.5:   *The growth rate of new manufacturing export capacities*

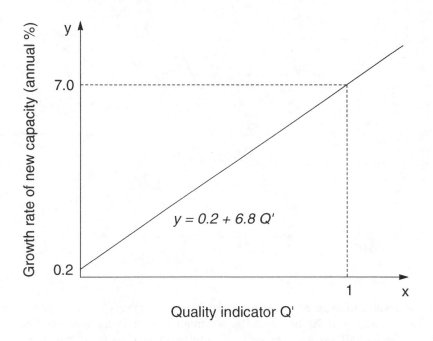

2.3   Medium-term Projections and the Pattern of Catching Up

The assumption underlying the medium-term projections – i.e. from 1995 to 2000 – is that no more conversion of East European capacities previously oriented towards Eastern Europe will take place. Whatever has not been converted up to 1995 will play no further role in the growth of exports to the West. The growth rates of exports of the different industries to EC markets will be entirely driven by its target share for 2010 derived from the long-term projections in sections 1 to 3, and the positions achieved by 1995 determined by the short-term projections. On the basis of these assumptions, the time profile of the catching-up process is going to look like Figure 16.6. g_j^c refers to the industry j's growth rate of exports to EC markets derived from conversion of existing capacities, g_j^n refers to growth in exports to EC markets from new capacities, and g_j is simply $g_j = g_j^c + g_j^n$. We can see that, by assumption, $g_j = g_j^n$ for the period after 1995.

Figure 16.6:   Growth Path of Exports between 1987 and 2010

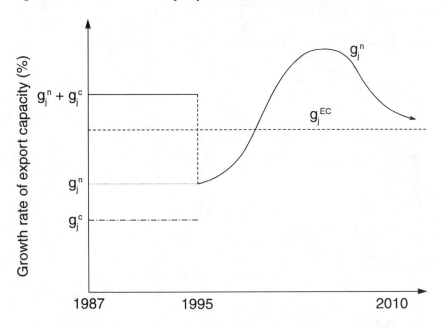

For comparative purposes we have also drawn the average annual growth of the expansion of the EC traded goods market for industry j, denoted by g_j^{EC}. The overall catching-up process implied by our analysis, which re-quires a substantial increase in the market shares of EE countries in EC markets, implies that g_j^{EE} (where EE stands for an East European country) is substantially above g_j^{EC} over much of the period 1987 to 2010. Whenever there is a shortfall in one sub-period there must be a compensating speeding up of growth in subsequent periods. The main reason for the catching-up process as postulated in our model was that there is a quality gap, expressed by our indicator $Q'_j(t)$, which closes over time. Literature suggests (see e.g. Verspagen, 1991) that when a quality gap is very high, it is difficult to start a catching-up process; when the quality gap is less than this threshold level but still large, a country can achieve the highest differential growth rates between the advanced competitors and themselves, and as the quality gap closes (i.e. $Q'_j \rightarrow 1$) the growth rates also asymptotically approach the rate of overall market growth (in our case $g_j^{EE} \rightarrow gj^{EC}$). In algebraic terms, the differential in export growth rates can thus be made a function of a closing quality gap, such as:

$$g_j^{EE}(t) - g_j^{EC}(t) = \lambda_j (1.0 - Q'_j(t)) \text{ where } Q'_j(t) \leq 1.0$$

The above discussion is quite consistent with the assumption made in the short-run projections where we assumed that investment into new capacities is inversely related to the quality gap, that is, the higher the quality gap the lower the rate of initial export expansion. This is what characterizes the short-run differential expansion of new export capacity over the period 1987–95. Over the medium to long term, however, the relationship reverses and we assume that the higher the initial quality gap the greater the scope for catching up; the differential growth rates of exports as described by the equation above express this relationship. The switch from a negative short-run relationship between the size of the quality gap and differential export growth in the short run to a positive relationship over the medium to long term is compatible with the threshold phenomenon mentioned above.[16]

The quantitative estimates of the respective average annual growth rates over the periods 1987–95, 1995–2000 and 2000–10 as well as the levels of exports achieved at each target date are summarized in Table 16.15.

In the last column of this table we present for comparative purposes a long-run steady state growth rate of exports (g_i^{8710}) of an industry if it were to attain the 'target' market share in EC markets at a continuous steady state rate of expansion starting in 1987. If the short-run growth rate (g_i^{8795}) is below that steady-state rate, the medium- to long-run growth rate would obviously have to exceed that steady-state rate to achieve the final 'target'. The information on total manufacturing gives a clear picture of the implied short-run and medium-run growth rates of exports to EC markets which is compatible with our analysis of catching-up processes discussed above and summarized in Figure 16.6.

Table 16.15: Projections for Growth 1987–95, 1995–2010

POLAND

NACE		1987	g_i^{8795}	1995	2000	g_i^{9510}	2010	g_i^{8710}
Metal Ex.	21	10 101	6.17	16 553	25 178	8.39	58 251	7.62
Metal Pr.	22	299 820	8.02	569 492	903 254	9.23	2 272 241	8.81
Miner Ex.	23	2 777	7.60	5 102	12 853	18.48	81 556	14.70
Miner Pr.	24	54 575	6.86	94 457	183 580	13.29	693 442	11.05
Chemicals	25	236 895	9.58	509 917	1 030 258	14.07	4 205 714	12.51
Mn-MD FBS	26	3 567	7.59	6 549	19 762	22.09	179 938	17.05
Metal Pds.	31	65 761	6.45	110 157	230 596	14.78	1 010 480	11.88
Mech Eng.	32	83 705	8.64	167 149	407 477	17.82	2 421 583	14.63
Office Eq.	33	1 170	14.42	3 708	28 561	40.83	1 694 976	31.65
Elec Eng.	34	82 902	8.30	161 087	418 016	19.07	2 814 860	15.33
Motor Veh.	35	96 006	6.44	160 755	374 102	16.89	2 026 009	13.26
Other Tran.	36	46 252	6.59	78 329	65 938	-3.44	46 725	0.04
Instr Eng.	37	8 970	8.53	17 748	57 763	23.60	611 877	18.36
Food	41	355 038	6.59	601 655	871 145	7.40	1 826 319	7.12
Food, Dri.	42	4 010	7.01	7 027	22 125	22.94	219 336	17.40
Textiles	43	87 288	4.78	127 905	239 301	12.53	837 647	9.83
Leather	44	11 674	5.63	18 310	29 352	9.44	75 432	8.11
Ft., Cloth.	45	306 518	4.97	456 095	545 741	3.59	781 355	4.07
Timb., Furn.	46	196 108	5.00	292 620	387 492	5.62	679 483	5.40
Paper	47	30 538	7.68	56 452	177 228	22.88	1 746 792	17.59
Rub., Plast.	48	23 537	6.74	40 343	123 831	22.43	1 166 694	16.97
Oth. Man.	49	40 826	10.27	92 858	221 933	17.43	1 267 738	14.94
Total Man.		2 048 038	7.02	3 592 169	6 372 880	13.38	26 718 449	11.17

HUNGARY

NACE		1987	g_i^{8795}	1995	2000	g_i^{9510}	2010	g_i^{8710}
Metal Ex.	21	66	11.97	172	4 458	40.69	76 921	30.70
Metal Pr.	22	162 437	7.88	305 116	671 095	9.85	1 337 560	9.17
Miner Ex.	23	1 748	7.34	3 145	15 122	19.63	59 749	15.36
Miner Pr.	24	39 365	6.96	68 676	191 451	12.82	469 518	10.78
Chemicals	25	204 555	8.90	416 956	1 096 761	12.09	2 556 414	10.98
Mn-MD FBS	26	6 701	6.71	11 465	46 873	17.60	160 708	13.81
Metal Pds.	31	55 656	7.11	98 312	311 503	14.42	854 500	11.88
Mech Eng.	32	92 774	10.15	209 025	746 278	15.91	2 272 562	13.91
Office Eq.	33	3 675	5.87	5 878	64 454	29.93	523 902	21.56
Elec Eng.	34	115 629	9.11	239 613	804 322	15.14	2 320 648	13.04
Motor Veh.	35	120 442	9.29	25 323	260 808	29.15	2 006 895	22.24
Other Tran.	36	1 544	10.27	3 511	14 499	17.73	50 144	15.13
Instr Eng.	37	8 811	8.21	16 991	93 755	21.35	417 867	16.78
Food	41	338 586	8.35	660 426	934 832	4.34	1 267 009	5.74
Food, Dri.	42	989	8.59	1 966	19 544	28.71	145 801	21.71
Textiles	43	105 791	6.12	172 618	379 416	9.84	755 772	8.55
Leather	44	22 826	7.53	41 678	55 547	3.59	71 420	4.96
Ft., Cloth.	45	283 250	8.13	542 711	750 015	4.04	995 425	5.46
Timb., Furn.	46	83 633	5.14	126 205	241 417	8.11	425 841	7.08
Paper	47	15 979	5.00	23 839	109 196	19.02	413 526	14.15
Rub., Plast.	48	37 588	7.15	66 400	264 008	17.25	883 354	13.74
Oth. Man.	49	46 449	7.11	82 048	204 781	11.43	455 886	9.93
Total Man.		1 639 994	8.05	3 122 076	7 280 136	11.87	18 521 424	10.54

CZECHOSLOVAKIA

NACE		1987	g_i^{8795}	1995	2000	g_i^{9510}	2010	g_i^{8710}
Metal Ex.	21	2 465	6.94	4 296	17 255	17.38	58 751	13.75
Metal Pr.	22	228 991	8.41	448 744	1 010 176	10.14	2 054 686	9.54
Miner Ex.	23	28 706	6.68	48 993	59 557	2.44	70 652	3.92
Miner Pr.	24	125 026	7.78	232 888	348 095	5.02	494 800	5.98
Chemicals	25	223 339	9.20	466 124	1 400 994	13.76	3 669 691	12.17
Mn-MD FBS	26	17 332	9.60	37 373	99 923	12.29	236 255	11.36
Metal Pds.	31	42 441	9.09	87 856	328 968	16.50	1 044 389	13.93
Mech Eng.	32	130 395	10.14	293 391	1 069 340	16.17	3 315 706	14.07
Office Eq.	33	1 822	8.91	3 718	67 916	36.31	862 897	26.78
Elec Eng.	34	65 668	11.10	159 646	767 167	19.62	3 029 735	16.66
Motor Veh.	35	68 944	11.23	169 320	586 495	15.53	1 739 309	14.03
Other Tran.	36	12 071	10.48	27 913	29 402	0.65	30 770	4.07
Instr Eng.	37	8 320	16.53	31 217	187 811	22.43	902 892	20.38
Food	41	79 279	9.16	165 019	685 864	17.81	2 385 630	14.80
Food, Dri.	42	13 397	6.34	22 242	61 745	12.76	150 873	10.53
Textiles	43	133 864	5.87	214 078	450 176	9.29	862 839	8.10
Leather	44	20 667	5.38	31 774	45 976	4.61	63 395	4.87
Ft., Cloth.	45	142 848	7.88	268 385	476 271	7.17	786 707	7.42
Timb., Furn.	46	187 855	6.00	303 648	472 522	5.53	695 772	5.69
Paper	47	111 824	7.26	199 910	949 898	19.48	3 714 607	15.23
Rub., Plast.	48	53 397	8.30	103 708	371 287	15.94	1 133 360	13.78
Oth. Man.	49	74 163	9.54	159 059	443 239	12.81	1 086 633	11.67
Total Man.		1 772 814	8.43	3 479 252	9 930 026	13.99	28 389 849	

BULGARIA

NACE		1987	g_i^{8795}	1995	2000	g_i^{9510}	2010	g_i^{8710}
Metal Ex.	21	13	4.77	19	460	39.81	7 468	27.62
Metal Pr.	22	72 801	8.00	138 097	247 039	7.27	410 937	7.52
Miner Ex.	23	729	6.37	1 214	4 390	16.07	13 520	12.70
Miner Pr.	24	5 771	6.83	9 970	36 835	16.34	115 574	13.03
Chemicals	25	57 136	7.97	108 086	278 867	11.85	639 104	10.50
Mn-MD FBS	26	3 500	8.67	7 005	19 864	13.03	49 449	11.51
Metal Pds.	31	4 304	6.60	7 298	39 891	21.23	176 325	16.14
Mech Eng.	32	23 450	9.56	50 389	164 972	14.82	465 689	12.99
Office Eq.	33	2 984	10.87	7 121	58 539	26.33	369 813	20.96
Elec Eng.	34	13 959	7.45	25 343	108 421	18.17	386 775	14.44
Motor Veh.	35	1 383	7.55	2 531	32 641	31.96	305 813	23.47
Other Tran.	36	242	3.99	333	929	12.82	2 279	9.75
Instr Eng.	37	868	9.63	1 876	20 368	29.81	164 162	22.79
Food	41	41 775	5.67	65 742	137 581	9.23	262 533	7.99
Food, Dri.	42	340	4.74	497	3 825	25.52	22 821	18.29
Textiles	43	28 838	5.20	43 707	97 102	9.98	195 241	8.32
Leather	44	2 982	2.77	3 720	4 269	1.72	4 815	2.08
Ft., Cloth.	45	34 354	4.74	50 206	82 857	6.26	128 442	5.73
Timb., Furn.	46	13 613	3.94	18 658	42 780	10.37	88 426	8.14
Paper	47	5 214	7.12	9 219	56 719	22.71	278 061	17.29
Rub., Plast.	48	4 819	6.02	7 802	39 936	20.41	166 671	15.41
Oth. Man.	49	26 432	5.16	39 952	58 314	4.73	81 185	4.88
Total Man.		345 507	5.43	598 785	1 536 598	13.97	4 335 102	11.00

ROMANIA

NACE		1987	g_i^{8795}	1995	2000	g_i^{9510}	2010	g_i^{8710}
Metal Ex.	21	0	4.21		0	14 189		
Metal Pr.	22	140 940	7.50	256 730	435 978	6.62	692 953	6.92
Miner Ex.	23	59	5.17	89	1 507	35.33	17 881	24.84
Miner Pr.	24	41 243	5.08	61 901	93 314	5.13	133 632	5.11
Chemicals	25	116 100	7.97	219 716	557 130	11.63	1 257 591	10.36
Mn-MD FBS	26	24 347	6.79	41 919	57 390	3.93	75 547	4.92
Metal Pds.	31	42 514	5.95	68 417	158 939	10.54	332 306	8.94
Mech Eng.	32	40 387	6.14	65 991	270 786	17.65	931 378	13.64
Office Eq.	33	1 584	2.44	1 925	19 932	29.22	154 089	19.90
Elec Eng.	34	40 736	4.84	59 977	184 705	14.06	494 212	10.85
Motor Veh.	35	51 878	6.72	88 776	260 668	13.46	668 965	11.12
Other Tran.	36	27 073	3.46	35 701	16 054	−9.99	7 977	−5.31
Instr Eng.	37	3 385	4.33	4 787	29 975	22.93	149 238	16.46
Food	41	62 345	5.58	97 441	222 069	10.30	456 580	8.66
Food, Dri.	42	92	4.94	137	3 163	39.28	49 446	27.33
Textiles	43	134 219	5.03	200 792	260 653	3.26	327 501	3.88
Leather	44	9 985	5.01	14 913	17 838	2.24	20 864	3.20
Ft., Cloth.	45	320 874	4.63	464 816	307 393	−5.17	214 070	−1.76
Timb., Furn.	46	340 077	4.06	470 733	261 117	−7.37	155 909	−3.39
Paper	47	18 092	6.07	29 286	187 128	23.18	948 259	17.21
Rub., Plast.	48	24 031	5.22	36 485	107 144	13.47	275 006	10.60
Oth. Man.	49	11 102	5.21	16 843	58 672	15.60	174 860	11.99
Total Man.		1 451 063	5.41	2 237 375	3 511 549	8.11	7 552 453	7.17

YUGOSLAVIA

NACE		1987	g_i^{8795}	1995	2000	g_i^{9510}	2010	g_i^{8710}
Metal Ex.	21	344	6.89	597	6 284	29.42	49 289	21.59
Metal Pr.	22	574 152	6.60	973 329	1 092 478	1.44	1 208 639	3.24
Miner Ex.	23	8 255	6.22	13 574	29 451	9.68	58 005	8.48
Miner Pr.	24	100 385	5.24	152 664	245 490	5.94	372 003	5.70
Chemicals	25	310 159	8.19	597 078	1 262 981	9.36	2 432 717	8.96
Mn-MD FBS	26	47 826	6.21	78 625	114 594	4.71	159 335	5.23
Metal Pds.	31	99 021	5.71	156 379	365 012	10.60	766 337	8.90
Mech Eng.	32	182 014	6.07	295 853	850 402	13.20	2 142 169	10.72
Office Eq.	33	18 503	5.35	28 395	209 303	24.97	1 201 892	18.15
Elec Eng.	34	393 447	5.77	624 145	1 085 591	6.92	1 761 973	6.52
Motor Veh.	35	429 029	8.31	833 936	1 645 283	8.49	2 981 673	8.43
Other Tran.	36	70 791	4.14	98 600	49 758	−8.55	27 351	−4.13
Instr Eng.	37	27 461	5.31	41 981	168 286	17.36	567 106	13.16
Food	41	279 376	6.32	463 151	712 530	5.38	1 038 719	5.71
Food, Dri.	42	2 753	5.74	4 356	26 712	22.67	130 587	16.78
Textiles	43	401 307	5.88	642 186	754 668	2.02	869 137	3.36
Leather	44	43 562	5.46	67 399	61 622	−1.12	56 975	1.17
Ft., Cloth.	45	1 059 117	6.40	1 766 805	1 232 302	−4.50	899 093	−0.71
Timb., Furn.	46	345 523	4.87	510 298	460 650	−1.28	421 187	0.86
Paper	47	138 263	5.03	206 769	402 258	8.32	720 106	7.17
Rub., Plast.	48	129 602	5.64	203 550	408 086	8.69	750 018	7.63
Oth. Man.	49	73 276	9.65	158 561	378 860	10.89	811 852	10.46
Total Man.		4 734 166	6.43	7 918 232	11 562 601	5.98	19 426 165	6.14

SOVIET UNION

NACE		1987	g_i^{8795}	1995	2000	g_i^{9510}	2010	g_i^{8710}
Metal Ex.	21	6 036	5.63	9 473	35 995	16.69	115 755	12.84
Metal Pr.	22	572 595	7.70	1 060 535	2 114 543	8.63	3 164	8.15
Miner Ex.	23	21 004	6.34	34 880	68 950	8.52	101	7.52
Miner Pr.	24	7 492	6.41	12 507	129 947	29.26	665	22.52
Chemicals	25	453 095	8.26	877 166	2 674 122	13.93	14 164	15.90
Mn-MD FBS	26	7 571	6.43	12 662	80 546	23.13	637	20.10
Metal Pds.	31	13 109	4.46	18 734	167 537	27.39	609	20.37
Mech Eng.	32	58 959	6.39	98 284	893 613	27.59	3 311	20.37
Office Eq.	33	1 102	5.42	1 700	88 386	49.39		0
Elec Eng.	34	43 140	5.06	64 690	516 450	25.97	1 146	21.14
Motor Veh.	35	291 636	5.46	451 507	1 166 337	11.86	1 457	8.03
Other Tran.	36	8 105	6.16	13 266	40 645	14.00	80	11.84
Instr Eng.	37	13 449	4.51	19 291	163 395	26.71	166	12.04
Food	41	142 074	7.01	248 864	985 754	17.21	2 995	15.44
Food, Dri.	42	18 892	4.96	28 094	92 744	14.93	468	13.90
Textiles	43	78 618	5.08	118 025	492 553	17.86	1 853	15.02
Leather	44	2 138	3.53	2 835	15 749	21.44	80	18.77
Ft., Cloth.	45	13 480	6.96	23 515	246 883	29.39	1 846	22.97
Timb., Furn.	46	648 591	6.95	1 130 535	1 361 040	2.32	1 584	4.00
Paper	47	186 337	7.35	335 470	881 633	12.08	3 924	14.49
Rub., Plast.	48	4 318	5.30	6 599	123 053	36.57	1 932	26.93
Oth. Man.	49	568 125	4.42	808 838	766 159	−0.68	107	−6.16
Total Man.		3 159 866	6.65	5 377 468	13 106 033	13.86	40 416	11.35

Notes:
g_i^{8795} is the average annual growth rate (%) required from 1981 to 1995.
g_i^{9510} is the average annual growth rate (%) required from 1995 to 2010.
g_i^{8710} is a hypothetical average rate for the whole period.

2.4   Import Projections

The projections of imports proceeded in the following way:

Firstly, we limited ourselves to projecting the composition of imports, i.e. the shares of different commodities in total imports. We denote these shares as $\mu_j = m_j M$ where m_j are imports of commodity j and M total imports. The import structure is then defined by the vector μ. Furthermore, we will henceforth confine ouselves to imports from EC producers (where the elements of vector μ refer to the shares of commodities i in imports from EC producers).

For projecting the recursive structure of imports, we make use of a relationship between the composition of imports and GNP per head. Support for this relationship is presented in Table 16.17. There we can see that the distance (using the same distance measures as described in section 2.1.1 of the chapter) between a country's composition of imports from the EC and total EC exports correlates with GNP per head. That is countries with a high

GNP per head are closer to the typical composition of EC exports. The distance of EE import from total EC export structures in 1988–90 is given in Table 16.16.

Table 16.16:   Distance from Total EC Import Structure (Manufacturing) –
1988–90

Hungary	Poland	Czech.	Bulgaria	Romania	USSR	Yugoslav
3.371606	3.304031	5.269147	4.721357	3.762459	4.858143	1.988682

Table 16.17:   Regression: Relationship between Distance in Import
Structure from Total EC Exports and Level of Development

Dep. variable: Distance from EC import structure
Regressor: GDP/Pop in 1985
Data Source: Kravis et al. (1988)

Constant	9234.81
Std Err of Y Est	2679.99
R squared	0.419
No. of observations	19
Degrees of freedom	17

X coefficient(s)	−1266.61
Std err. of coef.	361.35
t-ratio	3.51

Data:	GDP/Pop	Distance
Austria	9 023	1.445823
Switz.	10 670	1.109208
Finland	9 266	1.541039
Sweden	9 780	1.430149
Denmark	10 893	1.196869
Spain	6 385	2.069718
Portugal	3 622	1.828976
Greece	4 511	2.22261
Turkey	2 521	2.738768
Israel	6 183	5.938709
Egypt	1 197	3.032227
Iran	3 884	3.545099
Korea	3 034	5.151653
Japan	9 363	2.408773
Taiwan	3 556	2.712993
Malaysia	3 351	3.275756
Philippi	1 364	3.932764
India	757	7.659656
Brazil	3 253	4.27359

Our long-term projections of imports use, on the one hand, projections of GNP per head for both the EE and the group of reference countries (the same as those used in the exports projections) for the year 2010 (these projections are based on Rollo and Stern, 1992, supplemented by complementary projections derived from the Kravis et al. set of statistics, see Summers and Heston, 1988) and, on the other hand, the relationship just established. The projected import structures for the year 2010 are thus determined, for each EE country, as a weighted mix of the import structures of the reference countries. The weights are given by the formula:

$$\omega^{c'} = |1 - |((GNP/head)^{c'} - (GNP/head)^{ee}) / (GNP/head)^{c'}||$$

where c' refers to the reference country and ee to the East European country in question. Table 16.18 presents the weights of the different reference countries for each East European country in order to determine its import structure for the year 2010. The resulting import structures are presented in Table 16.19.

Table 16.18: Weights for Target Import Structures

	Hungary	Poland	Czech.	Bulgaria	Romania	USSR	Yugoslavia
Austria	0.109	0.075	0.115	0.076	0.068	0.067	0.069
Switz.	0.055	0.031	0.060	0.031	0.023	0.023	0.024
Finland	0.101	0.069	0.107	0.069	0.061	0.061	0.062
Sweden	0.085	0.055	0.090	0.055	0.047	0.047	0.048
Denmark	0.048	0.025	0.052	0.025	0.017	0.017	0.018
Spain	0.196	0.146	0.204	0.147	0.139	0.139	0.140
Portugal	0.137	0.216	0.126	0.215	0.213	0.213	0.214
Greece	0.166	0.197	0.156	0.197	0.189	0.189	0.190
Turkey	0.101	0.187	0.089	0.185	0.243	0.243	0.235
sum	1	1	1	1	1	1	1

2.6 Summary of Results

Part Two of this chapter has described a scenario of East–West European integration which corresponds to a successful economic transformation in all EEFSU countries and successful trade integration between all European economies.

The principal assumption behind the projections is that, by 2010, all the EEFSU countries will be at or approaching the leves of economic and trade performance currently displayed by those market economies which have

Table 16.19: Projections of Import Structures for the Year 2010

NAIVE	HUNGARY			POLAND			CZECHOSLOVAKIA		
NACE	Target	Orig.	Diff.	Target	Orig.	Diff.	Target	Orig.	Diff.
210	0.13	0.19	-0.06	0.13	0.13	-0.01	0.13	0.40	-0.27
220	7.63	4.99	2.63	7.86	5.39	2.47	7.59	3.29	4.31
230	0.42	0.18	0.23	0.36	0.30	0.06	0.43	0.33	0.10
240	2.33	2.46	-0.13	2.26	1.78	0.49	2.34	1.86	0.49
250	12.08	18.06	-5.98	12.34	17.17	-4.83	12.04	17.68	-5.65
260	0.62	1.26	-0.63	0.68	0.52	0.16	0.61	0.58	0.04
310	5.49	4.67	0.81	5.27	3.21	2.06	5.52	2.80	2.71
320	15.08	24.45	-9.37	15.81	26.88	-11.07	14.99	34.18	-19.19
330	2.73	1.89	0.84	2.46	1.76	0.70	2.78	3.83	-1.05
340	9.77	10.10	-0.33	9.66	7.92	1.74	9.81	10.58	-0.77
350	14.02	6.27	7.75	13.80	5.07	8.74	14.09	1.94	12.15
360	2.38	1.52	0.87	2.43	1.97	0.47	2.37	2.12	0.25
370	1.96	2.68	-0.72	1.90	2.15	-0.25	1.97	2.88	-0.91
410	4.66	1.66	3.00	5.04	5.90	-0.87	4.54	4.07	0.48
420	2.70	1.64	1.05	2.77	4.67	-1.90	2.67	2.55	0.12
430	5.88	4.95	0.93	6.15	4.61	1.54	5.81	2.69	3.13
440	0.83	1.41	-0.58	0.92	0.35	0.58	0.81	0.16	0.66
450	2.92	1.49	1.44	2.58	1.45	1.12	2.97	0.85	2.12
460	1.53	0.69	0.85	1.28	0.37	0.91	1.57	0.79	0.78
470	2.80	3.10	-0.30	2.59	1.98	0.62	2.83	1.61	1.22
480	4.05	3.41	0.65	3.71	3.34	0.37	4.11	2.33	1.78
490	3.52	2.93	0.59	3.46	3.07	0.39	3.54	2.50	1.04

NACE	BULGARIA			ROMANIA			SOVIET U		
	Target	Orig.	Diff.	Target	Orig.	Diff.	Target	Orig.	Diff.
210	0.13	0.41	-0.28	0.14	3.39	-3.26	0.14	0.21	-0.07
220	7.85	7.30	0.55	8.03	7.83	0.19	8.03	15.45	-7.42
230	0.36	0.19	0.17	0.35	0.94	-0.59	0.35	0.04	0.31
240	2.26	2.26	0.01	2.23	4.34	-2.10	2.23	0.53	1.71
250	12.34	16.58	-4.24	12.56	22.55	-9.99	12.56	13.03	-0.47
260	0.68	0.85	-0.17	0.69	0.18	0.50	0.69	1.36	-0.67
310	5.28	3.53	1.75	5.23	3.44	1.79	5.23	4.25	0.97
320	15.79	32.12	-16.32	16.36	7.26	9.10	16.37	32.57	-16.20

310

NACE	Target	Orig.	Diff.	Target	Orig.	Diff.	Target	Orig.	Diff.
330	2.46	0.88	1.58	2.39	0.53	1.86	2.39	1.93	0.46
340	9.66	8.12	1.54	9.75	5.05	4.70	9.75	7.72	2.03
350	13.80	3.03	10.76	13.63	2.53	11.10	13.63	1.59	12.04
360	2.43	2.22	0.22	2.43	1.45	0.99	2.43	3.23	-0.80
370	1.90	2.31	-0.41	1.90	1.29	0.61	1.90	2.11	-0.21
410	5.04	4.62	0.43	4.93	16.27	-11.34	4.93	4.73	0.20
420	2.77	2.31	0.45	2.72	3.50	-0.77	2.72	0.84	1.89
430	6.15	2.34	3.81	6.01	6.97	-0.96	6.01	1.66	4.35
440	0.92	0.24	0.68	0.94	0.46	0.48	0.94	0.51	0.43
450	2.58	1.05	1.54	2.40	1.76	0.64	2.40	1.46	0.94
460	1.29	0.68	0.61	1.21	1.37	-0.15	1.21	0.51	0.70
470	2.60	3.07	-0.47	2.52	1.59	0.93	2.52	1.80	0.72
480	3.72	2.88	0.83	3.58	2.55	1.03	3.57	2.09	1.48
490	3.46	3.03	0.43	3.49	4.74	-1.25	3.49	2.39	1.10

YUGOSLAVIA

NACE	Target	Orig.	Diff.
210	0.13	0.27	-0.14
220	7.73	5.83	1.91
230	0.34	0.29	0.05
240	2.16	2.04	0.12
250	12.11	16.35	-4.25
260	0.66	0.90	-0.24
310	5.06	4.00	1.05
320	15.74	17.47	-1.73
330	2.32	2.00	0.31
340	9.41	8.54	0.87
350	13.20	10.14	3.06
360	2.35	2.11	0.24
370	1.84	2.00	-0.17
410	4.78	3.00	1.78
420	2.64	1.97	0.66
430	5.82	7.92	-2.10
440	0.91	3.29	-2.38
450	2.34	2.50	-0.16
460	1.18	0.90	0.28
470	2.44	1.94	0.50
480	3.47	3.11	0.37
490	3.37	3.42	-0.06

fairly recently joined the European Community or border on the Community. By associating each EEFSU economy with those economies most closely approximating its employment structure we hope to have identified areas of long-run comparative advantage. We also take into account each country's size and location, the current quality of its exports and the relative starting date at which its economic reform process is firmly established.

(i) Long-term export projections

Chart 1 summarizes the interim results for exports from the whole of manu-facturing industry in each EEFSU country. It shows multifold increases in most countries' shares of EC imports between 1987 and 2010. For the EEFSU as a whole, market penetration rises from 2 per cent to 8.5 per cent.

Experience is, however, likely to vary greatly between countries. In 1987 the former USSR provided only a minute share (0.5 per cent) of the manu-factured goods imported by the EC. Allowing for the size of the former USSR, and its employment structure, quality and expected technological catch-up, however, produces an expected increase in market share to 2.2 per cent by 2010. By contrast, the market share of Yugoslavia is projected to rise only from 0.7 per cent to 1 per cent. Relative to its modest projected position in 2010, its current market share benefits greatly from its relatively advanced trade integration with the EC.

The Central European economies of Poland, CSFR and Hungary are ex-pected to gain substantial increases in EC market share as they become much more like other advanced European economies. Hungary's share, in particular, is expected to rise five-fold from 0.2 per cent to 1.0 per cent.

The aggregate projections conceal substantial differences between indus-trial sectors. Some sectors in some countries are already producing output at quality close to that of the major Western nations; others lag a long way behind. In some sectors the orientation has been so firmly towards former CMEA members that, despite conversion problems, the scope for penetrat-ing EC markets in a successful reform scenario may be sufficient for them to exceed the growth rates of sectors which have already been competing effectively. In addition, some sectors tend to be more open than others to competition outside Europe.

Chart 2 displays the seven industries which we expect to benefit most under the optimistic scenario. They are ordered by the size of the change in the EC market share for their own sector. The strong performance of these industries reflects relatively weak starting positions as a result of past pat-terns of specialization and trade within the former CMEA.

On the basis of these interim figures, the paper industry is the biggest beneficiary. Other industries showing high relative growth in market pen-etration are chemicals, mechanical engineering, metal and mineral products and mineral extraction.[17] On average, their share of EC markets rises from 2 per cent to 10 per cent. Only in the paper industry and the metal processing industry is the EEFSU projected, on the basis of the interim results, to achieve a market share above 12 per cent by 2010.

Compared with the 6 percentage points rise in average EEFSU penetration of EC markets over the period, some industries are projected to lag substantially. Chart 3 picks out the six slowest performers for the period up to 2010 as a whole. A rise from only 0.5 per cent to 4.5 per cent is projected for instrument engineering despite its particularly low starting level. Other relatively poor performers are office machinery, leather, motor vehicles, other transport and other goods. Implicit in the analysis is the assumption that most EEFSU countries will be at a comparative disadvantage in these sectors because the relative quality of their exports and features of their industrial structure mean that, like other neighbouring countries, they will continue to face particularly severe competition in these sectors from the older members of the EC or other parts of the world.

(ii) Short-term export projections

In our short-term projections (up to 1995) we concentrated on supply side considerations. The issue is how fast additional export capacity for EC markets can be brought on stream. We assumed that some capacity previously used for CMEA trade can be converted (the greater the previous emphasis on intra-CMEA trade – particularly exports to the former Soviet Union – the slower this process will be) and we also assumed that new capacity can be added (the higher the current 'quality' attained in the relevant industry, the more attractive that sector will be to new investment). Growth in exports to EC markets is then simply the sum of the growth rates arising from each of these sources (the 'conversion' growth rate plus the 'new investment' rate).

Charts 4 to 6 show, for Hungary, Poland and CSFR, how these projected growth rates vary across the different sectors of manufacturing industry (20 NACE categories are displayed). The lower panels identify both 'conversion' growth rates (darker-shaded areas) and 'new investment' growth rates. The assumptions behind our methodology imply that exports from most industries will grow at rates in the range of 5–10 per cent per annum. There are some notable exceptions – CSFR instrument engineering, for instance, at 16.5 per cent per annum or Polish electrical engineering at 14 per cent and man-made fibres at 12 per cent – but we are not projecting growth rates less than 4 per cent per annum in any individual sector.

Looking in more detail at the lower panels, we can see that most of the differences between industries can be explained by differences in 'conversion' growth rates rather than 'new investment' rates. For the CSFR in particular, we can also see that higher 'conversion' rates amongst the heavier industries (NACE categories 22–37) lead to higher average growth rates overall despite generally lower 'new investment' rates than in the lighter industries.

These high conversion rates reflect, in the main, the relatively higher levels of export capacity directed toward intra-CMEA trade in 1987. The upper panels in the chart show that, for Czechoslovakia, over 85 per cent of exports in NACE categories 31–37 went to other EEFSU countries in 1987. Although we assume that this concentration itself implies lower effective speed of conversion (even slower if a high proportion of intra-EEFSU trade went to the former Soviet Union) the higher levels of available export capacity in 1988 dominate the calculations.

(iii)   Export path

The different considerations underlying the projections of short-term rather than long-term export growth mean that the relative performance of different industries may vary considerably over time. For example, we saw that relatively strong growth is expected in exports to the EC from the CSFR instrument engineering sector up to 1995. However, by 2010 it is projected to have gained less market share than most other industries. Charts 7 to 9 bring out these discrepancies for three major sectors.

The charts display, on the upper panel, our projected relative change in market shares for each country. Thus we see, for example, that mechanical engineering sectors in most countries are expected to increase their market shares more than the industry average (Chart 7) whilst motor vehicles will show lower increases than the average (Chart 8). In the lower panels, we contrast long-run annual growth rates beyond 1995 (black columns) with short-run growth rates (shaded columns) up to 1995.

Looking at mechanical engineering (Chart 7) we see that, for all countries except Romania, long-term growth rates after 1995 and short-term growth rates before 1995 (relative to averages across all manufacturing industry) are in opposite directions. Where short-term growth is faster than the industrial average (the Poland, CSFR and Hungary), longer-term growth is slower.

However, it is not always the case that relatively slow long-term growth after 1995 reflects slower than average projected growth in market shares. We see for CSFR and Hungary, for instance, that growth is relatively slow whilst market share rises relatively faster. The explanation lies in our provisional projections of the export markets themselves: EC imports of mechanical engineering products are projected to grow slower than manufactured imports as a whole.

The relative long-term growth of exports in the textile sector (Chart 9) is also influenced strongly by projections of market growth. Market shares in most countries either rise faster or only just slower than the industrial average. However, all long-term growth rates after 1995 are slower than the industrial average, reflecting the fact that EC textile imports are projected to rise less quickly than manufacturing in general. One interesting feature of the projections for textiles is that relative short-term and long-term growth rates are always in the same direction for every country because they previously had relatively high exposure to Western markets. For both time periods, textile exports increase at rates slower than the industrial average.

Chart 1: Change in Total Manufacturing Shares in EC Markets 1987–2010

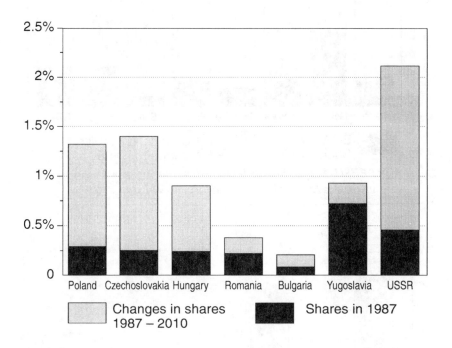

Chart 2:   EEFSU–Export Shares by Industry; Industries with highest
           growth in EC market shares between 1987 and 2010

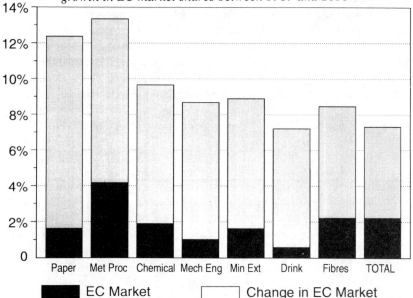

Chart 3:   EEFSU–Export Shares by Industry; Industries with lowest
           growth in EC market shares between 1987 and 2010

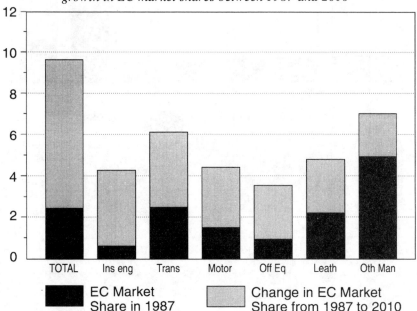

Chart 4:   Hungary

4A: Share of exports in 1987 going to EE and former USSR by sector

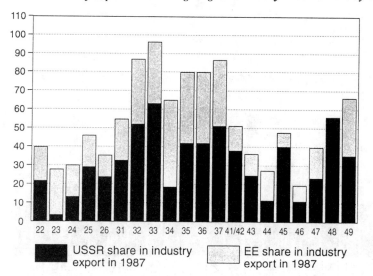

4B: Annual growth of exports to EC markets, 1987–1995

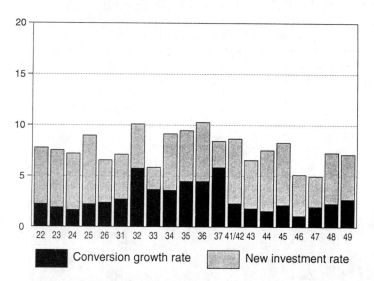

Note:
The two bar charts above, together with the succeeding four bar charts, provide information on manufacturing industry disaggregated into NACE '2-digit' categories 22–49. Categories 41 and 42 are combined.
Data are derived from Table 16.8.

Chart 5:   Poland

5A: Share of exports in 1987 going to EE and former USSR by sector

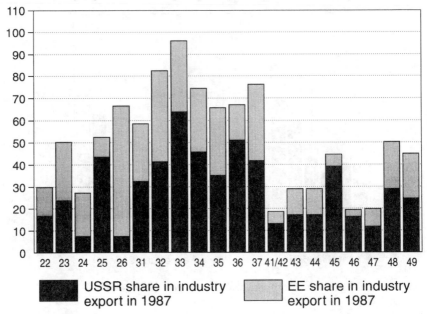

USSR share in industry
export in 1987

EE share in industry
export in 1987

5B: Annual growth of exports to EC markets, 1987–1995

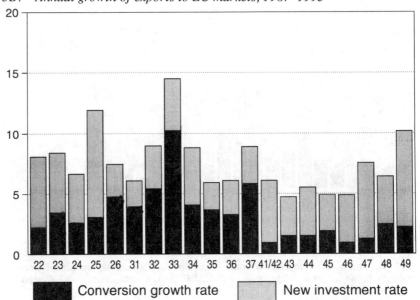

Conversion growth rate   New investment rate

Chart 6: Czechoslovakia

6A: Share of exports in 1987 going to EE and former USSR by sector

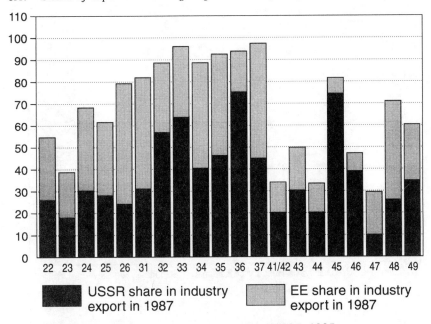

6B: Annual growth of exports to EC markets, 1987–1995

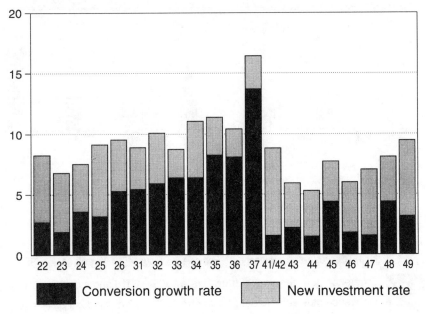

Chart 7:   Mechanical Engineering
7A: EE market share change 1987 to 2010 compared to industry average

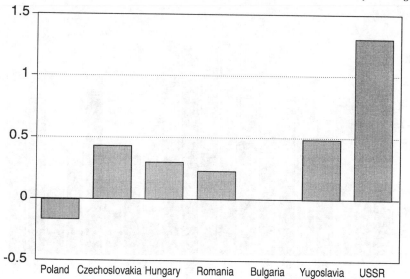

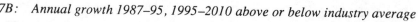

7B: Annual growth 1987–95, 1995–2010 above or below industry average

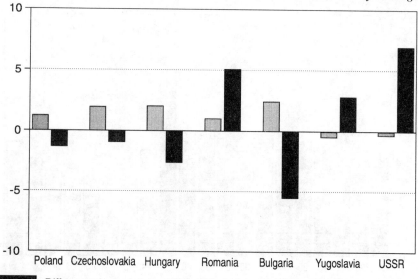

Difference between annual growth rate 1995 – 2010 and industry average

Difference between annual growth rate 1987 – 95 and industry average

Chart 8: Motor vehicles
8A: EE market share change 1987 to 2010 compared to industry average

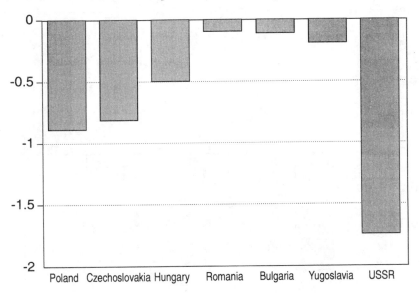

8B: Annual growth 1987–95, 1995–2010 above or below industry average

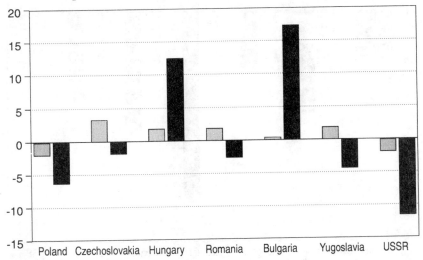

Difference between annual growth rate 1995 – 2010 and industry average

Difference between annual growth rate 1987 – 95 and industry average

Chart 9:   Textiles

9A: EE market share change 1987 to 2010 compared to industry average

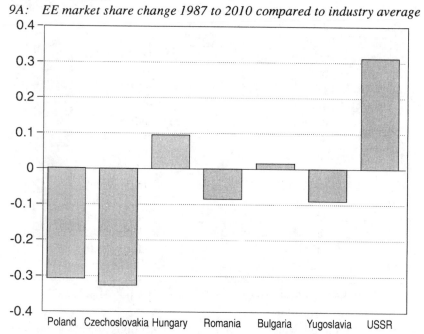

9B: Annual growth 1987–95, 1995–2010 above or below industry average

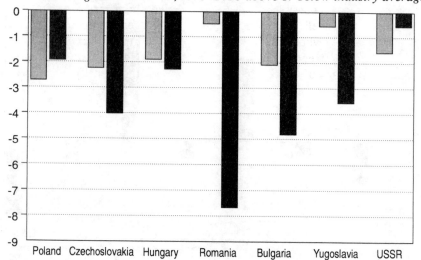

■ Difference between annual growth rate 1995 – 2010 and industry average

▨ Difference between annual growth rate 1987 – 95 and industry average

APPENDIX (PART TWO)

B1: Natural-Resource-Based Industries

The paper industry is treated as a special case in Step 1 because of the peculiarly high proportion of EC imports currently provided by two of the reference countries (Finland and Sweden). For each EEFSU country taken in turn, consideration is given as to the appropriateness of including these countries within the reference group for the paper industry.

In Step 2, some other natural-resource-based industries are also treated as special cases. This occurs where we thought that their comparative advantages as expressed by conventional calculations of $Q_j'/Qbar$ would be misleading in producing market share projections. For the mineral extraction sector (NACE 23) in all countries (often distorted by precious stones), we simply set Q_j' equal to the average (Qbar) for the remaining industrial sectors. We adopted a similar procedure for the footwear and clothing sector (NACE 45) in the Soviet Union (distorted by the influence of the fur trade).

This is not necessarily the best approach because there will be substantial differences in performance between countries. However, it minimizes any potential distortions caused to the projections of *other* industrial categories by a faulty averaging procedure.

We also considered whether to adjust the projections for other natural-resource-based sectors where the chances of statistical distortion were lower but where it seemed possible that the transformed economies of some EEFSU countries might benefit more than they had in the reference economies as a whole. The sectors where this seemed possible were mineral extraction, both 'food and drink' categories and the timber sector. However, in looking at how the economies of Greece, Spain and Portugal had actually developed, no consistent pattern could be identified. No further adjustments were therefore attempted.

B2: Calculations Corresponding to Table 16.9 for Bulgaria, Romania, Yugoslavia, USSR

In the following description superscript C is used for each of the four countries whose data is being calculated, and C' will refer to each of the three reference countries (Poland, Czechoslovakia and Hungary) for whom UNCTAD data was available.

A. EC/EE/USSR shares in total manufacturing export for all industries

The EE and USSR shares for country C could easily be calculated from the data in Table 16.6. The EC share for country C was calculated as the weighted average of EC shares for countries C'. The weights measure the degree of similarity of country C's export structures (to EC markets) with each country C'. The methodology of deriving the weights ($W^{cc'} = 1/D^{cc'}$) is the same as the one used to derive the weights for calculating the 'target structure' in our Step 1 calculations, except that here we are using a comparison of export structures rather than employment structures. (For industries 26, 33 and 37 these weights had to be renormalized since there were zero exports for Hungary).

B.   EC/EE/USSUR shares by industries

First we calculated the distribution of industry export shares (exports to EE, EC, USSR in total exports) around the shares for total manufacturing for the reference countries C':

$R_j^{c'} = XS_j^{c'}/XS_{tot}^{c'}$ where XS refers to shares of exports to EE, EC and USSR markets

The weighted average (using as weights the $W^{cc'}$ defined above) of these gives the distribution of industry shares around the total share for country C:

$R_j^c = R_j^{c'} * W^{cc'}$

In order to get the share of each industry, R_j^c has to be multiplied by the respective total shares for country C:

$XS_j^c = R_j^c * XS_{tot}^c$

C.   Export levels

The export levels in 1995 could then be calculated from the actual export levels for country C in 1987 given by the EUROSTAT data, and from the EE, EC and USSR share figures.

NOTES

*   I wish to thank Istvan Szekely and Anna Hont for their splendid collaboration on Parts One and Two respectively of this chapter.

1.   The data used are described in Appendix A1. We are grateful to the Industrial Statistics and Sectoral Surveys Branch of UNIDO for so kindly and promptly providing us with the UNIDO Industrial Statistics Data Base on diskette.

2.   It is perhaps worth mentioning that in Hungary after 1968, in contrast to Czechoslovakia and Poland where central control of producer prices was preserved, the major part of producer prices was no longer controlled directly.

3.   After an extensive international comparison of the Hungarian economy, Bekker (1988, p. 206) comes to a similar conclusion.

4. For the description of the indicators, see the Appendix A2.
5. Although their final conclusion, as pointed out below, is rather different from ours, Hare and Hughes (1991) also emphasize this characteristic of Hungarian prices. Van Brabant (1987a, p. 182) makes the same point, adding that it was only in Hungary and Poland that some prices provided market information.
6. Van Brabant (1987a, p. 96) also points out that one of the main characteristics of traditional CPEs, a system which was largely preserved in Czechoslovakia, but not in Hungary, is the delayed and muted response to the changing external (and internal) economic environment. He also rightly points out that this characteristic is intimately related to the nature of CMEA trade relations to which, as mentioned earlier, Czechoslovakia (and the other CPEs also preserving the traditional system of central planning), was much more exposed than Hungary and Poland.
7. Dyba (1989) comes to the same conclusion in both aspects. He attributes the present problems of the Czechoslovak economy to effects of maladjustment to lasting changes in the international economy and also stresses the apparent link between the lack of industrial restructuring and trade performance on competitive foreign markets.
8. At a later date it may be desirable to adjust the reference countries so that they all have the same expected population as the CSFR, which we take as our reference EE country. This can be done by scaling the trade share of each country by the ratio of the (total) manufacturing export share, correcting for population alone (but not level of development) to its actual export share. Note that the relation between export share and population is non-linear.
9. The group of reference countries includes both more or less industrially advanced West European (WE) economies. The distance in current industrial structures relative to the different WE economies reveals therefore the current level of development as well as pattern of specialization of each EE country relative to each WE country. It thus gives an indication of the location of each EE country in the spectrum of more or less developed economies of an integrated Europe. It is true that specialization structures as revealed by current information are affected by past development strategies of the socialist economies and their position within CMEA trading structures and that these features will become less relevant in shaping the EE countries industrial structures in the future. Nevertheless, we assume that some of the past legacy will continue to shape specialization of EE economies in the future, although the boundaries of such specialization are defined by the group of (WE) reference economies. In our analysis we used employment structures as proxies for output structures since value-added data for EE economies were and still are affected by relative price distortions.
10. NIMEXE and NACE refer to Eurostat's trade and industrial classifications respectively. From 1988 onwards Eurostat has adopted the Combined Nomenclature (CN) as a basis for its trade classification. Hence any use made of detailed Eurostat trade statistics after 1988 in this chapter has adopted this classification.
11. Table 16.7(c) shows the distribution of the Q_j^c around of the East European economies, i.e. Q_j^c/Y_j^{EE}.
12. This figure can of course be adjusted downwards if we wanted to assume, say, an 85 per cent catching up in the mean; in this case all the other countries will automatically be adjusted downwards as well.
13. Geoffrey Horton of National Economic Research Associates (NERA, London) remarked that the fact that we already scaled the different countries overall market shares up or down by their current levels of total manufacturing exports makes this additional scaling factor superfluous. However, we should remember that the 'size' scaling factor referred to differences in total manufacturing export capacity, while the global 'quality' adjustment factor makes use of relative 'quality gaps' observed in exports to EC markets only. This indicator for a 'technology gap' with respect to exports in this important segment of export trade in advanced Western markets would not be sufficiently taken account of if only the 'size' variable (referring to overall export capacity, a large proportion of which went to CMEA markets) were used for global adjustment.
14. The help of Istvan Szekely in this work is gratefully acknowledged.

15. To do it absolutely properly we should use a mapping at a 6 to 8 digit level.
16. Parameter (λ_j) is thus itself a non-linear function of Q'_j to arrive at a pattern of catching-up processes as described by Figure 16.6.
17. Mineral extraction excludes energy-producing materials but includes, for example, building materials and phosphates.

REFERENCES

Bekker, Zs. (1988), *Growth Patterns, Dynamic Branches*, Budapest: Akademia Kiado.
Brabant, J.M. van (1987a), *Adjustment, Structural Change, and Economic Efficiency*, Cambridge: Cambridge University Press.
Brabant, J.M. van (1987b), 'Production Specialisation in the CMEA – Concepts and Empirical Evidence', *Journal of Common Market Studies*, **26**, (3), 287–315.
Chenery, H. and Syrquin, M. (1975), *Patterns of Economic Development 1950–70*, Oxford: Oxford University Press.
Cohen, D. (1991), 'The Solvency of Eastern Europe', *European Economy*, Special Edition, No. 2.
Dyba, K. (1989), 'Understanding Czechoslovak Economic Development: 1968–1988: Growth, Adjustment, and Reform', *Jahrbuch der Wirtschaft Osteuropas*, **13**, (2), 141–65.
Hamilton, C. and Winters, L. (1992), 'Opening up International Trade in Eastern Europe', *Economic Policy*, No. 14.
Hughes, G. and Hare, P. (1991), 'Competitiveness and Industrial Restructuring in Czechoslovakia, Hungary and Poland', *European Economy*, Special Edition, No. 2.
Köves, A. (1985), *The CMEA Countries in the World Economy*, Budapest: Akademia Kiado.
Landesmann, M. (1991), 'Industrial Restructuring and Trade Reorientation in CSFR', *European Economy*, Special Edition, No. 2.
Landesmann, M. and Snell, A. (1990), 'Structural Shifts in the Manufacturing Export Performance of OECD Economies', DAE Working Paper, No. 9011; forthcoming in *Journal of Applied Econometrics*.
Landesmann, M. and Székely, I.P. (1991), *Industrial Restructuring and the Reorientation of Trade in Czechoslovakia, Hungary, and Poland*, Discussion Paper 546, Centre for Economic Policy Research, London.
Levcik, F. and Stankovsky, J. (1985), 'East–West Economic Relations in the 1970s and 1980s', in C.T. Saunders (ed.), *East–West Trade and Finance in the World Economy*, London: Macmillan.
Rodrik, D. (1992), 'Foreign Trade in Eastern Europe's Transition, Early Results' Centre for Economic Policy, Discussion Paper No. 676, June, London.
Rollo, J. and Stern, J. (1992), 'Growth and Trade Prospects for Central and Eastern Europe', *NERA Working Paper*, No. 1.
Slama, (1983), 'Gravity Model and its Estimation for International Flows of Engineering Products, Chemicals and Patent Applications', *Acta Oeconomica*.
Summers, R. and Heston, A. (1988), 'A New Set of International Comparisons of Real Product and Price Level Estimates for 130 Countries, 1950 to 1985', *Review of Income and Wealth*, **34** (1).
Verspagen, B. (1991), 'A New Empirical Approach to Catching-Up or Falling Behind', *Structural Change and Economic Dynamics*, **2** (2).

Author Index

Subject Index